"The narrative trajectory is something like a cross between a Martin Scorsese film and a Greek tragedy: the omnipotence, partying and carnal escapades slowly give way to feuding, executions and revenge killings. . . . It's a testament to Moorehead's precise, empathic prose that Edda emerges not as the Duce's devilish scion, but as a wounded, fragile being. . . . There is nuance and paradox: [Edda] appears not only an enabler and beneficiary of fascist crimes, but also their victim. It makes for a profoundly satisfying, albeit wistful, read." —*The Guardian* (London)

"Caroline Moorehead writes with her characteristic elegance, eye for detail, and authoritative knowledge about a monster and a survivor. The story of Mussolini's glamorous daughter is certainly a fascinating one."
—Miranda Seymour, author of *Mary Shelley*

"Painstakingly researched and vividly told, this engrossing history turns the spotlight on the deeply conflicted Edda Mussolini, brilliantly balancing the big picture with a wealth of telling detail."
—Clare Mulley, author of *The Spy Who Loved: The Secrets and Lives of Christine Granville*

"Timely. . . . An engrossing portrait of a young woman forced to become a public figure. . . . Moorehead has a spirited turn of phrase, a keen eye for the telling detail and pungent quote, and a gift for marshaling complex material."
—*New York Review of Books*

"Interesting and original. . . . Moorehead is a fine writer and a conscientious historian." —*The Spectator* (London)

"Wide-ranging and compelling . . . this book will take a leading place in all studies of the reality of Fascism and all authoritarianism."
—Richard Bosworth, author of *Mussolini and the Eclipse of Italian Fascism*

MUSSOLINI'S
DAUGHTER

MUSSOLINI'S
DAUGHTER

THE MOST DANGEROUS
WOMAN IN EUROPE

CAROLINE MOOREHEAD

HARPER ⬤ PERENNIAL

NEW YORK • LONDON • TORONTO • SYDNEY • NEW DELHI • AUCKLAND

HARPER PERENNIAL

Originally published as *Edda Mussolini* in the United Kingdom in 2022 by Chatto & Windus, an imprint of Vintage.

Map by Bill Donohoe

FIRST HARPER PERENNIAL EDITION PUBLISHED 2023.

Library of Congress Cataloging-in-Publication Data has been applied for.

ISBN 978-0-06-296726-8 (pbk.)

23 24 25 26 27 LBC 5 4 3 2 1

For Wolf and Basil

The Gods move very fast when they bring ruin on misguided men.

Sophocles, *Antigone*

Contents

Principal Characters

The Mussolini family

Benito Mussolini, dictator 28 October 1922–25 July 1943
  head of the Salò republic October 1943–25 April 1945
Alessandro and Rosa, his parents
Rachele, his wife
Arnaldo, his brother
Edvige, his sister
Edda, his daughter, married to Galeazzo Ciano
Vittorio, Bruno, Romano, his sons
Anna Maria, his daughter
Claretta Petacci, his last lover

The Ciano family

Costanzo Ciano, patriarch and supporter of Mussolini
Carolina, his wife
Galeazzo, his only son
Maria, his daughter
Fabrizio, Raimonda and Marzio, Edda and Galeazzo's children

The gerarchi

Roberto Farinacci, vulgar, corrupt and cynical *ras* of Cremona
Augusto Turati, suave party leader
Achille Starace, devoted Mussolini acolyte and enforcer of Fascist
  behaviour
Giuseppe Bottai, the most cultured of the *gerarchi*
Dino Grandi, ambassador to London

Other Characters

Eugen Dollmann, SS officer and interpreter
Curzio Malaparte, author, and friend of Galeazzo's
Emilio Pucci, devoted companion to Edda
Leonida Buongiorno, Edda's lover on Lipari
Isabella Colonna, doyenne of Roman society

Foro Mussolini

Parioli
(Via Angelo Secchi)

Villa Torlonia

*Borghese
Gardens*

Piazza del Popolo

Tomb of
Augustus

Corso d'Italia

Palazzo
Chigi

Via del Corso

Vatican

Palazzo Venezia

Piazza Navona

Pantheon

Victor Emmanuel monument

Roman Forum

Colosseum

Via dell'Impero

*Palatine
Hill*

Baths of Caracalla

N

River Tiber

EUR

FASCIST
ROME

0   1   2 miles

0   2   4 km

Foreword

The Villa Carpena was the Mussolini family home. An ochre stuc-
coed square house, it stands behind iron gates, with two immense
bronze eagles, their wings outstretched, outside Forlì in Emilia
Romagna, in northern Italy, not far from the hamlet of Predappio
where Mussolini was born and grew up. Rachele, the Duce's wife,
lived in the villa until her death in 1979. It is now a museum, with
something of a used-car lot about its surroundings, since over the
years the family possessions have been discovered and brought
back: rusty cars and bicycles, the tractor which Mussolini took
pride in driving during his occasional holidays from Rome, even a
small aeroplane he once piloted.

The neglected garden is laid out with paths, marked by lines
of small white stones, each bearing the name of one of Mussolini's
senior Fascists, and in-between stand life-sized statues in the classical style. There is a stone cottage, built on a miniature scale, in
which his children played; the benches on which Mussolini and
Rachele sat; the gravestones of the many dogs and cats owned by
the family. The gift shop sells Mussolini memorabilia: mugs, plates,
aprons, knives and even teapots engraved with Fascist insignia;
busts of the Duce in a hundred different heroic poses; replicas of
the caps and hats worn by him; books and framed pictures; knives.
In the niche by the front door stands the statue of a Roman matron,
clutching to herself a sheaf of corn, but otherwise naked. A pair of
peacocks was introduced some years ago and their many descendants, some of them pure white, utter their raucous and eerie cries
from somewhere behind the trees.

But it is the villa itself that is the true shrine to a cult that has
now endured for almost a century. When Rachele was allowed to

return here in the 1950s, she devoted herself to retrieving the many possessions looted from the house in the closing months of the war. Placing a chair by the gates, she sat and waited; sheepish neighbours appeared with a plate, a sewing machine, a cup. Mussolini's motorbike stands in the narrow hall, by the side of the primitive switchboard on which his aides fielded his calls. In his small dark study there are his caps, medals, trophies, pens, inkstands. In Rachele's modest kitchen, restored to its state during the years she rolled the pasta by hand on the travertine table, gleam rows of copper pots on the walls. Everything is dark, pokey, covered in a thick layer of dust, with very little light coming from the small-paned windows.

On the first floor are the bedrooms, each door marked with the name of a Mussolini child. On the bed in Mussolini and Rachele's room lies one of his many khaki uniforms, complete with fez and dagger, laid out as if waiting for his return. Edda, his eldest and favourite child, had her room at the front, overlooking the courtyard. Her bed has a white cotton cover, and on the pillow lies a doll in a frilly dress, with a worn ceramic face. The 1930s art deco cupboard contains some of the dresses, with their bold patterns, big shoulders and pinched waists, that she wore as an adult when her clothes were the models for chic Fascist women. On the dressing table are little trinkets and bric-a-brac that might have come from village fairs.

On every wall of this musty, chilly house, in every room, corridor and staircase, hung closely one to the next, are photographs: the family at banquets, in the streets, playing sports, on bicycles, on horseback and in fast cars; the older boys bold in their pilots' uniforms, the girls demure in their print dresses. Rachele shoots pigeons. The Mussolinis smile, frown, look serious, laugh; they get married, go to parties, raise their arms in the Fascist salute. The portrait of Edda in her early twenties gives her a handsome, stern, quizzical look.

The Villa Carpena is not the only place of pilgrimage for those interested in Mussolini and his family. In nearby Predappio, transformed from a poor, remote, agricultural hamlet into a thriving tourist centre, Mussolini's mother Rosa's schoolroom is also a museum, and visitors can inspect the dingy rooms of the *Casa Natale* in which the Duce was born. Nearby, in the cemetery of San

Cassiano, is the family crypt. On 28 October every year Italians nostalgic for the Fascist past come here to remember and celebrate the anniversary of the birth of Fascism, before processing with flags and banners down Predappio's main street. The gift shop in the village, which sells many of the same things as the Villa Carpena, does good business; alongside the busts and the knives are copies of *Mein Kampf* and Nazi insignia. None of this is illegal in modern Italy, where these pilgrimage sites have come to be seen as an integral part of the country's cultural and political heritage. Many thousands of people make their way to Predappio every year, some from as far away as Japan and Australia, others brought by coach from all over Italy. This year, 2022, 28 October is the 100th anniversary of the March on Rome.

A century on, it is not easy, in Italy, to forget the Fascist years. Mussolini devoted much time and many resources to engraving Fascist ideology on the landscape, stamping his new era of nationalism and a return to the grandeur of ancient Rome on to buildings, sports arenas, offices and even entire towns. Ridding the country of these monumental, intimidating buildings made of limestone, travertine and marble, with their flat surfaces and sharp lines, was considered impractical in the wake of the Second World War, when the Allied Control Commission recommended the removal of only the more 'unaesthetic' buildings and the destruction of the busts and statues of the dictator. They were more interested in putting their energies into limiting the powers of the Communist Party; in any case, the inter-party Christian Democrat bloc that took over the government included among its members many former Fascists. In the years since then, Fascist architecture has come to be regarded as an attractive form of modernism. In 2015, the fashion house Fendi moved its global headquarters into what had been the Palazzo della Civiltà Italiana at EUR, the overbearing Fascist suburb that lies between Rome and Ostia. Its gleaming white arches and rows of life-sized naked marble statues sparkle.

During the nineteen months of the Mussolini Salò republic on Lake Garda, between Mussolini's fall and Italy's surrender to the Allies in October 1943 and the liberation of Italy in April 1945, Mussolini and his family lived in the late-nineteenth century Villa Feltrinelli, a pink turreted and crenellated house on the edge of the lake. Claretta Petacci, his last mistress, occupied the pretty Villa

Fiordaliso not far away among the olive and lemon groves. Having preserved their Venetian glass, mosaic floors and burnt-sienna walls, these villas are now five-star hotels, and Mussolini's and Claretta's bedrooms are said to be booked up for many years in advance.

The cult that surrounded and sustained Mussolini during his years of power has lingered on in these places. His words and images continue to resonate with people unhappy with the instability of the sixty-six governments – which have lasted on average 1.4 years each – that have ruled Italy since the war. And, aside from Mussolini himself, no one is better remembered than his elder daughter Edda, who was twelve when he came to power, married his Foreign Minister, Galeazzo Ciano, and, all through the 1930s and into the war, took her reluctant mother's place as the image of what a true Fascist girl and woman ought to be. It was, as it turns out, a deceptive one.

I went in search of Edda. I found her in newsreels, in the photo magazine stories so beloved of Italians, in archives and libraries, in memoirs and autobiographies, including her own and those of most of the members of the Mussolini clan. One day, I followed in her footsteps to a seventeenth-century coaching inn at Cantale, on the border between Italy and Switzerland. It is called the Madonnina, and Garibaldi is said to have changed horses here as he left for exile after being sentenced to death for his part in the uprising in Piemonte.

On the first floor, down a dark corridor, I saw a sign that I was not expecting: the Edda Ciano suite. Inside were the rooms Edda occupied on the night of 9 January 1944, as she fled from the Nazis who were on their way to arrest her. The large bedroom and adjoining *salotto* have been left as they were then, with their Egyptian-style art deco furniture: the bed has posts in pale mahogany and the walls are painted blue and deep red. Towards the back of the room stands an immense iron bath. Edda's suite is much in demand. It costs twice the price of the inn's other rooms.

Edda was not just Mussolini's favourite child and Fascism's most exotic star. She was the most like her father, with her staring, hypnotic eyes, and she was also eccentric, clever and mercurial. Her will, like his, was of steel. She came to prominence at the age of nineteen and for the thirteen years that she stood at the forefront of the dictatorship, she was at times her father's closest confidante and only friend. But the misogynist culture she grew up in, and which became more pronounced with every Fascist year, was something she was never prepared to accept. Power intrigued her, but she played with it, as she did most things, erratically, with little understanding of her own strength.

All dictators leave myths in their wake. What made Mussolini different was that even before he came to power he was laying down and fostering his own cult, and that once he became dictator the cult came to obsess Italy. How the Duce looked, what he said, wrote, thought and did was known throughout Italy.

Edda is not so easy to pin down. The myth that enveloped her father spread to include the whole Mussolini family, and especially the cleverest and most enigmatic of his children. Even during their lifetimes, their words and actions were embellished, distorted, romanticised and often imagined; and they themselves contributed to a sometimes fanciful retelling of events. Unravelling fact from the fiction handed down by successive generations of followers, relations, journalists and historians is a bewildering task, made more so by the myths that swirled about Edda; and it is certain that not every incident or quotation in this book is true. But what follows is as close to the truth as I have been able to get.

Edda is intrinsically bound up with her father, and a true representative of what Fascism did – and did not – do to Italians. Sometimes, misfortune struck so quickly that her life seemed to follow the arc of a Greek tragedy. Mussolini and Fascism made Edda what she was: to understand her, you have to understand what Italians call *il ventennio Fascista*, the twenty years of Fascist rule, when Mussolini's vision and will ruled over every facet of Italian life – sport, education, leisure, health, culture, work – and most of all over Edda, who loved, admired and, for a while, hated him.

Part One

PROLOGUE

1

La cavallina matta

When Edda Mussolini was a girl, leading a band of small children across the wastelands behind Milan's tall apartment blocks, she was known as '*la cavallina matta*', the mad little horse. Wilful, bold, contemptuous of authority, the name stayed with her. Even in the years when Fascism was servile to the Mussolini family, when to speak of any of its members disparagingly was to invite police investigation, and Edda herself had become an awkward, capricious young woman, Italians repeated it to themselves, quietly. As they saw it, Edda was never tamed, and her restless, strident nature made her feared. But they did not forget her. 'I never felt liked,' she said, towards the end of her life. 'I had no ability to please. I lacked constancy in all things.'

Though Edda was born, on 1 September 1910, in Forlì, a small town in Emilia Romagna, the nearby village of Predappio was the true birthplace of the Mussolinis, 'our Galilee,' as Fascist historians would later say, 'because it was there that began our new history.' Both her parents were born in Predappio: Mussolini in 1883, thirteen years after Rome became the capital of the newly united Italy, and Rachele Guidi in 1890. Emilia Romagna, one of the poorer regions, was a land of labourers and share-croppers beholden to the Vatican and distant feudal landowners. Its villages, in the foothills of the Romagnole Apennines, were reached by narrow, rocky tracks, lined with poplars. The local Sangiovese wine, produced in hundreds of small vineyards along the valleys, was too strong and too acidic to travel. It was a grey, empty landscape, with crumbling medieval fortresses perched on crops of rocks, and cypresses, which gave it a look of Tuscany, but poorer, harsher, its colours paler. Between the fields of maize ran the River Rabbi, fast flowing in winter, a series of little pools in summer, where the village children played. Few of them could read or write.

Emilia Romagna had given its men to Garibaldi's cause, and even after unification they were litigious, conspiratorial, impatient for reform and anti-clerical - '*mangiapreti sovversivi*', subversive eaters of priests. Almost every family had a father or husband who had spent time in prison, protective custody or under house arrest. Superstition was fed by village witches. Rome lay far to the south, a place of incompetence and alien rule. When the harvests failed, people starved. By the year of Edda's birth, many hundreds of thousands of Romagnoli had emigrated to France and Austria, or further afield, to America, and sad little families could be seen trudging down the roads and through the villages on their way to the coast.

Edda's grandfather, Alessandro, was the local blacksmith, a hard man with a long face and a thick moustache, who in later life drank heavily. He was almost entirely self-taught, with a burning passion for international anarchism, and his pugnacious and brawling ways had taken him on several occasions to prison, while his own father Luigi had served time in a papal jail, when Emilia Romagna was still part of the Papal states. As Mussolini would later say, having served several prison sentences himself, he came

Rosa and Alessandro

4

from impeccable rebellious stock, and every self-respecting revolutionary needed to have been to jail. In time, Alessandro became a councillor and deputy mayor; he also formed a village band, with wind instruments.

Edda's grandmother, Rosa Maltoni, was a teacher, a thrifty, pious woman with a square face and deep-set eyes, but determined enough as a girl to force her parents to send her, the only one of their six daughters, to school. In 1877, having qualified as an elementary school teacher, she was posted to Predappio's sister village, Dovia, where the schoolroom, in a dilapidated but handsome palazzo, was so dark that it was hard to read a book. A small vineyard yielded a few grapes and there were three fig trees. Dinner was often nothing more than soup, wild radishes and bread. Rosa's mother gathered wild greens and boiled them with a few drops of oil.

Rosa with Mussolini as a baby

Rosa gave birth to Mussolini in 1883; then came Arnaldo in 1885, a pale, timorous boy who took after his mother, and Edvige, born in 1888. In the rooms above the schoolhouse, the boys shared an iron bed. They spoke to each other in dialect as the Italian national language, born with unification, was still unfamiliar to most Romagnoli, and they walked to school barefoot, carrying their shoes. Sitting on the steps of the foundry on summer evenings, Alessandro read Marx and Bakunin to his sons. In a hole in the cellar, he had buried a large red revolutionary flag. All three children had the same square faces, strong jaws and heavy eyebrows.

Moody, obstinate and averse to any kind of discipline, Mussolini grew a little wilder every year, confrontational with other children, sneering with teachers. He never cried. When he was nine, his father despaired and took him to a Church-run school in Faenza, hoping that it might subdue him. Mussolini felt humiliated and hated it all: the sermons, the rules, the monks, the rich boys who ate better food at separate tables in the refectory. Teachers noted that he liked to make the other boys afraid of him.

At the beginning of his second year, he was expelled for stabbing a boy with a penknife, having first been shut up in the dark with the dogs and told that his soul was as black as coal. But the Salesian fathers took him back to finish the year: what had become clear to them was that for all his surliness and disobedience, Mussolini was an unusually clever boy with a prodigious memory. From here, he moved to the College Giosuè Carducci in Forlimpopoli. He seemed, so his contemporaries later claimed, to thrive on drama, violent spectacles, epic sagas. He played the cornet and cultivated a small moustache. In January 1901, Verdi, the last great hero of the *Risorgimento*, died, and it was telling that it was Mussolini who was invited to deliver a memorial speech to the college: he was discovering oratory, the power to dazzle an audience, using rhythmic cadences, unexpected metaphors and a passionate delivery, and he took the occasion to attack Italy's governing class. At eighteen – a dishevelled, unshaven, violent young man, not very tall, with piercing black eyes, a pale face and a floppy black cravat – he left school with a teaching diploma but few friends. On the blackboard he had allegedly written: 'The most noble calling of man is to be a leader.'

His first posting, as a substitute teacher, was to Pieve di Saliceto, 100 kilometres from Predappio. He was too self-obsessed, too distracted and too prone to lose his temper to be a good teacher and he liked neither the children nor the noise they made. At the end of the year, his post was not renewed, but that may have been in part because of an affair with the wife of an absent soldier. Sex, first encountered with a prostitute when he was sixteen, obsessed him;

he liked it quick and casual, a conquest without demands. He raided Edvige's pocket money to pay for it.

In 1902, borrowing a little money from his mother, he decided to try his luck in Switzerland, where he wandered, aimless and often hungry, taking jobs here and there as a waiter, a builder, an errand boy and a butcher's assistant. One day he almost strangled an English tourist when trying to snatch her picnic. He began to explore the art of propaganda, and wrote fiery articles, finding that journalism suited his exhortatory style. At one Socialist conference he met Angelica Balabanoff, the daughter of a rich Ukrainian land-owner, five years his senior, who spoke six languages and was friends with many of Europe's revolutionary leaders.

Almost all émigrés were poor and eccentrically dressed, but what struck Balabanoff about Mussolini was how dirty and obviously starving he was, his black hair thinning, his eyes heavily shadowed. She thought that once he had learnt more, he would surely lose his overwhelming ego. She liked him, for all his boastful, blasphemous bravado, and recommended him for the post of secretary to a Socialist organisation in Trento and editor of its paper, *L'Avvenire del Lavoratore*. In the stormy, rivalrous world of European left-wing politics, where every faction had its own clique, Mussolini's brand of heated radicalism found many listeners. He liked to think of himself as '*vivere pericolosamente*', living dangerously.

Mussolini had dodged military service in Italy. He was now considered a deserter and was sentenced in absentia to a year in prison. But when, in 1904, King Victor Emanuel declared an amnesty in honour of his new son Umberto, Mussolini was able to return home. He reported voluntarily to the military and was serving with the 10th Bersaglieri regiment in Verona – with surprising docility and *esprit de corps* – when his mother Rosa fell ill with what was probably typhus. She seemed to be recovering, but then pneumonia set in and she died. His mother's death upset Mussolini profoundly; for the rest of his life he would refer to it as the saddest of his days.

Vociferous against both the monarchy and the Church, Mussolini brawled and railed his way through the next few years, moving between Italy and Switzerland, writing, teaching, calling for war between the classes, supporting strikes, writing angry articles for small papers. Violence, he announced, was 'useful, fruitful and decisive'; the Vatican 'a cadaver' and a 'gang of robbers'; and the political leaders in Rome 'asses, liars, microbes'. The authorities kept a close eye on him, and, when he went too far, put him in jail. He was permanently crumpled, his clothes threadbare, his language abusive, and in his spare time he read Nietzsche and Sorel, played the violin and wrote short stories. He seldom left home without a knife.

Mussolini was proving an excellent journalist. His style was spare, his tone angry, his imagination wild, and he had a talent for concision and analysis. Nor was he without irony and humour. He returned to Forlì, where Alessandro, having been forced to give up the rooms above the schoolhouse in Predappio after Rosa's death, was now running Il Bersagliere, an inn near the railway station. His new companion was Anna Guidi, a widow left destitute with five daughters by her husband's early death. The youngest of these was fifteen-year-old Rachele. Like Rosa, Rachele had fought hard to get an education and had eventually been allowed to attend Rosa's school. Family lore has it that on one of the occasions when Mussolini had taken his mother's place in the schoolroom, he had noticed the very blonde little girl, with her almost turquoise eyes and delicate hands, who kept asking questions. He had seen her again during a visit home from Switzerland, been drawn to her pale ringlets and pretty, bold looks, and had asked her to wait for him: he would return, he said, to marry her.

Rachele waited. The courtship was brief, an importunate suitor was seen off, and, in the face of considerable disapproval from her family, Mussolini carried Rachele off to Forlì. One of the many stories that have attached themselves to the family myth is that Mussolini, impatient with her parents' reluctance, produced a revolver and threatened to kill them all unless they let Rachele go. She was already pregnant. There was no talk of marriage. In the heavily Catholic, moralistic Italy of the early 1900s, it was a bold move on her part. 'Il matto', the mad man, as the locals called him, had no income and very few prospects. The couple took with them four sheets, four plates and six knives, spoons and forks, and walked the five kilometres to Forlì in silence, through driving rain. Later, Rachele said that she had been afraid only of the storm and the snakes.

It was January 1910. Mussolini and Rachele's first home, two scarcely furnished rooms in the shabby Palazzo Merenda looking out over a dark courtyard, was reached by steep stairs. It was also full of fleas. They found fruit boxes to use as a table and chairs. Since Mussolini tended to cut himself, Rachele shaved him. He had just found a job as secretary to Forlì's Socialist Party and editor of their paper, *La Lotta di Classe*. Calling himself '*il vero eretico*', the true heretic, he wrote many of the articles himself, on freemasonry, the Vatican, political assassination, anything that caught his eye, while also editing, correcting proofs and laying out the pages. He was ruthless with his red pencil. His own articles combined revolutionary fervour and Socialist politics, and though many dismissed him as a mere political agitator, he was read and listened to. At meetings, he stirred audiences with his hotchpotch of Hegel, Sorel and the Bolsheviks, fusing seemingly unconnected theories into electrifying diatribes, inviting their chanted replies. His voice veered between raucous and warm, bullying and cajoling, playing with his listeners, offering them something to believe in. In his scruffy Bohemian clothes, talking very rapidly, he was impossible to ignore.

Seven and a half months after their arrival in Forlì, on 1 September 1910, Edda was born. Mussolini had already decided that she would be a girl and the name Edda may have come from the fashionable *Hedda Gabler*. On her birth certificate, her father's name was given as Mussolini, but her mother's remained blank since they were not married. Mussolini's first act, the family later boasted, was to spend half his salary on a handsome wooden cradle. The baby had clearly inherited her father's genes: she was quick and demanding and her father was proud of his lively daughter, taking her everywhere with him: to the office, to bars, to his interminable political meetings. Edda's birth seemed to unleash a burst of frenetic energy in him. For her part, Rachele, never given to physical affection, found her daughter difficult. Edda was too restless, too fearless; once she learnt to walk there was no peace. When at night the baby refused to sleep, Mussolini played his violin to her, loudly and erratically. After himself, Edda was the person in the family who counted most. 'Within me,' he noted, 'I recognise no one superior to myself.'

Alessandro's health had been failing. He had a stroke, became paralysed and died aged fifty-six. He had almost nothing material to leave his children, but as Mussolini wrote later, 'of spiritual possessions, he left us treasure: ideas'. Rachele's mother Anna, 'soft as a sweet cake', came to live in the two rooms in Forlì. Mussolini was often drunk when he came home late. After Rachele threatened to leave him, taking Edda with her, he promised to stop; and in this he largely kept his word. He slept very little. After the cafés closed for the night, he sat crouched at the kitchen table, writing by the light of a candle. They were often short of food. In later years, when his fortunes changed, he would speak of Edda as '*la figlia della povertà*', the daughter of poverty.

In late September 1911, when Edda was just over a year old, Giovanni Giolitti's government, without any formal declaration of war, dispatched troops to Tripolitania and Cyrenaica – which later became Libya – ostensibly to protect Italian interests, but in reality to replace Turkey as the occupier. There were protests all over Italy, some of them violent. Among those demonstrating was a young republican called Pietro Nenni, and during an attack on a train carrying troops to the coast, Mussolini and Nenni were arrested together and charged with inciting rebellion.

At their trial on 18 November, the two men were given heavy fines and sentenced to a year in prison, later reduced on appeal to five and a half months. They spent their days companionably, playing cards and discussing politics. Mussolini studied German. He missed his daughter and his violin. He had borrowed money to give to Rachele, but it was confiscated and life at home in the Palazzo Merenda was bleak. To provide for the family, Mussolini was writing articles for the Socialist *La Lotta di Classe*. It was said later that Edda, just walking, was coached by her mother to hug and cling on to her father, while he slipped the folded pages of his columns into the pocket of her apron to be smuggled out of the prison. Rachele developed excema, and Mussolini advised her to shave her head.

By 1912, the Liberal Giolitti had been in power for the best part of the last twenty years, at the head of coalitions which sought to preserve the existing social order and isolate the extremes of both left and right. The Italian Socialist Party, which had hitherto refrained from opposing Giolitti, was now splintering into three sections: the revolutionaries or maximalists, who favoured militant action; the reformists, who called for universal suffrage and an overhaul of parliament; and the syndicalists, who wanted radical change to the economy. Mussolini's instincts lay firmly with the revolutionaries. Emerging from prison on 12 March 1912 as something of a local hero, and given a banquet by Forlì's Socialists, he attended the 13th National Congress of the Socialist Party, held in Reggio Emilia in the early summer. From the platform, he railed against parliamentary democracy and demanded the expulsion from the party of the soft and accommodating reformists. Italy's parliamentarians, he declared, were slothful, corrupt, insincere charlatans, an opinion which resonated strongly with the discontent of the times. The reformists were successfully ousted and departed to form a new, more moderate wing. Mussolini, with a heavy beard and threadbare coat, was now regarded as a coming star, a 'transcendent intellectual'.

The new revolutionary executive of the Socialist Party had voted to sack Claudio Treves, the reformist editor of the party's prestigious paper, *Avanti*. After some hesitation, they invited Mussolini to take his place. It meant moving to Milan. Mussolini went on ahead, leaving Rachele and Edda to follow.

On taking over *Avanti*, Mussolini had insisted that Angelica Balabanoff join the paper as his assistant. Whether or not they were lovers, she taught him a great deal; in his more generous moments, Mussolini would say that she had been his 'true political teacher' and that she continued to steer his thoughts. One cold and windy day in February 1913, Rachele appeared unannounced in the office with Edda in her arms. They were soaking wet and shivering. Rachele's hair had not yet fully grown back and she looked like a bedraggled child. Balabanoff later described the sudden arrival of this 'very humble-looking woman' with an 'undernourished, poorly dressed little girl', in clothes so wet they looked transparent. Mussolini insisted that they return to Forlì, but Rachele, whose will behind the soft blonde hair was also of iron, refused. They found a flat on the fourth floor of 19 Via Castel Morrone, near the railway lines, sharing it with her mother Anna. Balabanoff lived in the same street, at number 9.

The flat had a lavatory, but no bath. Mussolini seldom washed and Rachele went to the public baths, taking Edda with her and trying to wash out the nits in her hair. Their building, dark and crumbling, had three immense stone staircases and a series of courtyards in which Edda played. There were very few toys. The eccentrics and misfits who occupied the dingy flats included a young woman preparing to become a nun and an impoverished count. A small boy, very taken by the bold Edda, set up a pulley with a basket between their neighbouring flats in which he sent her presents.

Mussolini, Rachele and Edda

Edda was becoming increasingly wild and unruly, and Rachele chased her round the flat with a broom, delivering slaps. To keep the peace, Mussolini took the little girl to his office, where she played on the floor under the desk, and where he began to teach her letters, written in chalk on the tiles. With Rachele so much in the background, rumours circulated that Edda was in fact Balabanoff's daughter, born when Mussolini was still living in Switzerland. When the story reached Rachele and she repeated it to Mussolini, his reply was scathing. Balabanoff, he said, did indeed have a 'generous and noble soul'; but should he ever find himself on a desert island with just her and an ape for company, 'I would choose the ape'. Balabanoff was a mesmerising speaker, strong and warm, but she had a long body, short legs and a slight hunchback. One of her rivals noted waspishly that she had 'very little familiarity with water'.

Mussolini had discovered that, along with his political charisma, his grubby forcefulness was very attractive to women. Not long after arriving in Milan, he had been introduced to Leda Rafanelli, wife of a Zionist Socialist, an Arabist and novelist of some fame. Rafanelli had a salon and preached free love. They met on Tuesday afternoons to read Nietzsche together and exchanged infatuated, overwrought letters, in one of which he told her: 'I need to be someone, do you understand me? . . . I need to rise high.' Later, Rafanelli would write him into one of her novels, as a handsome though rather brutal lover, with an insatiable craving for admiration.

A more lastingly important woman in his life was Margherita Sarfatti, who came from a rich Venetian Jewish family and was married, with two sons, to a lawyer. Already somewhat matronly in appearance, she had a round face, abundant auburn hair and striking grey-green eyes. She was elegant, worldly and dressed expensively; she was also highly cultured and very clever and Mussolini liked clever women. Sarfatti, too, had a salon, and after initial hesitation over his rudeness and uncouth appearance, she began to introduce him to the luminaries who gathered in her house in the fashionable Corso Vittorio. Like her, the guests were soon intrigued; most noted Mussolini's extraordinarily piercing eyes and unsmiling stare.

Rachele was never invited to these gatherings. But she was taking pleasure in her relative new prosperity; she now employed a maid and could send Edda to school in shoes. Mussolini had bought a bowler hat and took to frequenting the cafés in Milan's Galleria, where journalists and artists held court. Sometimes Edda went with him. Milan, home to many literary and cultural journals and to crusading left-wing writers and editors, had prided itself since unification on its reformist, politically enquiring spirit.

Edda was now three and had started violin lessons. When she played she looked exactly like her father, pursing her lips, jutting out her jaw, her cheeks prominent in her strong face. Sometimes they played together. To win her often absent father's attention, she found ways to challenge him. When one day she refused to take some medicine, he slapped her and she slapped him back. What she would remember later was the day when he realised that she was terrified of frogs. Mussolini went to the marshes, got hold of a frog and put it into her hands insisting that she keep it there. No one, he told her, and especially no Mussolini, was allowed to indulge in fear. And nor was she permitted to cry.

What Edda would also remember were the duels. How real they were, how potentially lethal, is impossible to know, for they too occupy a place in the family lore. Mussolini was said to have a special shirt, with a single sleeve, that of his duelling arm cut away. Sometimes he came home with wounds from a gun or a sword, none of them very serious. He fought his predecessor on *Avanti*, Claudio Treves, calling him a 'nauseating' rabbit and a 'little old woman', and returned from that duel with his head covered in blood and a piece of his ear torn away. His style was not to parry and thrust, but rather to make spectacular, impulsive lunges. Fought surreptitiously in Milan's parks, in clearings and cemeteries, none of the duels ended with a death. Coming home victorious, he asked Rachele to make spaghetti instead of the usual tagliatelle. Spaghetti, for Edda, became the food of duels. Rachele, who hoarded Mussolini's possessions, insisted on keeping his bloody shirts and even the pieces of shot from his wounds.

Political discord throughout Italy was taking the form of strikes, demonstrations and brawls in the streets. Writing most of *Avanti* himself, Mussolini breathed revolutionary fire into the Socialist movement and increased the paper's circulation at an impressive rate. The name 'Duce' had been murmured before, perhaps with irony. Now it began to stick. At the Socialists' congress in Ancona in April 1914, Mussolini's irrepressible energy strengthened his political position. Disaffected Italians were looking for a leader.

Then, on 28 June, Archduke Ferdinand and his wife were assassinated in Sarajevo. Austria declared war on Serbia, which had ties to Russia, Britain and France. Italy's position was complicated. An ally of Austria for the past thirty-two years and with Germany a member of the Triple Alliance, it also had links of friendship with France and Britain. However, Austria held the '*terre irredente*' of the Italian-speaking city of Trento and the partly Italian city of Trieste, with their large ethnic Italian population, and their recovery was regarded by many as the unfinished business of the *Risorgimento*. Courted by both sides, Italy, for the moment, chose neutrality, a decision passionately endorsed by Mussolini and the Socialists, along with the King, most of the army, much of Parliament, and the new Pope Benedict XV, who refused to sanction this war as 'just'.

Not everyone shared their views. Nationalists and futurists were strident in their calls for action, along with a number of intellectuals who hoped that war would sweep away a governing class many now saw as dysfunctional and bring in its wake a fairer and healthier Italy. Listening to them, Mussolini's views began to change. He began signing his articles '*L'homme qui cherche*', the man who seeks. By September he was starting to refer to neutrality as backward-looking and feeble. Did Italy, he asked, really want to remain 'an inert spectator of this huge drama'? Within pacifist Socialist circles there was fury at his rejection of the party line. There were more duels; the adulation soon turned into hatred. Ousted from *Avanti*, Mussolini chafed for an outlet for his new-found militarism and found it when backers helped him set up a new paper, *Il Popolo d'Italia*, in which he agitated fiercely for war and social revolution. Neutrality, he told his sister Edvige, 'will make us all die of hunger and shame'. When he went to visit newspaper vendors to see how the paper was selling, he took Edda with him. 'Every new creation, every step forward,' he told a rally, 'is marked by blood.' He now kept a revolver in his desk and employed two bodyguards. Around this time, Rachele paid a visit to their home in Predappio, and she was hounded out of the village as the wife of a traitor to socialism.

Mussolini's switch had already alienated Balabanoff, who remained deeply opposed to war and contemptuous of his 'infamous' betrayal of neutrality. Years later, she wrote that without her, he would have remained 'an insignificant *arriviste* ... a Sunday socialist'; and that he had become nothing but a cowardly, hypocritical, vulgar, devious braggart and a Judas. Edda was not sorry to see her go. She had hated the way that in the office Balabanoff kept stroking her tenderly and whispering, '*Che bella bambina, che bella bambina.*'

By now Mussolini had found a new mistress. Ida Irene Dalser was Austro-Hungarian, with a dimpled chin and thick glossy hair, and by 1914 she was running an 'Oriental salon of Hygiene and Beauty' in Milan. She was also somewhat unstable. She had met Mussolini briefly while they were both in Trento, but she now came to the offices of *Il Popolo d'Italia* to place an advertisement for her business. They became lovers. In the tumultuous disarray of his life, Mussolini found her calm and orderly. When he needed more money for *Il Popolo*, Ida sold her flat and her beauty salon and gave him the proceeds. But the relationship soon started to sour and Ida took to turning up in his office and making scenes. He found the money to install her in a small flat. She called herself Signora Mussolini.

As Rachele described it later, one day when Mussolini was away in Genoa trying to raise money for his campaign there was a knock at the door. Outside was 'an ugly signora, much older than me, lean and cadaverous and making flamboyant gestures'. The visitor refused to give her name but, prowling around the room, began to question Rachele about her husband. Turning to Edda, she asked whether her father loved her mother. On Mussolini's return, Rachele asked him who the woman was. An Austrian, he told her, a hysteric, with whom he had had a brief affair while in Trento, and who was now persecuting him. Edda was becoming accustomed to the jealous rows; but she was also learning the lesson that great men could not be expected to be faithful.

Bit by bit, many of the Italians who had initially supported neutrality were turning towards intervention. From balconies and in crowded city squares, the poet, pamphleteer, novelist and strutting chaser of women and awards Gabriele D'Annunzio preached war, the 'beauty of triumphant Italy' and the grandeur of *la patria,* the Italian homeland. War was the future, a necessary evil to awaken the somnolent and disorderly Italians. In April 1915, Italy had been promised not only Trieste and the Trentino, but also South Tyrol, part of Dalmatia, a bit of Albania and islands in the east Adriatic in return for joining the Allies, and had signed a secret treaty in London. In return, Italy declared war on Austria, even if in parliament the interventionists remained in the minority. There had been ample time to observe the carnage already caused by machine guns, and Italy's leaders knew perfectly well that the country lacked guns and good officers; but these thoughts were put aside.

In September 1914, Mussolini left his family to join the Bersaglieri on the front line at Monte Nero, by now thirty-two and a little old for war. 'It is for this,' he wrote in one of his first articles sent home to *Il Popolo d'Italia*, 'that we are fighting today in Europe: a war that is at the same time a great revolution.'

2

A country ungoverned and ungovernable

Mussolini had been an unexpectedly diligent soldier back in 1905. He now asked to be considered for officer training but, unlike his brother Arnaldo, was turned down, on account of his unpredictable political views. Instead, he was offered a place at regimental headquarters, producing the Bersagliere war diary, but this he refused, saying – more family lore – that he was there not to write but to fight. He wrote his own diary, in his lively, discursive style, and sent it back to Milan to be published in *Il Popolo*. 'I live for tomorrow,' he wrote. 'I live for after tomorrow. The struggles that will come with the end of the war will be magnificent.'

The Italian army had confidently expected to defeat the Austrians in the valley of the Isonzo in Friuli, after which it intended to press ahead and take Trieste. But the war was not turning out as D'Annunzio had predicted – glorious and heroic – nor, as the futurist F. T. Marinetti preached, 'the world's only hygiene', but rather messy and murderous, the front line advancing and retreating, leaving in its wake piles of corpses. Eleven battles were fought on the Isonzo, the elderly and inflexible General Cadorna sending waves of men to be mown down by machine guns. By late November 1915, 110,000 Italian men were dead. Rats, fleas, hunger and the cold tormented the survivors.

When the first air raids sounded in Milan, Rachele, Edda and Anna took shelter in the basement. One day, two policemen knocked on the door. There had been a fire in a small hotel not far away and a Signora Mussolini was believed to have caused it. By the time Rachele had established that the culprit was Ida Dalser, and that she had just given birth to a boy she called Benito Albino, she decided to act. Typhus was spreading through the army at

Isonzo and Mussolini, who had caught it, had been sent to a hospital at Cividale del Friuli. Taking Edda with her, Rachele set out across the plains, past military convoys and lines of wounded men.

At three o'clock on a November afternoon, in a little side room off the ward and in the presence of the local mayor and witnesses, Mussolini and Rachele were married. The groom's eyes were yellow from the typhus and he was able only to whisper. He had not shaved for several days and wore a woolly beret. For a moment, enjoying her advantage, Rachele held back her '*Sì*'. The ceremony lasted five minutes. A nun produced a slice of panettone and a glass of wine. Edda, at four and a half, was now legitimate; she also had an illegitimate half-brother, Benito Albino. As Rachele said, the marriage might never have taken place at all had it not been for '*quella maniaca*'.

Mussolini was back at the front by Christmas Day, reporting piteously that all he had to eat was five chestnuts. 'Snow, cold, infinite boredom,' he wrote. 'Order, counterorder, disorder.' Then he was given leave and returned to Milan. Ida was still pursuing him and, backed into a corner, he set her up in a room in the Hotel Gran Bretagna and, before a notary, acknowledged Benito Albino as his son. By the time he returned to the front, to the ice and cold of the mountains at Carnia, Rachele herself was pregnant. On 16 March 1916, Mussolini was promoted to corporal. His letters to Edda, full of pressed flowers and leaves, were more those of a lover than a father. Rachele used them to teach the little girl to improve her reading.

To provide nourishment for Rachele when the baby came, Anna had acquired a cockerel. They fattened it up in the courtyard and Edda grew fond of the bird, stroking it, feeding it, taking it for walks with a string tied to its leg. One day she was kept away from the flat. When she was allowed back in, the cockerel had vanished. In its place was a baby, a boy called Vittorio. The silence around certain family events was a significant feature of Mussolini family life. Later, Edda would write about the confusion she felt and her acute rage at the loss of her pet.

Almost a year later, in February 1917, Mussolini was behind the lines in the rocky valley of the Caruso when the barrels of a mortar overheated and exploded. Five men standing near him were killed, and the explosion shattered Mussolini's thigh and left his body riddled with shrapnel. He was put on to a stretcher and taken to a field hospital. One of his first visitors was Sarfatti who described his '42 wounds ... like St Sebastian's arrows'. With the help of a friend, Rachele got hold of a Red Cross uniform and infiltrated herself into the hospital. By chance she was there when Ida appeared, carrying Benito Albino. Seeing her rival Ida began to shout, crying that Mussolini had seduced and abandoned her and that *she* was his real wife. While the soldiers in the nearby beds looked on and laughed, Rachele lost her temper and leapt at Ida, pulling her hair and pummelling her until Mussolini, powerless under his bandages, called for the orderlies to come and separate the two women. Ida fled.

In April, Mussolini was transferred to a hospital in Milan for a series of operations. For a while it looked as if his leg would have to be amputated. He lay in bed, studying Russian and English, boasting of his stoicism in the face of intolerable pain. He was discharged in August on crutches and spent a few days with Edda and Rachele on Lago Maggiore, fishing. When he returned to his desk at *Il Popolo d'Italia*, having been decorated with a bronze medal, Ida turned up outside with their son, shouting up at the windows: 'Wretch, pig, assassin, traitor.' She had cards printed in the name of Signora Mussolini. The police became involved and Ida was exiled from Milan as a threat to the Mussolinis and a danger to public order, and sent to Casette in the south, where she was interned as an 'enemy subject'. No longer his 'little Ida', she was out of Mussolini's life, at least for a while.

Edda, enraged by the attention paid to her brother Vittorio, had become even wilder and more irascible, terrorising the other small children in the building. When gypsies set up camp on the nearby wasteland, she was enchanted by their gold rings, many-coloured dresses and stories of life on the road, and begged them, as she wrote later, to take her with them. They refused, telling her she should stay with her parents. One day, having exasperated Rachele beyond endurance, her mother suggested that she go to live with the gypsies. Since she now had permission, the little girl hurried off to the camp only to find her new friends gone. Too proud and stubborn to go home – qualities she said were later her salvation – she hung around the empty wasteland long after dark, until rescued by her grandmother.

Edda was constantly covered in cuts and bruises and her minor acts of disobedience were becoming more spiteful. One day, seeing her grandmother nursing Vittorio on her lap, she suddenly pulled Anna's chair from under her, tipping her on to the floor. Her grandmother beat her. Rachele, hearing the noise, beat her again. Many years later, Edda would say to Vittorio, referring to the difference in their ages: 'You were lucky. You were saved six years of beatings.'

A photograph of Edda taken at this time shows a surly, sturdy child with a helmet of thick hair and rage in her eyes, sitting on a bench, her feet dangling. The fact that she had become a little despot delighted her father. He indulged her capriciousness and would have kept her at home to teach her himself, had Rachele not insisted on her going to school. Remembering this time, Edda would later say: 'I was barefoot, wild and hungry . . . a miserable child.'

The 12th Battle of the Isonzo at Caporetto, between 24 October and 7 November 1917, when the Austrian and German troops were armed with gas and flame-throwers, had resulted in the collapse of the Italian forces. Some three hundred thousand men had been killed or wounded in the last two years; many thousands of others had deserted or been taken prisoner. One of the dead was Margherita Sarfatti's eldest son, Roberto. By the time the war ended in 1918, Italy was a country of widows and orphans. The Italian army had been among the worst led and worst equipped, front-line soldiers were abandoned by their officers, and at one point reduced to cutting through barbed wire with garden secateurs. The government refused to send food parcels to those taken prisoner, on the grounds that it would only encourage others to surrender. Most of the fighting men had been stoical, but when they faltered their punishments were barbaric. Caporetto became a symbol for all that had been rotten at the heart of Italy's war.

The working men who now returned were angry, conscious of their sacrificed comrades, and they had seen what violence could achieve. They wanted a reward for all that they had suffered. Many of the Socialists among them had opposed the war in the first place. Promised jobs, land and better conditions in the factories by parliament, they received nothing, while those who had stayed behind and not gone to war had acquired skills and prospered. Back at home, living in a country they no longer felt a part of, these veterans talked of betrayal and dreamt of action. A sense of exclusion and a desire for some kind of justice, feeding on envy and resentment, spread across Italy, and it became a perfect breeding ground for the strikes that started in Umbria, Emilio Romagna, Tuscany and Lombardy. In the north, workers occupied the factories; in the south they took the land. Trains and trams were halted; bakers, nurses, electricians, teachers and printers went on strike. Production plummeted, inflation rose and there were shortages. The value of the lira fell to one quarter of what it was worth in 1914. Any increase in wages was quickly eaten up by surging costs.

The returning soldiers were not alone in feeling betrayed. The middle classes, those who had given their men as officers, felt squeezed by the 'pescecani', the sharks who had grown rich on war production, by the government which had allowed them to do so, and by the 'Bolsheviks', the agitators arising from below. In April 1919, fights broke out between striking Socialists and nationalists in Milan; the offices of *Avanti* were set on fire and four people died. A bomb went off in a theatre, killing and injuring many more. The government, fearing that any response might set off a Socialist revolution, did nothing. Eight-year-old Edda, who was often with Mussolini, witnessed many street fights; sometimes she helped patch up the casualties.

In Mussolini's absence, sales of *Il Popolo d'Italia* had fallen, and he now launched a drive for money and investors. He was at a low ebb, despised by many Socialists, ignored by the right, distrusted by the moderates. In the pages of his paper he warned that the returning men would want more than empty promises. He spoke of a 'trincerocrazia', a higher aristocracy of the trenches, a clan of men forged on the field of battle who would create a new Italy. To deny these men recognition for their sacrifices, he said, would be to invite the social fabric of Italy to 'splinter into smithereens'.

In April 1918, Rachele gave birth to a second son, Bruno. Mussolini, away at the time trying to raise money in Genoa, had instructed her to delay the birth until he got home, and when he arrived to find a new baby in the crib he scolded her. For a day or so, he tried to make himself useful, but Rachele soon chased him away from the kitchen, complaining of his extravagance and the mess he made. In the summer, they moved into a larger, more comfortable flat in Via Foro Bonaparte, not far from the Castello Sforzesco; it had a proper sitting room and long corridors down which Edda held sliding competitions with the local children. Arnaldo, Mussolini's brother and now his right-hand man at *Il Popolo d'Italia*, found a flat nearby. The returning soldiers brought the Spanish influenza with them and, while still breastfeeding Bruno, Rachele fell ill. Bruno developed diphtheria, then bronchial pneumonia and nearly died. He was a pretty baby, but had become scrawny and fragile, with an enormous head.

What Mussolini had understood, but which many politicians in Rome had failed to, was that once peace came, Italy would be profoundly split between those who had fought in the war and those who had not. Tellingly, he changed the subtitle of *Il Popolo d'Italia* from 'socialist daily' to 'daily of combatants and producers'. The moment had come to step on to the political stage. On 23 March 1919, before a group of followers, many of them Arditi, the veteran shock troops, carrying daggers and staves and wearing black shirts under their military jackets, he launched a new movement, the Fasci Italiani di Combattimento, in Milan's Piazza San Sepolcro. He had planned to stage the rally in a theatre, but since the turnout was so low he held it in a meeting room instead.

The men, plus a few women, who came included futurists and nationalists, disaffected pre-war socialists, anarchists and revolutionary syndicalists, and their numbers would later be greatly inflated by all those who wished they had been 'Fascists of the first hour'. Somewhat fuzzy in its goals, which ranged from a radical overhaul of Parliament to the confiscation of the property accumulated by war profiteers, the Fasci were to be not a party but a movement, an 'anti-party', free of the corruption and inertia of Roman politics. Mussolini pronounced the word '*Fascisti*' as '*fassisti*', the Romagnolo way.

Italy, as one of the victors of the war, expected the territorial gains it had been promised in the secret treaty of London in 1915. At Versailles in June 1919, the Italians found that the American President Woodrow Wilson did not intend to honour much of the treaty. The whole Dalmatian coast went to the Kingdom of Serbs, Croats and Slovenes, while Italy received Trentino, Venezia Giulia, Istria, Trieste and several islands along the eastern Adriatic, but was denied expanded colonies. It was, in D'Annunzio's much repeated phrase, which soon became a rallying cry, a 'mutilated victory'. When in January Wilson had passed through Milan, while he was still a hero in Italian eyes, Edda had been taken to see him in the central arcaded Galleria. There was a terrifying crush of cheering people and a soldier lifted her on to his shoulders; but the experience left her, she later claimed, with a life-long fear and dislike of crowds and crowded places.

Italy had risen in rank to become one of the four Great Powers at the Versailles Peace Conference, along with Britain, France and the US, but not getting Fiume, where the Italian speakers were in the majority, became a symbol for all it had been denied. Gabriele D'Annunzio, now fifty-six, was regarded by his admirers as a modern *condottiere*, a man who had lost an eye in a flying accident and led a squadron of nine planes on a 700-mile round trip to drop propaganda leaflets over wartime Vienna. The Italian victory, he claimed, should have caused the world to revise its view of Italians as ice-cream makers and tenors; but because of the humiliating peace terms, this view remained unchanged. On 12 September 1919, to prevent Fiume from being absorbed by what would later be known as Yugoslavia, D'Annunzio arrived to lead some two thousand 'legionaries' into the city, where from the balcony of a palace he proclaimed its annexation and himself the head of the new Regency of Carnaro. The 'Free State of Fiume', greeted with considerable excitement by its Italian population, covered just 11 square miles. In Rome, the government faltered, and meanwhile did nothing.

Mussolini, though wary of being eclipsed by the more dazzling D'Annunzio, hailed the venture in the pages of *Il Popolo d'Italia* as a grandiose revolt against the 'plutocratic Western coalition'. Italy, he declared, had acquired a new capital. He also took note of the way in which the Italians in Fiume were responding enthusiastically to D'Annunzio and his lyrical speeches, how the young in particular thronged around him singing old Arditi songs, and how they seemed drawn to Roman salutes and the cult surrounding this new leader.

Elections were called for November, the first in Italy under proportional representation. Prime ministers had been falling at a rate of one a year, and the Socialists and the centrist Catholics, brought together by their earlier neutralist stand, as well as the nationalists were all challenging the long rule of the Liberal elites. The strikes across the north of the country and D'Annunzio's exploits in Fiume gave Mussolini the chance to stand as a candidate. But the results for the Fascist movement were catastrophic: not a single seat was won, despite the presence of the acclaimed conductor Arturo Toscanini on its list. Discontent with the existing ineffective leadership in Rome played a part in bringing into parliament a high number of Socialists and Catholics from the People's Party, but for the moment the Liberals clung to power through a minority government.

On the night of the elections, Mussolini's opponents gathered in a funeral cortège with empty coffins of the defeated candidates. Carrying flaming torches and chanting '*Ecco il corpo di Mussolini*', here is Mussolini's corpse, they processed up the Foro Bonaparte before banging on Rachele's door. She gathered up the children and retreated upstairs to the attic, telling people later that she had taken with her two grenades in her apron pocket. They spent the night, terrified, listening to the cries and shouts in the streets. Edda became distraught at the thought that they had killed her father. Next morning, a policeman appeared to say that Mussolini was alive, but in custody, having been arrested in the chaos of the night. He was freed with the help of Toscanini but for a while there were fears that both the movement and *Il Popolo d'Italia* would go under. He now kept guns in his new offices in Via Paolo da Cannobio and began to talk of emigrating. Meanwhile, he took flying lessons, but caused further terrors for Edda when one day his plane caught fire and he came home limping with wounds to the same leg that had been injured in the war, his head bleeding and covered in bandages.

The turmoil and sense of imminent danger in the streets was matched by the disquiet at home. Mussolini had started a new affair with Bianca Ceccato, the curly haired eighteen-year-old office secretary, taking her to a performance of *Aida* and on a romantic weekend to Venice. Rachele, he told Bianca, was really only a peasant. Bianca got pregnant and had an abortion. Meanwhile, Mussolini had grown closer to Margherita Sarfatti. The few letters between them that survive – they were said to have written over a thousand each – chronicle delight in each other's company;

they spent most of their days at *Il Popolo d'Italia*, Mussolini drinking endless glasses of milk, into which he dunked biscuits. But the long-suffering Rachele saw Sarfatti's byline in *Il Popolo d'Italia* and, having been told that she was no longer on the paper, sent two telegrams – one to Mussolini, one to Arnaldo – threatening chaos. She said that she would throw a bomb into the office if she ever saw Sarfatti's name again.

Weary of the scenes, Edda built herself a little house in a nearby tree and took to spending hours in its branches reading. One day, deciding that she could bear the rows no longer, she ran away, but was soon tracked down and brought back. She was not a bad student, good at mathematics and literature, but she was undisciplined and excitable. At home she protested wildly if anyone touched her things, especially her violin. She begged to be allowed to take ballet lessons, but was told that it was the first step to a brothel. When Mussolini complained that she was sucking her plaits, Edda had her hair cut short, like a boy, which only increased her farouche, defiant look.

Mussolini family on the beach

Whenever he could, Mussolini kept her by him, taking her to La Scala and to the fashionable cafés in the Galleria. Edda was becoming conscious that she had an uneducated mother and a father around whom fashionable, clever women thronged. Later she would say that he taught her things that she never forgot: to value sympathy, to hate affectation, to behave naturally, to tell the truth at all times and never to cry, to feel pride in being Italian, and to stand up, always, to bullies. I learnt, she told a biographer many years later, putting a pious and poetic gloss on to the words, 'never to be mean or envious, to be intransigent, to despise the masses and to judge men coolly and to take responsibility, always, for one's own actions, accepting the consequences without looking for excuses, even when they were caused not by you, but by the wickedness of men and the malevolence of things. And the difficult art of silence, and man's inexorable solitude, which is born and dies with him.' Fine words and admirable sentiments, but they do not seem to come from the heart.

For her, Mussolini was a father who was heroic, strong, gentle and permissive, giving her what she wanted and indulging her whims. She began to divide her world into ordinary mortals and larger-than-life people, of whom he was the only one. She was too thin to be pretty, with ears that jutted out and very little neck, and she was neither gentle nor amiable, though she was intelligent and full of curiosity. At nine, she was already very like her father, passionate, jealous and possessive, unpredictable and volatile, and she had his very black, very round eyes and his imperious stare, all the more striking in her small, angular face.

The first *squadristi* appeared in 1920 in the province of Bologna. These were nationalists, former army officers and young landowners, united in their fears of a left-wing coup. There had been anarchical violence of every kind since the end of the war, everyone resorting to force as a means to express their grievances, but this was something different. Specialising in 'punitive raids', they roamed the countryside in old wartime troop transporters, armed with the *manganello*, a stave with a metal tip which they used to beat their victims, administering doses of castor oil with which to humiliate them and 'expiate' their sins, and they attacked labour unions and socialist headquarters. Some wore the Arditi black shirts and shouted the Arditi slogan '*Non me ne frego*', I don't give a damn. They called their weapons, an eclectic mix of pistols, shotguns and old rifles, '*mezzi energici*', doughty tools, and their raids 'hunting parties'. Occasionally women were raped, in front of their families. Those who stood aside and did not intervene felt ashamed and bitter.

From Bologna, the *squadre* spread to Tuscany and Emilia. Fascism was still a broad church and as they multiplied, they drew in students, adventurers, nationalists and futurists, and they saw themselves as warriors and apostles on a mission. By the end of the year, there were ninety separate Fasci in Italy, with twenty thousand members between them, but they had not yet coalesced into a political party. A journalist called Mario Missiroli, with whom Mussolini was said to have fought the last of his duels, wrote that it was like being at a party that was turning into an orgy, everyone uttering meaningless phrases and unable to find the exit. Italy, he wrote, was becoming 'everyday more a country ungoverned and ungovernable'.

Failing to quell the violence and unable to make common cause with the Socialists and the *Popolari*, the minority government fell and Giolitti was again made Prime Minister. But Giolitti, though canny, was tainted by his earlier neutrality, and was now nearing eighty. His attempts at fiscal reform were soon abandoned, and he proved no better at controlling the lawlessness; nor was he able to assuage the fears of socialist revolution, and he chose not to call out the army, or the carabinieri, or the police. Many Italians, terrified of total anarchy, began to look around for a leader with authority.

None of this was lost on Mussolini, who was using the pages of *Il Popolo d'Italia* to marshal his followers, churning out articles at great speed, yelling that he would shoot anyone who disturbed him and emerging from time to time 'like a bear from its lair'. Neighbours complained that the office was 'a cage of madmen'. A police report described Mussolini as an adversary to be feared, articulate, a skilful orator, shrewd, indifferent to money. Watering down his earlier absolutism against Church and state, he was deftly moving to the right, firing up his readers with attacks on the 'socialist barbarians'. Some trade unionists drifted towards the Fascists, along with more landowners and industrialists, and Catholics terrified of communist atheism. One of Mussolini's real skills lay in putting together and controlling disunited groups, even when it meant changing direction and contradicting himself. 'I am obsessed by this wild desire,' he wrote, 'to make a mark on my era with my will, like a lion with its claws.'

On 12 December 1920, having established a new border with the future Yugoslavia, Giolitti decided that the moment had come to deal with D'Annunzio, still perched in his palazzo in Fiume, still attracting a following and still crying out, '*O Fiume o morte.*' The end came quickly. D'Annunzio, accused of 'armed plotting against the state', declared war on Italy itself, and the Royal Italian Navy was dispatched to bomb the city. The legionaries surrendered and D'Annunzio, treated with surprising leniency, was allowed to return to Italy, where he was given the hereditary title of Principe di Montenevoso and a mansion called Il Vittoriale on Lake Garda. For Mussolini, who shrewdly did not oppose the government attack on Fiume, D'Annunzio was no longer a threat. The nationalist card was now his to play.

There were yet more elections in May 1921. This time, thirty-five Fascists were elected to the Chamber of Deputies. Mussolini was one of them. Though the Fascist squads around the country remained essentially local, with their own political bent and with powerful local leaders – or '*ras*' as they were known, after Ethiopian war lords – these were the men now gathering round him. Many of them were younger decorated war veterans, who had learnt to kill in the trenches of the Trentino and looked up to Mussolini as older and wiser. One of them was Roberto Farinacci, a quick-tongued, bad-tempered railway worker, who had risen to control the Fascists in Cremona and was now one of the new Fascist deputies. Another was Italo Balbo, the tall, striking-looking, neatly bearded son in a family of teachers, who wore a perpetual mocking smile and ruled with an iron hand over six thousand Fascists in and around Ferrara. Balbo conducted his punitive expeditions with savagery and military precision. As a member of the Arditi, he saw himself as part of the new elite, an aristocrat of war. Friends called him a '*testa calda*', a hot head.

By the summer of 1921, Mussolini was no longer the nomadic, scruffy, Bohemian agitator, but the proprietor and editor of a successful newspaper, a family man with three children and a comfortable house, and the leader of a quickly growing political movement. He had bought a car, a white Torpedo with folding seats he named Bianca, and on Sundays he took Rachele and the children for spins around the countryside. He was a fast but competent driver. He now wore carefully chosen black or grey suits, shirts with a stiff collar and garters, and Rachele went about in black button boots. Mussolini had started yet another affair, this time with Angela Curti, the daughter of an old companion from earlier days, who came with her father to ask for help in securing the release of her husband, who was in prison for murder. Angela was sophisticated and very pretty, and she had a two-year-old son. She was also an excellent listener. Years later, she said that she had found that, for all his exuberance and need for constant admiration, Mussolini was timid and averse to physical violence, and that he told her: 'I want to rise, and keep rising.' She soon found herself pregnant.

For Edda, there were fewer visits to the Scala or the Galleria, but in her thoughts, her father was becoming ever more heroic and adventurous, while the prosaic, stable Rachele, who looked delicate but was in fact adamantine, enforced discipline with her broom, prodding the children out of their hiding places and delivering painful slaps. Mussolini had wanted to teach Edda to drive, but she was too small to reach the pedals or to see out of the windscreen.

Though the May elections had brought him thirty-five parliamentary seats, Mussolini now had to navigate a tricky path between warring blocs of syndicalists, Socialists, Fascists, conservatives, landowners and industrialists – appeasing and courting some, threatening others, alert to the violence raging in the streets, while coming across as the only man who could control the chaos. To gain the power he sought, he had first to destroy the Socialists' hold on labour and local government. Events played into his hands. Just at the moment when unity was most crucial for the left, a schism among the Socialists ended with its revolutionary wing splintering off to form an Italian Communist Party.

By the summer of 1922, the general state of anarchy had grown worse. Across the country, Prefects, magistrates and police swung between turning a blind eye to the violence and actively supporting it. Those few Prefects who attempted to control the fights and punitive expeditions were frustrated by lack of men and equipment. In Rome five successive governments were voted in and quickly fell. Then a journalist and long-term Liberal deputy from the north called Luigi Facta was sworn in with yet another alliance of Liberals and *Popolari*; but his government proved even feebler than its predecessors. On 1 August, the socialist workers across the north called a general strike. It was a fatal move.

The Fascists were now no longer little bands of thugs, but had been incorporated into a loose paramilitary body and given ranks drawn from the legions of ancient Rome; they had set aside the *manganello* for revolvers, rifles and machine guns. Mussolini announced that if the government failed to stop the strike, then the Fascists would step in. Orders went out to his militiamen to wait forty-eight hours in order to allow Italians to witness the full impotence of the state, and then to act decisively.

When the moment came, the Fascist *squadre*, calling themselves '*Satana*' or '*Disperatissima*', went on the attack. In the days that followed they moved inviolate against left-wing political head-quarters and trade union offices, taking over and ransacking buildings, setting fires, commandeering buses and even trains. They did so openly, no longer bothering to raid by night. On the Lido in Venice, where the staff of the Excelsior had gone on strike, the Fascists moved in and restored order; foreign and Italian guests alike were delighted. And by the time it was all over, and peace of a kind had returned to the streets, the socialist workers had effectively been beaten, while the Fascists had positioned themselves as the champions of law and order, the defenders of the *patria* against '*il pericolo rosso*', the red menace. Fascism itself had become a strong, patriotic alternative to what were widely perceived as years of corrupt and inept Liberal rule. Beyond irreso-lute protests, its opponents appeared to have little to offer in terms of government.

Mussolini had played a clever game by ostensibly disassociating himself from the violence. At the Fascist Party conference, held in Naples on 24 October, conscious of the fierce jostling for leader-ship among the *ras*, he emerged as stronger than his rivals. He was not the most brilliant of them, but he had never wavered in his aims and he had seen better than anyone what could be achieved by playing on the fears and ambitions of ordinary Italians. He had been offered two ministerial posts by the Facta government, but turned them down, saying that the Fascists would take six or noth-ing. Before the conference ended, he told a cheering audience of tens of thousands of men: 'Either the government will be given to us or we shall seize it by marching on Rome.' A cry went up: 'Roma! Roma! Roma!'

Whether it was Balbo, as he later claimed, or Mussolini himself who decided that the moment had actually come to take the battle to Rome is not clear. But four '*quadrumviri*' – Balbo; Michele Bianchi, a revolutionary syndicalist; Emilio De Bono, a decorated career general with a luxuriant beard, and the head of Turin's Fasci, Cesare Maria de Vecchi – were appointed, each to lead a column of marching men, with Perugia as their headquarters. They began to marshal their forces and to plan a pincer movement on the capital for 28 October. Mussolini, increasing the pressure, issued an ultimatum: what he demanded now was to be made President of the Council. For his part, Facta had also decided that the moment had come to act. He proposed to impose martial law and arrest the Fascist leaders, but for this he needed royal assent. The King was summoned and returned reluctantly to Rome from hunting on his country estate at San Rossore. Whether because the King had little faith in either the Liberal state or the army, or because he feared ensuing anarchy, or even because he sensed that he might be deposed in favour of his cousin the Duke of Aosta, who was openly supporting the Fascists, he now refused to ratify the order. Facta and his government resigned. The Liberal regime, with all its equivocations and compromises, had been in power since unification; now its days appeared to be over. It could have been otherwise. There were some 25,000 soldiers from the regular army ready to defend the capital. They were not called out.

In Milan, Mussolini had planned his tactics carefully. Young Fascists, some barely teenagers, had been detailed to guard over the family home in Foro Bonaparte. Rachele kept her revolver by her at all times, and later claimed that she had placed grenades wrapped in cotton wool on top of a cupboard. Mussolini appeared to be in a cheerful mood, constantly whistling, helping Edda with her homework. He told Rachele that he was organising 'something special'.

In later years, Edda would say that she remembered little of the turbulent events of her childhood. But she never forgot the eve of the March on Rome, the night of 27 October 1922. That afternoon, Mussolini had instructed Rachele and herself to dress up, as they were going to the theatre. Molnar's *The Swan* was playing at the Manzoni theatre. They took their places in a box, conscious that from all over the auditorium binoculars had been trained on them. Every few minutes there was a discreet knock on the door of the box. Mussolini would slip out into the corridor, then return to his place.

The second act had just begun when he whispered in Rachele's ear: 'It's time.' Taking Edda's arm, he hurried them home. The telephone never stopped ringing with people asking for orders. One caller wanted to know whether the Fascists should blow up the offices of *Il Corriere della Sera*, which had been hostile to the Fascists. Mussolini said no. Then came the call he had been waiting for: the King wished to see him to ask him to form a coalition government. Mussolini asked Rachele to pack a suitcase for him, then left to catch the slow night train to Rome. He refused the special train offered to him by the government.

By train, by car, on foot, in lorries and on horseback, men dressed in every kind of military and civilian clothes, some wearing black shirts, others knee-high black boots and spurs, with the Arditi sporting their death's head insignia, had been descending on the capital. They had orders to occupy post offices, radio stations, newspaper officers and the police and carabiniere headquarters. The Romans standing at their windows looked on. Mussolini's train was an hour and forty minutes late, and he emerged on the platform to declare that he intended to make certain that the trains henceforth ran on time. Dressed in a bizarre combination of black shirt, bowler hat and spats, he was duly received by the King – explaining his odd costume as having come 'from the battlefield' – and asked to form a government.

Edda and Vittorio, who had not been sent to school that day, were with Rachele in their flat when Mussolini rang to tell them the news. Edda was now just twelve. The father she loved and admired had gone from blacksmith's son and political brawler to becoming, at the age of thirty-nine, the twenty-seventh and youngest prime minister in Italian history. On 31 October, after parading his followers through Rome to the Quirinale, where the King and the royal family were standing on the balcony, Mussolini was sworn in. The sun shone brightly; the crowds lining the streets cheered.

3

A path full of traps

Perched at their windows and on their balconies, watching Mussolini's rag-tail army parade jubilantly through their streets, the Romans were not at all certain what to expect. Politicians, aristocrats, the legions of bureaucrats in this excessively bureaucratic city, nationalists, monarchists and most ordinary citizens had come to feel that the coup that had taken place had probably been inevitable, and they welcomed what they saw as an end to the chaos and the threat of a communist takeover. They were also looking forward to a time when ministers of justice did not come to power and fall again the next year. But they equally believed that Mussolini's reign would not last long, that they could get rid of him whenever they wanted, and then return government into the familiar, conciliatory hands of the Liberal coalitions that had ruled Italy since unification. Meanwhile, for the short time it would take, the new prime minister would surely set Italy to rights.

Mussolini did not see it that way. He settled quickly into a suite in the Grand Hotel, set up his office in the Palazzo Chigi, formerly the Ministry for Colonial Affairs, and began to rule. His dreams and ambitions were limitless and he had no time to lose. For the moment, Rachele, Edda, Vittorio and Bruno were to remain in the Foro Bonaparte in Milan.

The country he had inherited was bankrupt, and its Parliament was a place of factions, poor attendance and 'trasformismo', the bartering of votes for favours. There was a profound divide between north and south, the northerners of the industrial triangle regarding the southerners as more African than European, inferior in every way, physically, morally and socially. Landowners and the Mafia between them exercised unimaginable power across the

Edda, Rachele, Vittorio and Bruno

south. The Spanish influenza, which started in 1918 and lasted two years, had killed 600,000 Italians, and the war slaughtered over half a million of its men. A quarter of the population could neither read nor write. Trachoma, syphilis, malaria, rickets and all manner of skin diseases were widespread. In Rome, the children of the poor, who lived in hovels around the city walls or in decaying buildings without running water or electricity, went around barefoot. The most recent census had found that 45,000 Romans – a little less than a tenth of its population – lived in penury.

Rome itself, crumbling and dilapidated, was also a city of princely families, with generations of intermarriages and immense palaces full of magnificent art and small armies of liveried servants. Many of these palazzi, in every style from late Renaissance to rococo, lay along the Corso, the street considered by Stendhal to be the finest in Italy, which ran for a mile from the Piazza del Popolo in a straight line to Piazza Venezia, over which loomed the monstrous, gleaming white monument to Victor Emmanuel II, known to Romans as the wedding cake or the *pisciatoio nazionale*, the national urinal.

At the apex of this Roman nobility, split between the Black, or papal, and the White, which owed its allegiance to the ruling house of Savoy, was the retiring, pedantic Victor Emmanuel III, who was unfortunately also spineless and deeply irresolute, and so small that he barely reached the shoulder of his stately queen, the Montenegrin Elena. Regal in public and dressed for another era, Queen Elena was good natured and frugal at home. She liked to cook, play the violin and brew up herbal concoctions from Montenegrin recipes for her ailing friends. There were five children and she was said to prefer the 18-year-old son and heir, Umberto. The Royal family rarely left the rococo Quirinale, on one of Rome's seven hills, but when forced to travel, they took the court and nobility with them. Whenever he could, the King went to his country estate to hunt; when in Rome, he gardened. The family ate sparingly and lived modestly, having moved into the least grand wing of the Quirinale. The few visitors invited to court receptions reported acute boredom and disgusting *spumante*, the fizzy wine of Piemonte.

And there was the Vatican, at war with the Italian state since September 1870, when Italian troops broke through the Aurelian walls, expelled the Papal rulers, and claimed Rome for the new united Italy. In some of the palaces of the Black nobility, the chair in which the Pope sat when visiting was kept turned to face the wall, in memory of the day when the papacy lost its power. For the most important Church occasions, the Holy Father was carried on a ceremonial throne by bearers dressed in red with white peacock feathers, with a bodyguard from the Black nobility in ruffs, capes and knee breeches.

What this enclosed, deeply privileged and gossipy Roman world, with its exquisite courtesy, perfect taste and snobbery, would make of the boorish, loud and unsophisticated Fascist men, and their ill-dressed and little educated wives, speaking every kind of regional accent but seldom the accepted Florentine one, remained to be seen. Nor was it clear what they in turn would make of the Romans. That he had to rid his party of all its rabble rousers, and tame its thuggish, aggressive foot soldiers, was immediately obvious to Mussolini. But he also knew that to woo the hostile Catholics, he had to find some kind of arrangement with the Vatican, and that to neutralise the disdainful monarchy he had to co-opt it, however much he longed for a republic, and even if, in private, he was heard to say that the King was 'by definition, a useless citizen' and 'too small for an Italy about to become great'. He intended, he announced, to make Rome 'marvellous to the whole world, vast, orderly, powerful as in the days of Augustus'; and he planned to turn Italy once again into an Empire. The King already found Mussolini both fascinating and terrifying.

Within a very few days, Mussolini had appointed his first cabinet, rewarding the *ras* who had brought him to power and bringing in all the major parties, except for the Communists and his old friends the Socialists, and reserving just four portfolios for the Fascists. For himself, he took the Interior and Foreign ministries. On 16 November, his party members ominously dressed in militia uniforms, he addressed an apprehensive Parliament. He was firm, purposeful and not a little threatening. He told the assembled deputies that, had he so wished, he could have turned 'this grey and gloomy chamber into a bivouac for my men. I could have bolted the doors of Parliament and had an exclusively Fascist government'; but he had chosen not to, then he paused, 'at least for the moment'. The Sardinian deputy Emilio Lussu noted that Mussolini reminded him of a cat with a mouse in its paws, 'holding it now gently, now letting it go, then snatching it back'.

In the vote of confidence that followed, only the Communists and Socialists opposed Mussolini; a very small number of deputies abstained; and all five former prime ministers voted with the majority to support him. When he asked for an entire year in which to deliver 'essential reforms', he was granted it with a handsome majority. Exceptionally, Mussolini now had the necessary powers to govern without having to seek parliamentary approval. His rise from virtually unknown journalist to head of the government had taken less than two years.

After his first unmistakable threat, Mussolini moved cautiously, conscious of the need for a smooth transition from *squadrista* bullying to legitimate governance. Those *ras* now recognised as *gerarchi*, party leaders, were for the most part small-minded, self-interested and not especially clever men, and some were given under-secretaryships. The spirited and ambitious Balbo was put in charge of forming a new national militia, reporting to Mussolini alone. Since the idea of youth and vitality lay at the heart of Mussolini's vision for Italy, the philosopher Giovanni Gentile was appointed Minister for Public Instruction and asked to put together far-reaching educational reforms, with an emphasis on new, communal values and beliefs. But having wrested power for himself, Mussolini did not seriously propose to share it, and nor did he want the men around him to imagine themselves his friends. He wanted them respectful and a little frightened, and sometimes spoke of them as 'pygmies'. Arnaldo, now editor of *Il Popolo d'Italia*, which he was busy turning into the mouthpiece of the regime, was his only confidant. The brothers spoke on the telephone every evening, at ten o'clock. He did not always remember to speak to Rachele in Milan, and Edda was finding his absence painful.

Since Fascism was claiming to be something spiritually new, born out of the comradeship and sacrifices of the war, it needed to forge a past, a national story. For this, Mussolini intended to turn to the myths of ancient Rome, reconstructing its memories and rituals as substitutes for democratic choices. The themes of blood and martyrdom were wound into the official narrative, Fascist violence recast as 'saintly and moral', and what was perceived to be the Fascist revolution as Mussolini's rise to become head of government.

The so-called anniversary of the foundation of Rome was proclaimed a national holiday, the Roman eagle and the she-wolf suckling Romulus and Remus became symbols of veneration, and the *fascio* – from the Latin *fascis*, a bundle of rods tied to an axe and representing authority in ancient Rome – was made the emblem of the Italian state. To solve the many contradictions inherent in the great mix of his backers, Fascism, Mussolini declared, would be at once modern and traditional, nationalist and syndicalist, conservative and revolutionary, looking backwards to classical Rome and forwards to industrialisation and technological advance. In this byzantine new world of opposites, faith was to count more than reason, spirit more than matter, action more than thought. 'Our myth,' Mussolini declared, 'is the greatness of the nation.' As a canny and seasoned journalist, Mussolini understood better than anyone 'the tremendous magic of words'.

One of his first pronouncements had been to promise 'a truly

Fascist foreign policy'. He wanted, he said, Italy to be treated 'like a sister and not like a waitress'. Exactly what this meant was not clear but foreign governments, relieved to see a measure of stability return to Italy, greeted Mussolini with tentative approval. His first appearance on the international stage took place three weeks after coming to power, at a conference to settle Turkey's borders in Lausanne. Surrounded by bodyguards and keeping the delegates waiting, he appeared ill at ease and remained largely silent. In London to discuss German war reparations a few weeks later, he was serenaded by military-style parades of black-shirted Italian Fascists who had made England their home, and complained bitterly about the all-pervasive 'grey grime' of the city, before voting first one way and then another, and making fiercely anti-British remarks. There was talk of him being a 'dangerous rascal' and possibly 'slightly off his head'.

A more serious test of this truly Fascist foreign policy came when an Italian general, working with an International Boundary Commission, was murdered on Greek territory in August 1923. Mussolini ordered the bombardment of Corfu from the sea and occupied the island. Most of the few dozen casualties were children. Greece imposed martial law. The British government, initially bellicose, called on the League of Nations to arbitrate but, after Mussolini threatened to withdraw from it, they were forced to climb down, incensed by what they regarded as Mussolini's bluster and bad faith. Mussolini emerged stronger, the League weaker. In the *Manchester Guardian*, Robert Dell warned that an 'unfortunate precedent had been set'.

Tired of being pestered by journalists, Mussolini moved from his suite in the Grand Hotel to a flat on the Via Rasella not far from the Quirinale, found for him by Margherita Sarfatti, who also provided him with a housekeeper, Cesira Carocci. Bit by bit, he was feeling his way into Roman life. There had been much ridicule when he was first seen in his assortment of top hat, black shirt and spats but, on the advice of a fashionable young diplomat, he was now getting his clothes made – and advising his *gerarchi* to do the same – by an expensive tailor. The British Ambassador, Sir Ronald Graham, gave a dinner in his honour, then the Principessa Marianna Giovanelli, lady-in-waiting to the Queen, gave another. The guests professed themselves amazed at the correctness of his manners. They had already remarked that Dino Grandi, the new under-secretary in the Interior Ministry, looked like a 'handsome pirate', and that the sprightly, bearded Balbo shone like 'burnished steel'. They also liked the way that the *gerarchi* seemed genuinely to appreciate women, and there was none of the usual gossip, so prevalent in Roman society, about impotence and sodomites.

Margherita Sarfatti

Mussolini was constructing a routine that he would follow for the next twenty years. He rose early, exercised, ate sparingly and worked extremely hard. His energy, to his flagging associates, appeared inexhaustible. Two of his recent mistresses had now had his babies – Bianca Ceccato a boy called Glauco, Angela Curti a girl called Elena – and he continued to pursue other women vora- ciously and seemingly indiscriminately, providing they were not too thin. As he put it, 'my sexual appetite does not allow for mon- ogamy'. He enjoyed it when they smelt a little, whether of sweat or scent and, often not very clean himself, did not mind them grubby. Edda now had two illegitimate half-brothers, Glauco and Benito Albino, and one illegitimate half-sister, Elena.

What he was discovering was that dozens of women – the wives of Fascists, diplomats and civil servants – were perfectly willing to put up with his rapid, sometimes brutal sexual transactions. The noble women of the Corso may have laughed at his earlier uncouth manners, but some at least were happy to drop in to the Via Rasella. In public, Mussolini could still be very unkempt, not always bothering to shave, chafing at butterfly collars and having his shoes made with elastic sides, so that he did not have to waste time tying laces. Ever unpredictable, he swung between warmth and rudeness, caution and impetuousness, ferocity and forgiveness. But his smile could be very charming. As one British visitor noted, Mussolini came across as a somewhat sinister figure, 'fundamentally vulgar and not so much strong as violent', but he was full of attractive ideas.

Perhaps not surprisingly, Mussolini was in no hurry to have Rachele and the children in Rome. He paid fleeting visits to Milan, where he spent more time in the offices of *Il Popolo d'Italia* than in the Foro Bonaparte, and quarrelled violently with Rachele. In his absence, Edda's streak of rebelliousness had become more pronounced, and she was now constantly at war with her mother. If in so many ways like her father, it was from Rachele that she appeared to have inherited a second strain of toughness, a quick temper and a tendency to sulk. She found her grandmother Anna easier and more loving. Edda had set herself up as the leader of a pack of local children, conducting them on perilous escapades across the rooftops, though she had little time for the girls among them. They nicknamed her Sandokan, after the hero of a popular children's book. At school, she was considered clever and got high marks in everything except for Latin and Greek; in gymnastics, she scored 10/10. She refused to wear stockings, preferring to show off her cuts and bruises. All Mussolinis were deeply superstitious and Edda especially so: black cats, spilt milk and umbrellas opened inside the house were all to be avoided.

Possibly under the influence of the religious-minded Arnaldo, or as a sop to the Vatican, Mussolini decided to have the three children christened. The ceremony took place at home in Milan and was conducted by Arnaldo's brother-in-law, Don Colombo Bondanini. It was getting harder for any of them to escape public attention – both good and bad – and Edda complained that some of her teachers fawned over her, while others treated her with unwarranted severity. As Mussolini's eldest child and only daughter, she felt herself to be the most scrutinised and subject to higher expectations than her brothers.

King George V and Queen Mary paid a state visit to Rome in the spring of 1923, increasing Mussolini's international respectability, and before he left the King bestowed on him the Order of Bath, causing much merriment among the children when translated into *l'Ordine del Bagno*.

Victor Emmanuel had also given him the most prestigious Collare dell'Annunziata, which made him his nominal cousin, and offered him titles, but Mussolini refused them. When the Queen Mother, Margherita, visited Milan, Rachele and the children were invited to attend a screening of a film about the life of Christ at the Palazzo della Sport. An equerry appeared to invite Edda and her mother to the royal box, where the Queen Mother stroked Edda's hair and told Rachele that she was grateful for everything that Mussolini was doing for Italy. But Rachele, too, was in no hurry to move to Rome to be observed by the malicious Romans. In any case, she declared, she was, and was proud to remain, a peasant. She called Mussolini 'professor', the Romagnolo way.

The family spent the summers of 1922 and 1923 in Levanto, in a hotel by the sea. On one of his visits, Edda was told that her father, piloting his own plane, would fly low over the beach to wave to them and she duly positioned herself on the sands to wait. A plane appeared on the horizon, drew near and she began to wave her handkerchief. Suddenly, it faltered, tipped to one side and plunged to the ground. Terrifying minutes passed before it was discovered that the dead pilot was not Mussolini, but a young aviator, come to salute his fiancée on the same beach. Edda later confessed that she found it hard to get the spectacle of the slowly cascading plane out of her mind.

Mussolini had repeatedly boasted that Fascism was not a party, but an anti-party. The moment had now come when Fascism itself needed to take shape; it was no longer enough to have ousted the old Liberal elite and his socialist rivals. He had asked for absolute power to rule for a year, and did not intend to squander it. Italy was still riven by a degree of *squadrista* violence and angry political opposition and before anything else could be done, both had to be crushed. All over the country, the leading *ras*, dictators in their own regions, continued to force citizens they deemed subversive to drink castor oil, to go on murderous punitive expeditions, and to sing of conquest and force. A much-loved priest, Don Giovanni Minzoni, was beaten to death in August 1923 in Argenta while trying to organise a rural cooperative in the province of Ferrara.

To contain the violence and bring some kind of order to the *squadristi*, a new Milizia Volontaria per la Sicurezza Nazionale, founded on 1 February 1923, enrolled men between the ages of twenty and fifty into Roman-style military units, with 133 legions, one for every province. They had uniforms of black shirts and fezzes, and swore allegiance not to the King but to Mussolini. Many were already well versed in violence and coercion. Relieved to see an end to the chaos, Italians made very little protest, though the army leadership branded these irregulars 'fanatics'. Needing something closer to him, Mussolini also approved the establishment of a secret group, with outposts all over the country but the most important one in Rome, which quickly became known as the '*Ceka*' after the Russian secret services. Its job was to intimidate political opponents, by collecting incriminating information on them and conducting its own punitive expeditions.

In January 1923, Mussolini appointed a Gran Consiglio – in theory the pre-eminent consultative body on matters of state, in practice little more than a rubber stamp for his decisions – and he merged the Fascist and nationalist parties, hitherto separate, into one. If by now it was becoming clear that the menace of a communist takeover had been much exaggerated, it was also plain that Mussolini was a superlative puppeteer, a plotter and manipulator, quick to adapt, skilfully using friends and enemies alike, while presenting himself always as the restorer of law and order.

In pursuit of creating Fascist ideals, he was no less attentive to culture. Sarfatti had followed him to Rome and, though they were forced to meet secretly until her husband's death in 1924, she was quickly nicknamed the 'Duce's muse'. She was now editor of *Gerarchia*, the party's monthly journal, and she was helping prepare for Italy's participation in the forthcoming Paris Exhibition of Decorative Arts. In her salon, hung with Picasso drawings, Rome's writers, artists and architects met to discuss the Novecento Italiano, a movement fusing the ancient and the modern to produce a new modernist classicism. Sarfatti intended to smarten Mussolini up, not only in appearance but also in culture: she forced him to visit exhibitions and go to the theatre. He called her Vela, the sail that guided his intellectual journey, steering him to subtler thoughts.

He had also appointed the philosopher Giovanni Gentile to come up with a Manifesto of Fascist Intellectuals, a guide to a new Enlightenment touched by the 'grace of Fascism', with a steely message between its velvet paws. 'Culture', in Gentile's credo, meant obedience to the state and artists, inspired by the Roman principles of discipline and duty and uncontaminated by foreign or democratic influences, were to put their talents entirely at its service. No other culture, it was understood, could exist any longer outside Fascism. Benedetto Croce, Italy's most regarded liberal philosopher and historian, who had earlier supported Mussolini, now acted swiftly to put together a reply, signed by academics and writers, who dismissed the Manifesto as incoherent, banal, absurd, sterile, cynical, aberrant and full of demagoguery. An unbridgeable rift opened between the two factions.

In April 1924 Italy went to the polls. The elections were overshadowed by Fascist intimidation and saw opposition candidates wounded and a number killed, but they brought Mussolini a comfortable majority. The Socialist vote virtually halved; the other parties splintered. His position seemed unassailable; even his former critics grudgingly conceded him the title 'Duce'.

But there were still a few brave, determined opponents and they found their champion in Giacomo Matteotti, the courageous, doggedly anti-Fascist thirty-nine-year-old secretary of the newly formed moderate Socialist Unitary Party who, having to shout above the jeers in the Chamber, demanded that the elections be annulled. He had evidence, he said, of illicit arms deals and bribes from an American oil company, as well as information on widespread election fraud. He promised to bring it before Parliament. He had no time to do so. On 10 June, as he was leaving his house on the banks of the Tiber, he was seized by members of the *Ceka*. Not long after, the car they had used was discovered spattered in blood, and six weeks later Matteotti's body, covered in stab wounds, was found in a shallow ditch not far from Rome.

No proof was ever found that Mussolini had ordered Matteotti's murder; as with Henry II and St Thomas a Becket, words he had uttered were thought to have been misinterpreted as a call to murder. But there was no doubt that the Fascists were responsible, and Matteotti's disappearance and death were profoundly damaging to Mussolini. A huge groundswell of revulsion gathered strength and Fascist Party members returned their cards. At ten o'clock on 27 June, millions of Italians stood bareheaded for a moment's silence. To diffuse the mounting tension and show that he was not involved in the subsequent inquiry, Mussolini gave up the Ministry of the Interior portfolio. He also brought in a decree suspending newspapers which printed 'sedition': his old paper, *Avanti*, would be shut down thirty-six times in the next few months. But neither his resignation nor the arrest of the *Ceka* assassins calmed the sense of national disgust. The corridors of Parliament, usually thronged and noisy, were deserted. The Socialists declared him a broken and defeated bandit chieftain. 'There are two dead people,' wrote the journalist Ugo Ojetti, 'Matteotti and Mussolini. Italy is divided in two, half crying over the death of the first, half over the second.' To his followers, Mussolini appeared anxious and uncertain, prey to the first signs of the ulcer that would torment him for the rest of his life.

His opponents in Parliament were now in a strong position to challenge him. But they could not agree on a strategy. They havered and squabbled. A hundred deputies retired from the Chamber, saying that the government was no longer constitutional and that they would stay away until democracy was restored; they called themselves the Aventino, after the last stand of the Aventine Plebeian secessionists in 494 BC. The King, invited to dissolve Parliament, refused. The Socialists proposed an alliance with the Catholic *Popolari* but the Vatican backed off. After five turbulent months, Parliament reconvened. The crisis was not over. The sales of *Il Popolo d'Italia* plummeted. But then a Fascist deputy called Armando Casalini was murdered by a communist shouting 'Vendetta for Matteotti': it provided the Fascists with a useful martyr, and the *squadristi* with the pretext for a fresh wave of violence. Mussolini held his nerve, telling his unruly followers that they must abandon their bullying tactics.

Rachele was kept informed of events in Rome by Mussolini, and she claimed to believe him when he told her that he had nothing to do with Matteotti's killing. The heightened tensions had, however, made the family vulnerable, and bodyguards were assigned to watch over her and the children. For fourteen-year-old Edda this meant more control, more accountability, more encroachment on her wild ways. She felt on display, criticised. But she was also revelling in her father's approval of her. In the summer, when the sea was very rough, she had saved the life of an older girl who had swum out too far. Mussolini proudly awarded her one of Fascism's silver medals for courage but, knowing what she felt about being the centre of attention, he allowed her to skip the usual ceremony that went with it. Edda was missing him. She felt that he had modelled her and had now chosen to abandon her. Still fighting with her mother, and feeling herself to be considerably older than her brothers, she mourned the days when her father had taken her everywhere with him.

In the midst of these months of unease and uncertainty, two of Rachele's sisters, Pina and Giovanna, died within weeks of each other. Giovanna had gone into labour in the middle of a hailstorm with no possibility of reaching the distant hospital, then given birth to a daughter before an infection set in. Rachele arrived as she lay dying and Giovanna handed her the baby and asked her to look after her. Rachele found a wet nurse and took the baby home, but she died soon after.

Not long before she had paid a visit to Predappio and Forlì, where this time she received an excited welcome, with crowds turning out to cheer her. But she did not fail to notice the way that the local grandees, who had once scorned her, now came to pay her court and ask for favours. She had recently inherited a small legacy and used it to buy the Villa Carpena, a *casa colonica* with land not far away, which she planned to turn into a working farm, planting new varieties of fruit trees and wheat and keeping cows for milk.

Shortly before the March on Rome, Mussolini had told his followers: 'The dictatorship card is a big one, and can be played just once. It carries terrible risks and once played, it cannot be played again.' On 3 January 1925, he judged that the moment had come to play it. Before a largely silent Parliament – the deputies recalled from their Christmas holidays but still missing the 100 Aventine members, who made the fatal mistake of believing that they could still triumph by legal means but who would in reality never be allowed back in – he declared that the solution to the crisis was 'force'. He promised to deliver it. Though not of course personally responsible for Matteotti's death, it was up to him alone, he said, to take responsibility, and now up to him alone to put Italy back on its course to greatness. The country, he told them, 'wants peace and quiet, work and calm. I will give them these things with love if possible and force if necessary.'

That night, telegrams went out to the Prefects in all the regions to order the closure of associations, clubs, left-leaning institutions and opposition newspapers, along with the arrest of 111 well-known 'subversives'. One of the last papers to shut was *Il Corriere della Sera*. 'I consider,' said its renowned editor, Luigi Albertini, 'the Italian nation in a state of permanent war.' But Mussolini's own party also had to be dragooned into obedience. The most powerful and dangerous of the Fascist extremists were co-opted and silenced. Farinacci, the fanatic from Cremona, the most hated and feared of all the *gerarchi*, who went around with a revolver visible on his belt, was neutralised by being made party secretary. The King approved a cabinet in which Mussolini had taken for himself not just the prime ministership, but the Foreign Ministry and the Ministries of War, the Navy and Aviation. Sparked by Matteotti's brutal death, a new chapter was opening. Fascism was back in control and Mussolini, with his springy, cat-like step and the mannerisms – the jutting jaw, the scowl, the large bald head thrown back, the staring eyes – that would define his long tenure, was not about to cede any corner of it. Discipline was to be just another word for dictatorship. The 'fascistisation' of Italy had begun.

Mussolini's visits to Milan continued, but there were fewer of them and he sometimes stayed with the newly widowed Sarfatti in a hotel, fuelling rumours that he and Rachele had separated. When in the Foro Bonaparte they had furious rows, Rachele attacking him for his persistent infidelities, and both parents used Edda as their witness, calling on her to take their side. After one particularly savage explosion, Edda decided to run away again, cycling 20 kilometres before she was found and brought home. Later, she would say that it was a 'double betrayal . . . both my father and my mother did me harm'. She had become aware of the rumours, ignited by the fact that her parents had only married after her birth – and with only Mussolini's name on the birth certificate – that she was the daughter not of Rachele, but of Balabanoff. She knew it not to be true, but it only intensified her feeling of being constantly scrutinised.

There was in Rachele a tacit assumption, shared by many Italian women, that men, and especially powerful men, were somehow entitled to their mistresses. But the open secret of Mussolini's philandering, snidely alluded to in the popular scandal sheets, was more than she could always bear. In public, the Duce was often heard to say that his mother Rosa was his model for perfect motherhood, and that matrimony was 'indissoluble'. In the spring, Rachele and the children moved to the Villa Carpena, and schooling was arranged for Vittorio and Bruno in Forlì. Edda, announcing that she could no longer stand the arguments and recriminations between her parents or her role as go-between, asked to be sent away to boarding school. She also knew that her mother had an admirer, perhaps a lover, which only increased her intense wariness about the faithlessness of adults.

The school Mussolini chose for Edda was the most prestigious establishment for girls in Italy. It was called the Istituto Femminile della SS Annunziata and it occupied the summer residence of the former grand dukes of Florence, with gardens designed by a pupil of Le Nôtre. Its pupils were the daughters of the nobility, and its many rooms were frescoed, with silk hangings and ducal crests. Before Edda arrived, Mussolini wrote to the headmistress: his daughter was to be treated 'the same, exactly the same, as all the other girls'. The plain, severe uniform was grey, with a collar and belt of different colours to denote family ranking, and pupils were told to arrive with three hats, two pairs of gloves and twelve pairs of black cotton stockings. They were taught French and Italian literature and history, drawing, sewing, mending and embroidery, religion and morality. There were regular outings for the study of worthy causes and works of art.

Edda hated it all. She found the excessive formality and strict orderliness, after fifteen years of chaos and improvisation, painfully stultifying. She was treated with disdain by the other girls, who, for her part, she considered prim, frivolous, and their white gloves and decorum absurd. On a day of a widely publicised threat to Mussolini's life, everyone stared at her in the refectory; she pretended total indifference, but when the meal was over she fled to her room and cried. She mourned her freedom. She fought with her teachers, sided with the domestic staff and was rude to the headmistress, calling her a polecat and a witch, for which she was repeatedly punished. The headmistress struggled, but she was no match for the '*cavallina matta*' who had decided that insolence would force her father to free her. Eventually Mussolini agreed to take her away. No one was sad to see her go.

Edda was still in Florence when Anna, who had moved with the family to the Villa Carpena, died in her sleep. Not long before, she had told Rachele that she should be less strict with her children, and, as perhaps the only constant and reliably loving person in Edda's life, who – unlike her parents – showed real emotion, Anna was very important to her granddaughter. Edda was home again when, on 29 December 1925, to complement the civil one that had taken place during the war, Mussolini and Rachele had a religious wedding. It was a characteristic Mussolini event: Rachele was rolling out pasta when Mussolini appeared with his witnesses. She grumbled, took off her apron and joined them. It was all over in five minutes. There were no photographs, no celebrations, and Mussolini left soon after the ceremony. With a reconciliation with the Vatican on the cards, he needed to shed all taint of being a '*mangiapreti*', an eater of priests, and he had also insisted on a confirmation for the three children, a ceremony carried out by Cardinal Vincenzo Vannutelli in a private chapel. To everyone's relief the family were now back in Milan, in a larger and more elegant rented flat in Via Mario Pagano, though the children missed the livelier, more popular Foro Bonaparte.

What people would later remember about 1926 was that it was the year of repeated attempts on Mussolini's life, and that they heralded a whole new level of repression. Edda had not been with her father when, the preceding April, sixty-two-year-old Violet Gibson, the daughter of an Irish peer later declared mad and shut up in an asylum, drew a pistol from her bag and shot Mussolini as he was leaving the Campidoglio in Rome. He received a slight wound to his nose, which he made light of, but enjoyed sporting a

Edda

blood-stained bandage and maintaining that he was invincible, protected by a higher power.

But Edda and Rachele were both with him in Bologna for the opening of a new stadium, when sixteen-year-old Anteo Zamboni shot at Mussolini's open car as it drove slowly through the streets. The Duce was unhurt but the crowds, angry and agitated, lynched the boy and dragged his body along the road before anyone had a chance to discover who he was or why he had wanted Mussolini dead. Edda and her mother were in a separate car taking them back to the station when a panic-stricken official arrived to describe the scene. There was an agonising wait, no one certain about whether or not Mussolini was alive, before he eventually appeared, unhurt. The train carrying them home stopped at every station to show the crowds who gathered that Mussolini was unharmed. For Edda, it was yet another incident marking the unsafety of life. It contributed to her feeling that she had to be strong, or at least to show every appearance of strength and self-reliance.

Coming very soon after another attack, when an anarchist marble worker called Gino Lucetti threw a bomb at Mussolini in Rome, which bounced off his car, leaving him shaken but unhurt, the Bologna shooting became the catalyst for a fundamental review of the police forces.

As a young man in the 1890s, Arturo Bocchini, the youngest son of a southern landowner, had been good-looking, with deep-set eyes, a sensual mouth and a long, interesting face. A career rising through the civil service in the Ministry of the Interior to become first Prefect of Brescia, then of Bologna, had seen him grow corpulent and greedy, with a taste for salacious gossip and women. When, shortly before the Bologna attack, he had been appointed chief of police, he had found the entire system antiquated, underfunded and almost unchanged since it was set up in 1852 to 'watch over vagabonds, ne'er-do-wells, beggars, women of loose morals and recidivist gamblers'. It became Bocchini's life's work to reform the police service, to put in place a coherent, disciplined organisation and to make certain than never again would Mussolini's life be in danger. His reforms sounded the death rattle of the liberal democratic state.

Seldom rising from his desk in the Palazzo del Viminale except to eat gargantuan meals, the shrewd and extremely clever Boc-chini, who had a prodigious memory and a character riddled with vengefulness, began to put in place an apparatus of repression so perfect, he would say, that he could sometimes permit himself a certain tolerance and leniency. He overhauled the police force, cre-ated new divisions, asked for and was granted more money and greater powers, and set up a special department of political police – known as PolPol – and later a special inspectorate to deal with political dissidents, public order, Communists and the Mafia. Soon, there were also border policemen, and a squad of agents to protect Mussolini and his family day and night, along with fat files on the lives of individual Italians, their habits, opinions and morals. The most interesting of these Bocchini took every morning for Musso-lini to pore over. In order to do anything at all, whether buy a car or rent a house, an Italian now required a permit from the Pub-blica Sicurezza, to be renewed every year, for which he needed a certificate of good conduct, issued by the local police. Into Boc-chini's private office came a steady flow of gifts, from baskets of fruit and vegetables to valuable pictures and silver ornaments.

On appointing Bocchini police chief, Mussolini had asked him for a system of control that had the 'tentacles of an octopus'. Over and above the political police, there was a new secret service known as OVRA, which provided a whole other layer of surveil-lance and investigation, with agents both inside Italy and abroad. Its acronym was not spelt out, on the grounds that the letters alone made it sound more frightening. In Rome, Bocchini's ante-rooms, like those of the French Kings of the *ancien régime*, teemed with avaricious and needy people: policemen, military officers, inform-ers, industrialists, Prefects, and a great many pretty young women. He thought of himself as a doctor, at the bedside of a sick man, monitoring his every change of pulse and heartbeat. Italy was his patient.

Not that Bocchini was the only man watching over Italy's remaining freedoms. The army put in place its own information service, SIM, coordinating it with those of the navy and air force, with its own subsections for such things as counter espionage and censorship. The militia appointed Provincial Investigative Officers. And Mussolini himself, not quite trusting anyone, not even Boc-chini, set up his own information office, to ward off 'hostile attacks'. Meanwhile, in Rome, typists were put to work intercepting and transcribing telephone conversations and their numbers grew rapidly, along with their skills and their knowledge of foreign languages. These transcriptions made their way to Bocchini's desk. As did the reports from agents placed on the mail trains to steam open suspicious-looking letters, using quartz lamps and ultraviolet rays.

Hand in hand with this formidable array of new police powers came the 'special' laws, passed in two long sessions of the Gran Consiglio in early November 1926. With them came the revocation of all passports, the death penalty for attempts on the life of the royal family or the head of state, a Special Tribunal for the 'defence of the state' – with no redress – and the banning of all political parties. The Aventino dissidents were expelled from Parliament. The press lost its few remaining freedoms. In every province, a new commission was created, consisting of the Prefect, the public prosecutor, the heads of the police, the carabinieri and the militia, bodies soon infamous for their zeal, their corruption and their vendettas. Italy was now not just a dictatorship, but a fortress.

Rachele had never yet been to Rome, an earlier visit having been postponed after Mussolini had an ulcer attack, when it was feared that her presence would suggest a dangerous condition and provoke panic in the public. But she and the children joined him for the first time in Via Rasella for Christmas and Rachele cooked the meal she always made for special occasions, *cappelletti*, chicken and fried potatoes and a home-made cake. Later, what ten-year-old Vittorio would remember was that their father was especially nice to them, giving them money to spend, as if to make up for all the months apart. Rachele took an instant dislike to the housekeeper Cesira, who she judged impertinent and far too possessive of Mussolini. And she firmly refused all the obsequious invitations showered on her by the Roman nobility. Mussolini, constantly receiving presents of every kind, had been presented with a puma cub which, loving cats as he did, he had brought back to the flat and tied to the piano leg. For sixteen-year-old Edda, Rome seemed to offer limitless possibilities.

By the time Rachele and the children returned to Milan – Rachele concluding that 'being important was no fun' – she was pregnant.

Hearing the news, Edda commented: 'Aren't you ashamed, at your age?' Mussolini had said that he wanted a child of the '*giorni belli*', the days of prosperity, in contrast to the days of 'penury' that accompanied Edda's birth. He was certain that the child would be a boy and wanted him born in the Villa Carpena, so that he would be a true Romagnolo, and it was in the Villa Carpena that Romano was duly born in September 1927. This time Mussolini arrived in time for the birth, having driven himself at great speed from Rome in his Alfa Romeo.

The new baby had an uncanny likeness to his father, with very round staring eyes and a forceful jutting chin. Flowers, baby clothes and gifts of every kind arrived from all over Italy, some dropped over the house from small planes. Edda, who gave everyone nicknames, named the new baby Tampussino. Local children gathered at the gates to sing hymns of praise. The King and Queen sent their congratulations. The fake medieval fortified castle of the Rocca delle Caminate above Predappio, from whose battlements you could see the Adriatic, had been presented to Mussolini by the grateful local municipality. That night its great revolving beacon, which threw its light 60 kilometres over the surrounding countryside, was lit up for the first time.

4

The tentacles of an octopus

Edda was growing up. Journalists, constantly following the family's every move, spoke of her grace and charm. In reality, she was awkward, prickly and combative, with an excellent memory and a habit of caricaturing her own defects, hiding her skills and virtues as if she were ashamed of them. Her aunt Edvige called her 'exuberant and fey'. She blushed easily. Her interest in applying herself to anything fluctuated wildly, and she pleaded ill health to avoid exams. She was learning to conceal her thoughts, dealing with emotion by pretending it was not there. In any case, displays of warmth, sentimentality or exhibitionism were frowned on by both Rachele and Mussolini. Too forceful to be pretty, she was certainly handsome, staring at people with her father's insistent glare, which gave her, wrote one reporter, a look that was both melancholic and also 'demonic', without which she might have resembled an 'English aristocrat or a German countess'. Edda was, he added, '*spavalda*', arrogant, defiant and very sure of herself, though also very averse to being 'observed'. She risked becoming, he concluded, a 'tragic figure'. Feeling her way into the advantages of being the daughter of the most powerful man in Italy, Edda was also learning to shop, to run up small debts, particularly with a dressmaker, who eventually sent the unpaid bills to Mussolini.

Permissive over some things, strict over others, Mussolini allowed her to cycle, swim and wear trousers, but certainly not to smoke or to accept invitations to dances. He was teaching her to observe everything and to remember what she saw, and to describe things without exaggeration. Noting her wildness and restlessness, which he suspected concealed a strong romantic streak, he worried that it would not be long before she embarked on ill-judged escapades with boys. 'Edda is an imperious child who has very much a mind of her own,' wrote a correspondent for the *Chicago Daily News*.

Every evening, Mussolini rang the flat in Milan and the children took it in turns to speak to him. On the rare weekends he came north, they went to the Villa Carpena where on Sundays, after playing cards, they rode their bicycles along the straight roads between the vineyards with Rachele, who was prone to fall off, bringing up the rear. Like Edda, the boys missed their father who, when he came, spent most of his time attending to business and talking to local Fascist grandees. One summer they wrote him a joint letter: 'We are waiting for you ... we promise that we won't tell anyone when you come so that you will spend a bit of time with us.' When they saw photographs of him in Rome in his bowler hat, they laughed, saying it made him look exactly like Laurel and Hardy. One Christmas, Mussolini took them to the zoo in Rome, where he had just sent his most recent pet, a lion cub, after driving around the city with it in his open-top Alfa Romeo, to the delight of photographers. He urged ten-year-old Vittorio to enter the cub's cage. At first, it nuzzled him, but it grew playful and then rough, scratching his leg and drawing blood. Mussolini struck the beast hard on the nose and dragged Vittorio away. He wanted toughness in his boys.

Her parents had been right to worry about Edda's erratic behaviour and choice of suitors. Mussolini asked Bocchini to keep a close eye on his daughter, and disquieting reports began to reach his desk. They spoke of fortune hunters, spendthrifts and drug addicts, and an apparent allergy on Edda's part to suitable young men. There was Marino Vairani, 'of dubious moral conduct', unemployed and a 'lover of pleasure and women', given to calling himself Conte or Marchese; Muzio Conradi, the twenty-eight-year-old son of a rich industrialist from whom he was estranged on account of his 'dissipated and megalomaniac' ways. Conradi, who had been in a clinic for cocaine addiction and was 'believed to be syphilitic', was boasting openly of his friendship with Edda. And there was Pacifici 'of the worst behaviour', who took Edda on moonlit drives during which, according to her somewhat fanciful police escort, the two of them 'in the midst of infinite poetry and charm give every appearance of loving each other'. Most of these romances were conducted at the seaside town of Riccione on the Adriatic, where the family now regularly spent the summer months. Hearing that Chiavolini, Mussolini's private secretary, was opening all her post, Edda 'peremptorily' ordered him not to. He replied that he had no choice. What he did not tell her was that Mussolini had also instructed him to find ways to make certain that the young men in question were not seen around Edda again.

To tame his wild daughter, Mussolini arranged for her to join a cruise to India, taking with her a carabiniere as bodyguard and her maid Pina. Cables were sent ahead that she was to be '*assolutamente inosservata*', totally anonymous, but this did not prevent a huge turnout of dignitaries when her ship, the *Tevere,* left Brindisi. 'Whole city saw her off', cabled one reporter. 'Great enthusiasm. She stood topmost desk acknowledging cheers with Roman salute.' Every time they went ashore, messages were dispatched back to Italy. 'Everything proceeding smoothly,' Signor Conti, a senator into whose care Mussolini had placed his daughter, reported home.

At eighteen, Edda was one of the youngest passengers on board. To fill her days, she joined in the sports and made herself popular with her simple manners and lack of airs. A telegram arrived from the Palazzo Venezia urging her to study English, which she would find essential in India. A correspondent for *Il Corriere della Sera* wrote that Edda was tall, thin, slender and never seasick. Her face had a sweet expression, teasing and quick to laugh but also a little quick to take offence. She struck him as both very young and very knowing: she was '*un tipo*', a character. Other reporters were more openly adulatory. 'You are sacred to us,' declared *L'Unione*. 'You are the Duce's daughter. And Edda, we love you.'

In India, there was a visit to a temple on elephants dressed in gold and silver, and a 200-mile tour through the jungle, once again accompanied part of the way by elephants. A prince offered her two tigers. Conti cabled to say that Edda was 'happy, enthusiastic, affectionate'. Going around some ruins in Ceylon, her eye was caught by a young poet; but her behaviour remained impeccable. Even Mussolini, on reading the many reports, was pleased. The cruise had been intended as a demonstration of the successes and virtues of Fascism and at every port local *fasci* turned out to greet the *Tevere*. But the performance of her fellow travellers seemed to the Duce to have lacked true Fascist fervour. To Edda, Mussolini now sent one of his characteristically formal telegrams: 'You saved the situation brilliantly and upheld the prestige of Fascist Italy. I am grateful to you, as father and head of government.' What Edda herself would piously later say about the trip was that it had taught her how to behave in society, and given her a chance to improve her English. She brought back with her tapestries, rugs, gold and silver jewellery and a miniature temple made in ivory. Her brothers complained that she had come back a '*signorina*' and was no longer their third musketeer. Certainly, it had been a valuable lesson in public performance.

Rachele was experimenting with new strains of wheat at the Villa Carpena. She had bought a tractor, and when Mussolini came to stay he had himself photographed driving it around the property. Rachele was keeping a diary on squared paper and had decided that, now that her husband was surrounded by constant adulation, she would keep him informed about what ordinary Italians really felt about Fascism. On her bicycle or by train she travelled around the province of Forlì, taking with her little packets of salt, a luxury at the time, telling people that it came from Il Duce. Occasionally, if the road was too rough, she went by mule.

One winter, when the River Rabbi was in spate and a number of houses along its bank had flooded, she perched on the back of a security guard's motorcycle and had herself driven to a local monastery, to ask the Abbot to take in the families who had been made homeless. The Abbot, flapping his arms furiously, told her to write to the Pope. Rachele was driven back to the post office in Forlì and rang Mussolini. Two hours later, a shamefaced Abbot went to collect the families. Like her daughter, Rachele was testing the reaches of her new power. As Edda would say many years later, Rachele was not the mild, patient woman portrayed by so many historians, but on the contrary authoritarian, forceful, desperate to keep what she called the 'bohemianism' of her husband and children under control, and that, long after she grew up, her mother continued to hit her. But then, Rachele was not the parent whom Edda loved.

When Edda turned eighteen, Mussolini had been in power for six years. He had, with some difficulty, weathered Matteotti's murder, and was now '*il Duce del Fascismo*', responsible only to the

King and not to Parliament. The unshaven look, with a casual assortment of ill-fitting clothes, had been replaced by well-tailored suits and a variety of military uniforms chosen to match his mood and the occasion, though he seldom wore the black shirt and retained a fondness for spats, two-tone shoes, berets, jodhpurs and belted pullovers. He looked, noted one observer, like a corpulent, working-class British man. He was still close to Sarfatti, now widely regarded as Italy's premier ambassadress of *italianità*, the essence of being Italian, and was reliant on her cultural enthusiasms. Edvige would say that Mussolini loved her more than he ever loved any other woman and that Rachele, for all her unworldliness, instinctively understood her to be more dangerous than any of his other lovers and consequently hated her the most. Sarfatti considered Rachele to be, as she told a friend, 'an ignorant, boorish peasant'.

There had already been a number of hagiographies of Mussolini, but Sarfatti had written her own encomium. She described him as a man of exceptional powers and charisma, embodying both modernity and the grandeur of the ancient Romans – thoughtful, resolute, realistic, ever young, ever energetic, 'an aristocratic Plebeian' – who had weighed his fellow men and found them wanting, and whose destiny was to command. The Duce's ambition, she wrote, 'sustains and devours him'. Choosing to overlook what snideness lay concealed beneath her smooth and admiring words, Mussolini loved the book. *Dux*, published in 1925, was a vast success, rapidly translated into eighteen languages and selling well over a million copies. It did much to feed the growing Mussolini legend.

Now, alone in Rome, with the ferocious Cesira as his gatekeeper, Mussolini was becoming ever more eclectic in his choice of mistresses. There was a dancer called Cornelia Tanzi, who ran a salon on the Via Margutta, later dismissed by him as 'frigid, coldness personified'; a talented pianist with untidy ringlets, Magda Brand, who fed his love of music but complained that he ate like a pig; and a sultry Sicilian princess, Giulia Alliata di Monreale. As his valet Quinto Navarra would say, Mussolini needed a woman a day, often chosen from the river of letters that poured every day to his office, and it was up to those around him to make certain that they made no demands and caused no embarrassment. With women, Navarra said, Mussolini used a special voice on the telephone, 'soft, weak, gentle'.

Ida Dalser

Ida Dalser, the mother of his son Benito Albino, who had returned to Trento after the war, came to Rome hoping for money and recognition and unwisely went to petition a magistrate, who had her arrested, put in a straitjacket and confined on the grounds of dangerous 'over-excitement'. Ten-year-old Benito Albino had been living with relations and was quickly removed, had his name changed and was put into a shelter for the destitute. Ida would spend the rest of her life in mental asylums; Benito Albino, too, would die in one. In her book, Sarfatti tactfully avoided drawing attention to Mussolini's ruthlessness.

The image *Dux* projected, together with the many photographs of the Duce with his lion cub, his tractor, his stunts and his many sporting activities, endeared Mussolini to Italians. But what they were really beginning to appreciate was his programme of public works, and his vast plans for social welfare, all of which had largely been neglected by previous governments.

Leisure activities and sports were laid on in after-work clubs, known as Dopolavoro, which had taken over the defunct socialist organisations, while children were being enrolled in after-school activities. There was already much discussion about the 'new Italian'. Leisure was no longer to be an end in itself, but a means of improving the health and state of mind of the country, turning its citizens from lazy sheep into audacious fighters, prepared to live dangerously, 'to act, fight and if necessary die', and to love the patria as a mother. Under the slogan of 'many participants, few spectators', these new Italians of all ages were to sing, bicycle, swim, do calisthenics, dance and engage in tugs-of-war. Fascism was to bring style into people's lives, '*il stilo Fascista*', which was to be picturesque, unexpected, mystical and full of rituals, enshrined in laws and decrees emphasising the supremacy of the state over the individual. And at its apex, the Duce himself, serenaded in every hymn and song with the words, taken from the Greek battle cry, and used at Fiume by Gabriele D'Annunzio: '*Per Benito Mussolini, eja, eja, eja alala.*' He expected Edda and his family to lead the way into the new Italy.

To keep the singing, jumping, running new Italian from getting into trouble, Bocchini, the hefty, sinuous chief of police, had put in place a spider's web of spies, informers and agents provocateurs, and their stringers, the *tombettieri* – buglers – with himself as the spider at its centre. These were men and women coerced by fear, lured by greed, inspired by jealousy or resentment, who fed their stream of information into Bocchini's office, to be distilled, typed up, filed and, where appropriate, passed on to Mussolini. On the basis of these reports, dissidents, would-be emigrants, people who had foolishly bad-mouthed the Duce in public, were making their way in their hundreds to the penal colonies on the islands off Sicily and in remote villages in the mountains. The dwindling number of remaining dissidents were trying to regroup and fight back but, one by one, Bocchini's spies picked them off. Some of the courageous anti-Fascists had managed to smuggle themselves abroad; others were already dead; others again, like Antonio Gramsci, the Marxist philosopher, were in prison serving long sentences. And after a bomb exploded by the Fiera Campionaria in Milan – where crowds had gathered to see the King – killing twenty people, Bocchini's grip grew heavier. When Mussolini was filmed dancing with peasant women, at bucolic festivals, it was said that they were female police officers in disguise, Bocchini intending to take no risks.

A few years earlier, when he had been upstaged by a mobster while on a visit to Sicily in 1924, Mussolini made the decision to take on the Mafia, declaring that he refused to countenance any authority but his own. A Prefect from Lombardy called Cesare Mori was dispatched to Palermo, where clans ruled unchecked, holding magistrates, politicians and absentee landlords in their thrall. Though referred to as the '*Prefetto di Ferro*', the iron man, Mori had struggled to understand the labyrinthine nature of the problem he was dealing with, or to keep his head above the rising water of blackmail, petitions, claims, denunciations and complaints that threatened to drown him. He put in place sweeping police operations, arrested thousands of suspects and conducted impressive trials. Many mafiosi did indeed fall into his net, but so did many innocent Sicilians. Mori's callous methods proved to be excellent recruiting grounds for the Mafia. Neither he nor Mussolini appeared to have understood that it was not enough to liquidate the culprits without changing the social milieu in which the Mafia thrived. When Mori was pulled out four years later, he left a Sicily just as destitute as it had been before, corruption flourishing at every level, banditry out of control, a place where fear of reprisals kept people quiet, and where favouritism, protection, extortion and *omertà* emerged stronger for their new links to Fascist power. The Mafia leaders he had imprisoned were soon amnestied.

Soon after the March on Rome, to make certain that the Fascist Party did not get away from him, Mussolini had replaced elected mayors across Italy with non-elected *podestà*, Fascist loyalists. Though not at first greatly interested in courting the old aristocratic families, whom he both despised and felt intimidated by, Mussolini now cleverly co-opted them by making a few of them *podestà* in their own regions. When he decided to establish a governorship of Rome, he turned to the Roman princes with their close connections to the court. Slowly, gingerly, aristocrats and Fascists were inching towards each other. Richard Washburn Child, a recent American Ambassador to Rome who had helped Mussolini write his autobiography, noted that the Duce 'has not merely ruled a house: he has built a new one'. No one else 'stands in the orbit of his personality. No one. The only possible exception is his daughter Edda.' A remark made all the more intriguing by the fact that Edda had not yet appeared in Rome.

Nothing of what Mussolini did, however, would have been possible without the *gerarchi*, the Fascist leaders who had brought him to power and who now circled him like hungry dogs, snapping at each other, vying for position and advancement, though it would be a while before they were allowed to rise. 'Either no one speaks,' Mussolini declared, 'or I speak, because I know how to speak better than anyone else.' He took great pleasure in ferreting out his *gerarchi*'s secrets and their lies, storing away their misdoings in the drawers of his desk for future use, playing on their ambitions and rivalrousness. Disagreements between them flared up into battles, which saw one or another demoted, or even exiled or imprisoned, but never for long.

In the wake of the Matteotti murder, the vulgar, cynical and infinitely corrupt Roberto Farinacci had been rewarded for his loyalty with the secretaryship of the Fascist Party. But it was not long before his over-heated, bullying ways saw him replaced, returned to his fief in Cremona where he made trouble from the sidelines, bombarding Mussolini with tales of malfeasance by his former comrades until he was warned that he had become 'spiritually undisciplined'. Farinacci, backed by local landowners grateful for his *squadrista* intimidation tactics, filled the pages of his paper, *Regime Fascista*, with attacks on everyone, including, unwisely, Arnaldo, Mussolini's brother. What he did not know was that Mussolini had been informed that, as a student in Modena, Farinacci had spent more time brawling than studying and earned his degree through plagiarism. This useful information was filed carefully away.

The man who took over from him as party leader was Augusto Turati, an elegant, suave figure, who came from Brescia and had his black shirts made of silk. Turati disapproved of drink and 'negro dancers'. He was given the job of improving the image of the party and laying to rest its aura of violence. No less keen on suppressing dissent than Mussolini, he wanted a new ruling class established, 'orderly and unquestioning in its belief in Mussolini'. Farinacci was said to be the Dominican, a believer in strength and power; Turati the Jesuit, austere and wily.

Farinacci's bitter enemy was the debonair Italo Balbo, the only *gerarco* who dared to address Mussolini as '*tu*', who sat perched on his desk, stroking his pointy beard, knowing that Mussolini hated beards. Balbo was made undersecretary for the Aeronautica in 1926 and its Minister not long after. But he had begun to view the excesses of the Fascist victory, in which he had played such a violent part, with misgivings. Mussolini was deeply jealous of the shadow Balbo cast, recognising a charisma that matched his own.

There was Achille Starace, a small, dark, fanatical gymnast, dog-like in his devotion to Mussolini, humourless and obsessed with medals and uniforms. To a rivalrous *gerarco* who pointed out that Starace was also remarkably stupid, Mussolini famously replied: 'He is indeed a cretin, but an obedient cretin.' Then there was Giuseppe Bottai, said to possess the best mind of all the *gerarchi*, to be both poet and economist, a devoted family man in a vast clan of twenty-eight close relations. Bottai started a journal, *Critica Fascista*, to give Fascism a cultural and ideological basis. It was, he said, a 'revealed religion', that needed 'to be codified'. He was regarded as a rising star, even if he remained outspoken against the 'so-called men of action, all muscle, all nerve, all guts', and, as the most devoted of all Mussolini's men, he kept repeating, 'I met Mussolini and my life was decided.' And there was Dino Grandi, perhaps the most personable and more interesting of all the *gerarchi*, a much decorated veteran of the Alpini, who had won one of the first Fascist seats in Parliament but been too young to take it up. Grandi was sycophantic and sly.

There were others, but these six were the men who mattered. They had in common that they came from the lower bourgeoisie, were nationalists, had fought in the war and become more or less brutal *squadristi*, and were now in their early or mid thirties. Each contributed something: Grandi and Bottai brought intelligence; Balbo energy and courage; Starace the theatre of politics. All were extremely ambitious and, as Edvige remarked, essentially provincial and small-minded 'self-interested agitators'. Some were freemasons, at least until freemasonry was banned, and in any case they knew that Mussolini, a past master of secrecy himself, had made it clear that he was averse to the occult and to things that took place in secret, underground. But what they really shared was one simple fact: they were entirely dependent on Mussolini. To survive, to remain in favour, meant being constantly alert. They would thrive, or fall, solely on his whim, which none would ever forget or forgive. Ultimately, Mussolini trusted none of them, except perhaps Costanzo Ciano, a heavy, jowly, moustached man who had performed heroic acts as a naval officer in the war, and who, though rough and unsubtle, was unequivocally loyal. Arnaldo remained Mussolini's one friend and confidant. His brother's 'secret fire', Mussolini wrote later, 'a fire that fed my will and my faith' was what accompanied and sustained him.

The family spent Christmas 1928 together and soon after Rachele found herself pregnant yet again. This fifth child gave her a reason to press harder for them all to move to Rome, though Mussolini was not exactly enthusiastic. The Italian public – and grand Roman society – for a long time extremely curious about the Duce's private life, were about to see for themselves just what his family was like, and in particular Edda, rumours of whose strong character and wild ways preceded her to Rome. Both shy and full of curiosity, Edda welcomed the decision.

Despite the impending move, Mussolini was in an extremely good mood. The general election of March 1929, which took the form of a referendum, a single Fascist Party list either approved or rejected by voters, saw him endorsed by over 98 per cent of the men – women did not have the vote – who marched to the booths set up in piazzas to the sounds of town bands playing 'Giovinezza' the Fascist party hymn. And, after almost four years of tricky negotiations, the Vatican was again an independent enclave.

The stand-off between Church and state had been at the centre of Italian affairs since the *Risorgimento*, when the papal territories were seized for the new liberal, united, Italy. In May 1926, urged on by the pious Arnaldo, and recognising the usefulness of the Church to his plans, the formerly anti-clerical Mussolini had opened delicate talks with the papal secretary of state, Cardinal Gasparri. Held up for a while by disagreement over the extent to which the Catholic youth bodies were to cede power to the Fascist ones, the pact was signed at a magnificent ceremony in the Lateran Palace on 11 February 1929, with people straining to catch a glimpse of Edda and her mother. Hardly surprising, perhaps, that Church and Fascism had made common cause since they shared the same enemies – liberalism, freemasonry and communism – and both called for discipline, hierarchy and order. Mussolini's model citizen was also the Church's.

Both sides professed themselves delighted. Catholicism was declared the state religion, compulsory religious education was restored and the Vatican acquired a voice on the international stage and authority over marriages. Italy recognised the inviolability of the 108.7 acres of the Vatican state, separated from the city of Rome by an enormous wall. Extraterritorial status was granted to the capital's three other basilicas, along with many other buildings. The papal nobility could again turn the chairs they kept for the Pope to face the room.

In return, the Vatican recognised the kingdom of Italy, with Rome as its capital. Pius XI declared that Mussolini was 'the man whom Providence had sent us' and for a while endorsed 'Catholic totalitarianism'. Mussolini chose to see this as another step towards the cult of Fascism and, perhaps more importantly, the cult of himself. He boasted that though the Italian state was now indeed Catholic, 'it was also, in fact before all else, exclusively and essentially Fascist'.

With the signing of the Concordat, Mussolini told Rachele, a golden decade of Fascism had begun. Edda was about to discover the part he intended her to play. The 'agnostic, paralytic' Liberal state had been routed, and a new, virile, Fascist one born. He was revered at home and accepted abroad. Churchill, who had visited Rome in 1927, declared that had he been Italian he would certainly have supported Mussolini's 'victorious battle against the bestial appetites and passions of Leninism'. Increasingly, the Duce drew parallels between himself and Napoleon.

5

The virago

In early September 1929, to celebrate his growing status, Mussolini moved his office out of the Palazzo Chigi and into the Palazzo Venezia, the immense fifteenth-century papal palace at one end of the Corso, with windows that looked out on the gleaming Victor Emmanuel monument and across to the Capitol. The vast Sala del Mappamondo became his private office and he placed his desk carefully at the far end, so that visitors would have an awkward and intimidatingly long walk to reach him. Outside was the frescoed Sala del Gran Consiglio, with its high ceilings and marble floor inlaid with mosaics, the seating arranged in a horseshoe with a throne in the middle for himself. There was a balcony high above the Piazza Venezia, from which he would be able to play out the role of Duce, addressing the crowds below, his words beamed out by radio to piazzas all over the country.

Hearing of the family's planned move to Rome and their need for somewhere to live, the Roman nobility had pressed their unoccupied palazzi on Mussolini. He let it be known that he was looking for somewhere quiet, imposing, surrounded by greenery. Without consulting Rachele, he settled on the Villa Torlonia on the Via Nomentana, at a peppercorn rent of one lira a year, and its owner, the Principe Torlonia, moved into a small house on the property. The villa was grand, but odd, a neoclassical nineteenth-century pastiche of Greek, Roman, Egyptian and romantic Renaissance, with pillars, mosaic floors and chandeliers, reached by broad stone steps leading to a terrace, more a stage set than a home. There was a loggia on the first floor with a suite of rooms on either side. But it had the advantage of sitting in the middle of a large park with palm and pine trees, statues, outhouses, stables with a riding ring and an obelisk, and it was enclosed by a high fence with a gate house, useful for the dozens of agents now detailed to guard the family.

Whole family, including Romano and the baby, Anna Maria

Anna Maria was born on 3 September 1929 in the Villa Carpena, Mussolini again insisting on a Romagnolo birth. He was not present, but when Rachele rang to tell him it was a girl and ask him to name her, he settled on that of his mother-in-law. Edda nicknamed the new baby Zabughina. On 15 November, Rachele and the five children arrived at the Villa Torlonia. Appalled by its size, complaining that it was like a museum with too much empty space and furniture that fell apart when you looked at it, Rachele set to work. Workmen, some of them friends and relations from Predappio, were summoned to Rome, and the vast kitchens in the basement moved upstairs and split into two, half for the cooks, half for herself. Rachele's side was turned into a replica of her kitchen in the Villa Carpena, complete with marble table and copper pots and pans. The formal furniture was replaced by more homely pieces; cupboards were built, walls repainted, curtains hung. Being both practical and strong, Rachele helped with the work.

Then she turned to the landscaped gardens, formal parterres and exotic shrubs and trees. Delighted with the size of the park, which she declared was reassuringly like proper countryside, she selected a suitable area not far from the villa and, overriding the loud protests of Principe Torlonia, she had her workers create a vegetable garden and a chicken coop. There were sties for two pigs and hutches for rabbits. Cesira Carocci, Mussolini's possessive housekeeper, had come with him from the Via Rasella, but she did not last long, Rachele saying that she treated her more like the governess than the wife. Mussolini protested but was told: 'You rule Italy, but I rule here.' Two Romagnole women, Irma and Nerina, arrived to help. In the house, the Romagnolo dialect was spoken. To celebrate the family's arrival, photographs were taken in the garden. Mussolini, in jackboots and jodhpurs, is holding two-year-old Romano in his arms. Vittorio, who looks rather fat, and Bruno are ungainly in shorts; and Edda seems serious, with her thin face and slightly hooked nose.

Family life, in the Villa Torlonia, changed remarkably little. To the annoyance of the Romans, who longed to get a glimpse of the family, Rachele avoided all formal occasions and very few visitors came to the house. She kept the accounts as she always had, made all the pasta, and watched over the two younger children. Most days, she kept on her apron and wound her hair, peasant style, in a scarf. Bruno and Vittorio were sent to the prestigious Ginnasio Liceo Torquato Tasso in nearby Via Sicilia, driven there by the chauffeur. Mussolini rode in the park, then left for the Palazzo Venezia, returning at two o'clock to bolt down, on his own, boiled vegetables and spaghetti with tomato sauce. No meal, he said, should last more than ten minutes. The children had to eat what was on their plates and lateness was not tolerated. By three thirty he was back in the Sala del Mappamondo. After another rapid meal of soup, vegetables and fruit, served at eight o'clock in the evening, he read the papers, circling things that interested him, then threw them on the floor. Edda, who had abandoned all education, hung about the house, gradually resuming her position of supremacy in her father's life.

Most evenings, the family, servants and some of the bodyguards gathered in the large room on the ground floor that had been turned into a cinema to watch newsreels and light comedies. When *gerarchi* appeared on the screen, Mussolini enjoyed pointing out their defects, but not their virtues, saying that they had none. Twice a week, Italy's most famous Disney cartoon mouse, Topolino, was screened. Mussolini often dozed through the films.

On Sundays, there might be games of ping-pong or billiards in the ornate dining room under the chandeliers, occasional outings to Ostia with Mussolini at the wheel, or football matches on the gravel drive, in which Edda, rapidly learning the ways of upper-class Roman girls, played in high-heeled shoes. During the opera season, he took the children to the Teatro Reale, to hear Wagner, Rossini and Puccini, though not Verdi, whose works he disliked. Rachele stayed at home. During the intervals, he left the box and wandered up and down the corridors, talking to acquaintances. No more than at the Villa Carpena did Mussolini seem to care much for family life. Long silences filled the times he was at home and when he did speak, a rare visitor noted, he addressed Rachele and the children as if he were at a meeting. Edda was heard to remark that her father had gone into politics in order to be at home as little as possible and that in the house Rachele was the dictator.

Having won round the disapproving Principe Torlonia to her kitchen garden, Rachele and he talked, she said later, about the ghosts said to wander the villa at night – all food for pleasurable discussion with the deeply superstitious Mussolini and Edda. Alongside the smallholding of chickens, rabbits and pigs, sprang up a menagerie to accommodate the many animals and birds presented to the family. There were at any one time gazelles, a jaguar, more lion cubs, eagles, tortoises, falcons, monkeys and parrots, together with an ever growing number of horses, on which Mussolini conferred heraldic and imperial names.

The summers were spent at Riccione, where Edda celebrated her birthdays on 1 September at the Grande Hotel Lido. In July 1929, a Contessa Treuberg sent a perceptive article to the *Prager Tagblatt*, a German-language newspaper in Prague, describing Edda as a prisoner of her role as the Duce's eldest daughter. 'She possesses great charm,' she wrote, but she was full of self-doubt and 'despises mankind. That is the tragedy of the children of great men. They are either imitations or wretched wanderers.'

Edda knew perfectly well that she was constantly under scrutiny and that her father's secretary, Chiavolini, was still reading her letters. Avoiding the surveillance had become a game she revelled in. Mussolini had given her an Alfa Romeo. The moment had come, he now decided, to prevent further unsuitable attachments and to find her a husband. He turned to Edvige for suggestions. The young man she proposed, Pier Francesco Mangelli, was the son of a respectable industrialist from Forlì, a good Romagnolo, honest, healthy and teetotal. Edda found him painfully dull and complained that the one time he kissed her, her lips swelled up. When suitable young men were produced, she behaved appallingly, trying to put them off with her erratic ways and telling their mothers that she planned never to have children.

She decided that she was in love with Dino Mondolfi whom she had met, like her earlier boyfriends, at Riccione and informed her father that she planned to marry him. Mussolini asked Edvige to investigate, discovered that the young man was Jewish – which Edda probably knew all along would annoy her father – and told Edda that such a marriage would be 'scandalous' and that mixed marriages did not work out. It 'cannot', he announced, 'and will not take place'. If she continued to meet Dino, he informed her, he would take away her car. Evidently preferring the charms of the Alfa Romeo, she agreed to give him up, after a last tender meeting outside a church in Bologna, while her police escort waited in the car, later reporting to Bocchini that 'she remained with him for rather a long time'. Finding a husband for Edda, Edvige remarked, was very hard work.

Edda had remained friends with Pier Francesco Mangelli, whose parents were now pressing for an engagement. She spent a holiday with them in Spain, during which she behaved in a spoilt and obnoxious way but, after too much wine one evening in Seville, she agreed to marry him. They returned to Italy engaged and Mussolini presented her with a large bunch of flowers and gave a lavish party for the young couple. But Pier Francesco had read the family wrong. Presenting himself to Mussolini one day, he asked what Edda's dowry would be. It was an unpardonable gaffe. Mussolini informed him curtly that there would be no dowry; Mussolinis did not do such things. 'It's finished,' he told Edda. Pier Francesco loitered around the house for a few days, his family furious at his clumsy stupidity. But it was indeed over, and on 17 January 1930,

Edda told him so. 'So there I was,' she wrote later, 'free again and rather happy.'

Galeazzo Ciano was the only son of Costanzo, the heavy, jowly, whiskered naval hero ennobled at Mussolini's request in 1925 as Conte di Cortellazzo, appointed his Minister of Communications and designated his heir in case of his sudden death. Never drawn into Mussolini's inner circle, possibly on account of his boorishness, Costanzo consoled himself by becoming the self-styled '*Granduca di Livorno*', owner of *Il Telegrafo* and a shipping company. Born in 1903, Galeazzo was a timid boy, insecure, browbeaten, venerating but fearing his coercive and spartan father, who demanded that his only son be strong and decorous, unlike his modish and frivolous peers. Since the family moved constantly when Costanzo was posted to different ports, Ciano had few friends. His main companion was his younger sister Maria, a gentle, religious girl with whom he played cards. He cried easily, and hated his father's absences. His mother Carolina, a pragmatic, even-tempered woman, deferred in all things to her husband. Margherita Sarfatti, a keen observer of Fascist affairs, described Costanzo as a sinister figure, with watchful eyes and the only jaw in Rome more prominent than Mussolini's. He was, she said, totally unscrupulous, but could be witty; Carolina she dismissed as ignorant and vain, with all the affectations of the *nouveaux riches*.

Costanzo would have liked his son to pursue a naval career, but Ciano had problems with his ears and throat. After doing well at school, he enrolled in the law faculty at Rome university, and lived in his parents' house in Prati, home to many of the rising *gerarchi*. Rome in the 1920s was an agreeable city for an ambitious young man, and in the Caffè Aragno on the corner of the Corso, he listened to writers and artists, gathered in an inner sanctum, talk about themselves and their work. He was a quick learner. Though not greatly interested in politics and indifferent to Fascism, he took in what he heard, soon adopting their debonair manners, though he remained neater and more old fashioned in his clothes and kept his hair slicked back. To his contemporaries, he gave the impression of being the perfect biddable son, expressing no interest in rebellion. As the only one with money in his pocket, he sometimes felt a little uneasy with his Bohemian friends, and a little envious of their freedom. At night, when he got back late, he often found Costanzo waiting up for him.

The young Ciano had charm and good looks, with a high forehead and full lips, even if his eyes were a little too close together, and, when he threw his head back in a characteristic gesture, he reminded his friends of a Roman emperor. He was discovering in himself a useful talent for saying nothing, while giving the appearance of saying everything. One of his poses was sobriety – he neither smoked nor drank; another was to appear somewhat snobbish and affected.

A first job was found for him writing occasional theatre reviews for *Nuovo Paese* and *L'Impero,* Fascist papers, but he was not a natural writer; he tried his hand at plays, which were worse. The first to be staged – *La Felicita di Amleto* – ran for three nights and was received with boos and jeers. Though enjoying the Roman literary world too much to engage seriously in anything, Ciano began to perceive that, with his money, his connections and his looks, a delightful future beckoned.

Costanzo would have accepted a literary son, had Ciano been successful. As he was not, his father urged him to think of practising law in Livorno, and when that was rejected, persuaded him to sit for the diplomatic service. There were thirty-four places for six hundred candidates and though Ciano did not excel, he passed. For a young man so pleasure-seeking, he had a genuine aptitude for hard work. His first posting was to Rio de Janeiro, his second to Buenos Aires. He blended in well with his colleagues, was diligent and deferential with his superiors and found that his Roman ways were attractive to women, though he was careful to avoid entanglements. Respectful towards Fascism in public, denouncing anti-Fascists as 'pigs', he was quick to mock Mussolini in private, enjoying the role of mordant, funny *enfant terrible*. He wore his black Fascist suit only when forced to do so.

In 1926, possibly after complaints about his womanising, Ciano was transferred to Peking, where Chiang Kai-shek's Nationalist Revolutionary army had launched a campaign against warlords in the north and the east. China was regarded as a nursery for high-flying young Italian diplomats, and the head of the Italian legation, Daniele Varè, was an engaging, erudite man who had spent many years in China and had two teenaged daughters. Living inside the legation district, Ciano explored a world he found fascinating and desirable. The walled city, in which the rich lived in palaces filled with exquisite art, had become a magnet for writers and artists from all over the world. In the surrounding hills the foreign diplomats rode and had picnics, waited on by armies of servants. Ciano visited temples, picnicked with Varè's daughters, walked along the Great Wall and fenced. As Varè would later write, 'for him, as for the rest of us, the days were all sunshine and the nights all stars'.

Just over two years later, mourning the pleasures and the freedoms of Chinese diplomatic life, he was summoned back to Rome to take up the post of attaché to the Italian Embassy to the Holy See. He complained to a friend about the 'forced sanctity' of his new job and mourned Peking, but he was a natural chameleon and attended the innumerable receptions without fuss. He believed that to rise to the top in Italy, you needed the friendship of the Church.

Edda had just parted from Pier Francesco. Mussolini was pressing hard for her to find a husband, if possible from the 'new Fascist aristocracy'. Ciano's name was mentioned by an old friend of Arnaldo's, and his sister Maria showed Edda a photograph. Edda agreed that Ciano was a good-looking man. At a charity ball held in the Grand Hotel towards the end of January 1930, Maria introduced them. Neither seemed much smitten, but they looked each other over and recognised that there were possibilities. Edda told Ciano that she had heard he was very intelligent. A few days later they went to the cinema together to see a film about pearl fishermen in Polynesia, Edda's bodyguards, whose presence never failed to irk her, stationed in a row not far away. Ciano leant across and whispered: 'Do you want to marry me?' Edda, reportedly, smiled and replied: 'Why not?'

Edda returned to the Villa Torlonia and went to tell her father, always her first confidant. Mussolini was putting on his trousers and, holding them in one hand, dashed to Rachele's room shouting, 'Edda is engaged.' She wrote later that she had been sure that 'with Galeazzo everything would be beautiful, clean and pure'. There was no mention of love.

After this matter-of-fact and impulsive exchange, things moved quickly, even if for a while Edda toyed with the idea of running away with another man with whom she was currently infatuated.

The *cavallina matta* appeared almost unnaturally calm. Vittorio and Bruno thought they perceived signs of her being in love, and Edvige insisted that there had been a *coup de foudre*, but Edda herself remained inscrutable. In her diary, Rachele wrote: 'Up till now her temperament has been more that of a boy ... keen on sports, lively and headstrong, Edda does not seem to me sufficiently mature yet to marry.'

Ciano, in an impeccable grey suit and gloves, came to pay the customary call on her father, and had to suffer the fate of many of his visitors, forced to stand nervously while Mussolini pretended to be unaware of his presence. The one person who took against Ciano was Rachele. By instinct and upbringing she was repelled by all manifestations of easy bourgeois charm, and she declared that he was snobbish and vain and that he walked like a goose, with his flat feet pointing outwards. On the evening of the engagement, she took Galeazzo to one side and spelt out Edda's character to him: her daughter was loyal but very 'arrogant and wilful'; she was intelligent, but she could neither sew nor cook, nor mend. Edda was, in short, '*un maschiaccio*', a virago. There was much laughter. Remarking that he had never succeeded in taming Edda, Mussolini set the date for the wedding: 24 April 1930.

It was to be the wedding of the century. The rather pallid Crown Prince, Umberto, had recently married Maria José, a Belgian princess who had also been a pupil at Edda's Florentine school. The Royal wedding in the Quirinale had been grand, stately, sumptuous, with the three hundred ladies of the court dressed by Milan's finest couturiers and squadrons of planes circling the skies over Rome. Edda's Fascist nuptials were to be more restrained, in the modest church of San Giuseppe on the Via Nomentana, yet more imposing, more impressive, planned with military precision. It was to be a demonstration of Fascist might and rituals and a celebration of fecundity, as distinct from the decadence of other countries. Rachele begged feebly for no more than thirty guests but was overruled. Five hundred and twelve invitations were sent out for the reception, to be held on 23 April at the Villa Torlonia. They went to Italy's Black and White nobility, to the ambassadors and chargés d'affaires of over thirty countries, including those of Afghanistan, Egypt and Ethiopia, to the representatives of the eighteen most prestigious international newspapers and press agencies, and to the senior *gerarchi*, who were instructed to turn up in their black shirts, with 'opaque black silk cravats'.

Presents began to arrive, to be displayed in one of the villa's large downstairs rooms. The King and Queen sent a valuable brooch and the King signed himself 'your most affectionate cousin'; King Zog of Albania sent a 'vibrant telegram'; the government a ruby bracelet and the Duke of Aosta a pair of heraldic lions to remind the bride and groom of the 'tempered steel of their illustrious fathers'. D'Annunzio dispatched a 'winged messenger', whom Edda and Ciano hoped would come bearing treasure but instead delivered a pair of red pyjamas embroidered with dragons and lotus flowers. School children in their thousands sent poems and cards with angels. Gardens all round Rome were stripped of their flowers and the Villa Torlonia turned into a bower of lilies, azaleas and roses, and they kept on coming until they overflowed from the house out into the gardens under the pine trees. Mussolini announced that every child living in poverty in Rome, Livorno, Forlì, Predappio, Forlimpopoli and Faenza would receive a gift of 500 lira.

To ensure that there would be no trouble, 1,500 policemen were detailed to check on all houses and buildings from which it was possible to see the Villa Torlonia or the church of San Giuseppe. Roads were closed. An order went out to take note of the whereabouts of 'subversives, people of insane mind and anyone known to be an enemy of the Regime'.

On the day of the reception, Mussolini and the young couple received the guests in a room 'transformed into a flower garden'. Many had never even glimpsed Rachele before. They declared themselves surprised, both by her appearance – she wore an elegant dress and looked considerably younger than forty – and by her pleasant, natural manners. A reporter wrote that her eyes were as blue as the sea and her hair 'as fair as wheat'. For her part, Rachele was curious to see them all, and to study the glorious uniforms and furs and jewellery. The ambassadors kissed her hand. The Papal Nuncio arrived, bearing the Pope's present: a malachite rosary (later, to everyone's mirth, misspelt in the newspapers as a *rasoio*, a razor, rather than a *rosario*), and sat drinking tea with Mussolini. Edda wore a pale pink chiffon dress and shone, according to the gushing and sentimental news reports, like a 'fragrant flower of youth . . . radiant with pleasure'. In fact, she looked pale and handsome, guests telling each other that she had her father's frown and his forceful chin, but also his magnetism.

Choir girls waving flowers at Edda and Ciano's wedding

On 24 April, the wedding cortège of six large Fiats took the family the few hundred yards to San Giuseppe, built not long before 'in the Byzantine style'. Vittorio and Bruno were in shorts. Edda, with a veil of lace from Burano and a garland of pearls and orange blossoms, was followed by two pages carrying her very long train. Her wedding dress was severe and plain. Her witnesses were her uncle Arnaldo and Principe Torlonia; Ciano's were Dino Grandi and Cesare Maria de Vecchi, a somewhat surprising choice in that, despite being a family friend, he had recently described Ciano's sister Maria as being 'a capricious kitten prone to temper tantrums' and was fast coming to consider Ciano vain, lazy and superficial. In keeping with Romagnolo custom, Edda cut a silk ribbon held across the church by women in peasant costume.

After the ceremony, Edda and Ciano left under an arch of raised swords, choirs singing Romagnolo hymns and strewing flowers before the bride, the girls in their white pinafores, the boys in their black shirts. In the official wedding photograph Ciano is grinning;

Edda looks stern and wary, as if struggling not to be overwhelmed. Then came a prayer in St Peter's, before the tomb of the Prince of the Apostles, for which Edda wore a black veil over a tight-fitting hat, which made her look a little like a nun. They kissed the saint's bronze foot, as was the tradition for young couples. Later the Pope presented her with a copy of Thomas à Kempis' *The Imitation of Christ*, bound in pergamon, with a papal seal. As she walked back to the Villa Torlonia, she raised her arm in the Fascist salute.

Addressing the couple kneeling before him in San Giuseppe, the priest had told them that it was their duty to become the 'standard bearers of the Fascist Italian Christian family': Edda, healthy, virtuous, dutiful and surely soon mother to many little warriors and housewives; Ciano, strong, ardent and ambitious. That, indeed, was the point. At nineteen, Edda was to stand for everything that was best about Fascist womanhood, while Ciano carved out the path of the 'new Italian man'. Whether either of them wanted this role, or were at all suited to it, no one paused to consider.

Three cars were waiting for them at the Villa Torlonia. There was Edda's white Alfa Romeo, which she was to drive south herself to Capri for their honeymoon; the second car was for her maid and the luggage, and the third for the bodyguards. The cars took off at great speed down the Via Nomentana and would have disappeared from sight had Edda not noticed a fourth car behind. In it were Mussolini and Rachele. She pulled over and said to her father: 'What kind of honeymoon is this? You're being absurd.' A sheepish Mussolini said that he had been 'accompanying her a bit of the way' and had just been about to turn back. It was a measure of how dependent he had become on her. When in Milan not long after, Mussolini told Angela Curti that his new son-in-law was intelligent and would go a long way on his own merits. He also told her that Edda was definitely his favourite child.

A vast turnout awaited the Cianos on Capri, along with a telegram from Mussolini, saying that he would be happy if he were the first to send her greetings. The *podestà*, Marino Dusmet, was a renowned choreographer of events and used to receiving celebrities. There were bands, flags, cheering people, a profusion of flowers, a display of folk dancing. Edda appeared shy and ill at ease and the couple escaped into the mid-nineteenth-century Hotel Quisisana as quickly as they could, where they occupied the imperial suite. They seldom emerged, taking many of their meals in their rooms. Whenever they were seen, crowds gathered. The couple refused invitations to concerts, art galleries and people's houses, and when processions of local Fascists came to the hotel with flowers, hoping to be received, they were sent away. A first faint stirring of public misgiving surfaced: was the Duce's daughter really very timid and reserved, or was she perhaps arrogant and superior?

Whether the nineteen-year-old Edda was or was not a virgin, no one knows. But her parents' ceaseless rows and Mussolini's brazen affairs had left her wary and deeply confused about sex and fidelity. On the first night in the Quisisana, she dawdled over dinner and kept ordering more food, then locked herself in the bathroom, telling Ciano that, if he touched her, she would throw herself over a cliff. 'Nothing in you surprises me,' Ciano replied, 'but I would like to know how you plan to get there.' They laughed. 'And so began,' Edda wrote many years later, with her usual candour, 'our first married night, which, to be honest, was not much fun. I hated it all. Later, things improved, but it took time.'

They stayed on Capri for two weeks, then continued their honeymoon on a yacht belonging to Giuseppe Volpi, a rich Venetian industrialist and former Minister of Finance. Edda had caught an ear infection swimming in the cold sea, but she had fallen in love with the island. As they pulled out of the harbour, every house in the Marina Grande sported flowers and flags, while a son et lumière played over the rocky mountainside and its Roman remains. On Rhodes, they bumped into an earlier boyfriend of Edda's and she injudiciously kissed him. A scene in the rain with Ciano left her vowing never to let herself be devoured by the demon of jealousy.

To the envy of his peers in the Foreign Ministry, Galeazzo had been leapfrogged to the job of Consul General in Shanghai. As for Edda, it promised a miraculous escape from everything now expected of them in Fascist Italy.

6

La prima signora di Shanghai

Edda and Ciano were seen off on the *Tevere* from Brindisi by
Rachele, Costanza and Carolina, amid much Fascist fanfare; Mussolini had said goodbye to them in Rome. While Ciano waved and
blew kisses as they pulled out, and his parents on the shore wept,
Edda stood still and silent, a slightly irritated expression on her
face. Ciano was not yet accustomed to her reserve and apparent
indifference, his own family being given to tears and elaborate displays of emotion. As they steamed south and it grew hotter, Ciano
said he was perfectly content to keep the portholes shut; Edda
announced that she needed a cool room, where she could wrap
herself up in several layers of sheets and blankets, pulling them
over her head. She moved into a separate cabin. Telegrams from
Mussolini pursued them at every stage, and when they were not
answered he fumed and fretted. In Hong Kong they were met by
Daniele Varè, under whom Ciano had served in Peking in 1927.
He took them on a brief tour of the city. Ciano told him that he
had never expected to be so happy.

A month after leaving Brindisi, the *Tevere* reached the mouth of
the Yangtze and steamed up its tributary, the Huangpu, towards
Shanghai through a dense thicket of funnels and masts, past ferry
boats, sampans, junks and every kind of steam launch. After the
factories and warehouses came the Bund, the seven-mile stretch of
banks, hotels and merchant buildings, with their distinctive neoclassical domes and their bronze and granite art deco facades. It was 10
October, China's national day, and flags flew from every building.
Skyscrapers stood on what not long before had been muddy wasteland. Rickshaws sped in their thousands along the packed streets.

Perfectly placed between North and South China, within a delta flowing through major tea- and silk-producing areas, midway between Atlantic Europe and America, Shanghai was the richest port in Asia, its 'Paris of the east'. The nerve centre of industry and commerce, it lay far enough from the sea to be protected from coastal typhoons, with the Yangtze, as 'long and sinuous and dangerous as a dragon', not far away. When it rose, the water spread 40 kilometres each side and buffaloes could be found wallowing in mud with only their muzzles showing. Having grown from a village into a city of three million people occupying some 20 square miles in less than ninety years, it was split between the foreign concessions and the Chinese districts. Shanghai was everything that Fascist Rome was not: chaotic, racy, messy, cosmopolitan, garish, smelly, insanely noisy, a perpetual 'jenao', as the Chinese put it, a 'hot din of the senses'. 'Shanghai,' wrote the reporter Emily Hahn, 'is for now, for the living me.' Its gossip was 'fuller, richer and less truthful' than anywhere else in the world. For Edda, it meant freedom.

The Italian consulate on Bubbling Well Road stood in the International concession, the most pleasant area of the city, lined with tulip trees, roses and magnolias and wide avenues with plane trees, two miles from the Bund. The house itself was large and airy but, as Edda wrote to Mussolini, it was 'dirty, dusty and full of ill matching old furniture'. The bed in the main bedroom was made of iron and reminded her of a Corpus Domini procession. 'In the kitchen,' she wrote, 'there are just four pots and saucepans and two broken enamel ladles.' She set about pulling it together. Ciano was extremely interested in the appearance of things and furthermore very conscious that he and Edda had been posted to Shanghai to demonstrate the power and success of Fascism. With extra money willingly sent by Mussolini, the house was transformed. An excellent Italian cook was quickly found. Because Edda was so young, Ciano told her she was at a disadvantage in the diplomatic world; but the fact that she was pretty could be turned to advantage. Her duty was to keep the Chinese and foreign diplomats happy, Ciano said, to do her best to be sweet and kind and to preside over a lavish table, somehow overlooking the fact that sweetness and kindness were not perhaps her main strengths. She was, however, both energetic and efficient and had finally found a role.

The timing of the Cianos' arrival could not have been better.

Sun Yat-sen, who had overthrown the Manchu dynasty in 1911, sweeping away two thousand years of imperial rule and setting up a Nationalist government, had died in 1925. When Puyi, the last emperor, was expelled from the Forbidden City, his eunuchs left with him, carrying their testicles in boxes so that they could join their ancestors whole. They smuggled out the Pekinese dogs bred especially after an Empress requested a dog as clever as a monkey, as brave as a lion, and with the pop eyes and flowing tail of her favourite goldfish. Sun Yat-sen's successor, Chiang Kai-shek, having defeated the competing warlords and established his government in Nanking, converted to Christianity and married a girl with impeccable missionary connections, had declared himself impressed by the energy of Fascist ideology. 'Fascism,' he told his followers, 'is a stimulant for a declining society. Can Fascism save China? We answer, yes. Fascism is what China needs most.' Though it needed to be adapted to Chinese traditions and classical Confucianism, he shared Mussolini's taste for hierarchy, orderliness and militarism. He was in the process of distancing himself from the communist disturbances in forty-three of China's provinces, where 'reds' and bandits were looting and setting fire to villages.

Italy was looking for new markets and wanted to import raw materials; China, emerging from decades of political conflict, needed to modernise its economy. Collaboration between the two countries, brokered by the Cianos, would bring great benefits to both. Ciano was eager to work hard and, as he wrote to a friend, what delighted him about China was that it was the place where, uniquely, you could say exactly what you liked. Though Edda herself was rather lazy, she was full of curiosity and excitement. Both spoke some English and French, and Ciano also spoke Spanish and Portuguese and was planning to learn Chinese. They were the perfect Fascist emissaries.

What Edda discovered as she explored her surroundings was that Shanghai was in fact several cities, distinct but coexisting, with, as Daniele Varè described it, an unforgettable smell of 'cooking with sesame oil, incense, lotus flowers, garlic and humanity'. There was the city of the foreign legation: each of the Great Powers had extracted treaty port rights from the weak and tottering imperial dynasties, thus exploiting their own spheres of influence. They were averse to any thought of a strong and united China, or any attempt to clean up the immensely lucrative opium trade. The foreigners enjoyed great power and great wealth, occupying land and property deemed 'extraterritorial', governed and policed by them alone from their banks and merchant houses along the Bund, enjoying privileges that the Chinese were now contesting.

Along with the Japanese, the British were the most numerous. They owned the largest banks and trading houses, and also ran the trams, the water works and the municipal courts along British lines. The Russians had built railroads. The meticulously tended gardens along the Bund banned 'Chinese, dogs, flower picking, ball games and bicycling' and Sikhs kept the chaotic traffic moving by leaping from their boxes to beat the rickshaw men with their truncheons. Though very modest in comparison with the other European or American presence in Shanghai, Italy nonetheless had forty-seven firms, and six hundred residents, most of them men from the North of Italy, the first Italian Chinese treaty having been signed by the government of Savoy before unification. The British dealt in tea and opium; the Italians in marble, textiles, hats and clothes, but most of all in silk and healthy silk worm eggs, having forged close ties with the Chinese when Lombardy was hit by a disease among its silk worms in the nineteenth century.

The foreigners also owned clubs, restaurants, shops and newspapers and lived for the most part in luxury, in houses that looked like Brooklyn brownstones, Bavarian castles and neo-Gothic mansions, though Noel Coward, passing through in 1929, described the city as a 'cross between Brussels and Huddersfield'. The Cianos' arrival coincided with the start of the hunting season – paper chases rather than foxes – which came soon after the cotton and bean harvests. These hunts, noted the *North China Herald,* were the 'best protection against luxury, idleness, debauchery and effeminacy'. Horses played a central role in the social life of the city; wild ponies were driven down once a year from the grasslands of Mongolia, looking like small woolly bears with powerful backs and shapely legs, but once broken in they proved exceptional race horses.

The exclusive Shanghai Club had a marble staircase, a colonnaded hall, teak-panelled rooms and a Turkish bath, as well as the longest bar in the world, 300 metres of gleaming mahogany at which members sat in order of seniority. The Hong Kong and Shanghai building, which stretched along 300 feet of waterfront, was decorated with mosaics, with Shanghai portrayed as a damsel looking across the Bund, her left hand on a ship's wheel, her right shading her eyes as she gazed down the river. The national balls were the grandest of the social occasions and were held in the Majestic Hotel, where the ballroom was in the shape of a four-leaf clover, with pieces of real gold inlaid in the main hall. Here, in the heat of the summer months, blocks of ice were placed in the middle of the dance floor and guests sweltered to the sounds of Ragtime, Dixieland Swing, the Turkey Trot and the Grizzly Bear. Shanghai boasted the longest chorus line in the world. Each year the Americans produced ice cream in the colours of their flag, and the Scots shipped in haggis. In the Palace Hotel, you could get cereal, poached eggs and bacon for breakfast, and in the Chocolate Shop, thirty-one flavours of ice-cream sundaes. By a long way the youngest of the diplomatic wives – she had celebrated her twentieth birthday on the journey out – Edda was now called on to shine in this feverish, chaotic, rivalrous world. Though shy and still prone to blush, she had no choice.

Just streets away from the frenetic niceties of legation life, there was a second Shanghai, a place of unimaginable poverty, exploitation, corruption and gang warfare. Organised crime of every kind thrived, as did spies, informers and secret societies. The city had a leper colony and an almost medieval level of squalor; tuberculosis, smallpox and scarlet fever were rife. In 1930, the life expectancy of a local Chinese inhabitant was twenty-seven, the same as in Europe in the thirteenth century. Shanghai was reported to have a hundred thousand heroin addicts, their skin papery and grey, their teeth falling out. On cold nights, corpses looking like bundles of rags lay in the streets, and in the factories that surrounded Shanghai were small children, many sold by their destitute families to contractors, their gums blue from lead poisoning, working sixteen-hour days to produce crêpe de Chine, brocade and chiffon. There were also brothels, with thirteen-year-old girls in silk pyjamas, their toes broken to keep them no more than three inches long, so that they looked like pigs' trotters in embroidered silk slippers.

But there was also an in-between Shanghai, a city of nightclubs, cabarets and casinos, most of them served by the White Russians. Many of these were Jewish and had fled the pogroms and the

Bolshevik victory and had arrived penniless in successive waves from Vladivostok having lost families and homes and suffered terrifying journeys, some of them by camel. They tended to be despised by the other Europeans, who spoke of them as emotional and untrustworthy and worried that they would sully the 'white man's prestige', but allowed them, as Edda was informed, to do their hair, make their clothes and teach their children to dance. The Russian men, former military officers, teachers and office workers, taught languages, horse riding and fencing. Some played in Shanghai's many bands and orchestras. Avenue Joffre, in the French concession, was known as 'Little Russia' and smelt of fresh bread and cakes from the White Russian bakery. There were two Russian schools and several Russian newspapers. The Italian writer Mario Appelius called Shanghai the 'Babel of Asia', where promiscuity and vice were the 'putrescence of both worlds', but added that no one city could 'equal her formidable charm, that of a lavish and joyous gal, dressed for an endless dance party that begins on 1 January and ends on 31 December'. Once you knew Shanghai, all other cities appeared dull and colourless. Edda revelled in the in-between Shanghai.

And there was Chinese Shanghai, neither quite foreign nor quite Chinese, where rich, educated Chinese lived in foreign-looking houses with verandas. Freed from the strict traditional mores of their childhoods, they thought they saw China's future in Shanghai's glitter and modernity. For a long time wary of each other, foreigners and Chinese were now learning to mix. Daniel Varè observed that when grand Chinese officials attended receptions in their full imperial dress, 'society women grovelled before the brocades, the furs, the velvet boots, the coral and jade buttons, the peacock feathers and the general sartorial magnificence'.

Shanghai, along with Peking, Hankow, Tientsin and Canton, remained an oasis of relative tranquillity, surrounded by a country descending into civil war, overrun by brigands and pirates, the foreign colonies protected by gunboats. Italy, through a treaty of friendship and commerce signed with the Nationalist Republican Government in 1928, was liked by the Chinese, who considered that she had not been tainted by the imperialism of the Greater Powers.

For Edda and Ciano, it was all of it, the good and the bad, the extraordinary splendour and the enticing entertainment, an exotic paradise, a spectacle, a vast market in which everything was for sale and anything was possible. They fell in love with it all. Edda would later remember it as the happiest time of her life.

H.G.W. Woodhead was a pipe-smoking, canny reporter, working for various English-language newspapers in Peking and Shanghai, of which there were many, the early missionaries having brought with them printing presses in order to disseminate Christianity, and the merchants reading them in order to learn business news. Known for his reports on the opium trade, Woodhead was also a keen observer of the diplomatic world, and an outspoken critic of international affairs. The Italians, he had decided, were not to be trusted, and in Shanghai his word went a long way. Edda quickly identified him as one of her first challenges. Inviting him to her newly decorated consulate, she wooed him with excellent Italian dishes and good wines. He was charmed. Edda, he was soon heard to say, to the annoyance of the older wives, was '*la prima signora di Shanghai*'. Soon, the Italian consulate teemed with foreign diplomats, nationalist leaders, journalists and pretty women. The crazy little horse was discovering how to please.

For all the years of the Manchu dynasty, Peking had been regarded as China's intellectual and cultural capital, the 'authentic' city – unlike the 'inauthentic' Shanghai – where foreign artists and writers came to settle in courtyard houses with little moats of water lilies and roofs in yellow, green and blue tiles. But after the warlords took the city in 1926, university professors and writers had moved to Shanghai, taking with them publishers and libraries. They were soon joined by filmmakers and by the early 1930s a Chinese film industry was flourishing, taking its subjects from legends and from the world of gangsters and detectives. With the development of the turbine engine, and the building of larger, faster, more comfortable ships, cruises had become popular and ships from the United States, bringing film stars from Hollywood to advertise the American film industry, regularly docked along the Bund. Douglas Fairbanks and Mary Pickford were among the earliest arrivals, as were André Malraux, Charlie Chaplin, Eugene O'Neill and Gloria Swanson.

With these cruises came women who shopped for silk, satin, embroidered linen, carved furniture and jade, often going on to visit the Great World Amusement Centre, six floors of slot machines, bird cages, acrobats, jugglers, ice-cream parlours, tightrope walkers and marriage brokers, with a stuffed whale perched in splendour on the fifth. The liners that brought them to China carried back morphine and heroin, to be smuggled into the US. Alert to the famous names among the passengers, and prompted by her father's repeated telegrams about the need to fly Italy's Fascist flag, Edda sent out invitations, held receptions and began to visit other diplomatic wives. She should never forget, one cable instructed, to cultivate 'that strength of will which is the prerogative of the Mussolinis'. Despite her youth Edda was, noted an admiring reporter, 'a most generous and solicitous hostess'. Thin and tall, she was an excellent model for fashion-conscious Shanghai, where the many newspapers now included women's pages. Edda's arrival coincided with the autumn collections: long black velvet wraps edged in black fox, soft pelts of astrakhan and karakul, a revival of squirrel coats, 'table bell' skirts with flared hems, muffs, beading, and white or pink chiffon. 'Style,' noted the *North China Herald*, 'will count above everything. And style will be smart.' Edda was good at style.

She was not, however, greatly interested in women's clubs or associations and her name was not to be found on the mastheads of any of them. She preferred to spend her afternoons playing bridge with other diplomatic wives. Then she discovered mahjong and poker, both played for high stakes, in spite of calls for bans on gambling from the Shanghai authorities. What she enjoyed was not just the sense of danger, but watching other players lose with perfect equanimity. She wanted to be like them, inscrutable. Ciano drank no alcohol, but Edda was acquiring a taste for gin.

Though she studied the methods of her poker-playing companions with great care, she was often a heavy loser, whereupon her polished manners would desert her and she reverted to the cruder language of Milan's backstreets. She went to great lengths to keep her mounting debts from Ciano, who frequently declared that gambling was pernicious, imprudent and silly, especially in women. When suffering a losing streak, she promised she would give it up, but then she invariably went back to it. And she was not able to hide from him one especially disastrous evening, when she lost 4,000 Mexican dollars at the poker table, and had no funds to pay off her losses. Dealing with her predicament with her usual mix of irony and histrionics, she informed Ciano: 'I am in despair. I am going to kill myself.' Ciano gave her the money, remarking drily: 'Children don't kill themselves.' His censoriousness maddened her.

Mussolini was constantly in touch and she learnt to deal with her father's diktats by waiting several days before she opened his telegrams. Signing himself not 'Papa' but 'Mussolini', he had stock phrases that he used over and over again. One was that 'I am, as usual, having to pull the cart behind me on my own'; another favourite: 'Italy continues to be an oasis of tranquillity in a world in chaos', and '*per tutto il resto*, all is calm'. He sent news of Rachele and what her brothers and sister were doing, football scores and the fact that he had taken up riding a motorcycle.

But he had other things on his mind. Not long after Edda's departure for China, Arnaldo's elder son, known to them all as Sandrino, had died of leukaemia at the age of twenty. Arnaldo had been particularly devoted to this boy and his death changed him. He became sombre and distracted, insisting on keeping Sandrino's place at the table laid for meals. 'Arnaldo is with me,' Mussolini wrote to Edda, 'but his thoughts are elsewhere.'

Arnaldo

Every day, Arnaldo appeared sadder and more hopeless, his mood darkened by rumours of financial irregularities. The end came quicker than anyone expected and, at the age of forty-six, he died. This is one of the 'saddest Christmases, perhaps the saddest of all', Mussolini wrote to Edda. Arnaldo had been not only his dearly loved brother, but the broker of the Vatican accords and the only person he really trusted and considered his friend. He immediately started to write a memoir about him, *Vita di Arnaldo*, which became a sentimental account of their childhood.

In Milan, the offices of *Il Popolo d'Italia* were turned into a mortuary and while Arnaldo lay in state, thousands came to pay their respects. Mussolini sat with the body all night. As the coffin was carried through the streets to the church of San Marco, flags and banners were dipped, bells rang out and people threw flowers on the coffin from their windows.

Not long after reaching Shanghai, Edda discovered that she was pregnant. Hearing the news, Mussolini replied, 'fills me with happiness and emotion. From now on I will think of you with even greater intensity.' Edda herself was not greatly pleased, and while Ciano went out dancing, she stayed at home writing her diary. She had vowed not to be jealous, but Shanghai was full of attractive and available women and she knew that her husband was having affairs, one beautiful Chinese girl replacing another as he tired of them. The diplomatic community was already gossiping about his dalliances behind the potted plants with pretty guests at receptions. There were rumours that he had an affair with Wallis Simpson when she came to China to escape an unhappy marriage and, like Edda, took to gambling. But the rumours were false.

Labour pains started on 1 September 1931, Edda's twenty-first birthday, then subsided. From Mussolini came a loving telegram, remembering the day of her birth, one of '*festa e grandissima gioia*', celebration and the greatest happiness. The whole consulate waited nervously. From Rome, a mountain of anxious telegrams poured in almost daily from Mussolini. Sending her 'wishes from the depth of my heart', he told her: 'Just as in the years of your adolescence, when times were hard, so today you are the favourite of my spirit. I embrace you with the love you know I bear you and which will accompany you always.' A month later, on 1 October, after a long and hard birth, a boy was delivered. When she saw the baby covered in blood, Edda screamed: '*Mamma mia! Quanto è brutto*', how hideous he is. Ciano, waiting next door, rushed in expecting to be confronted with a monster. The boy was healthy and weighed just over 3 kilos. Mussolini had cabled to say that he thought that Giorgio or Guido, 'plain, strong names', would be best. Edda, exercising her new-found independence, decided to call the baby Fabrizio, refusing even her father's request to spell it with two 'b's as a reminder that his own father had been a *fabbro*, a blacksmith. Always keen on nicknames, she called him Ciccino. Chang Su Lin, a friend of Chang Kai-shek, was made godfather and sent a gift of a small jade Buddha.

Not long before, the inventor and electrical engineer Guglielmo Marconi had put in place a wireless telephone connection between Genoa and Sydney, and on Mussolini's urging, managed to link Rome with Shanghai. Soon after the baby's birth, Mussolini and Rachele spoke to Edda. The King and Queen sent their congratulations and the Pope asked for news. Mussolini was extremely pleased with his new grandson, and sent him his first membership card for the Balilla youth organisation in Rome, while making a generous donation to the Fascist women's organisation. 'We're getting old. We're now grandparents,' he complained to Rachele. But word went out to the news agencies that he was never, under any circumstances, to be described as '*nonno*'. The baby was worryingly quiet and floppy until it was discovered that the wet nurse, along with her milk, was giving him opium.

It was lying in bed after Fabrizio's birth that Edda realised how deeply jealous she felt about Ciano's liaisons. It was making her ill with unhappiness. She spent part of a night outside on the terrace, remembering her mother's endless scenes with Mussolini, pondering what she should do, indulging in reflections that if she caught pneumonia and died, that would be the best way out. She suffered no ill effects, but reached a decision. Whatever happened, even if she found him in bed with her closest friend, she would never, by an act of will, allow herself to be sexually jealous again; and in Edda's case, will was paramount. She would cease to believe herself in love with him, but regard him quite simply as a friend, with 'fraternal affection'. Ciano, surprised and intrigued by her new coolness, tried to woo her back; for a while at least, she remained firm, a measure both of the strength of her willpower and her ability to control her emotions. There was something feline about Edda, a kind of sinuous, nervous energy, and, feeling freed from her marriage vows by Ciano's dalliances, she took to flirting more or less openly with men she found attractive. She preferred their company to that of women.

*

In September 1931, shortly before Fabrizio's birth, the Japanese, on the pretext of an attack on their railroad – which they had staged themselves – invaded and annexed Manchuria, where their political and economic interests had been growing since the Russo-Japanese War. Chiang Kai-shek abandoned the area and retreated west. The League of Nations, calling on the Japanese to withdraw, set up a commission of inquiry under Lord Lytton to investigate whether they had acted in self-defence. Diplomats were hopeful that if Japan's territorial gains were at least partly acknowledged they would stop there. But on 18 January 1932, a Chinese crowd in Shanghai, enflamed by students protesting against the occupation of Manchuria, attacked five Japanese monks belonging to the Buddhist Nichirin sect, a militant order pursuing Japanese dominance in Asia. One priest was killed. A Japanese mob set fire to a Chinese factory and the Japanese consulate demanded that the priest's murderers be punished. Japanese marines, armed with machine guns, roared up and down the streets on motorcycles. The Shanghai authorities declared martial law, erected barbed-wire barricades and called out the various volunteer militias. The Western powers sent warships and the city's international settlement was put on to a war footing. The Chinese Nineteenth Route Army, most of its soldiers young boys in faded cotton uniforms and tennis shoes, prepared to defend the city, supported by students.

The Japanese, meanwhile, began to shell the wharves. Bombs set alight churches, schools, densely packed apartment blocks, which collapsed. 'Situation becoming critical,' Ciano cabled Rome in an '*urgentissimo*' telegram, 'Chinese have gathered 30,000 men around the city.' The Shanghai municipal council now advised foreign residents to leave, but for a while many preferred to climb to the top of the sixteen-storey Broadway Mansions on the Bund to watch the fighting from its terrace. When it spread to the international settlement, and Chinese families began banging on the gates to ask for refuge, most of the diplomatic families prepared to depart. Edda, however, refused to leave. When her new admirer, Woodhead, heard that she had no intention of abandoning the consulate, he filed his report to the English-language newspapers, and the story went out under an enormous headline: 'The first lady of Shanghai refuses to go'. As Edda herself said later, not without a certain smugness, she had wanted to show what Fascists were made of. She was also curious and slipped out from the consulate to watch the fighting.

The Chinese could never have won, though many died defending the city. Their soldiers were ill equipped and poorly armed, firing at the Japanese planes with rifles. By early March, Japanese reinforcements had pushed the Nineteenth Route Army across the city and on the 8th they raised their flag over the North Station. Packs of dogs, abandoned by their owners, roamed the streets, the Japanese bayonetting those they caught. Eight thousand Chinese were dead and a further 10,400 people were missing; in the international settlement, one hundred people had lost their lives. Nineteen of Shanghai's thirty-nine cinemas had been destroyed.

The French and British governments asked their consuls to set up a peace commission, under the auspices of the British Minister, Sir Miles Lampson. Ciano sensed an opportunity to make his mark and cabled Rome for instructions; then, without waiting to hear, he joined in the peace talks. When the answer came it ordered him to play a part, but to be certain not to compromise Italy's position of being on good terms with both sides. Lampson would later complain that he found Ciano very irritating, but he was nonetheless appointed the commission's chairman. Forced to navigate in subtle, complicated waters that were incomprehensible even to many China experts, he turned out to be better informed and more able that most of the other members. Peace was duly brokered and signed but the Chinese were forced to accept that they could not garrison their troops in and around Shanghai; they regarded the deal as yet another humiliation imposed on them by the Western powers. The Japanese on the other hand emerged more assertive, and soon after renamed Manchuria 'Manchukuo', making it a puppet state under China's last emperor, Puyi. The League of Nations had shown itself weak. 'Where,' asked a Spanish delegate, his words confused but his meaning clear, 'is going the peace of the world?'

Within days, Shanghai had returned to its frenetic pace. The diplomatic families had sailed back up the Yangtze and returned to their mahjong, horse races, cocktail parties and Sunday rounds of golf. In his gleaming new Cathay Hotel, Sir Victor Sassoon was planning a fancy dress party, the guests to come as if caught in a shipwreck. One came in a flannel nightdress, with curlers in her hair; two others in shower curtains. It was in the Cathay Hotel that Edda discovered that she could finally cross a room without blushing. For the tenth anniversary of the March on Rome in October 1932, the Cianos gave a vast reception.

As for Ciano himself, his position among the various consulates had been much enhanced. His reward was to be promoted to Minister Plenipotentiary and Envoy Extraordinary. Mussolini sent him a telegram: 'You have increased Italy's prestige abroad.' Ciano now set about promoting further economic and cultural exchanges between China and Italy, inviting Italian scholars and scientists to visit Shanghai. In Rome, an Italo-Chinese league was founded and plans put in place for an Italian Institute for the Middle and Far East. A party of Chinese officials left for Italy to study the workings of the Fascist government. A Fascist law course was established at Soochow University. Ciano was also spending considerable periods of time dealing with the increasing number of restrictions and taxes imposed on foreign concerns, and on ensuring the safety of Italy's nineteen Catholic missions, prey to constant attacks by bandits who made exorbitant ransom demands for the missionaries they kidnapped. It was, as one Fascist diplomat noted, all rather like Italy, a question of '*accomodazione*', finding your way through the undergrowth of conflicting interests.

What the hostilities had done was to show up the extreme weakness of the Chinese military forces, and especially its air force. China was still paying indemnities from the Boxer Rebellion, its internal taxation was chaotic, and Chiang Kai-shek's government continued to be threatened by the strong and autonomous warlords. But moves were made to ease the remaining indemnities, and Ciano began successful negotiations to reduce the money due and to spend the rest on buying Italian goods and setting up hydroelectric plants and factories. Orders for military aircraft were put in to Fiat and Savoia-Marchetti, and two courses to train pilots were set up, one in China and one in Italy. To celebrate this new closeness, and to further his own ambitions for Italy to retain a privileged position in the east, Mussolini sent Chiang Kai-shek the present of an aeroplane, while also signing a contract for a factory and aerodrome in Jiangxi province with lavish Italian grants, regarded as a triumph for Ciano over German and American competition. The '*panFascismo*' he preached found ready listeners among the Japanese and Chinese.

Towards the middle of May, the Cianos gave a ball. (
recovering from a first attack of asthma, which would
for the rest of his life. Talking of a return to 'the good ol
foreign community turned out in force, together with a number оι
Italian naval officers. A great deal of champagne was served and at
4 a.m. Ciano was still urging the revellers to stay a little longer.
Next day, the *North China Herald* reported: 'The abilities of the
host and hostess in the matter of entertaining are already too well
known to require further testimonial.' Edda was singled out as a
'most generous and felicitous hostess', and the Cianos as a particularly devoted couple, a compliment that Edda would deflect, in her
usual acerbic way, by saying that many considered Ciano showy
and uncultured and herself as interested only in reading American
gossip columns – 'the perfect couple, he imbecilic and I trivial'. By
early June, peace in Shanghai was considered sufficiently restored
to hold the annual flower show, which this year bestowed its medal
on sweet peas.

Edda played her own part in furthering Italy's commercial interests. During the talks held by the Lytton Commission, she
accompanied Ciano to Peking. One night she found herself seated
at dinner next to an unusually tall, slim, young Chinese guest with
a sensual mouth and large eyes, who spoke excellent English and
was reputed to be the first Chinese man to adopt tweed suits. This
was Hsueh-liang, the 'Young Marshal', who had been privately
educated by tutors and had wanted to become a doctor, but had
been obliged by his Manchurian warlord father, Chang Tso-lin, the
'Old Marshal', to command his personal guard instead. At fifteen,
Hsueh-liang had been married by arrangement to the daughter of
a landowning friend of his father's, by whom he quickly had three
sons and a daughter.

In 1928 the Old Marshal had been murdered by a bomb placed
on a train by opponents wanting a warlord more amenable towards
Japan, and Hsueh-liang had returned to his father's palace in Mukden and emerged as the new leader of a Manchurian political and
military clique, trying to remain neutral in the various conflicts. In
the walled city of Mukden, he lived in great splendour, with two
immense stuffed Manchurian tigers in the great hall.

When Edda met him, Mukden had been overrun by the

Japanese and the Young Marshal had been forced to leave. He was now in his early thirties, with two wives and a concubine. All four were opium addicts. Hseuh-liang, described by a malicious reporter as a 'pallid ghost in dandy's clothes', was fighting his addiction with tennis and golf and daily morphine injections. A report sent back to Rome described him as 'very dedicated to drugs and women', with an appearance 'more degenerate than martial', but added that he had a certain 'nervous energy' and 'simple, courteous and impulsive manners' which made him attractive. Edda had immediately struck him as glamorous and interesting and during this first dinner he passed her a note inviting her on a tour of the summer palace. They met again and he gave her presents. There were also several meetings between the Cianos and the Young Marshal and his retinue of women, during which Ciano was able to sell him a considerable amount of war *matériel*, having been instructed by the Foreign Ministry in Rome to convince him of the glories of the new Italian technology. Hearing that he wanted to buy aeroplanes, Edda praised those made by Fiat and Marchetti and talked to him about helpful links with Fascist Italy and her father. Hseuh-liang put in an order for three planes and talked of getting more.

But this was not the end of Edda's friendship with the Young Marshal. Pei-ta-ho was a village on the Bay of Pei-Chu-Li, some nine hours journey from Peking, originally home to missionaries but now a fashionable summer resort for diplomats and foreigners. With Ciano kept in Shanghai by his work, Edda took Fabrizio and joined two women friends, Hui-Ian Koo, the wife of a senior government minister, and Laura Chieri, who had been born in Chicago and lived for some time in China, taking a house just outside the village on the side of a mountain. The area was rugged and very beautiful, with no cars or carriages allowed. Though surrounded by legation staff and bodyguards, she slipped away and the three women swam naked from the rocks. Having lost a lot of hair when Fabrizio was born, she had what was left cut very short, and struck her friends as exaggeratedly thin and elegant. Laura, wrote Hui-Ian Koo later, was 'cheerful as a cricket', but Edda was 'razor sharp'.

What her two friends liked about Edda was that, endearingly lacking in poise and self-confidence, which might have made her wary and snobbish, she was on the contrary always eager to put others at ease. In the evenings, the three friends danced on the

Edda and Young Marshal

terrace to the gramophone and played mahjong and poker. Whenever he could, the Young Marshal joined them. He was clearly infatuated with Edda; she called him '*mon béguin*', my crush.

He met Edda again in Peking, where he took her up in his new plane, and often walked with her along the city walls, Edda in a sedan chair, the Young Marshal pacing by her side, to the consternation of the Chinese who thought subservience far below his dignity. She worried that Ciano would get to hear of their daily meetings and be angry. Since reporters and photographers often trailed their outings, even Mussolini was able to follow her life in the foreign papers. A letter full of heavy innuendo, sent by Ciano's deputy Anfuso to the Foreign Ministry in Rome, spoke of the Young Marshal's 'exceptional attentions' to Edda, and the way that he paid her the kind of notice that he had never shown before to any other foreigner.

A moment came when Edda decided that she needed to hold an official dinner in Peking for the diplomatic corps. She arranged it with great care and lavishness. On the appointed night, not one of the wives turned up. Assuming that this was a mark of their disapproval for her closeness to Hseuh-liang, she was amused and reassured to discover that she had been shunned because she had breached a simple matter of diplomatic etiquette: she had failed to deliver personal visiting cards to each of them before the dinner. But Edda, still just twenty-one, had scored a coup with her sale of Italian aeroplanes, and neither they nor their husbands quite liked or trusted her threatening glamour.

Edda had kept to her resolution and spurned Ciano's advances for months, but some time in the winter of 1932 she relented and soon, to her great annoyance, found herself pregnant. Mussolini had been hinting that he thought she needed a rest, and now started to talk about recalling them to Rome. She was appalled and protested strongly. Hui-Ian Koo and Laura Chieri had come to Shanghai and the three friends, after supper at any one of half a dozen fashionable clubs, had taken to ending the night in the Del Monte, where sausages were served all night.

Orders finally came that the Cianos were to leave Shanghai in April 1932. After thirty months, Mussolini wrote to Edda, he was delighted to note that the 'temperature of your Fascism has grown. It is the only powerful and original thing in our current century.' He had not altogether abandoned his habit of addressing his children as if they were at a public meeting.

Ciano hoped to secure more aeroplane orders from the Young Marshal and arrangements were made for him, his wife, concubine and children to travel to Italy with them on the new and very plush SS *Conte Rosso*, all oak and leather panelling and Ionic columns. The crossing took twenty-three days. A doctor, nurse, secretary and various advisers accompanied the Young Marshal's party, and there were plans for him to meet Mussolini in Rome before putting his children into school in Brighton and settling somewhere to study politics and military affairs.* Edda, pregnant and furious at leaving China, was in low spirits and sulked for much of the way home.

* In 1936, the Young Marshal, having thrown his lot in with the Kuomintang, had Chang Kai-shek kidnapped, earning a stern rebuke from Ciano. When he agreed to release him, he was himself arrested and spent many years in jail.

Part Two

EPISODES

7

The cult of the Duce

Edda and Ciano arrived back in Brindisi in late June 1932, walking down the gangplank with Fabrizio between them, each of them holding on to one of the little boy's hands. Mussolini had repeatedly told Edda that she would find Rome altered beyond recognition. After the chaotic colours and turbulence of Shanghai, her first impression was of silence, sobriety and infinite dullness.

Edda and Ciano

In the three years she had been away Rome had indeed changed greatly. Though parts of the city were still building sites, piazzas deemed 'without value' had been cleared away, along with towers, roads, alleyways and entire popular quarters where goats had still grazed. Their former inhabitants were now living in new suburbs outside the city walls. Many churches had been razed, as had the Pantanella in the Circo Massimo, home to ten furnace steampowered mills, cottages, sheds, haywicks, rag-picking dumps, bakeries and pasta factories. Pavements had been mended and rubbish cleared away. As Mussolini put it, the time had come to clean up the 'picturesque filth'. In its place were wide avenues, vast new public edifices, banks and post offices. In July 1931, a regulatory plan more ambitious than anything that had gone before had been approved by Royal Decree, paving the way for forty-five new schools, twenty-two covered markets, two hospitals and two cemeteries. Though there had been no precise architectural policy, the 'spirit of Fascism' had dictated grandeur in all things: monumental size of buildings and inscriptions everywhere, in lettering that was an eclectic mix of nineteenth century and pseudo-classical, proclaiming the triumphs of the new order. Eagles, lictors' fasces, crests and statues, a great many of them of Mussolini himself, were to be seen on every street. Rome was now a city of messages.

The Via dell'Impero, inaugurated on 28 October 1932, the tenth anniversary of the March on Rome, running past the Colosseum and through the forums of Trajan, Augustus and Nerva, had provided Mussolini with a theatre for his patriotic celebrations. Fascist Italy, he declared, must come first everywhere, 'on earth, on the sea, in the skies, in material things, in people's spirits'. In the new Foro Mussolini, between the Tiber and Monte Mario, a 'marble temple to the young forces of Italy' with its huge nude white statues in sporting poses and a monolith of Mussolini that had taken sixty oxen to drag through the streets, twenty thousand spectators could now watch public games. 'Obelisks,' remarked Edda when she saw the 20-metre column of marble, 'are a phallic symbol of dictatorship. Always erect.' There was a new Museo di Roma, a partially rebuilt Teatro Reale dell'Opera, a dozen new Fascist associations and institutes. Thirty thousand vehicles sped through the streets. There were new parks and new gardens.

To ensure that everyone should be aware of these architectural and civic glories, an Exhibition of the Fascist Revolution had filled twenty-three rooms with photomontages, sculptures, sounds and vast inscriptions, remembering the Great War and heralding the achievements of Fascism. Four giant copper fasces bathed in a 'radiant red mantle' rose 25 metres into the air. Visitors, referred to as pilgrims, were invited on a journey of regeneration, from melancholic, decadent liberalism to the awakening forces of faith, idealism and national glory, from agitation and disorientation to symmetry and clarity. The exhibition was eventually visited by almost four million people. 'Harmony, order, cleanliness,' noted one dazzled spectator, 'discipline in the streets, at home, at school.' Or, as a journalist remarked, 'The new Italy is called Mussolini.'

It might not be, as Mussolini boasted, 'vast, orderly, powerful as in the times of Augustus'. But Rome, with its tons of marble hauled from Carrara by sea and then up the Tiber, its glass and steel, its electric lighting, its newly excavated ruins, places of 'meditation and ecstasy' fused with sparkling modernity, was a new kind of city. As one visitor rather sourly put it: 'Eternal Rome, eternal din.' The once slow-moving, indolent capital had swollen – almost half a million new inhabitants in less than twenty years – and speeded up. It did, indeed, look different, but it was still sedate and provincial; and this was precisely what Edda had taken such pleasure in escaping from. She yearned for Shanghai.

Edda, Ciano and Fabrizio moved back into the Villa Torlonia to await the birth of the new baby. Vittorio was now seventeen, and with a school friend had been producing a magazine, *La Penna dei Ragazzi*; he had also grown interested in film, making shorts in the gardens of the villa. Bruno, at fifteen, was more reserved and pessimistic by nature. School reports from the Liceo Tasso, pored over obsessively by their father, reported Vittorio as unruly and very weak in Latin, and Bruno as clever and idle. The younger boy, wrote his headmaster, was 'extremely lively, impertinent and a devil' and when scolded 'not above lying'. Both boys were disobedient with their bodyguards and the chauffeur, did not like to be told off, and 'do not always follow the lessons or do their homework'. Perhaps, the headmaster suggested cautiously, this might have something to do with the fact that they had so much else to occupy their time – riding, fencing, the theatre, boxing – which did not leave them enough time to study. Increasingly, it was a question of the teachers adapting to the boys, rather than the boys obeying the masters; if something displeased them, they simply walked out.

Like Edda, the boys were closely watched by the secret services, their every movement noted and reported back to Bocchini, who passed the information on to Mussolini. The '*signorini*' were known to truant, to spend hours playing billiards in a bar on the Via Buoncompagni and to frequent theatres and cinemas where the managers kept seats for them. Vittorio was said to visit brothels, to smoke and to use bad language. Even their friends' families were investigated, their phones tapped and their finances checked. Two brothers, Leone and Radius, were thought to be 'leading them down a very dangerous path'. The mother of another school friend, Maria Filomena Bastioli, was described as being of 'dubious morality': one of her daughters had been arrested at sixteen, and another was exhibiting signs of 'clandestine prostitution'. When the moment came to send six-year-old Romano to school, thought was given to who should sit next to him in class. After rumours that a criminal gang in Genoa had made plans to kidnap the child, he was kept at home while Bocchini strengthened the network of spies and guards around the family. Once again, Edda could do nothing unobserved in Rome: it was this constant surveillance, after the freedom of Shanghai, that she found especially intolerable.

In the Villa Torlonia, Rachele ruled. Edda called the atmosphere 'peasant fanaticism'. Her mother supervised the maids, tended the vegetable garden and the chickens, and tried to cope with the avalanche of presents that descended on the villa, from antique weapons to stuffed eagles, tooled leather books, bronze busts and model aeroplanes, sending some to charity, others to Rocca delle Caminate to be displayed in what the children called 'the tower of horrors'. Admirers also offered houses by the sea and in the countryside, along with any amount of flowers, cakes, baskets of vegetables and fruit. As reluctant as ever to engage in any form of social life, Rachele had been forced to attend one reception at the Quirinale where she observed the décolletés of the court ladies with disapproval, and found the ladies themselves prim, solemn and full of repressed jealousy. They gave her 'supercilious little smiles' and she laughed to herself about all the men who flocked around her, kissing her hand, hoping that she would put in a good word for them with Mussolini. She came home saying that the King was a 'smiling rascal' and that he had told her that to him the court felt exactly like a 'chicken coop'. He had offered the Mussolinis the use of his estate at Castel Porziano, which was full of deer and wild boar. Rachele had a wooden hut built there and sometimes went to shoot pigeons. Shooting, she said, was her 'greatest passion and only distraction'.

Rachele had another enjoyable occupation. Since arriving in

Rome, she had continued with her own spying activities, calling them '*missioni di fiducia*', missions of trust, and saying that she had learnt many good tips from the *One Thousand and One Nights*, which she knew almost by heart. Few Italians knew what she looked like, which meant she was free to go on expeditions on Rome's buses and trams, eavesdropping on what people were saying about Mussolini. She never lost her Romagnolo accent and, if questioned, she called herself Margherita Guidi. She also built up her own little network of useful informers, mainly to spy on the *gerarchi*, most of whom she profoundly mistrusted. Mussolini pretended that he had no interest in her discoveries and dismissed them as '*spionaggio femminile*', female spying; but he listened. Rachele very seldom visited the Palazzo Venezia and when she did it was usually while he was away, when she would take a picnic and sit in one of the window seats in the Sala del Mappamondo, watching the crowds in the Piazza Venezia below.

To the pleasure of the whole family, Gandhi had paid them a visit on his way back to India from the second Round Table Conference in London in 1931. Having inspected a march of young Fascists and gymnastic displays in the Piazza Venezia, and called on Mussolini in the Sala del Mappamondo, he came to the Villa Torlonia. Both boys later recalled watching from the windows as their father, Gandhi and his famous goat, which went everywhere with him to provide him with milk, walked up and down the paths, the goat nibbling at the flower beds until it slipped its lead, ran away and was at last lured back by Rachele, who gave it some salt. When Gandhi left, Mussolini told Rachele that he was a true saint, using goodness as his weapon. 'That man and his goat are making the British Empire tremble.' Later, Gandhi described Mussolini as having the 'eyes of a cat', which swivelled around in a terrifying manner, and said that he had bombarded him with forty-four separate questions about India. The Duce had expressed sympathy for his cause, he said, but had not committed himself to anything concrete.

Edda found life in the Villa Torlonia intensely boring. She was now six months pregnant, with a baby she did not really want, and she embarrassed the servants by walking around naked, a habit learnt in China. The precise routine of the days in the villa never altered and the family lived frugally – though Mussolini did not deny himself a plane, an expensive sports car and a string of horses. Meals were taken largely in silence, Edda being the only one of Mussolini's children who dared to treat him like an ordinary father, challenging his assertions and disagreeing with his opinions. Mussolini ate rapidly and with terrible table manners. Then the family, the staff and the bodyguards filed into the room with the film projector for the nightly newsreels. Mussolini studied his own appearances on screen minutely, to see how his speeches were going down with the public. After the newsreel came a feature film, which he seldom sat through unless it was slapstick, when he would say *'bene, bene',* when plates were broken over people's heads. Fabrizio played with Romano and Anna Maria, who were not much older than himself. Edda's aunt Edvige was often there, having moved to Rome after Arnaldo's death, when Mussolini asked her to be near to him as 'we two are now the only survivors of the old block'.

In all this, Ciano was a somewhat awkward participant. While the Mussolinis liked all forms of physical activity – swimming, riding, playing tennis, fencing, and even Rachele joined in the football – he enjoyed no sport but golf. He was sleek, lazy, extremely conscious of his good looks and well-cut clothes, worried about getting fat, and essentially gregarious, genial and self-consciously bourgeois in his tastes. The Mussolinis were reserved, cool, little interested in discussion or intimacy and averse to social life. They gave each other no presents, Mussolini presenting Rachele each year with a framed photograph of himself at Christmas. Ciano liked to spend money. He was aware that Rachele disapproved of him, and that she considered him too charming, too slick and ultimately untrustworthy. She hated his brilliantined hair. For his part, he referred to her in private as an *'ammazza galline',* a killer of chickens.

Rome was not the only thing that had changed. The dictatorship itself had taken on new forms and spread into every corner of Italian life. The *'fascistizzazione'* of Italy that had begun with the totalitarian state in 1926, codifying the passage of the cult of Fascism into the cult of Mussolini, had seeped into the army and the police, into schools, businesses, industry, the civil service, even into family life. Brave anti-Fascists, labelled traitors, were in jail, in internal exile or had fled abroad. The more violent and angry of Mussolini's early supporters had been purged, tamed or co-opted. Toscanini, regarded as a good Fascist until 1931, had refused to play 'Giovinezza' at a concert in Bologna, been kicked and hit until rescued by the carabinieri, then constantly heckled until he left for the US, saying, 'I can't wait to leave ... We have become white slaves.' Even the former ruling classes seemed to have forgotten that they never planned for Mussolini's rule to last beyond the moment he dealt with the Communists and Socialists.

A recent series of ministerial shake-ups had underlined the essentially Fascist nature of government, incorporated the increasingly toothless Fascist Party into the regime and consigned the *squadristi* heroes to history as *la Vecchia Guardia*, the old guard. Many of the men who replaced them were less clever but more biddable. The party itself had been '*epurata*', purified, and thinned down, the lazy and uncommitted removed along with those who had failed 'in ardour, responsibility and danger'. Mussolini's famous slogan was everywhere: 'Everything for the state, nothing against the state, nothing outside the state'.

And Italy was weathering the Depression, that had begun in the US and spread to Europe, better than many had expected. Though a number of small businesses had gone under, a series of loans from the government had helped others stay afloat. Industrial production was growing, as was that of the agricultural sector. Mussolini's 'corporative' state had seen the establishment of corporations to combine the representatives of both management and unions in the same bodies, effectively eliminating the bargaining powers of the unions, and banning internal competition in order to challenge international competitors. A series of 'battles' had been launched: 'of wheat', to raise wheat production so that Italy would no longer have to import as much of it; 'of the lira', revalued to show the world that Fascist Italy was stable and had a strong, desirable currency. South of Rome, the Pontine Marshes were being drained, 80,000 hectares of land reclaimed and made fertile, and unemployed families were being settled in the new towns of Sabaudia and Latina, where they were instructed to become model citizens, imbued with civic pride and purpose. Working hours had been reduced and a system of pensions and sick pay introduced.

Unemployment had risen, in keeping with other European countries, but protests were aimed not at Mussolini personally, or even at his politics, but rather at the world order, while hardship had been mitigated by relief measures, often labelled 'gifts of the Duce'. There were school lunches for children and 'popular trains', laid on to carry workers to the seaside. Indoctrinated by the slogans, kept in check by police vigilance, Italians seemed to have reacted to the Depression as to a natural disaster, something entirely beyond their control.

Even the young appeared to accept the regime, either because it suited them or because they genuinely wanted to believe Mussolini's boast that Italy was the most powerful and admirable nation in a world of decadent and weak states. They had been told that they were revolutionaries and that Fascism had shaken Italy out of torpor and cowardliness, showing them a new path, and that only the faithful would be accepted and rewarded. Obedience, valour, discipline were the new catchwords. With considerable guile and stealth, Mussolini had created a new, profoundly illiberal state, convincing those Italians who were neither in exile nor in detention that censorship of the press, emasculation of parliament and the violent suppression of dissent were in fact a small price to pay for new roads, sanitation and a programme of public works unrivalled in modern Europe. For the moment, they felt proud.

As for Mussolini himself, he was fast turning into a living God. The Italians were told that he was a genius, but at the same time modest, simple, a loving family man and to prove it he cried when he visited needy peasant families and stripped to the waist to help them in their fields. Never having shown much interest in sport, he was now the 'first sportsman' of Italy: he rode horses and motorcycles, flew and boxed, sometimes using animals as props, his lion cubs travelling with him in his car. He also fenced, declaring that it honed the physique and was all about courage and cunning and that it smacked of *Romanità* and *Latinità,* and he expected Edda and her brothers to be sporty and competitive. He had a presidential train of six carriages, with a dining room and a kitchen, and when he set off on his many visits to schools and factories he stood at the window so that he could be seen by the people.

Having created a public character – a tone of gravitas and solemnity, messianic eyes, a shaven head (after he found that he was going bald and there were no restorative lotions to prevent it) – he had adopted the manner to go with it: he walked with longer strides and practised theatrical gestures to appear more forceful. Though Sarfatti maintained that he had no sense of irony and very little humour, he would say of himself that what he really enjoyed, after their admiration, was the laughter of the people, hearty and spontaneous. A manicurist called Gina came every other day to do his nails and regale him with the gossip of Rome. To help Italians feel, but not think, he became a man of symbols, incantations, mystical visions and powers, and they were duly fascinated and admiring. As the popular slogan put it '*Mussolini ha sempre ragione*', Mussolini is always right.

The new vogue for photography helped – it would be claimed that during the twenty years of Fascism, thirty million pictures of Mussolini in 2,500 poses were taken – as well as the nascent taste for film stars. The unsocial, passive and homely Victor Emmanuel III and his wife, who were both singularly without charisma and had no taste for acquiring any, were also helpful. The ruling Savoy family had always been lofty, remote: their lack of public presence allowed Mussolini to move into an arena that could, and should, have been theirs. He was a man for whom the private was public, a man just like ordinary Italians and their neighbours, and he made certain that they knew him: he travelled more widely than any of his predecessors, orchestrating his visits as magical moments of communion with his people. Mussolini's children – and most especially Edda – were extensions of his persona. Wherever she went, there were photographers to capture her appearances; she had conquered her shyness and now no longer blushed, but she hated the attention.

So powerful had the cult of Mussolini become that when the family went to swim off the beach at Riccione, so many fully dressed women rushed into the water after him that the sea was full of floating garments. A special unit of guards was detailed to swim round him, keeping them at bay. Rather than touch him, these admiring women were encouraged to write to him, which they did, in their tens of thousands, a whole department of secretaries hired to send back signed photographs and sometimes a little money. Now, when spelt out, DUCE was always written in capital letters. The understanding was that he was as great as

Napoleon, as far-sighted as Hadrian, and a philosopher greater than Marcus Aurelius.

Though Rome was the heart of the cult, other sites proved useful in emphasising the religious overtones of Fascism. Forlì was '*la provincia del Duce*'. Even before the March on Rome, Mussolini's mother's grave at Predappio had become a place of pilgrimage for his followers. In the 1920s, a new village, Predappio Nuovo, grew up around the *Casa Natale*, the house in which he was born and the building in which Rosa, '*la più santa delle maestre: sua mamma*', had her schoolroom. Rosa was the mother of the new Italy, who protected and nurtured her children.

After this came an imposing new Fascist headquarters, a bridge over the Rabbi, a family chapel and a church dedicated to Rosa. Mussolini's father Alessandro was rather harder to canonise and for a while was portrayed with just a bronze bust and an anvil; as time passed his image was burnished, the heavy drinker and brawler transformed into an honest artisan and a strong, virile father. To all these altars to the Mussolinis came senior *gerarchi*, official groups, ordinary people arriving at the rate of five thousand a day in the summer months, on foot, by bus and bicycle and train, to be shepherded around by a new tourist office. Mussolini gave Predappio's *podestà* money to provide 'decent uniforms for the local people', who greatly enjoyed their new-found prosperity. Rachele, meanwhile, had been awarded the title of '*prima massaia*' of Italy, the country's foremost housewife, though unlike Mussolini she remained essentially unchanged, as full of rancour, vindictive and mistrustful of everyone as she had always been.

It was not long before Edda understood that a clear and binding role had been prepared for her. She and Ciano were to be the golden young couple of the new Fascist aristocracy, models of the '*stile Fascista*', dutiful, efficient, moral and fecund. Edda herself, independent, resourceful and spirited, had already produced one son and would surely produce more. But everything in her nature rebelled against it. The split between what was expected of her and what she herself wanted, between experiencing emotion and showing it, was growing more pronounced. And she was still just twenty-three.

With idolatry had come a growing sense of isolation. 'Now,' Mussolini had been heard to say at Arnaldo's funeral, 'there is no one left whom I can trust' – except perhaps for Edda. He very seldom convened the Grand Council and when he did it was to lecture them. To the German writer Emil Ludwig, who came to interview him in 1932, and described him as a man of 'finely tempered steel', a 'lion, mighty but high strung and nervous', Mussolini said that he had no friends, 'firstly because of my temperament, secondly because of my view of human beings. That is why I avoid both intimacy and discussion.' He had said as much to Sarfatti not long before: 'I don't want any [friends], I hate even the thought of them.' And though she continued to hover at the edges of his life, and made a furious scene on the doorstep when she was not invited to the opening of the Exhibition of the Revolution, he ceased to consult her. Sarfatti had moved into a house not far from the Villa Torlonia, where on Friday evenings she continued to receive foreign guests, among them Ezra Pound, André Malraux and André Gide. She had turned fifty and was not as beautiful as she had been.

Mussolini once told D'Annunzio that he felt like the 'national mule', an expression he often used with Edda. Having lost Arnaldo and got rid of Sarfatti, he was wary, sceptical, convinced that he had to do everything himself, that only he was the leader and Italy depended on him alone, though Edda's return from Shanghai provided him with someone he felt that he could talk to. An obsessive need for control meant that he wasted a great deal of his day scanning foreign newspapers to see what they were saying about Italy, reading reports from the party, Bocchini, OVRA and the ministries. When out in the car, he looked out of the window for things to change or criticise. Many decisions were now taken on the run with very little preparation. Orders, directives, reprimands flowed out of his office. Italian visitors to the Sala del Mappamondo were warned that they would have to cross the 60 feet of echoing marble while he ignored them, though with foreigners he could be charming, advancing towards them with his springy, feline step, his conversation fluent, sometimes witty, rich in metaphors. Though he had now reached fifty, and was neither happy nor content, he was still the 'man of providence' who never seemed to age.

And he still had time for women. In the Palazzo Venezia they continued to pass through, vetted by his *maggiordomo* Quinto

Navarro. They were admitted, wrote Navarro later, in the late afternoon for a quick coupling in the Sala del Mappamondo, either on the carpet in front of the desk or on a cushion on one of the stone window seats. All 'new' ones, whatever their rank, were checked by Bocchini and had their telephone calls intercepted. The dossiers piled up.

And then on 24 April 1932 a new figure entered Mussolini's life. As he was driving at great speed down the Via del Mare, he overtook a chauffeur-driven Lancia. Inside were Giuseppina Petacci, the wife of a successful society doctor, and her two daughters, twenty-year-old Claretta and eight-year-old Myriam. Claretta's fiancé, Riccardo Federici, was with them.

Claretta

Among the fifteen hundred or so letters sent to the Palazzo Venezia every day were many effusive and passionate ones from school girls and young women. Several of these had been from Claretta, who wrote: 'Duce, my life is yours!' and sent him her poems. Recognising Mussolini at the wheel of his red Alfa Romeo, she now waved frantically, shouting, 'Duce! Duce!' and urging the chauffeur to speed up. When they reached Ostia, the two cars pulled up together. Claretta sprang out and hurried across to him; no one stopped her. Three days later, Mussolini phoned the Petacci house and invited Claretta to the Palazzo Venezia to read her poems to him. She was driven there by the chauffeur and her mother waited in the car while she went in.

When Edda returned from Shanghai, Mussolini and Claretta had not yet become lovers; but she was already an important presence in his life, calling on him frequently in his office in the afternoons and exchanging as many as a dozen phone calls every day. Claretta was dark-haired, round-faced, with a husky voice, green eyes, a large bust and a somewhat prominent nose. She liked scent from Lanvin and was fond of fur coats and chocolates, which she ate lying on her bed. She told Mussolini that what she felt for him was 'ecstasy of my heart'. She was two years younger than Edda.

On 12 December 1933, Edda gave birth to Raimonda, immediately bestowing on her the nickname of Dindina. Never one to hold back her thoughts, however pessimistic, and in keeping with the Mussolinis' habit of dating their children's arrivals to events or moods, she referred to her daughter as '*la figlia dell'errore*', her mistake. Ciano had become '*Gallo*', cock, as in the lord of his hen coop of amorous women. She herself was now 'Deda'. The Cianos moved out of the Villa Torlonia and into a flat in the attics of an old house in Parioli, at number 5 Via Angelo Secchi. The two children lived with a nanny on the floor below. Edda was a cool mother, interested but not greatly attached; neither Fabrizio nor Raimonda seemed to break through the careful barrier of emotional self-protection that she had put in place. They had brought back with them from Shanghai carpets and furniture, which Ciano carefully arranged in the empty rooms. Edda, who cared nothing for domesticity, left the house to him: he masterminded the decorations, selected the staff, kept the household accounts and decided on the menus.

Almost from the moment they arrived back in Rome, Ciano had been chafing for a job. In June 1933 Mussolini had sent him to the World Economic Conference in London to discuss the Depression. The Italian delegation stayed in Claridge's and Ciano struck his colleagues with his affable manners and eagerness to please. What one remembered later was that when someone mentioned a friend who had just had the good fortune to marry an heiress, Ciano had broken in: 'No one could say that about me. As everyone knows, Edda came to our marriage without a penny.' The dowry had indeed been very small.

No money, perhaps, but soon he had a prestigious job. Edda went to tell her father that Ciano's restless pacing about the house was driving her mad. 'Send him wherever you want! Give him work! He's fed up, and so am I.' Mussolini obligingly appointed his son-in-law as the head of his Presidential Press Office, to promote the glories of Fascism, and indeed those of the Duce himself. He was given the rank of Minister Plenipotentiary and an office in the Palazzo Chigi, where he immediately had a bed made up for himself, to be on hand at any moment of crisis. Ciano was a willing servant, trained by his overbearing father to follow and carry out orders, and Edda, struggling to escape Mussolini's tutelage and ever more determined to go her own way, found his obsequiousness to Mussolini infuriating. She had thought that Ciano would be her ally; instead, he was clearly more concerned with pleasing his father-in-law. She hated it when she caught him imitating his gestures, mimicking his staccato soundbites, adopting his martial tread and authoritarian demeanour, whereas his natural walk was clumsy and his usual expression was kind and somewhat timid.

For Mussolini, Ciano was the perfect choice: a hard worker, a good linguist, dynamic and full of initiative. The moment had come to soften the oppressive control over the press, in place for almost ten years, and to find more sophisticated ways of putting across the Fascist regime. Ciano was given a generous budget; and he began to assemble his court.

Contacts between the Italian Fascists and the German National-Socialists dated to before the March on Rome, when Hitler had made overtures to Mussolini. Though there were no closer ties between the two men until Hitler came to power in the elections of January 1933, Hitler was known to find Mussolini inspiring. For a while at least he had referred to him as 'my master' and kept a life-sized bust of the Duce in his Munich office. For his part, Mussolini considered *Mein Kampf* 'unreadable', and the Nazis fanatical and lacking in subtlety, but he particularly enjoyed Hitler's obvious admiration for him and his desire for a friendly relationship between their two countries. While all over Europe Hitler's rise had been greeted with consternation, in Italy the reaction was largely positive. Ciano, however, was sceptical. 'Hitler in power?' he was later quoted as saying to Edda. 'What a catastrophe.'

Two months after becoming Chancellor, Hitler had appointed Goebbels to head a Department of Propaganda, with control over journalism, the arts and radio, as well as a brief to celebrate Nazi achievements. Goebbels had come to Rome, and at various dinners Edda was called on to demonstrate the diplomatic skills she had acquired in China. With Rachele refusing all such engagements, Mussolini was discovering Edda to be a skilful hostess. Shanghai had softened her, made her less wary and politically more adroit. She found Goebbels interesting. Despite his disdain for Hitler, Ciano produced a detailed and admiring analysis of Goebbels' new department, proposing that the Italians adopt a similar model.

Mussolini was in no hurry to encounter Hitler in person but finally agreed to a meeting in June 1934. Ciano's first important job was to arrange the press coverage and he courted and managed the two hundred journalists who had been invited with lavish and efficient care. In him, Shanghai had had the effect of increasing his desire to be liked. The encounter between the two leaders took place in the immense royal palace of Pisani at Stra, on the Brenta canal in Venice. It was, from the start, a disaster, both men having misjudged the formality of the occasion. Hitler arrived in Venice nervously twisting his grey felt hat in his hands, dressed in a yellow mackintosh and patent leather shoes. Mussolini was resplendent in full black Fascist uniform, complete with dagger and silver spurs, surrounded by his *gerarchi* turned out like peacocks with all their decorations. Mosquitoes, reported humorously by one journalist to be the size of quails, ravaged the company.

When left alone, the staff standing at a distance noted that the two men barked at each other like dogs, possibly because Mussolini's German was only adequate and Hitler's Bavarian-Austrian accent made communication difficult. On a boat trip across the Venetian lagoon, Hitler rambled on about Nordic superiority, observing that the Italians had 'Negro blood in their veins'. Asked later what he thought of his guest, Mussolini dismissed Hitler as a 'silly little clown' and a 'garrulous monk', who kept talking about 'taking Europe by surprise'. He had, however, he reported smugly, given Hitler some good advice, and 'now he'll follow me wherever I want'.

In any case, Mussolini was dreaming of quite another form of conquest. The moment had come to carry out a promise he had made to the Italians repeatedly in speeches over the years: that of making Italy 'great, respected, feared'. For this, he needed colonies, an empire, to rival those of France and Britain and to prove that Italy had a legitimate place at the high table of the great powers. He had long had his eye on Ethiopia, the last remaining potential colony in Africa, and he longed to hear again the mighty tread of the Roman legions. From London, Dino Grandi, now ambassador at the Court of St James, assured him that the British would not go to war over it.

Before making a move, however, he wanted to be certain of Britain's position. In July 1933 Italy had signed a pact of four with France, Britain and Germany agreeing to preserve the peace in Europe. He believed the British to be friendly, having heard that British visitors to Rome regularly went home commenting on his air of authority and strength of character. Had Lady Chamberlain not commented on his vitality and his muscles? And Lord Rothermere, owner of the *Daily Mail*, not compared him to Napoleon? Mussolini had the perfect emissary close to hand. He decided to send Edda to London, with her good English, her polished diplomatic manners and above all with the powers of observation that he had drilled into her. Her task, he told her, was to convince the British that Italy really *did* have ambitions of invading Ethiopia, and then to study their reactions closely.

Edda left Ciano and the children in Rome and arrived in London in late June 1934. She was twenty-three, but her sophistication made her appear older, and here, at last, she had a job to do. The social season was at its height and the British were enjoying Wimbledon, the Russian ballet and a sudden vogue for swimming pools. She stayed with the Grandis at the embassy, was invited by Lady Astor to Cliveden, and by Sir Philip Sassoon to Port Lympne in Kent, and she was the guest of honour at the Lyceum Club and at a lunch given by Marchesa Marconi at The Ritz. She was received by the King and Queen at court, where she marvelled at the uniforms and the ceremony and where she perfected, she said later, her curtsey. At Ascot, George V offered her a cigarette. At a ball at the Italian embassy, she wore a black tulle dress with a red sash, and the Prince of Wales asked her for the first dance.

Edda in London

Grandi was a flatterer: the reports he sent back to Mussolini were unctuous. The British, he wrote, were saying that Edda was not only 'beautiful, intelligent and extraordinarily interesting', but, 'what is rarer, possessed of perfect harmony between luminous youthfulness and a natural, exquisite aristocratic dignity ... You should be very proud – Duce – of this girl of yours.' Newspapers remarked on her close resemblance to her father so that her chin and her eyes 'give one a strange sensation of masculine power in a fragile setting'. The *Sunday Chronicle* wrote that she looked as slim and 'as modern as any of our debutantes'. People who met her expressed surprise at her apparent candour and openness and her unguarded and sometimes caustic remarks.

Edda fulfilled her mission conscientiously. She was shrewd and observant and had not been unduly overawed, taking the deference and admiration as her due as Mussolini's daughter. She had well understood that her role was to come across as the perfect young Fascist woman, both fashionable, with her hair cut short, and yet feminine, without the decadent androgyny so loudly derided by her father. She returned to Rome to tell Mussolini that for the most part, the British appeared absolutely indifferent to the idea of an Ethiopian campaign. She reported that Lord Rothermere had told her: 'Get out there and take in hand those wretched blacks! . . . After all we too built up our empire.' The one unfriendly voice came from the Prime Minister, Ramsay MacDonald, who gave a lunch in her honour. In answer to her question about Britain's response to an eventual invasion, he was clear and decidedly chilly. 'Very good, but I assume that you have thought of the consequences?' Edda's reply, as she told it, took the form of another question. 'Will you declare war on us?' 'No,' said MacDonald, 'we won't.' All this was welcome news to her father.

In Italy the *gerarchi* and the public had taken note of Edda's diplomatic mission and she was beginning to be regarded as someone – perhaps the only person – who now had real influence over Mussolini. An aura of power seemed to settle on her; limited, certainly, by the fact that she was a woman, but power nonetheless. Edda herself was beginning to perceive that there might be a role for her in the regime, as informal emissary on the world stage. Easily bored, with no taste for formal social life and too little to do, it could perhaps give her a purpose.

In April 1933, the Chancellor and effective dictator of Austria, Engelbert Dollfuss, had come to Rome in search of support against Hitler's ambitions over his country. Dollfuss and Mussolini got on well, and the Duce told the Chancellor that he would stand up for Austrian independence. In the summer Dollfuss and his wife Alwine had been guests at the new Mussolini summer house in Riccione. The following summer the Dollfusses were invited again, but this time Frau Dollfuss came without her husband, bringing her two small children. Edda and her own children were there, as well as Romano and Anna Maria, and the days passed pleasantly. Then, on 25 July 1934, news came that Dollfuss had been murdered in his Chancellery by a group of Austrian Nazis. Mussolini and Rachele, who were in Cesena examining plans for a new hospital, hurried back to tell his widow. Outwardly calm, Mussolini said to his family over dinner: 'I believe that peace in Europe is over.'

The next day Mussolini mobilised four divisions and sent them to the Brenner Pass as a show of strength against further Nazi plans against Austria, and also to forestall any possibility of an advance on his Italian borders. Hitler, not wishing for a conflict with the Western powers, backed down. For a brief moment, the Italian newspapers were encouraged to print anti-German sentiments. The assassination had come only weeks after the murder of Ernst Röhm and the leaders of the SA paramilitary brownshirts. The Italian newspapers were instructed to run cartoons of blond SS men, showing them as women and calling them *'belli-nazi'*. Mussolini now referred to Hitler as a 'horrible, sexually degenerate creature'. Edda joined her father in calling him Attila the Hun.

Ciano's proposal that the Italians should adopt Goebbels' propaganda machine had gone down well. In September, the Presidential Press Office was made into a junior ministry and Ciano its under-secretary. The Depression had increased Mussolini's belief in the need for a new kind of civilisation, a new 'style of life', purposeful, robust and active, and, to live it, a new Italian. *Fascistizzazione* was to become not just coercive but also prescriptive and the press to be regarded as an orchestra conducted by the Duce. Ciano was installed in a large, elegant office in the Palazzo Balestra on the Via Veneto, given access to the Gran Consiglio and the right to issue his own directives and take over responsibilities previously held by other ministries. He now had power over book publishing, the press, the Automobile Club, theatres, the documentary film corporation LUCE, radio stations and film production. *'Veline'*, brief orders to newspapers on exactly what they had to say, down to the headlines, most of them dictated by Mussolini, began to spew out from his office. 'Please permit me,' Ciano wrote to his father-in-law, 'to tell you again my infinite and affectionate devotion.' He was now thirty-one, and he and Edda had both been given the title *'Eccellenza'*.

8

At Ciano's court

It was now thirteen years since the Roman noble families, peering out through their louvred shutters, had watched Mussolini's rumbustious army strut as victors through their city. They had been confident that Fascism would not stay long. But it had, infiltrating itself into every corner of political and administrative life, and in 1935 there was no suggestion that the Fascists ever meant to leave. For the first years, there had been curiously little mixing between the nobility and the Fascist grandees, each side viewing the other with extreme wariness, though the nobility remained grateful that Mussolini had seen off the Communists and the Socialists. Mussolini had no taste for social life and said that he found the Roman aristocratic women discontented, opinionated and sickly. As he told Angela Curti, 'They want me to come to them, so that they can laugh at me behind my back.' It was Rome itself that interested him, and his plans to make it 'once again the ruling city of civilisation in the whole of Western Europe'.

A very small number of aristocratic families, conscious that they had squandered their vast patrimonies and depended too credulously on corrupt agents and administrators, had married their daughters to the more polished *gerarchi*, but few of these marriages had gone well. For the most part, Rome's three hundred or so noble families preferred to do what they had always done, sleep in their vast garlanded beds, meet in their magnificent frescoed palaces for bridge, mahjong and small receptions, dress their servants in livery, go fox hunting along the Via Appia Antica, wield their ancestral – if now much reduced – power, and patronise their clubs, some of which admitted only men with titles. They had no desire to see their sons parade in little black shirts. As the half-English Duchessa di Sermoneta wrote in her memoirs, they found it distasteful that Rome was now 'invaded by the Fascist *gerarchi* and their sycophants'.

As for the royal family, it was, if possible, even more averse to society than Mussolini and Rachele. The King himself abhorred worldliness and public life. But Mussolini, perceiving that the King's presence alongside Fascist dignitaries at ceremonial events lent lustre to the regime, and wanting to underline the link between Fascism and monarchy in a shared culture of war, heroes and remembrance, put increasing pressure on Victor Emmanuel to show himself to the people. Sometimes, on visits to industrial centres, schools or military academies, they appeared together, to shouts of, '*Per il Duce, o Patria, per il Re! A noi!*'

Mussolini visited the King at the Quirinale twice a week, wearing civilian clothes. They could not have been a more unlikely pair, the small moustached King, rigid and somewhat graceless, and the increasingly corpulent Duce who, ever the actor, choreographed every movement minutely, to show himself in the best light. Very occasionally, the King stole the show, summoning up unexpected reserves of military dignity despite his decidedly un-martial appearance. The collaboration between the two men was described on all sides as 'friendly', and after the King bestowed on Mussolini the prestigious Collare dell'Annunziata, he signed himself in his letters '*Affezionatissimo cugino*', your most affectionate cousin. Wherever he went now, Victor Emmanuel was no longer King of Italy, but King of Fascist Italy.

Crown Prince Umberto's marriage to Maria José was not happy. He was correct, kind and dutiful, little interested in culture, fanatical about etiquette and silently obedient to his father, with whom he went fishing at San Rossore and talked about kingship. For his entire life, he kissed his father's hand every time they met. Marie José, cultured, scatty and impulsive, was openly and physically affectionate with her own family, and found the Italian court extremely chilly. From time to time, there were rumours of an annulment, but the House of Savoy did not divorce. Mussolini, beginning to think about the succession, managed to push through a law giving the Gran Consiglio – that is to say, himself – a say in the choice of future monarch. Umberto regarded this as a sword of Damocles dangling above his head.

From long before the Grand Tours of the eighteenth century, Rome had been a source of delight and fascination to generations of travellers and scholars, who came to sketch the many churches and stroll through the grassy Forum. The Germans had established their own historical institute, the French an academy in the Villa Medici, and their embassy was in one of the most beautiful of all Roman palazzi, the Farnese. For a party given at the Austrian embassy, guests came as Persians bringing with them black pages, monkeys, peacocks and greyhounds. Though the First World War had seen the disappearance of many of the long-entrenched foreign colonies, they had left behind them libraries, art schools and colleges, and the years since had been filled with ever-growing numbers of international visitors. Some claimed to regard the transformation of Italy under the Fascists as little short of miraculous, admiring the new trains with electric engines, the polite and efficient officials, the excellent new roads and the absence of beggars. As one American put it, Mussolini was 'unwopping the wops'.

With these various forces at play there was, by the early 1930s, a change of heart towards the Fascists. Earlier it had been felt, as one woman put it, 'wise to wait, and waiting, to live as if nothing had happened'. But now that time had passed. After the signing of the Vatican accords, relations between Black nobility and Fascists became friendlier, the clerics and the nobility finding that not all the Fascist leaders were quite as gruff and vulgar as they had feared. It became expedient to court them. The College of Heralds, lamenting the lack of positions and recognition for their princes and dukes, convened a meeting to 'offer our services to the regime'. Mussolini had spoken warmly about their 'high destiny' and for a while these noblemen thought they might be on their way to new distinctions, though their hopes were dashed when their request to add 'Eccellenza' to their titles was met with icy disdain. 'Eccellenza' was jealously reserved for the leading Fascists. However, a number of these counts and marqueses had managed to slip their way into some of the Fascist jobs, and some joked that they were injecting a little 'artful snobbery into the Fascists'.

George Nelson Page, an Anglo-Italian journalist and the nephew of a famous US southern general, who returned to Rome after some years abroad and took Italian citizenship, found the capital a different place from the one he had known as a boy, busier, more efficient, more fun, even if muzzled in comparison with the clatter and gaiety of Paris. He noted that the Italians seemed proud to be Italian. The salons he frequented were beginning to open their doors to the *gerarchi*. Only a few of the aristocratic families, he wrote, continued to hold out: the Duchessa Olimpia Civitella della Porta received only the Black nobility; her rule was no foreigners and no Fascists.

The Fascists were not much interested either way, since they regarded themselves as the new aristocracy, not of blood but of the sacrifices of the First World War, and some at least, like Grandi and Costanzo Ciano, had taken titles of their own. As deeply provincial, family-minded men, reared on the *manganello* and hostile to all things cosmopolitan, they did not have a great deal to talk about in Rome's elevated social circles. They found it easier to leave the old noble families undisturbed while Bocchini's spies kept watch on them through their drivers, cooks, maids and friends. Though full of mutual wariness and disdain, each trying to profit from the other, aristocrats and Fascists were learning to live together.

When Hitler and Mussolini had met in 1934 it was clear that more differences than similarities existed between their two countries and the disparities seemed to Mussolini more pronounced when Hitler moved on Austria. As he said then, Hitler was nothing but a '*pazzo pericoloso*', a dangerous lunatic. And there was one enemy that the two countries did not share: the Jews. Pivotal from the start to national socialism, anti-Semitism and racial purity were concepts more or less totally alien to the Italian character, and indeed to Mussolini, if not to all sectors of the Vatican. At least for the moment. As Mussolini told Emil Ludwig, he considered anti-Semitism 'the German vice'.

Something new and significant had happened in Italian society. Fascism had found its golden couple, with impeccable Fascist pedigrees and the culture and sophistication to bridge the gap between the snobbish, enclosed Roman nobility and the uncouth, ambitious *gerarchi*. Edda and Ciano were everything Mussolini had dreamt of as his model Fascist family: young, healthy, fashionable, forceful and fertile. In the ever adulatory press, they were said to have been born 'for sun and rectitude'. Yet neither Edda nor Ciano, as it turned out, was destined to play their part in fusing the two worlds, though each of them in their own way took to the loucher side of Roman social life, the no man's land where the more adventurous of the nobility joined forces with the energy and excitement of Fascism. And here, they thrived.

Edda in Rome

Edda was certainly fashionable. She wore her hair rolled up around the crown, and was reported to go everyday to Attilio in the Piazza di Spagna, the most sought-after hairdresser in Rome. After the first Exhibition of Fashion, held in Turin in 1933, promoted the idea of a *'stile nazionale'*, forged by Italian designers and dressmakers, she dressed in Rome rather than in Paris, though she was known to like French perfumes. Still very thin, she looked well in the new *'abito serpentissimo'*, the slinky dress, sometimes worn in the evening with a train. She had grown into her severe and bony face, and her confidence gave her dignity.

However, as she had been as a girl – a wild cat, a crazy little horse – so she remained as a woman: wilful, rebellious, odd and restless, she was all the more fascinating to reporters. Though hostesses complained that Edda could be shy and brusque, they were happy to invite her to their dinners, and Edda was happy to go, though she was conscious that there were often guests there who, knowing how close she was to her father, and believing that she knew his secrets, wanted things from her. As an elderly Roman princess remarked, 'Roman society is divided in two: those who say "*tu*" to Edda, and those who would like to.'

Count Volpi di Misurata, the former Minister of Finance, and Edda's host during her honeymoon, had the idea of staging an annual festival of cinema in Venice where, with his palazzo on the Grand Canal, he was known as the Corsair or Doge. On one of Edda's visits, he gave a dinner for her on the terrace of the Excelsior. Guests fought for an invitation, begged to be allowed to sit next to her, and during the evening she came across as courteous, distinguished and a little distracted, surrounded by a distinct aura of unapproachability. Edda did not, however, charm everyone. The Duchessa di Sermoneta, who met her around this time, wrote in her diary that she was unattractive and took no pains to make herself agreeable. The way that the aristocracy had taken to fawning over her, and calling her 'darling', made the Duchessa feel sick.

In his new offices on the Via Veneto, Ciano was taking his job very seriously, always conscious that Mussolini was an excellent journalist himself and an obsessive reader of newspapers, both Italian and foreign, and that he was acutely alert to every nuance in the reactions of the world both to Fascism and to himself personally. His own task, Ciano knew, was to feed and shape the so-called 'new Italian', from cradle to grave, and to tell him what to think. As Mussolini put it, 'Italian journalism is free because it serves just one cause and one regime.' A jubilant Ciano told his friend George Nelson Page, 'Everything will go through me, we'll talk to the whole world!'

Through him, perhaps, but not *from* him: Mussolini called him at all hours, barked out orders, instructions laying out what arguments to push with the press, what topics to avoid, even what photographs to run. He informed his son-in-law that the word '*coniglio*' should never be used alongside 'Italian', because rabbits suggested feebleness, and that papers were to run no pictures of women wearing trousers because it made them look manly. (Edda's trousers were overlooked.) There were to be no lovers' tiffs, suicides or broken homes and no mention of venereal diseases. The weather was to remain universally good and all reports of storms avoided. As for the coverage of Mussolini himself, he was never, ever, to be shown as old or tired or any reference ever made to his ill health or birthdays.

Having studied Goebbels' propaganda machine with great care, Ciano proceeded to adapt it to the Italians, making it softer and less blunt. There would be no coercion, no sense of menace and intimidation, but rather inducement and persuasion. He never threatened and was very seldom overbearing. Genial and generous, he courted journalists and their editors, invited them to meals, slipped them little envelopes of cash, ostensibly to cover their costs on invented literary projects. Most of them, with perfect understanding of these ruses and subterfuges, were happy to go along with the fiction that in Italy crime and poverty did not exist, the sun always shone, and the country had no serious diseases. When Rome was struck by a severe outburst of typhus in the summer of 1935, only the barest mention appeared in the newspapers, in order not to alarm tourists.

Always apparently at ease, his hair smoothly slicked down with brilliantine, his modish clothes made by his English tailor, Ciano held court at the golf club of the Acquasanta on the Appia Antica, where he kept his own table and where petitioners waited like beggars for his greeting. As his friend Susanna Agnelli wrote: 'Ciano was the very image of worldly power.' He was regarded as Anglophile and unassailable. He was vain but not so stupid – at least in these early days – that he could not see that some of the admiration that swirled around him sprang from simple opportunism. Whenever he spoke, one friend observed, 'everyone fell about laughing. But I'm not sure that he did not hate them all.' It suited him to believe that everyone was his friend. He was attractive to women, not least because he was so attracted to them himself, despite his round, plump thighs and knock knees, his rather short arms and legs and a voice that rose to a falsetto when he got angry. And he had taken care to improve his Fascist credentials and join the party, getting a colleague to swear that he had been a member of the Disperata squad in Florence – a lie – which gave him the right to wear red bands on his uniform. 'He had the look,' remarked a friend, 'of a happy man.'

It was not long before a court formed around him, of journal-ists, writers, princesses, actresses, the *beau monde* of Rome, who met to drink in the bar of the Excelsior, and gave parties in their houses. Unlike many of the other *gerarchi*, Ciano was careful never to behave too grandly. Those who had known him as a student marvelled at the speed with which he had transformed himself. His inner circle was, as people said, a Petit Trianon, where he held sway and where Edda seldom appeared, and it was all very seduc-tive. Both Edda and Ciano, each in their own way, were both seducers and seduced.

Malaparte

Several new and lastingly important friends had entered their lives, but the most curious of them was an outrageous self-fantasist called Curzio Malaparte, who later wrote a vivid, mocking por-trait of Roman society. Born Kurt Erich Suckert to a German father in 1898, taking the name Malaparte when he became a writer, he had passed exams for the Foreign Ministry, only to become impa-tient with its formalities. He revelled, he said, in chaos. Drawn to the early populism of Fascism, he wanted to become the voice of its intellectual roots. With very shiny black hair, described by a woman friend as 'smooth as velvet', Malaparte was a good-looking man, with long eyelashes, a straight nose, a neat chin and the 'eyes of an angel'. His mouth was 'sad and cruel', and he was said to use powder to cover his wrinkles as well as a little mascara, and to put raw steaks on his cheeks to keep them firm and smooth. He needed women, but preferred young girls, and certainly never wanted an equal, claiming that women were there to enhance their men, and then to be abandoned by them. He allowed himself one sexual encounter a week, saying that each one shortened his life by an hour. His preferred kind of conversation was a monologue, and he did not like to be interrupted.

For the subtitle to one of his books he had chosen: 'The story of a chameleon'. Malaparte was indeed a chameleon, but he was also a peacock. He later called his house on Capri *Casa Come Me*', the house like me, and his women were all '*come me*'. More than women, he loved dogs, who fed his insatiable need to be liked; they were by definition '*come me*' and he celebrated their birthdays by laying a table on the floor and eating by their sides. His dogs, he said, were 'the best part of myself, the most humble, the purest, the most secret'.

In 1928 Malaparte became editor of *Il Mattino*, the Naples daily paper. Introduced to Giovanni Agnelli, owner of *La Stampa* as well as of FIAT, he was soon lured to Turin to edit his paper. He met Edda and they took to each other. A feud with *La Stampa*'s publisher cost him his job, but a far worse feud with Italo Balbo, the aviator *gerarca*, who had once been his close friend, earned him a stint in the Regina Coeli prison in Rome and a sentence of five years on the penal island of Lipari. With both Mussolini and Ciano's help, and shamelessly pleading ill heath, he got himself moved to the healthier and considerably more glamorous Forte dei Marmi, and then pardoned.

In the 1930s, Forte dei Marmi was a fashionable resort for writers and artists, and Edda and Ciano, whose family home was in Livorno not far away, became just one of the many famous couples who came to enjoy its pineta and swim from its long beach, the sand white and fine from the nearby marble quarries. Here, Malaparte started an affair with Agnelli's daughter-in-law, Virginia Bourbon del Monte, a tall, thin, fascinating but not beautiful woman recently widowed after the death of Agnelli's son Edoardo in a car crash, who had become one of Edda's friends. Perhaps at least in part to punish Agnelli for his sacking, Malaparte made no effort to keep their liaison secret. Virginia had seven children – one of them the memoirist Susanna. Furious with the man he had sacked, Agnelli started a judicial process to have her children taken away from her, which might have succeeded had she not appealed to Mussolini, who declared, perhaps not surprisingly, that no country governed by him could possibly tolerate children removed from their mother because she had taken a lover.

Not long after Ciano became minister of what was now known as the MinCulPop, Malaparte founded a glossy, stylish magazine, *Prospettive*, a 'prospective on Fascism', '*italianissimo*' in tone. Malaparte remained, at least at the time, a faithful courtier to Ciano, though he was critical of his court, saying that it was driven by vanity and fickleness and was a place of chicanery and bribes.

Principessa Colonna

Edda was never the queen of Ciano's court. But there was a queen: the Principessa Isabella Colonna, who probably understood better than most of the inward-looking Roman nobility what it meant to be an outsider. Born Isabella Sursock in the Lebanon, and brought up in Cairo and Istanbul, she was dismissed by Roman society as an intruder and a parvenu until she married Prince Marcantonio Colonna, senior member of a family that had given Italy a pope and twenty-two cardinals. Then she found herself much courted, living in one of Rome's most beautiful palaces, with frescoes by Pinturicchio, more valuable paintings than in any other palace in Rome, and a ballroom said to have been the model for the Galerie des Glaces at Versailles. The Palazzo Colonna, close to both Piazza Venezia and the Quirinale, had two large inner courtyards and gardens full of cypresses, fountains and old statues, connected to the palace by a stone bridge across the street. A giant Roman crocodile in porphyry squatted in the entrance. Isabella was now forty-six, not conventionally beautiful, but perceptive, full of vitality and pride, possessed of a strong streak of malice and a 'heart of iron', as one of her guests wrote, 'under a cloak of lace'. She was a keen student of human passions, which she claimed she no longer indulged in herself, and, together with her rank and her money, she had a 'unique aptitude for intrigue'.

Like Catherine de' Medici, Isabella surrounded herself with the most interesting men and the most beautiful women in Roman society, the '*gruppo cosi-detto super-elegante*' as Nelson Page put it, not greatly caring whether they were nobles or *gerarchi*, provided they sparkled. One of her earliest conquests was the bearded, handsome Italo Balbo, who sent her wild strawberries and white roses. By 1935 her court revolved entirely around Ciano, though it is doubtful that they became lovers. It was here in the Palazzo Colonna that he reigned as favourite, and here that he brought or met his mistresses, few of whom lasted more than six months, after which, known as 'Ciano's widows', they went to cry on Isabella's shoulder. In this corrupt court, as one of the sharper tongued visitors put it, Isabella was the servile queen and Ciano her pasha, 'fat, pink, smiling, despotic'. And it was here, at Isabella's dinner table, that Ciano spoke freely and injudiciously about politics and the foibles of the people he met, apparently oblivious to the danger of Bocchini's spies. These spies – the footmen? The butler? Other guests? – were quick with their reports, carefully picked over by Mussolini before being filed, anonymously, in dossiers. The princess, wrote one informer, was 'ambitious and very haughty', and in her salon there 'sometimes blew a little wind of rebellion, in the sense that the guests are very tepid *Mussoliniani*'. As Malaparte observed, Isabella's dinners were a 'talking table' and a ticking time bomb.

To their friends, it sometimes seemed as if the Cianos had made a pact of infidelity in which they competed to see who could have more fun. On their return from China, both sought out lovers. Edda was said to like pretty boys, but none played much of a part in her life and they were dismissed by Ciano as 'my wife's little flirts'. She really preferred gambling, spending long evenings at the poker table losing large sums and appealing on one occasion to Mussolini's private secretary for 15,000 lire for 'extraordinary expenses' and suggesting to him that it might come out of her petrol allowance, since she barely used her car. At the same time, she begged him not to tell either her father or her husband. But since Rome thrived on gossip and informers, letters from the public, usually anonymous, regularly made their way to Bocchini and then to Mussolini. His daughter, said one, was 'dishonouring Italian women'.

If Edda's affairs were 'flirts', Ciano's conquests were described as 'lionesses', many of them chosen without scruple from among his wife's friends, on whom he was said to pounce like a teenager. But what could pass as tolerable in Shanghai was not really acceptable in Rome, though neither Ciano nor Edda saw the need to be discreet. Women behaved around Ciano with astonishing lack of dignity; it became an honour, even a badge of distinction, to be seduced by him. As an obedient Fascist, he remained on the surface entirely faithful to his marriage, but the reports reaching Bocchini said otherwise. Delia di Bagno, a lady-in-waiting to the queen with whom he was spotted in a 'close embrace', was described as one of his more important mistresses, and her husband Galeazzo, previously living a 'quite modest life', was now buying expensive cars. Another courtesan was reported to be costing Ciano many millions of lire, in jewellery and furs. 'In Rome,' wrote an anonymous correspondent, directly to Mussolini, 'everyone is laughing about your disgraceful daughter and the whole circus who are stealing without shame and exploiting your name.' Relations between the two families, the Mussolinis and the Cianos, had reached a low ebb, with Rachele openly scornful of Ciano and Edda referring to her mother-in-law Carolina as 'the ape', saying that Costanzo had surely been driven to his heroic naval feats in order to get away from his sour wife.

Edda and her husband took to spending less and less time in each other's company. When they were together there were scenes, many of them emanating from Ciano, who did not believe in the same standards for men and women. One summer's day, Edda and a friend went to swim from the beach at Ostia, and Edda decided to try out her bikini, a new fashion she had brought back with her from London. Ciano was not expected but turned up suddenly, saw what she was wearing, grew furious and ordered her to follow him into the cabin, where he slapped her. Being accustomed to a lifetime of slaps from her mother, Edda was not greatly upset. Even so, his very public womanising was making her unhappy. Choosing to disregard her own adventures, and distressed and humiliated by his, the day came when she went to see her father to tell him that she wanted to leave Ciano. He looked at her: 'Does he not give you enough to eat?' 'No.' 'Does he give you no money?' 'No.' 'Is he unfaithful?' 'Yes.' 'Are you in love with someone else?' 'No.' 'Then go home and let me hear no more about it.' As Edda coolly noted, 'There was nothing left for me but to sort things out for myself.' Once again, she avoided shows of emotion. She and Ciano resumed what had become their normal lives.

For all his insensitivity, however, the person Edda remained extremely close to was her father. Sometimes they went swimming together, speaking little but feeling that they understood each other. She loved and respected him in many ways more than her husband, whom she was beginning to see as weak and indecisive. She admired Mussolini's canniness, even if she would tell friends that it was Rachele who was the more cunning of the two. When asked whether she was like her father, Edda would reply: 'I wouldn't be able to say the ways in which I do not resemble him. I am a faithful copy.' Both had explosions of anger and a taste for dramatic scenes. He would have wished her, she knew, to have been a boy and, wishing to have been one herself, she drank, smoked, swam, played golf and took lovers, living outside the rules as if life were a game she was playing with him. Mussolini seemed to love her rebelliousness and indifference to risk even if he scolded her for her behaviour. As he told a friend, 'I managed to bend Italy to my will, but I will never bend Edda.' On her birthday, he wrote to her: 'As in your adolescence, when times were hard, so today you are the favourite of my soul.'

Even Edda, prickly as she was, enjoyed the sense of admiration and stardom that grew up around herself and Ciano. It gave her a feeling of power, however fleeting, of having truly put behind her the poverty and chaos of her childhood. Hostesses vied for their company, and if the people they met were neither intellectual nor particularly cultured, they were rich, beautiful, elegant, sophisticated and unshockable. As the beady-eyed Duchessa di Sermoneta put it, 'It is probable that at no time, in any country, was there a more shameless display of toadying than the one we witnessed in Roman society during the period of the Cianos.' In later years, it became fashionable to claim that these hosts and hostesses had been at heart conspirators and anti-Fascists all along, but at the time, people were happy to fawn if not to befriend. For many of them, in this world of sexual encounters disguised as love, of recklessness and superficiality, of true and false aristocrats, of snobbish diplomats and adventurers posing as gentlemen, Edda and Ciano were too young, too sure of themselves, too arrogant, and in the end, they were neither good Fascists nor really acceptable to the upper echelons of class-Rome. The 'consort' or 'little son-in-law' craved too obviously to have been part of the *ancien regime*, and Edda, fundamentally timid and not good in crowds or at her best in large gatherings, was too reserved to be loved. As Malaparte put it, her mask was 'sometimes that of an assassin, at others that of a potential suicide'.

9

Lionesses without manes

Fascism had now been in place for over a decade. It was a world of diktats, arrangements and exhortations. Edda was not the only Italian trying to learn to negotiate its arcane rules and prohibitions.

Even before the end of the First World War, Mussolini was aware of the poor health of the Italian soldiers and the general physical inferiority of a people beset by tuberculosis, malaria, trachoma, syphilis, rickets and every kind of skin disease, further weakened by the war itself and by the Spanish flu. A strong Fascist state, with its feet firmly at the table of the Great Powers, required strong, healthy citizens, and it needed more of them – far more – than it had. To create such people, he reasoned, you had to exert total control not only over what they ate, but what they wore, what they studied and how they behaved, 'remake not only the forms of human life, but the content' – man, character, faith – though in reality it all came back to Mussolini himself.

Gathering around him a group of demographers, anthropologists, sociologists and psychologists, he asked them how best to produce the ideal man he had in mind, a synthesis of thought and action, '*libro e moschetto*', book and rifle, of sport and culture. Fascism, as Mussolini had told Edda, was the 'big idea' of the twentieth century, and it would act as a model for the rest of the world, a 'corporate state in a new ethical state', a moral revolution that catered to the whole person. Since Italians were so facile and credulous by nature, it was his duty to put them on the right path. Nowhere was this more true than with education, which, like culture, was by definition political and had to be harnessed to serve the state.

Since youth, and all the energy, vitality and optimism that it implied, was fundamental to his vision, one of Fascism's first moves had been to set up the Opera Nazionale Balilla. Boys from the age of eight, in their little black shirts, grey-green shorts, blue ties and fezzes, were enrolled to 'conquer' their egos and laziness, ignore illness and hardship, and learn to defend the nation as responsible patriots and soldiers. Vittorio and Bruno were members, but there are no photographs of Edda as a child in a uniform. The *gerarca* in charge of the ONB was Renato Ricci, an unstable, corrupt, little-educated *squadrista* from Carrara, with a penchant for the martial arts. What, went the catechism, is the child's first virtue? 'Obedience.' And the second? 'Obedience.' And the third? 'Obedience.' To this end, boys of every class and background from the tip of Italy to the foothills of the Alps, were organised into legions and cohorts, in which they exercised, played sports, sang and marched, brandishing their wooden replica rifles to rousing martial airs. Refusal to join meant a black mark against the family; in any case, many of its activities were fun.

After a brief moment when Mussolini had talked vaguely about giving women the vote – of the 120 founders of the Fascist movement in Milan's Piazza san Sepolcro in 1919, nine had been women – the idea had been comprehensively shelved. If a woman loved her husband, he declared, she would vote for him; if she did not 'she has already voted against him'. That women were biologically inferior to men was the message that now ran through every aspect of life, from health to politics. As Mussolini's much repeated remark to Emil Ludwig put it: 'The woman must obey ... she is capable of analysis but not synthesis', and then, even more damningly, 'In our state, she does not count.' Girls had their own forms of Balilla as '*Piccole Italiane*' and the daughters of the she-wolf, and they needed protecting from the horrors of feminism, and from the rough and tumble of the boys' war games. They practised 'doll drills' and ironed. Edda never ironed. And she was always conscious that, though the closest of the Mussolini children to her father, her opinions had somehow always mattered less than those of her brothers. Ciano also made no secret of his own sense of superiority to his wife.

In place of suffrage came a slew of decrees designed to make Italy into a nation of mothers and housewives, 'ready whatever the challenge and sacrifice to defend her sacred surroundings and work for the greatness of the patria'. Adultery was a crime, but only for women. The 'strength' of men had to be developed, so that they could fight and father children; women, 'lionesses without manes', needed 'energy', with which to confront their daily tasks and escape neurotic weaknesses. Mother and baby clinics, paediatric centres, welfare offices for women and their children were set up, though some of their good work was offset by the terrible conditions in which the poor lived, both in cities and in the countryside. Rare group photographs of prolific mothers show worn, shapeless, haggard women, looking far older than their years.

Italy was also awash with women's magazines, all peddling the same messages, crafted and scripted by the MinCulPop and Ciano. Filippo Tommaso Marinetti's futurist cookery book decried pasta as leading to fatigue, pessimism and even pacifism, and extolled rice, an authentic home-grown food that promoted pride and dynamism. Every dish, he said, had to be preceded by a different scent, peculiar to itself, to ensure 'a virgin palate'. Futurists also exalted 'aggressive movement, hectic sleeplessness, the quick step, the somersault, the slap, the blow'. Articles by doctors warned against lipstick (lip cancer) and kissing (germs). There were to be no very thin models – 55 kilos was the minimum permitted weigh and pronounced hips were encouraged. The foxtrot was frowned on, as were skimpy bathing suits, cropped hair, cigarette holders and small dogs (child substitutes). Edda loved these magazines, but paid little heed to their advice.

In an effort to avoid foreign influences, the word 'negligée' became '*disordine*', 'chignon' became '*cignone*', a sandwich '*tra i due*'. Rabbit and lamb coats were decreed good, since they were indigenous; as was squirrel fur. (Edda wore mink and sable.) Since fashionable Fascist men, like Ciano, kept their hair slicked back with a thick layer of brilliantine, antimacassars were recommended for the backs of sofas. The rules were straightforward: the good Fascist woman, a thrifty housewife, married, had children, obeyed her husband and kept out of trouble. (Edda obeyed no one, spent lavishly and courted trouble.) All of this had led to a raft of contradictions: spend and save, be sexually puritan and bear many babies, be a good Catholic but a better Fascist. When the sporting contests, the *Littoriali*, were opened to women, those who came forward to take part were treated like performing animals.

Men, women and children all had their own Fascist uniforms, for meetings and displays – '*vestire da Fascista*' meant dressing for modernity, discipline, leisure and speed – and for the '*sabato Fascista*', the after-work Dopolavoro clubs. Under the dictum 'no worker is to be left to his own devices in his free hours', leisure had ceased to be an end in itself: it was a means of improving workers in the national interest, curing their defects, inculcating self-control and self-discipline. As Mussolini aptly noted, there was little point in leaving such things to chance. 'Consent,' he said, 'is as unstable as the sand formations on the edge of the sea.'

Men and women alike, Mussolini declared, needed to be lean and sinewy. 'I have no pity,' he said, 'for fat.' (His own taste was for plumpness.) Displays of gymnastics were especially 'precious' gifts, wrote *Il Corriere della Sera*, because they substituted 'the cult of senility for the cult of youth' and restored the 'physical-psychological hormones of the Greeks and the Romans'. What was important was to be seen as Italian, and proud to be so. Certainly, Edda never doubted that she was the equal of any woman in Western Europe or America. When not praising the virtues of gymnastics, the women's magazines carried photographs of society beauties – Edda among them – languid and sophisticated, often modelling their own clothes. That there was a glaring difference between aristocratic ladies, with their mosaic-tiled bathrooms, silk décolleté evening dresses and yapping dogs, and the stalwart Fascist female foot soldier was somehow overlooked.

In the first years of Fascism, Giovanni Gentile had proposed a new curriculum to replace the fossilised school system based on much rote learning. Schools, he argued, should be places where pupils learnt to understand Fascism – in short, centres of indoctrination. To think was harmful to health. Using examples drawn from ancient Rome, popular fables and the tales of Fascist martyrs, pupils were to be made to see that the patria was not simply a place, but a set of laws, religion, language, tradition and customs, and to know no other ideology than that dedicated to the cult of the state, the family and the Duce himself. The years since 1922 had seen the introduction into primary schools of a '*libro unico*', a single Fascist textbook, with the Duce as hero. As Gentile boasted, it was now possible to tell precisely what any child in Italy was learning at any given moment of the day. '*Duce, a noi*', '*siam come tu ci vuoi*', we are just as you want us, sang the girls in their white pinafores, the boys in their black ones, which they complained bitterly looked like dresses. The Duce's day, they were told, 'is always a luminous triumph of fresh and virile youth'.

Mussolini's real concerns, however, lay with the universities, which he suspected were harbouring cells of anti-Fascists. His attitude towards intellectuals had always been, and continued to be, contradictory. He wanted to be welcoming to well-known artists and writers, yet at the same time he intended to tell them exactly what they could say and write. At the end of 1931, university professors were purged if they refused to sign an oath of loyalty to the regime. Some twelve hundred agreed to do so; just twenty refused and left their posts, but it was a measure of Mussolini's ambivalence that they retained a measure of intellectual freedom and were not punished for it, just as artists did not have their contentious works of art seized. Heterodox ideas, provided they did not threaten the regime, were seen as safety valves for intellectuals and idealists. Few, in any case, made much fuss, preferring obsequiousness to unemployment, practising occasional furtive acts of rebellion and waiting for better times. The best known liberal opponent of the regime, Benedetto Croce, was allowed to live, and publish, unmolested in 'aristocratic aloofness'.

By the mid 1930s, it had also become clear that it was probably unwise to squash all individuality, and there was much debate among the senior *gerarchi* about how total obedience could in fact be squared with a spirit of initiative. Gentile was given the task of preparing a new thirty-two-volume encyclopedia, and a Doctrine of Fascism now replaced John Stuart Mill, Hegel, Tolstoy and Rousseau as the essential topic for study. The *Littoriali* were extended to include culture in order to provide 'free, solar gymnastics for the brain'. In 1934, the first *Littoriali della Cultura*, held in an outdoor theatre on the left bank of the Arno, had brought intellectuals and university students to compete with one another in displays of literature and philosophy. The *Littoriali* would become the freest forum in Fascist Italy, perhaps the only place where serious criticism of the regime was aired.

Saying that he was sick of Italy's image as a country of 'eternal tenors and mandolinists', Mussolini also encouraged the establishment of musical events and orchestras, though he made it clear that he preferred symphonies to chamber music, as they provided excellent opportunities for 'collective group discipline'. By now Italy was boasting any number of travelling theatre companies, playing in piazze throughout Italy, to stir up, as Mussolini said, 'the great collective' passions through Greek drama and medieval mystery plays allied to new technology. But musicians and actors, like teachers and professors, had their lives circumscribed by byzantine laws and edicts, and by 1935 they had been dragooned into a Corporazione delle Professioni e delle Arti, and their lives regulated by an Inspectorate for theatre and music under Ciano and the MinCulPop. It was noticeable that neither he nor Edda seemed to have had much interest in culture. As for state art, its message of *romanità* and *italianità*, of homely, maternal women and robust smiling peasants, was to be seen on murals inside and outside most public buildings.

As Federale of Florence, Alessandro Pavolini had also been behind the Maggio Musicale, the musical month of May, and in late April 1934 a vast piece of mass theatre was staged on the left bank of the Arno on a set the size of six football pitches, complete with hills, trenches, pits, a model of books crowned with bayonets and several aeroplanes and tanks. Called *18BL, Mamma Giberna* – mother cartridge pouch – after the name of an Italian truck used in the First World War, it traced its story through the war, the March on Rome and Italy's subsequent glorious development in a series of orchestrated set pieces, sound effects and son et lumière.

Neither Mussolini nor Pope Pius XI were inclined to cede control over the hearts and minds of young Italians. The Azione Cattolica youth groups were a festering sore for Mussolini, who saw in them rivals to his own authority, while the Pope accused Fascism of filling the young with 'hatred and irreverence', and complained that female athletes smacked of paganism. In 1931, Mussolini had decided that the situation was intolerable and dissolved all youth organisations which were not part of the Balilla movement. The Pope, realising that to forbid the young from their oath to the Fascist regime would be tantamount to a declaration of war, came up with a compromise: while professing their oath, the young were to add a sentence undertaking to do nothing that went against the duties of a good Christian, but that they could utter the words not aloud but to themselves. Mussolini had every reason to be pleased. Catholic youth groups put themselves under the Fascist umbrella, and effectively withdrew from politics to become essentially arenas for religious discussion.

Of all the activities designed to shape his new Italian citizen, Mussolini loved sport best. It was for him the perfect expression of Fascism, the best way to project its dynamism, aggression and boldness and he encouraged his sons to practise every sport available to them. (Women's sports were essentially uncompetitive and sedate, not to distract them from their mission of motherhood.) As he said, 'The armchair and slippers are the ruin of a man.' Whether to curry favour or because they genuinely enjoyed sport, the *gerarchi* followed suit. Turati was an excellent fencer; Renato Ricci a skier, pilot, rider and athlete. Starace, the most sporty of them all, rode motorcycles and horses, skied and swam, saying that what counted was speed, risk and abnegation, 'because this is Fascism and this is what Italy has to be'. From time to time, Mussolini went to watch his *gerarchi*'s sporting competitions. You must be 'tenacious, gallant, bold', he told a gathering of sportsmen in November 1934, the year that Italy won the football World Cup. Italy's sporting heroes were Fascism's ambassadors on the world stage.

The sport dearest to Mussolini's heart – and the most personally problematic – was flying. Fascists were passionate about flying, and the futurist Marinetti's claim that aeroplanes were like a choir of mandolins and guitars, and pilots new men 'soaring over the pedantic realities of mere mortals' chimed well with Fascist hyperbole. Both Vittorio and Bruno learnt to fly; Edda wanted to but was not allowed to take lessons.

No one, however, was more passionate about conquering the skies than Italo Balbo, the handsome, rebellious, neatly bearded *squadrista* from Ferrara, who addressed Mussolini as '*tu*' and now saw himself as an accomplice to a regime he no longer quite believed in but could not free himself from. In 1926, Mussolini had made him under-secretary at the Aeronautica; in 1929, at the age of thirty-three, he became its Minister. There was no need to 'Fascisticise' the Ministry, because it was born Fascist. Balbo ruled over his little empire from a modern glass building with paternalistic severity, providing a canteen – a revolution among people accustomed to going home for lunch – and insisting on good table manners and no spitting. He gave his staff toothbrushes and tooth-paste to use after lunch.

Soon after joining the Aeronautica, in May 1928, Balbo led a formation of flying boats across the Mediterranean. Orders for planes, very lucrative for Italy, multiplied. Balbo improved the workshops, the equipment and the training.

Crossing the Atlantic remained the ultimate challenge. Balbo pre-pared his sortie with great care. Sixty-four pilots were chosen and rigorously trained. On 1 July 1933 a flotilla of seaplanes took off from the lagoon at Orbetello in the Maremma. A million people were waiting to greet it in Chicago, where the mayor proclaimed an 'Italo Balbo Day'. A few days later, in perfect formation, Balbo's twenty-four seaplanes circled above New York's skyscrapers. The traffic stopped. Balbo led a cavalcade of open-top cars down Broad-way to a cacophony of clapping, cheers, whistles and showers of confetti. *Time* magazine put him on their cover; Roosevelt presented him with the Distinguished Flying Cross; the Sioux made him Chief Flying Eagle. On his return to Rome, Mussolini embraced Balbo in public, led him on a victory parade through Constantine's Arch and down the new Via dell'Impero and bestowed on him the title of Maresciallo dell'Arma.

However, Mussolini had always been jealous of Balbo, con-scious that after himself, no one understood better how to charm and hold a crowd. Of all the *gerarchi*, he was the one whom Mus-solini felt most threatened by. Unlike the others, Balbo, while acknowledging Mussolini's political superiority, believed that when it came to personal relations they should be on equal terms. After his triumphant flight, he felt this more than ever, and Mussolini grew more jealous. He kept a wary eye on him, which became warier when reports made references to possible plots against him, which Balbo, provocatively, made no effort to deny.

Then suddenly, in November 1933, Mussolini sent Balbo to Libya instead, as Governor-General of the newly merged Italian colonies of Tripolitania and Cyrenaica. Balbo felt humiliated but was soon seduced by the grandeur of his new appointment and his quarters in a fifteenth-century castle built by the Knights of Malta. He invited out from Italy old *squadristi* friends and together they flew up and down the coast and went hunting. Visitors reported

Italo Balbo

Achille Starace

Roberto Farinacci

Dino Grandi

that his receptions were more sumptuous than anything seen at Europe's imperial courts, with dozens of liveried servants and vast, opulent meals. But Balbo proved a competent, modernising governor, with genuinely original ideas about meteorology and the need for a better understanding of climate. Mussolini grumbled and watched carefully, but at least Balbo was several thousands of miles away.

In 1931, the over-zealous Giovanni Giuriati had been replaced as party secretary by Achille Starace, the small, dark, fanatical gymnast whose adoration of Mussolini knew no bounds. Under his eight-year rule, a liturgy of Fascist dogma spread to encompass every corner of Italian life, regulated by a Vademecum dello Stile Fascista and shaped by directives, *fogli di disposizioni*. He was a man curiously without personality, which suited Mussolini perfectly. He was dogged in his obedience, never questioned orders and had neither scruples nor a sense of humour. He loved medals and uniforms, particularly military ones. Within five days of taking up his appointment, he had introduced the *'saluto al Duce'*, to be used whenever Mussolini entered the room, and to which the assembled people were meant to shout *'a noi'* in reply. After this came a slew of slogans, catchphrases, displays, sporting galas, military parades and competitions – for the most prolific mother or the most obedient Fascist. To test the physical courage of the senior *gerarchi*, Starace invented trials. Portly, ageing men were invited to prove their mettle by jumping over unsheathed bayonets and through hoops of fire. Mussolini called Starace 'the greatest choreographer of the regime' – even, Starace himself would add, 'of the world'.

As the head of the Fascist Party, Starace was effectively the most powerful man in Italy after Mussolini. But as the 1930s progressed he was increasingly regarded as a clown, especially as his diktats became ever more ridiculous, and no one regarded him as more absurd than Edda and Rachele. Later, when Starace finally fell, Ciano would say that Italians will forgive anything, even harm done against them; but what they never forgave was being bored and annoyed.

And, lest anyone fall seriously out of line, Bocchini and his machinery of repression were there to remind them. Bocchini was now in his mid-fifties and had grown large and florid, his face, as one waspish visitor to Rome put it, 'still youthful, but one on which burgundy and lobster seemed to have left perceptible traces'. He was reputed to possess eighty suits from Rome's most prestigious tailor. Bocchini's fief had expanded into every corner of Italy, now divided into zones, with an army of informers – rumoured at ten thousand – and a central database in Rome, with 'subversives' arranged into fourteen separate categories and cross referenced. As Bocchini said, 'The more the Italians are frightened, the more they will remain tranquil.' Over a period of six years, thirty-three million reports on individuals were filed. On many of the reports that landed on his desk, Mussolini added comments in his red pencil. Wherever she went now, Edda was escorted by motorcyclists and bodyguards, some of them OVRA spies whose reports sooner or later landed on Mussolini's desk, too. She may have chafed at the ceaseless surveillance, but she was not alone in feeling its heavy hand.

One of Bocchini's best informers was his mistress, an actress called Bice Pupeschi who, as Diana, spy number 35, provided him with salacious material on the aristocracy, foreign embassies and the world of film, theatre and newspapers. Pupeschi, who earned 20,000 lire a month from her spying activities, had forty subagents, including a number of the aristocracy, who were happy to spy on each other. Isabella Colonna's dinner parties were only one of the many social occasions she spied on. She recruited Monsignor Benigni, a tyrant when it came to insufficiently zealous junior priests and those lukewarm towards Fascism, to report on the Vatican. The 'Capi palazzi', the doormen of the apartment blocks, also proved excellent informers.

Bocchini visited Mussolini every day, taking care to feign astonishment when the Duce told him of Rachele's most recent discoveries from her own little network of spies, none of them unknown to him. By the mid 1930s, the 'vice-Duce', as he was nicknamed, had every reason to feel pleased. There had been no attempts on Mussolini's life for almost ten years. The troublesome Communists and Socialists had been silenced and the various networks of anti-Fascists had been largely dismantled and their members dispatched to confino or in exile abroad, where they lived in impoverished communities, especially in Paris, watching events gloomily from the sidelines. Deeply corrupt himself,

Bocchini had waged war against profiteers and black marketeers. He now turned his attention to monitoring the degree of Fascist fervour of the Italians, making certain that they remained faithful and obedient. His spies and informers were instructed to become barometers of public opinion and mood which was, for the moment, reported to be excellent.

Mussolini's 'new Italian' was loyal, obedient, martial, strong, sporty and sober; his wife thrifty, undemanding and generously proportioned. Edda and Ciano, who were meant to be the epitome of this Fascist ideal, were in fact in almost all ways its very opposite. Edda was unmaternal, thin, opinionated, a heavy drinker and a terrible housewife. She played no musical instrument and did not listen to music; she liked to travel abroad and followed French fashion. Ciano was soft, vain and uncertain, with expensive tastes, by instinct and education a good bourgeois, neither ruthless nor bloodthirsty and reluctant to take exercise or follow a sport. The higher he rose, the more pronounced the disparity became, while the deeper he allowed himself to be ensnared by Roman society the more isolated he became from the other *gerarchi*, many of whom in any case dismissed him as Costanzo's son and Mussolini's son-in-law. Both he and Edda had affairs, Edda saying that she did indeed sleep with other men, but had children only by her husband. She was outspoken, sometimes to the point of rudeness, saying that in a world in which everything was artificial and unspontaneous, she had decided that she would always behave naturally and say exactly what she thought. Neither was any good at something dear to Mussolini's heart: 'going to the people' – being close to the masses – and both knew themselves to be little liked. Neither was, or felt themselves to be, a good Fascist – Edda had not even bothered to become a party member – and they despised Starace's absurd rules and paid little attention to any of them.

On 11 May 1935, Ciano and Edda went to London, at least in part to test once again British feelings towards Mussolini's colonial ambitions, which were now hastening towards war. They stayed at the Italian embassy with the Grandis, attended a recital and a party at Covent Garden given by the Austrian embassy and a ball held in honour of the King. Grandi gave a reception for

Edda with seven hundred guests, and 1,300 Italian boys and girls from the Fascist youth organisations paraded before her. In another of his fulsome letters to Mussolini, he praised Edda's 'gift of a lively political intuition'. What Edda herself said later was that she knew perfectly well that she was useful: 'Ciano and Papà needed me.' But at this stage she seems genuinely to have believed that she had no power beyond that created by her own personality. She followed politics, she would say, as an 'enthusiastic dilettante', using her instinct rather than her reason, and she looked on international relations much as a game of poker – to win you needed cunning, quickness and pleasant manners. In fact, her power was considerable and growing all the time: both her husband and her father listened to her closely.

On the surface, the Mussolini family had never seemed more settled, nor Edda and Ciano more assured, the golden couple of the hour, who had everything: looks, money, health, perfect children. Like other couples, they lunched every Sunday with her parents and Fabrizio and Raimonda called their grandfather Nonno Duce. But something of the chasm between appearance and reality lay not just in their marriage, but at the heart of the increasing malaise of the regime itself. Though it had yet to reach its moment of greatest popularity, its parabola had already begun its descent. Ever attuned to the atmosphere she lived in, Edda was very conscious of the precariousness around her. 'We must deprive ourselves of nothing,' she told a friend, 'because we know that the guillotine awaits us.'

10

The most influential woman in Europe

War was one of Fascism's founding myths, for which mothers had been urged to produce sons and small boys had marched with their wooden rifles. 'It is blood,' as Mussolini said, 'that moves history's wheels.' The chance to demonstrate Italy's military might came with the invasion of Ethiopia.

It was one of the few remaining truly independent states in Africa, ruled since 1930 by the Emperor Haile Selassie, who was seeking both to modernise the country and to increase the authority of central government. Because of Italy's colonies in Eritrea and Somalia – both founded in the late nineteenth century – Mussolini believed he was entitled to occupy at least some part of it. In the Europe of the 1930s, few people knew or cared much about the country but, largely as a result of Haile Selassie, Ethiopia had joined the League of Nations in 1923, and it was the League's responsibility to ensure the country's territorial integrity. Though Mussolini had had his eye on colonial conquest since the early 1930s, it was only in 1934 – at the time of Edda's first London trip – that he appears to have begun to plan his move, conscious that a burst of military success would lift Italy out of the Depression and that Italy needed land for emigration. There was also the catastrophe of the first Italo-Ethiopian War to avenge, when at Adowa in 1896 three thousand Italian soldiers were ambushed, the single biggest loss of European lives in the scramble for African countries. And a pretext had just appeared in the form of a clash between Italian and Ethiopian soldiers at Wal Wal over the possession of oil wells.

At home, Mussolini's critics had been silenced and his popularity was high. Abroad, he continued to be admired for his subduing of communism, his disciplining of industry and for making peace with the Vatican. Fascism might be a little crude, but it was working. Mussolini was, so it was said in European political circles, a '*tipo umano*', a self-made man with a sense of destiny. Much of the earlier mockery was forgotten. As the *Daily Mail* put it, the Duce had 'inspired a sense of faith in Italians' by lifting them out of anarchical chaos. The first female Lord Mayor of Liverpool and campaigner for children and their mothers, Margaret Beavan, returned from a visit to Rome saying that she had never met a man so impressive: 'I was moved in every fibre by his dominating, magnetic, powerful, immense personality.' As an old journalist, finely attuned to the power of words, Mussolini knew how to give of his best.

Mussolini's invasion of Ethiopia could only happen, however, with the connivance of the French and the British. He believed that he had it, having observed international acceptance of Japan's occupation of Manchuria, as well as the fact that there had been no repercussions over his invasion of Corfu in 1923; and he had signed an accord with Laval and France, which included an understanding that he would be allowed a free hand in Ethiopia. (Laval later said that he had intended to leave Mussolini a free hand only in economic affairs.)

Britain was more problematic. The government, too, saw the need to reach a compromise with Italy, as an ally against German aggression, and at the Stresa Conference in April 1935 they believed that they had secured Mussolini's commitment to a common front. However, Anthony Eden, Lord Privy Seal and Minister for League of Nations affairs and long hostile to Mussolini, paid a chilly visit to Rome in June which ended in a violent quarrel and only reinforced their mutual antagonism. He came home more convinced than ever, as he said later, that Mussolini was a 'complete gangster'. Eden had offered the Duce concessions in the Ogaden and on the Eritrean-Sudanese border, to which Mussolini had replied: 'Mr Eden, Fascist Italy is not interested in collecting deserts.' As he told Rachele, Eden was a 'sworn enemy of Italy'.

However, Britain also wished to preserve the League of Nations, particularly since the recent Peace Ballot held in Britain in June had resulted in a vote of 86.8 per cent in favour of economic sanctions in the case of one of the League's members attacking another. Various other small concessions were offered to Mussolini, which he refused. By the time even better ones were suggested – a protect-orate or a mandate – it was too late. Mussolini's machinery of war was already rumbling into life. 'With Geneva, without Geneva, against Geneva', as he wrote anonymously in *Il Popolo d'Italia*.

The war was not without its problems. Though Mussolini believed that, faced with his clarity and decisiveness, Britain would do no more than grumble, he wanted neither to threaten European security nor to menace British interests in Africa, nor lose his repu-tation as peacemaker and statesman. Sanctions might block raw materials, so the war needed to be short and victorious. In Italy, some of the *gerarchi*, generals and the King were opposed. A vast propaganda exercise was launched by Ciano at the MinCulPop, involving radio, film, newspapers and schools. Cartoons of the Ethiopians, portraying them as shoeless savages with huge feet, appeared, along with accurate descriptions of their continued widespread use of slaves, exported to Arabia and Iraq. Britain was denounced for trying to deny Italy her 'place in the sun'. Under their desks, schoolboys passed around photographs of beautiful Ethiopian girls, naked, 'agile as gazelles'.

Both Vittorio and Bruno had been taking flying lessons and in mid July 1935, Vittorio was made a sub lieutenant and a navigator in the air force. Bruno, at seventeen still only a cadet, and not yet having finished school, begged his parents to let him volunteer. In mid August, the boys joined an early expedition of troops to leave for Africa, and a *velina* instructed Italian newspapers to put their photographs prominently on their front pages, under a two-column headline. Ciano went with them, as did the loudmouthed Farinacci and the fifty-eight-year-old futurist Marinetti, along with a group of politicians, journalists and *gerarchi*, particularly those who had missed out on the First World War. Edda travelled to Naples with her parents to see them off on the *Saturnia*, in their gleaming white air force uniforms and amid great fanfare; she gave them all lucky charms. The ship's captain presented her with an immense bouquet of flowers. Edda was never good at gestures, but as the boat pulled out she saw an elderly woman standing not far away in tears and went over and handed her the flowers. At seven thirty that evening, as Ciano's ship passed Capri, lights all over the island flashed on and off, and fireworks exploded in the shape of miniature volcanic eruptions.

The armada of Italian ships went through the Suez Canal – with the tacit acceptance of the British – where they were serenaded with patriotic hymns by a popular Italian singer, Maria Uva, while Italians resident in Egypt joined in the choruses. At their base at Asmara in Eritrea, the Mussolini boys were assigned to the 14th Squadron and began to train. Bruno finished school in a *lycée* in Asmara, which enabled him to become an officer. Ciano, detailed to command the 15th, took for its name La Disperata, with a death's head and crossed bones, after the Florentine *squadra* to which he had pretended to belong. The Fascists, with their love of speed, revered pilots as the equivalents of the ancient cavalry. As Mussolini said, 'every flyer is born a Fascist'. While waiting for hostilities to begin, the young men played bridge in the officers' club and went hunting on the border between Sudan and Eritrea, where they found a paradise of guinea fowl, gazelle and bustard. In photographs, Vittorio has a bushy beard; Bruno looks like a little boy.

On the late afternoon of 2 October, Mussolini came out on to his balcony above Piazza Venezia and told a cheering crowd that the moment had now come to take what was owed to Italy. The war, he promised, would not lead to fighting in Europe. In Predappio, Rachele listened to the church bells ringing through the valleys. At five the next morning, 110,000 Italians crossed the frontier and marched into Ethiopia. Eighteen airports had been built at record speed and Vittorio, Bruno and Ciano were sent to bomb a bridge over the River Tecazzè.

The reaction from the League of Nations was immediate. On 10 October, fifty-two members voted to condemn Italy's aggression and impose an embargo on arms, credit and imports and exports. The US, on the eve of presidential elections in which the Italian immigrant vote was important to Roosevelt, agreed to continue to supply Italy with petrol. Germany, who had withdrawn from the League of Nations in 1933 and was looking for ways to exploit the situation, saw the opportunity to split Italy still further from Britain and offered Italy steel and coal. Talks, meetings, consultations continued between Paris and London, the French arguing for more concessions to Italy, the British declaring that it was wrong to reward an aggressor.

The Italians rapidly occupied Adowa, which was seen as a great psychological victory, 'washing away the shame'. Cardinal Schuster in Milan gave thanks for a heroic new chapter in Italian history.

Fascist women were urged to make patriotic omelettes in green, white and red and told to save money on lipstick, face powder, silk stockings and Dijon mustard. At court, to save petrol, cars were replaced by the old court carriages, the large Queen sailing out in a tiny brougham, lined with blue brocade and little plush tufts. When it was noticed that the Palazzo Doria was the only building on the Corso not to fly a flag, a mob broke in, stormed up the staircase and found the princess making scones in an apron covered in flour. She told them that the family was out. They took her for the cook and left.

On 18 December, in response to Mussolini's calls for 'frugality and sacrifice', Italian women all over Italy joined Queen Elena in a *Giornata della Fede*, a day of faith, exchanging their gold and silver wedding rings for metal ones, which brought 37 tonnes of gold and 115 of silver into the national coffers. Never had the regime seemed more popular. Rachele contributed half a kilo of gold as well as many of the presents piled up in the Villa Torlonia. A map was hung in the hall, and Mussolini moved pins around as the war news came in.

It was a terrible war. Though the senior generals bickered and were changed about, though cranes smashed tanks as they unloaded them and burlap bags of spaghetti, flour and sugar dropped by parachute were left in the rain and rotted, the Italian forces pressed mercilessly on. Under the murderous General Badoglio, who had earlier 'pacified' Libya by waging a near-genocidal campaign against the resisters, they released high-explosive and incendiary bombs on tented villages of civilians and targeted Red Cross field hospitals clearly marked with large red crosses. Even before the invasion, Mussolini had authorised the use of flame-throwers and poison gas, despite having ratified a protocol forbidding gas or biological warfare, drawn up in 1925 by the International Committee of the Red Cross. At the end of March 1936, *The Times* published a telegram sent by Haile Selassie's daughter to the British government: 'The suffering and torture is beyond description, hundreds of countrymen screaming and moaning with pain. Many of them are unrecognisable since the skin has burned off their faces.' A delegate from the ICRC in Geneva wrote that women and children were being 'disfigured, blinded and burnt by gas sticking to their faces'.

The Ethiopians never had a hope. Crushed by Italian motorised troops, brought down in manhunts as they fled, strafed and bombed by Ciano, Vittorio, Bruno and their fellow aviators, they lacked even basic weapons. As Pavolini, a *gerarco* now rising in the ranks and a close friend of Ciano's, saw it, the blacks were simply another feature of the landscape – 'background, like the camels'. The Ethiopians, soldiers and civilians alike, died in their hundreds of thousands; the Italians suffered very few casualties. The 14th Squadron lost neither a plane nor a pilot.

Towards the end of 1935, Ciano, who felt nervous when away from Rome for too long, had returned to Rome for medical treatment, much to the irritation of Mussolini and the other *gerarchi*. His persistent throat and nose problems had left him with a significant loss of hearing in one ear. There were rumours that he had abandoned the front in order to enjoy himself in the arms of Delia di Bagno, a friend of Edda's, even as his companions were fighting. Delia, a spy reported, was a 'tireless and dissatisfied nymphomaniac'. One of the anonymous letters that reached Mussolini's desk spoke of a '*Cianaio*', a Ciano clan, which abused his name and position; another said that he was known to be spending millions on another mistress, Lola Giovinelli. The family spent an anxious Christmas in the Villa Torlonia playing solitaire and worrying about Vittorio and Bruno. Edda was photographed standing at a bus stop in Rome, her expression pensive, choosing to give up her car and 'live more intimately with the people . . . an Italian woman like so many others, with the same feeling of pride in her heart'.

Ciano went back to Ethiopia in the spring, to take part in a stunt with Vittorio, Bruno and Farinacci dropping leaflets, which nearly ended in disaster. As a pilot, Ciano was bold but reckless. When the Italian forces were 60 miles from Addis Ababa, he took off for the capital, planning to capture an enemy soldier. But he misjudged the enemy strength, his plane was hit twenty-five times by machine-gunners, putting two fuel tanks out of action, and he was fortunate to get back to base, having dropped a Disperata pennant in the main square. Mussolini sent him a telegram of congratulation: 'I am proud of your flight.'

But neither Ciano nor the Mussolini brothers joined in the triumphant entry of the Italian forces into Addis Ababa on 5 May, their planes having been grounded by bad weather. Ciano made his way there soon after, to find the city still on fire and marauders looting the foreign shops. He stayed in the old Imperial Hotel and announced that the Italian victory was proof that Britain's days of glory were over, 'or she would have taken a stronger stand against us'. Though in private he told Edda later that he believed the war had been a terrible mistake.

Edda was in the main square of Predappio on 9 May when she heard over the radio, beamed out to the entire town, first three trumpet blasts, then her father proclaiming, 'Italy, at last, has her Empire, created with her own blood.' Victor Emmanuel III was now an Emperor. At that moment, she later wrote, the people gathered around her seemed suddenly to grow ten centimetres taller. In Rome, Rachele, Romano and Anna Maria had slipped out to join the throngs in the Piazza Venezia. They watched as the crowds, in a state of almost frenzied excitement, shouted '*Du-ce! Du-ce! Du-ce!*', falling silent as the sirens sounded and Mussolini appeared high above them, stern, hand on parapet, until suddenly he smiled and pronounced his words of triumph. The sky above Piazza Venezia was turquoise, fading into rose, and the swallows wheeled and called. The cheering crowd went on to the Quirinale, where the King came out and waved and the royal hymn was played. Queen Elena sent Rachele a bunch of roses, causing Mussolini to remark crossly that she might have sent something more generous.

Ciano, Vittorio and Bruno all came home with medals, though Ciano regretted that his was not gold. He had made thirty-two sorties, to Vittorio's thirty-eight and Bruno's thirty-six. The turbulent Farinacci got a medal too, for an accident in which he lost a hand. He claimed it was a battle wound but it was, in fact, the result of fishing with grenades. Bruno remained in the air force, and Vittorio sat down to write a book of the campaign. Called *Voli sulle Ambe*, it perfectly conveyed the callousness and cruelty of the war, with descriptions of picking off Ethiopian women and children with machine guns from his plane and carpet-bombing villages, though he was later to profess himself a little ashamed.

The conquest of Ethiopia was to be Mussolini's '*capolavoro politico*', his finest political hour. Talks had continued between the League of Nations members throughout the campaign, though they had been distracted by Hitler's sudden remilitarisation of the Rhineland in March. Haile Selassie was present in Geneva, and Ciano, on Mussolini's orders, had arranged for a claque of Italians to barrack the session from the public galleries, a scene widely condemned throughout Europe. But on 6 July, the League voted to remove all sanctions against Italy. Later, Lord Perth, the first general secretary of the League who was made Ambassador to Rome in 1933, would say that he believed that Britain's failure to warn Mussolini strongly against invasion was 'one of the most criminal blunders in the whole course of diplomacy'.

In Italy, Mussolini's prestige had never been higher. It was, said Rachele, the best moment of her life, a 'profound peace, as never before, like a dream'. The fact that the Italian soldiers had lacked shoes, socks, proper guns and artillery was conveniently forgotten, as were the many massacres and orders to 'summarily kill' all who resisted. Mussolini's ruthless breach of the protocol on poison gas was allowed to pass unchallenged – for which the International Committee of the Red Cross was later much criticised. After an attempt on his life, General Graziani, having sanctioned the use of 317 tonnes of gas, unleashed bloody reprisals that took the lives of some seven thousand people, which earned him the title of the 'butcher of Ethiopia', but did not lead to prosecution for war crimes.

The Gran Consiglio hailed Mussolini as the 'founder of the Empire' and the King would have made him a prince had Mussolini not said that his family had always been peasants and that he was proud of it. Addis Ababa was to be rebuilt as an Italian city in Africa. 'Salute the Duce, the founder of the Empire' became the new greeting dreamt up by Starace. Every bookshop in Rome gave over its windows to photographs of Mussolini. A British journalist, Stephen Potter, visiting Italy, described a 'soldierish nation', so different from the 'boring, inhuman, German militarism', an Italy that was cheerful, cleared of rubbish, united and obedient.

Within Italy, the few remaining dissidents fell silent or fled abroad. 'The old anti-Fascism,' declared Carlo Rosselli, one of the political leaders trying to galvanise opposition to Mussolini from exile in Paris, 'is dead.' The cost of the war had been ruinous, taking a third of the country's gold and foreign currency reserves. But as General Badoglio, newly created 1st Duke of Addis Ababa, put it, with fatal self-delusion, 'with soldiers like these, Italy can dare all'.

A new map showing the Empire created by the taking of Ethiopia was added to the four in the Basilica di Massenzio tracing the expansion of Roman power since the first settlements. Now showing the Empire created by the taking of Ethiopia. Italy's legions were again conquering the world.

There had, however, been a change of mood in Europe. Germany was looking stronger, more menacing, and Italy, with its victory in Ethiopia, more powerful. An endless, dangerous, game of shifting alliances was about to begin, with Mussolini swinging first one way and then the other, towards accords with Hitler, back to accommodation with France and Britain.

And something new, or at least more sharply defined, had entered the lexicon of Fascist ideology: the question of race. Mussolini had repeatedly said that he was not drawn to the Nazi policy of eugenics, nor to Hitler's attacks on the Jews. But among the other plans for Ethiopia had been the idea that Italy would provide a 'civilising mission' to a country that had been 'immersed in centuries of darkness'. Not, of course, that the Italians and the Africans would mix: racial segregation was to be pursued as part of a wider attempt to encourage racial consciousness. Reporters were instructed to describe the Ethiopians as ignorant, idle, 'occasionally ferocious', with barbaric customs and living in 'primitive naturalness'. They were, wrote one, 'insensitive to physical and mental pain and they know few feelings of joy'.

The same reporters kept silent on the widespread prostitution, known as '*madamismo*', between the Italian soldiers and settlers and the Ethiopian women. Photographs in Italian newspapers showed the 'black Venuses' as naked, thus symbolically sinful and promiscuous, in contrast to the modest, respectable Italian women now arriving as colonists in their long, heavy dresses. Those who 'contaminated' the race – originally delinquents and criminals, but after Ethiopia also 'non-whites' – were declared somehow not Italian. To be Italian was to be 'racially pure'.

In June 1936, not long after Ciano's return from Addis Ababa, Mussolini sent Edda on another mission to fly the Italian flag and take the temperature of a potential ally. This time it was to Germany, where her brief was to be friendly, interested and alert. It was to be a '*mondano-politico*' visit, both social and political, and Edda, he had decided, had proved herself adept at such things.

Edda spoke no German and arrived in Berlin alone. The *Frankfurter Zeitung* reported that she had come 'to visit various institutions of the nationalist-socialist state', a task she often declared to be paralysingly dull. She stayed with Ciano's sister Maria and her husband Mario Magistrati, first councillor at the Italian Embassy. Berlin was draped in swastikas, which were stamped on everything from water glasses to bed sheets. The headlines of *Der Angriff* and *Der Stürmer* were relentlessly anti-Semitic, and most outspoken critics of the regime were already in Dachau and Buchenwald for 'treason'. Storm troopers roamed the streets. Goebbels made certain that newspapers only printed what they were told to, and Western diplomats struggled to follow events. The senior Nazis had taken over vast houses, in which they gave sumptuous parties.

Soon after Edda's arrival, the new Italian Ambassador, Bernardo Attolico, an astute and intelligent diplomat with a somewhat surly manner and glum features, gave a dinner in her honour. Bella Fromm, a journalist who was present, wrote in her diary that Edda's 'violently blonde' hair did not look natural. She seemed to Fromm to be very like her father, 'quite immoderate in her consumption of lovers'. 'Dashing flyers in snappy uniforms', under special instructions to make themselves pleasant, had been laid on to entertain her. There was much respectful talk about the Italian victory in Ethiopia. 'A large gathering,' noted Goebbels in his diary. 'Germany has embraced her.' He knew Edda from his visits to Rome, when she had proved an 'excellent hostess' at dinners in the Parioli flat, using the children's German nanny as interpreter.

Edda and Goebbels' wife Magda had become friendly during earlier meetings in Switzerland, Edda coaching the blonde, beautifully dressed Magda, who was several inches taller than her sardonic husband with his club foot and gnome-like face, to ignore his infidelities and see marriage as 'only one of the states of man'. Magda, who was sophisticated and spoke several languages, went to great lengths in Berlin to make a public show of their friendship and to keep Edda away from the predatory Ribbentrops, whom she referred to as 'the climbers'. Together, the two women looked elegant and assured, Edda holding her own with her strong face, basilisk stare and lean figure.

Though Edda was treated with respect, everything changed on 9 June when she heard from Magistrati that Ciano had just been made Foreign Minister in a cabinet reshuffle at home. The news came as a complete surprise to her. After this moment, she wrote later, the Germans treated her like a queen. The senior Nazis competed in courting her, and Edda fell for their flattery. Goebbels gave a tea party at his house on the Wannsee, which Hitler attended. He made himself very agreeable to Edda, offered her the use of his private train and told her how much he admired Mussolini. He invited her to go out on the lake with him. In his diary, Goebbels noted that Edda had been 'extremely taken by him'. Edda herself said later that she had liked the way that Hitler played with the Goebbels children, and that she had changed her earlier impression of him as a marionette, with a raucous voice and a Charlie Chaplin moustache. More elegant than she had remembered him, he now struck her as 'an amiable and cultivated man of the world' with 'charming' blue eyes, a pleasant sense of humour and a 'low and agreeable voice'. Edda, though watchful and quick, was highly susceptible to flattery. And she appears to have been oblivious to the many signs of Nazi repression, admitting later that her 'Germanophile sympathies' had led her to 'consider Hitler a veritable hero'.

As for Goering, she said later, he seemed to her a 'kind of condottiere who had degenerated into an extravagant satrap'. She was invited to Karinhalle, his vast hunting lodge north of Berlin, where his forest guards wore medieval costumes and she observed her host's constant change of clothes, one item a colour that 'oscillated between violet and rose', strutting about with sword, dagger, decorations and coloured ribbons. Goering took her to see his electric train set, laid out complete with tunnels, signal lights, switching points and bridges, and he told her that it was a replica of Germany's secondary railway lines and that it might come in useful in the event of the main lines being destroyed by fighting. If the war came, Edda reported him as saying, Germany should take Malta and occupy Britain but never, ever open an eastern front. Edda met his lion, who put a biscuit on Goering's knee, but she was spared his bison. For all his 'obesity', she found him 'extremely likeable'.*

Both Goebbels and Hitler commented that Edda was very nice

---

* Malaparte, who later had a sauna with Himmler, described a gathering of ten naked men, all with fat breasts and flesh that looked like lobster, 'pale and rosy, exuding a crustacean smell' with grim hard faces, sweaty, flabby and freckly, using switches with which to beat each other.

and 'sympathique'. But both deplored her excessive make-up, so out of tune with the plain, homely looks encouraged in Nazi wives. Goebbels remarked smugly that Hitler really valued Magda, who had remained 'a clear and simple woman', which was why 'Edda M did not impress him'. He and Magda gave another dinner in her honour. 'Many guests,' he noted. 'Very hot weather.' Goebbels, wrote Martha Dodd, whose father was the US Ambassador to Berlin, was a demagogue, who 'hisses like a snake and coos like a dove'. A visit for Edda to Potsdam with Magda soon followed, Goebbels noting that their friendship 'might come in useful one of these days'.

In diplomatic circles, Edda's visit to Germany was judged somewhat harshly. André François-Poncet, the French Ambassador, a master of diplomatic verbiage, innuendo and nuance, a man with exquisite manners and a black waxed moustache which he twirled constantly, was a keen observer of Berlin life. He reported back to Paris that Edda's 'conduct' had 'aroused profound consternation' – presumably referring to her warmth and enthusiasm for her hosts – while Grandi, ever jealous of the Cianos, declared that she returned 'inebriated' by her reception and that she was more than ever taken by the idea of a closer relationship with Germany. He was right: Edda had indeed been charmed by her German hosts, and it said something about the ease with which she could be seduced, about her need for admiration and longing to be listened to which somehow dulled her political intuition. At twenty-five, she was an odd mixture of worldly sophistication, self-absorption and artlessness. Too much had happened to her too quickly; she had neither the self-knowledge nor, perhaps, the intellect to understand it.

Edda might have stayed longer in Germany had news not come from Rome that Anna Maria, her seven-year-old sister, had come down with what was initially thought to be whooping cough. She left immediately for Italy, seen off by senior ministers, members of the Italian colony in Berlin and one of Hitler's aides, who arrived with a large signed photograph of the Führer for her. Rachele had taken Anna Maria to Tivoli, hoping that a change of air might do her good. But the little girl's headaches had grown worse, and her temperature had risen steeply. Polio was diagnosed and Anna Maria's legs became paralysed. Edda arrived from Berlin, and Vittorio and Bruno from their summer holidays in Riccione. Mussolini was distraught and abandoned all work to sit by his daughter's bedside, the older children remarking that they had never seen him so desperate or so furious to find himself so powerless. Never given to expressions of emotion, the family clustered around Anna Maria's bed, often in silence.

The specialists brought in from all over Italy warned that it was very likely that Anna Maria would die. The days passed and the family waited. 'Still no hope,' wrote Rachele in her diary. 'Benito is prostrate, shaken by Anna Maria saying that she would rather die than be paralysed for the rest of her life.' When Ciano arrived in Tivoli to discuss a matter of some urgency, Mussolini shouted at him to go away.

But Anna Maria, like Edda, had inherited her parents' steely determination. The crisis passed and within weeks she was being wheeled around the gardens, swearing that she would walk again. For a while, Anna Maria's illness was kept secret, but when the news got out, presents and telegrams flowed in. Queen Elena sent a talking doll. Overcome with relief, Rachele gave 200 lire to every poor family in Tivoli, where Anna Maria was referred to as 'our little Empress' and Mussolini as 'our earthly father'.

Anna Maria had sufficiently recovered for it to be judged safe to let Vittorio and Bruno attend the Olympics in Munich in September 1936. The boys were received with deference and invited to the Chancellery by Hitler, where Prince Umberto, also in Germany for the Games, was guest of honour. They attended a gala dinner given by Goebbels for a thousand guests, where the firework display was so extravagant and noisy that it sounded like artillery bombardment. Goering then held a ball, where the many servants wore livery and powdered wigs. As François-Poncet remarked, the Third Reich loved parties, and no one more than the obese Goering, with his costumes and jewellery, his art looted from museums or confiscated from Jewish collectors, receiving his guests in his immense white uniform, his fingers festooned in rings. Described by the acerbic Martha Dodd as a 'blob of flesh', his fine face lost in rolls of fat and his icy eyes merciless, Goering then hosted a tea party for the Italians, with his matronly wife Emmy, her golden hair wound in coils around her head in the approved German style.

As they sat holding their little cups, looking out into the gardens, a lioness suddenly wandered into the room and started nuzzling the guards. Vittorio and Bruno sat frozen to their chairs. Maria-Josè and Princess Mafalda, Victor Emmanuel's second daughter, who had accompanied Umberto to Germany, leapt on to theirs, behaving, wrote Vittorio later, very like women who had just seen a mouse. Like Mussolini, Goering enjoyed using his wild pets as props.

One hundred and eighty-two Italian athletes competed in the Berlin Olympics and Mussolini was very keen to see them do well. It was assumed that the Germans would triumph, and they duly took thirty-three medals, but the Italians came away with a satisfactory twenty-two. Watching Hitler, François-Poncet noted that he kept his eyes fixed 'with passion' on the German athletes, laughing and slapping his thighs when they won, frowning deeply when they lost. When Jesse Owens won his famous race there were complaints that it had been unfair to let 'non-humans' compete with fine human Germans.

Ciano's promotion was not altogether surprising. Though he was still just thirty-three, and now the youngest foreign secretary in the world, he had proved himself brave in Ethiopia, resourceful at the MinCulPop and had demonstrated diplomatic skill in China. Looking around at his quarrelsome *gerarchi*, Mussolini decided that Ciano was more dependable than Grandi, Bottai or Farinacci – who was trying to manoeuvre his way back to the centre of power – and, certainly, more biddable. He was young, someone he could teach, married to his favourite child and the son of one of the very few men he trusted.

News of his new appointment was not, however, greeted with universal acclaim. In Rome, a city renowned for its bitchy chatter, Ciano was judged too vain, too ambitious, even too intellectual. But to Mussolini he appeared respectful and grateful, and even pleasantly in awe of him. The '*generissimo*', the most son-in-law, as he was described in mocking Roman circles, a play on the *generalissimo*, Chang-Kai-shek, now held what was probably the most crucial political post in Italy, after that of Mussolini himself. The question Romans asked themselves was whether he had what was needed to fashion a coherent and effective policy, and to steer it at a time of spiralling international uncertainty.

The test came immediately. On 17 July 1936, General Francisco Franco had launched his uprising against the elected Republican government in Spain from Morocco and asked Mussolini for help in ferrying his men across the Straits of Gibraltar. Ciano was inclined to act immediately, but Mussolini held back, despite encouragement from both the militia and the Vatican, eager to go to the defence of the embattled Spanish clergy. When it became clear that France was helping the Republicans, and that Germany was planning to send aid to Franco, Mussolini agreed to send twelve planes to carry Franco's troops. It was to have been kept secret, but three of the planes crashed and the news got out.

France proposed that a non-intervention committee be set up, with Britain, Italy, Germany and the Soviet Union agreeing to stand back, but men and weapons continued to reach both the Republicans and the Nationalists. Fearing that a leftist Spanish government would introduce communism into the Mediterranean, and pleased that Franco was talking about setting up a Fascist-style government, Ciano and Mussolini began to call for volunteers to serve in Spain under the Nationalists. Whether the men who came forward actually knew where they were going or why, beyond responding to promises of making good money, was never clear. Both the Duce and his Foreign Minister were convinced that this would be another quick victory, from which Italy would emerge stronger. But the days passed, the war spread, Franco did not seem inclined to hurry, preferring to crush the country province by province and more and more Italians were dispatched to the front. The war was also proving a rallying cry for the Italian anti-Fascists, long feeling impotent, and many now came back from exile in the United States, France and South America to set up their own battalion against Franco. Italians were about to start fighting other Italians.

Mussolini had ordered brutal acts in Ethiopia. In Spain, when asked what should be done with captured Italian anti-Fascists, he said, 'Shoot them, dead men tell no tales.' A vicious militia leader, Arconovaldo Bonaccorsi, informed Ciano that he was emptying the local prisons with 'daily radical cleansing of places and infected people'. At first, Ciano made no protest. While the war was marked by carnage, Italian reporters continued to file stories about the defence of civilisation against the barbarism of communism. As the writer Leonardo Sciascia later said, the Spanish Civil War represented one of the lowest points in Italian journalism, preferring propaganda and triumphalist rhetoric to honest reporting.

As for Edda, her increasing status as her father's confidante and emissary was quickly felt. With Rachele seldom leaving the Villa Torlonia and in any case openly scornful of Roman society – she preferred her chickens and rabbits – Edda had moved more obviously into the role of first lady. Though she continued to repeat that her father would never let her meddle in the affairs of state, she was acquiring a reputation as a secret manipulator in Italian politics. Mussolini appeared to enjoy her growing fame. After an adulatory article appeared in the German *Weltwoche* describing Edda as someone with many admirers but few friends, he sent her the cutting with an affectionate observation that she was becoming the stuff of legends. 'Countess Ciano,' said the reporter, 'is one of the strangest and most attractive female figures of our age.' The sharp-tongued Duchessa di Sermoneta, who met her again at a ball, remarked that she was 'transformed, for she was now well dressed and her hair waved and curled; she had become almost good looking, but was not more gracious'. Power, even of an imprecise nature, had improved not just her confidence but her looks.

Rachele going hunting

Other papers spoke of Vittorio and Bruno as '*bravi figlioli*', nice lads, but said that only Edda, Mussolini's 'best counsellor', had her father's ambition, pride and inner fire. The Swiss *Berner Tagblatt* maintained that even when Mussolini had given firm instructions that he was not to be disturbed by anyone, Edda was still put through immediately, however trivial her question. 'Everyone knows,' wrote a journalist, 'that her father rules Italy and that Edda rules her father.' She had become, said a Zurich paper, 'the most influential woman in Europe'.

In October, Ciano paid his first official visit to Germany to sign a secret protocol of reciprocal collaboration with the Spanish nationalists, and to further Mussolini's growing links with Hitler. It was a tense moment for Italy: the wars in Spain and Ethiopia had estranged her from France and Britain and she felt isolated.

Hitler invited Ciano to Berchtesgaden. Ciano had brought with him from Italy thirty-two documents intercepted by the Italian secret services that demonstrated Britain's hostility to Germany. Hitler told him that Mussolini was the 'leading statesman in the world', and that the rapprochement between the Western liberal democracies should be countered by a German-Italian alliance based on anti-communism. Before they parted, Hitler gave Ciano a signed copy of *Mein Kampf*, but told an aide that he loathed the smell of his Chinese aftershave lotion. For his part, Ciano was heard to mutter 'idiot' under his breath. 'Should we really believe Ciano a great man?' a journalist enquired of the German press office. 'Not at all,' he was told, 'but he must think we think he is.' However, as François-Poncet reported back to Paris, another step had been taken towards the creation of a bloc of central powers. *'Ils marchent donc ensemble.'*

Unlike Edda, Ciano did not warm to the senior Nazis whom he met. He took an instant dislike to Ribbentrop, soon to be the German Foreign Minister, calling him a fool; he dismissed Goering as a 'fat, vulgar ox', capable, but interested chiefly in money and decorations; and he was wary of the 'small, olive skinned' cripple Goebbels, who lacked, Ciano said, the 'stupid frankness of his colleagues'. To his mind, it was clear that Hitler was bloodthirsty and a bit mad. Germany, he concluded, was in the 'hands of men of very inferior quality whom we must exploit'. Completely failing to see their determination and growing power in Europe, he returned saying that the brutal Germans could easily be outmanoeuvred by the sharper and wilier Italians. No more than Edda did he perceive the danger.

In July 1936, Hitler had signed an agreement with the Chancellor Kurt von Schuschnigg recognising Austrian sovereignty, but clearly had an eye on future annexation. Mussolini stood back, evidently prepared to abandon Austria as a disagreeable but necessary sacrifice to his growing closeness with Germany. Edda had not accompanied Ciano to Germany in October, but in November she went with him to Vienna. They were received coldly, Schuschnigg complaining about Nazi interference. Ciano was ill with his recurrent throat and ear problems. The journalist Giovanni Ansaldo, who accompanied them, observed that Edda stood out against the other diplomatic ladies. She was a *'tipo singolare'*, very much her own character.

Edda's reaction to the visit was telling: she was deeply bored. Saying that after her years in diplomatic circles in Shanghai 'I could have made a stone talk', she could find no conversation with Schuschnigg, and declared him tedious. An exhausting and dull programme of visits to schools, museums and institutions of the very kind she most hated had been laid on for her and every morning at eight, Princess Starhenberg, a woman in her sixties who had been a member of the Federal Council, collected her from her hotel in a black limousine. The Princess, Edda wrote later, was 'less affable than an automaton, rigid and detached' and it proved impossible to get beyond the most starchy formality. And it was not just the disapproving princess: everywhere they went, Edda was met with 'icy coldness'.

Suddenly, one morning, to her immense relief and delight, as they drove slowly down a street and through a courtyard, she saw that the windows above were lined with smiling, waving, laughing men and women. 'I felt,' she wrote, 'liberated from a nightmare.' She enquired who these people were and the princess told her that they were patients in a mental hospital. When, on returning to Rome, she gleefully recounted the story to Mussolini, 'he laughed like a child'.

Soon after Anna Maria recovered, Rachele asked Mussolini to consider stepping down from leading Italy. 'There are no black clouds to darken the horizon,' she told him. The Duce was now in his mid fifties and though apparently fit, he was prone to attacks from what appeared to be an ulcer. For a moment, he seemed to consider it, but a conversation with Starace brought some of the senior *gerarchi* to the Villa Torlonia, who persuaded him to remain. In any case, he told Rachele, there was still much to be done. He needed to complete his task. The truly Fascist Italy he dreamt of was not yet in place.

11

The Fascists at play

Once he was Minister of Foreign Affairs, Ciano told a friend that the Palazzo Chigi was going to be the 'most Fascist of all the Fascist ministries'. By 1936, the old-school traditional diplomacy, with its protocol and subtleties, its courtly manners, network of relations and common language, all geared towards equilibrium and a balance of power, was vanishing all over Europe. During the first decade of the regime Mussolini had made a number of changes to the Ministry, rewarding some of the younger prominent Fascists with jobs, and Grandi, while Foreign Minister, had made a few others. But in practice, Italian diplomats had continued to be recruited from a small, well-off, social pool. The Ministry remained what it had always been: nationalist rather than Fascist, continuing traditions laid down by successive Liberal governments. All this was about to change. Though foreign affairs now concerned him more than internal matters, Mussolini was prepared to let Ciano enjoy a certain freedom, while keeping a close eye on his every move. Ciano planned to make the most of it.

Ciano had many good qualities and they had so far served him well. He was an excellent organiser, worked hard and fast, was quick at mastering information, spoke well and knew how to please and charm. But he was also weak, spoilt, susceptible to flattery, narcissistic and extremely indiscreet, and he shared Mussolini's boundless impatience. He could be both impulsively generous and casually cruel, and he lacked political astuteness. As Bottai later said, he was a 'man of contradictions', with a lively intelligence and a lazy intellect and at the same time widely cultured and ignorant about life. He could recall superfluous details, but seldom bothered with substance. He was 'elegant in dress and vulgar in tone'. Trying to please everyone, trying to prove that he was more than Edda's husband and Costanzo's son, he ended up pleasing no one.

One of his first moves on reaching Palazzo Chigi was to concentrate power more closely into an inner cabinet. Older diplomats were ousted from the service or shunted to jobs in which they had no power, and with them went a measure of traditional caution and thoughtfulness. (But as an unsigned letter in Bocchini's files put it, 'As long as we have l'Uomo [Mussolini], we can rest easy. But afterwards?')

Those who replaced them were Ciano's creatures, younger and biddable. One of these was Filippo Anfuso, an ambiguous figure, clever, articulate and profoundly cynical, who had a long cold face and hard eyes and had served with Ciano in China. Anfuso was made chef-de-cabinet. Another was Raimondo Lanza, a wild, attractive, frenetic man, a wonderful mimic, with curly hair slicked down with brilliantine and arresting blue-grey eyes, the illegitimate son of one of the last great Sicilian princes. Lanza entered the Cianos' lives when he appeared with a collection of jazz records sent from America and took them around Rome to parties in a specially made crocodile-skin bag. He kept a permanent room in the Grand Hotel, which, together with the Golf Club at l'Acquasanta, the Palazzo Colonna and a bathing establishment at Castel Fusano, all became outposts of the Foreign Ministry.

Of all Ciano's new friends, Lanza was the closest to Edda. They were both anxious, restless, hated discipline and formality and determined to maintain their own freedom. Their friendship soon went as far as they themselves called a 'certain animal attraction', which led them to hug and kiss, but then draw back, conscious that getting closer would lead to impossible complications. As spies reported to Bocchini, Lanza was Ciano's 'latest fancy and so must be tolerated', but he was a dandy and man about town, and used Ciano's name too freely in his dealings. Lanza's life, they said, was dedicated to 'debauchery and gambling'.

For the many trips that now took him around Italy and abroad, Ciano liked to surround himself with a retinue of journalists, with whom he talked far into the nights. One of these was Alessandro Pavolini, the brutal former Florentine *squadrista*, now Ciano's *'uomo di fiducia'*, his right-hand man. Like Ciano, Pavolini had returned from military service in Ethiopia with several medals but he had also brought back with him a grudge towards his mentor, complaining that he had excluded him from one of his more spectacular exploits.

In the Foreign Ministry slow, thorough work was jettisoned in favour of rapid, ill-prepared action, Ciano preferring to listen to his intuition rather than to outside advice. Files went missing and important information was ignored. Traditional diplomats, Ciano insisted, had failed to convey a sense of the strong new Italy, its true '*tono fascista*'. When speeches were shown to him for his approval, he cut out the diplomatic niceties. The Palazzo Chigi was soon a nest of intrigue, jealousy and resentment, concealed under a blanket of collective enthusiasm while Ciano himself, trying to ignore his staff's ironic asides, put on airs that did not suit him. As one diplomat remarked, under Ciano there was no Foreign Ministry, 'only a minister . . . and no tradition but daily inventiveness'. Ciano, said his critics, was '*il cretino arrivato*', the cretin who had made good, who wanted too much, said too much, gave too many orders, made too many scenes; corrupted by his 'monstrous' power, he was destroying half a century of responsible Italian diplomacy.

Some of this hostility came from the other *gerarchi*, who believed that Ciano owed his promotion simply to the fact that he was Edda's husband, while Ciano himself made very little effort to conceal the fact that he considered most of them tedious and self-important. Though relations between the two men were courteous on the surface, Dino Grandi, who had thought the post of Foreign Minister would go to him, was soon remarking that Ciano was supine when it came to following Mussolini's orders and that power had only accentuated the flaws in his character. Ciano was heard to observe that Grandi was 'quite uninteresting and has the intelligence of a mosquito'. There were rumours that Edda was interfering in appointments; certainly she had strong views of her own about the *gerarchi* and expressed them readily to both her father and her husband. Though quickly irritated by diplomatic niceties, when she turned her mind to problems she could be trenchant and astute.

None of this feuding was lost on the foreign ambassadors in Rome who, accustomed to being wooed and flattered, now found themselves slighted and overlooked, particularly in the case of the representatives of smaller countries, to whom Ciano paid scant attention and very seldom consented to meet. William Phillips, the recently appointed US Ambassador, reported that it was hard to take Ciano seriously for he was 'less the Foreign Minister than a young man with a roving eye', with 'no standards morally or politically'. He came away more impressed by Edda, saying that she was obviously an 'intelligent observer'. There was talk of her paying a visit to the United States, a country about which, Phillips observed, Mussolini was 'astonishingly ill-informed'. At dinner parties he and his wife gave for the Cianos, Phillips noted coolly, the couple expected their 'youthful favourites' to be present, and were reluctant to pay much attention to older and more serious guests. 'They could do as they wished,' he wrote. 'It was not considered wise to criticise them openly.' Another important diplomat whom Ciano failed to impress was the German Ambassador, the aristocratic Prussian Ulrich von Hassell, a deeply Christian man at odds with Hitler and the Nazis. Von Hassell, Ciano said, knew his Dante too well, and 'I mistrust foreigners who read Dante. They want to massage us with poetry.' Von Hassell dismissed him as a 'boorish youngster'.

With the spotlight now falling more glaringly on them, and conscious that they had effectively become the bridge between Roman society and the Fascist administration, Edda and Ciano set the tone. It was gossipy, cynical and increasingly corrupt. As Eugen Dollmann, a German journalist living in Rome, said, the people who surrounded them were 'frivolous, libertine, irresponsible, endowed with physical charm but deprived of intellect'. Ciano's clique copied his every gesture, bought their suits as he did from Caraceni and had their hair cut by his favourite barber, Biancafiore. They were 'like beggars' observed Susanna Agnelli, 'waiting for Galeazzo's "ciao"'. They wore silk shirts, white jackets and two-tone shoes, and only appeared in Fascist dress when obliged to, preying on his guilelessness and the fact that he never saw that they were not really his friends but often simply using him. They called themselves CAC, the *club dei amici di Ciano*, and the circle included his harem of well-born, idle women. The Petit Trianon in Isabella Colonna's salon became the place where everything was a joke, where fortunes were made or lost and jobs secured, where betrayal was all part of the game, and where the aristocracy flirted with a few privileged *gerarchi* who came to fawn. Isabella herself was referred to as the 'tzarina of the Black nobility', despotic, generous and very religious. As Rachele said scathingly to Edda, 'Your counts and your marquesses stink like hairdressers.'

Edda and her sculpture

Edda herself rarely visited the Palazzo Colonna. She preferred to pursue her own life. She gambled, always for high stakes, and constantly lost, so that hostesses set up games in separate rooms and kept the disapproving Ciano from witnessing his wife's mounting losses. Together, she and Ciano gave sumptuous parties in the Villa Madama, the traditional residence of foreign ministers, and many hitherto disapproving and snooty aristocrats fell over themselves to embrace this modern, chic couple, who were doing so much to rid Italy of the reputation that the country had been turned into a 'barracks run by an ex-corporal from the Bersaglieri', and who spoke English with the English and French with everyone else. Like Ciano, Edda was much imitated but not always liked, and especially not by the other *gerarchi*. When invited to the Quirinale, she found court life excruciatingly dull and complained that there was never enough to eat: the moment the King finished his quick, frugal meal, all plates were instantly removed.

Even so, with their place at the centre of power, 1937 was proving a good year and Ciano, enjoying the choreography of power more than its substance, was still to realise that he was little more than a mouthpiece for Mussolini's designs.

*

Yet Edda was not exactly happy. She felt increasingly detached from Ciano, whose vanity had begun to annoy her and whose political sense she feared inadequate for his new position, and she seemed to take little pleasure in the company of her children. Ciccino and Dindina spent their time mostly with their nanny. China had given her a taste for heavy drinking and now she found that it lessened her sense of discontent – though she was too mindful of her father's disapproval to let it get out of hand. She shopped, she gave presents, she showed every appearance of indulging cheerfully in frivolity when she was for the most part deeply disgruntled. She went to bed very late and slept through the mornings, emerging towards lunchtime in dark glasses. Easily bored, profoundly irked by convention and affectations, she could be witty, ironical and lively with friends, abrupt and awkward with strangers, her moods of euphoria rapidly giving way to frustration and the self-doubt that had plagued her during her childhood. Often, her dissatisfaction took the form of anger, with herself and especially with her husband.

The rumours that reached her about her own scandalous behaviour left her feeling desperate and inadequate or defiant and miserable. Adulterous encounters provided her with moments when she felt alive, and the risk of being found out only added excitement. On one telling occasion her maid, knowing that she was somewhere in the house but unable to find her, went to ask Ciano where she had gone. Together they searched the various rooms and finally discovered her crouched inside a cupboard, crying as she had as a very small child. Tears were private affairs. Bottling them up, as she had been forced to do from earliest childhood, sometimes proved simply too hard. And she was still just twenty-six.

Edda felt better when she travelled. Venice had become one of the centres of Fascist society and its summer seasons were especially glamorous. Edda met Barbara Hutton there on one of her visits and the two women had become friends. When the Duke and Duchess of Windsor came to Venice on their honeymoon, the Cianos were guests at a small dinner party given in their honour. Hutton had a cabin on the Lido, in front of the Hotel Excelsior, and she and Edda lay on the beach and went to the parties and balls held every night in the palaces along the Grand Canal. Few were as entertaining as the one given by Elsa Maxwell who had decided to liven up her annual masquerade party in the Palazzo Vendramin with sound effects created by bees hidden in hives behind heavy curtains, whose harmonious buzzing would serenade her guests. But one hive toppled over, the bees escaped and started chasing the guests, some of whom leapt into the Grand Canal.

Where Edda really liked to go was Capri. She had been enchanted by the island on her honeymoon and returned whenever she could get away from Rome. Most often she went on her own, but sometimes she brought Raimonda and Fabrizio and a nanny with her.

Though Capri had drawn visitors since the seventeenth century and been a stop on the Grand Tour in the eighteenth, it was not until the late 1800s that it became popular with holidaymakers, who were brought by steamer across the Bay of Naples to marvel at the Blue Grotto and the twin Faraglioni rocks and climb the long ribbon of Augustus's seven hundred stone steps up to Anacapri. Many years earlier, while on holiday in Lapland, the Swedish doctor and psychiatrist Axel Munthe read that cholera had reached Naples and he travelled south to volunteer to work in its plague hospital. On a visit to Capri in 1902 he bought the ruined chapel of San Michele, high on the peak of Anacapri, where he grew grapes and fought against the local habit of blinding quail so that they acted as lures to the cranes, roller birds, ring plovers and flycatchers on their winter migrant routes over the island.

Maxim Gorky, recently released from prison after the aborted 1905 Russian Revolution, had come to Capri with his mistress. He liked the climate and decided that it was congenial for writing and had enough money to subsidise the penniless Russian refugees who followed him. Other foreigners, many of them German and American, came as tourists, fell in love with the island and stayed. As Norman Douglas, who first visited Capri in the 1890s remarked, it was a place of 'lovable freaks of various nationalities' living contentedly on next to nothing in their whitewashed, flat-roofed little houses scattered around the hillside, where they formed 'cantankerous little cliques' discussing the vast quantities of cocaine and heroin consumed at legendary parties. The Caffè Morgano in the main square had become what Joseph Conrad called a hub of 'scandals, international, cosmopolitan and biblical', and Capri itself a 'sort of blue nightmare traversed by stinks and perfumes'. Since there were no proper roads, small donkeys, given the names of Roman emperors, ferried provisions.

Most of the foreigners had departed after the First World War broke out. Douglas and Gorky were among those who returned when it was over, and they were quickly followed by many others. Capri in 1920 was still a rocky, primitive outpost, very short of water and extremely poor, but its grand hotel, the Quisisana, once famous as a sanatorium for typhoid and rheumatism, had been bought by a Milanese company called SIPPIC, along with the local electricity plant and the funicular which carried visitors from the port of Marina Grande up to the main piazza. Afraid of the damage SIPPIC's plans for development of the island might cause, the locals convened a meeting to which they invited writers, artists and architects from all over Europe. One of these was the futurist Marinetti, later remembered for having pranced around under a full moon praising skyscrapers. The island was fast becoming attractive to the Fascists, and most importantly to a young hotel owner called Teodoro Pagano, who had taken part in the March on Rome and co-founded the first *fascio* on Capri.

In September 1924 Mussolini visited the island, arriving by flying boat at the Marina Grande to be met by Principe Ruffo di Calabria, a permanent resident of the Albergo Splendido. He was taken by funicular to the terrace overlooking the Bay of Naples and professed himself enchanted. Capri, just five miles in length, he decided, would be the showpiece for his new Fascist Italy, where foreigners could be brought to admire the scenery, eat well and see for themselves just how cultivated and peaceful the regime really was. Having lunched at the Quisisana, he asked Pagano: 'What does Capri need?' 'Duce, a port and water,' replied Pagano. 'I will see to it,' said Mussolini.

With generous funds sent from Rome, the islanders built a proper harbour, set up vast cisterns to catch water, paved roads, started a bus service and put up more houses and hotels. The traditional small industries of silk, coral and lime vanished. And, most importantly, they planted: eucalyptus, almond, cypress and oak, oleander, rosemary, myrtle and juniper, wisteria and bougainvillea. The Hotel Quisisana installed central heating, lifts and a small theatre, and the ballerina Anna Pavlova was spotted dancing on its tennis courts. Its barman, veteran of transatlantic liners, invented a cocktail he called Milano-Torino, containing Punt e Mes, Campari, lemon juice and soda water. Archeologists arrived to excavate Tiberius's house. Gracie Fields came, as did Diaghilev and Stravinsky, Colette and Marguerite Yourcenar, bringing her lover Grace Frick. On hot summer nights, the Faraglioni and the Blue Grotto were illuminated for people dining on their yachts.

When Axel Munthe published his *Story of San Michele* in 1929, it rapidly went into seven editions and though its attack on the hunting of migrant birds infuriated his neighbours it pleased Mussolini, who decided to ban hunting on the island. Munthe turned his property into a bird sanctuary; the islanders took to calling him Il Caprone, as insatiable in his sexual advances as a billy goat. By the end of the 1920s, Capri had eight hundred foreign residents and any number of summer visitors who arrived to a cloud of trailing geraniums, petunias and trellised roses or, if they waited until September, to canopies of white cyclamen. Maurice Chevalier declared Capri 'worthy to be French'. The island, wrote Compton Mackenzie's wife Faith, was haunted by 'ghosts of revelry . . . and the tumult of festivals, orgies and saturnalia'.

The Fascists, meanwhile, had taken over. A Neapolitan aristocrat, Marino Dusmet, a very short but pleasant-looking man, was made Fascist *podestà*, and Teodoro Pagano party secretary. Alberto Fassini, the Piedmontese director of SIPPIC and another 'Fascist of the first hour', bought land, took over hotels and built new houses. Pagano was a zealot. Whenever possible, he staged parades of blackshirts. Bells rang constantly summoning the islanders to public meetings. Dusmet, an equally obsessive martinet, rose before dawn to check that the streets were clean and the island orderly. Barefoot children were turned into neat little Balilla boys and mothers with large families were given prizes. Capri, said Marinetti, was indeed VI-RI-LIS-SI-MA, exceedingly virile, but also *Fascistissima*, exceedingly Fascist. Efforts were made to play down Tiberius's long sojourn on the island since, as the novelist Moravia put it, he had been 'the pre-eminent master of vice . . . with the most fantastical perversions'.

Pagano, as he soon found, had a collection of oddballs and eccentrics to deal with, not always easy to marshal into Fascist neatness. Among the post-war arrivals had come many foreigners in exile from their own countries' repressive sexual mores, some at least drawn by Capri's appearance in the underground *Le Troisième Sex*, a Baedeker for sexual adventurers. Germany, in particular, was accused of sending 'pederasts and masochistic painters'; England its 'undesirables'.

Dusmet's wife threw herself into a campaign of 'moral disinfectation'. A number of more egregious exhibitionists were thrown out and Compton Mackenzie's novel *Vestal Fire*, which touched on trisexual scandals on the island, was banned. Homosexuality was not a crime in Italy, even under the new penal code of 1930, but it was regarded as on a par with other perversions – fetishism, zoophilia, necrophilia. Things got so bad that a Roman carabiniere with flourishing whiskers called Giuseppe Dosi, hitherto head of a Squadra del Buon Costume which mopped up prostitutes and bordellos on the mainland, arrived to carry out an investigation into the 'merry men', 'sexual degenerates ... pederasts, homosexuals and "*sporcaccioni*", filthy people'.

Dosi made himself unpopular by becoming fixated on the idea that an Irish priest who lived in Capri, surprised in the act of assaulting a young girl, was in fact also responsible for a recent series of child rapes and murders in Rome. Dosi's behaviour became increasingly erratic and he was recalled to the capital, where he wrote a four-hundred-page book of steamy revelations, with a long list of rapes, abortions and affairs with minors, quickly suppressed by Bocchini, who had him put into a lunatic asylum. When Bocchini forwarded the report to the Palazzo Venezia, Mussolini wrote on it: 'Act decisively.' But foreigners were crucial to Capri's economy, and no more steps were taken. Women gave up wearing monocles and carrying cigarette holders and became more discreet. Dusmet was far too clever not to realise that the charm of the island lay precisely in its mix of arts, culture and permissiveness.

Fassini's real social coup had been to invite Edda and Ciano to spend their honeymoon in 1930 in the Hotel Quisisana, for Capri was everything that Edda most liked: unconventional, tolerant and amusing. It was the nearest she could find to Shanghai. Whenever she could get away, she travelled to the island by train to Naples, usually in a special coach, then took the steamer across, sometimes bringing with her Roman friends and often accompanied by Ghita

Carrell, a photographer known for her portraits of society women. Rather than join the others on boat expeditions, she preferred to dance until very late, play poker and go to bed as the sun was coming up.

In 1937, Fassini, whose son Munzio was a friend of Ciano's, gave her a plot of land high above Capri's second port, the Marina Piccola, used when the north-easterly winds put the Marina Grande out of action. Edda commissioned Dario Pater, a builder friend of her mother's and renowned for putting up cheap and flimsy housing in Africa, to design a house for her. His first effort was pronounced so insubstantial as to be unsafe and was replaced by a box-like structure with magnificent views across the Bay of Naples. Edda liked modernist Fascist architecture. Her large house, two storeys high, was painted blinding white inside and out. It had an extensive garden, a small vineyard and a terrace, where she placed a rocking chair. The islanders complained that it looked out of place among the odd mix of Pompeian and Moorish styles beloved by the Capresi, and complained even more when she succeeded in having the public road to her house blocked off and made private. But on the whole they welcomed their illustrious visitor and were discreet about her behaviour, remarking chiefly on her long thin figure, low accentless voice and aquiline nose. Giorgio Campione, who ran the Quisisana, indulged her every whim, including that of building a cage in the hotel gardens for a jaguar sent to her from Brazil. The animal was not popular. One morning it was found dead, poisoned by some meatballs.

Wishing her house to be bathed in bright light, Edda filled it with light-coloured wooden furniture, flowery chintz sofas, a parquet floor, tiles decorated with little fish, and plates in different colours. She installed electric blinds, never before seen in Italy other than in American films. There were big open fireplaces for winter and she covered the house in wisteria. Two enormous stone eagles, their wings outstretched, perched on columns by the entrance. Her bodyguard, a former carabiniere called Costanzo Strina, was known locally as '*u maiale*', the pig, because he had won a bet that he would not be able to eat a hundred ravioli at a single sitting. Rumours of Edda's extravagance, few of them true, spread around the island. She was said to have spent 3,000 lire each on a number of coral door handles encrusted with gold.

When Ciano came to Capri, it was usually for less than a day, travelling by flying boat from Ostia to the Marina Piccola in his white safari suit and exquisite white shoes. As he was rowed to shore, those watching shot their arms up into the air in the Fascist salute.

Edda was only one of many Fascist celebrities drawn to Capri's permissive shores. Balbo had been a frequent visitor until his exile to Libya, and Farinacci and Bottai both took holidays on the island. Though jazz had been banned in Germany as 'negro music', there was nowhere on Capri where someone was not playing, at all times of the night or day, ragtime, blues or swing. But since Fascism demanded that all things be Italian, Louis Armstrong was renamed Luigi Fortebraccio and Benny Goodman became Beniamino Buonuomo.

Prince Umberto and Maria José also had a house not far from Edda's, to which they came from the Palazzo Reale in Naples in their own midnight-blue motorboat. Malaparte, in defiance of all regulations and using money that Ciano had given him for his health, was building a 'sad, hard, severe' house jutting far out on a cliff, accessible only by foot, which had a roof large enough to bicycle on and a sitting room left almost entirely empty so that he could concentrate on the view from his plate-glass windows. It was red in colour and its surroundings were treeless. In keeping with his other self-referential possessions, the red *Casa Come Me* resembled a huge brick dropped on to a reef.

In the wake of the fashionable Fascists came the Nazis, who were received by Edda in the port. Goering was an early visitor, greeted by a crowd on the jetty raising their arms and shouting 'Heil Hitler'. It was the first time the swastika was seen on the island. He came again with Emmy to a suite in the Hotel Quisisana, and had the misfortune to be bitten on the nose by a pet monkey belonging to one of the other guests. The Goerings spent lavishly in Capri's new boutiques. For a moment it seemed as if they might buy Axel Munthe's Villa San Michele, though rumour had it that Goering was acting as a front for Hitler who, fascinated by astrology and the Holy Grail, had decided that Anacapri might possess magic astral powers. Hess, Goebbels and his wife Magda, and Hans Frank all came, often in motorboats laid on by the Prefecture in Naples. A party of Hitler Youth swam out to the grottoes, showing off their muscly bodies.

Often, Edda would cross paths with Raimonda and Fabrizio as she emerged from her bed and they returned from the beach for lunch, and the children would observe her closely to gauge her mood. When black and heavy, their mother looked ugly and bony and fought with the governess. Edda mixed little with the locals, discouraged familiarity, refused to join the island's intellectuals when they went off with donkeys to picnic, and spent a lot of time playing solitaire with a pack of cards brought back from Shanghai. She seldom left the house without dark glasses. But she did make friends with one of Capri's more eccentric inhabitants, a jeweller called Pietro Capriano, known as Chantecler – from Edmond Rostand's play about a rooster – who sported bright red trousers and silk shirts in many colours and sunbathed naked. Capriano was a prankster, and only Edda's intervention saved him from being deported after he dropped a firecracker at Prince Umberto's feet.

It was not surprising, then, that Capri, a nest of eccentrics and Fascists at play, was also a nest of spies. Phones were tapped, people were followed, letters steamed open. Chief among Bocchini's men was the party secretary, Pagano – though OVRA spied on him, too – but there were many others among the waiters, the porters and even among the visitors. They spied on Capriano, accounts of whose excesses landed on Mussolini's desk in Rome, who finally ordered that the jeweller be sent away from the island whenever Edda was in residence. They spied on Edda, falling over themselves to establish whether it was really true that she swam naked from the rocks in the moonlight, slept with her male guests and attended parties at which the guests dressed up as wild animals and had orgies worthy of the Romans. And they spied on the shady Madame Carmen, a medium whom Edda made the mistake of confiding in and who pestered her constantly for introductions and favours.

Of the many things Edda was accused of, she may have been guilty of no more than difficulty in paying her poker debts. But as she said later, by now much of Fascist Italy, feeding avidly on rumours that Bocchini was somehow unable to quash, believed that she had slept with some forty thousand men, which would have made Madame de Pompadour, Ninon de Lenclos and Madame de Maintenon look in comparison like ingénues or nuns.

*

There was by the late 1930s something increasingly desperate, almost feverish, in the efforts to promote and extol Fascism. It was to be found in the excesses of the pedantic and absurd Starace, in his relentless efforts to rid Italian of foreign words – picnic had become '*picche nicche*' – and in his campaign to make people use '*Voi*' rather than '*Lei*' (too feminine). Because there had never been much original thought behind the 'doctrine of Fascism' and the Fascists had always been clearer about what they were against rather than what they were for, a jumble of campaigns – against very thin women ('*la donna crisi*'), liberals, socialists, trade unionists, unmasculine men – trickled out of the MinCulPop to be given flesh and shape in the pro-regime papers.

Prohibitions on mentioning Mussolini's age or ill-health were becoming draconian, and photographs of the Duce, the 'prince of youth', were carefully inspected and doctored before publication; those used were martial and often equestrian to evoke victorious Roman consuls. LUCE's documentaries regularly featured Mussolini addressing 'oceanic' crowds. The Duce was Italy's leading film star. As he said himself, 'the idea of trying to separate Mussolini from Fascism, or Fascism from Mussolini, is the most useless, the most grotesque, the most ridiculous thing that can ever be imagined'. Edda, his female shadow, was photographed whenever she allowed herself to be seen. That she shunned the limelight only fed stories about her hidden powers.

Rachele and Mussolini with grandchildren

The emperor Augustus's tomb in the centre of Rome, finally excavated and the area around it cleared of houses, was celebrated by an Augustan Exhibition of Romanità, and Mussolini was presented with a live eagle as a sign that imperial tradition had passed the baton to Fascism. The building of EUR, the Esposizione Universale Romano, on the road to Ostia, was underway. This new town of granite, marble and travertine, with arches and columns was designed to become a showplace of 'grandiosity and monumentalism'. Portrayed as both exceptional and yet also very human, the 'spiritual father' of the new Italy, Mussolini was omniscient and could right all wrongs. 'Where is the Duce?' asked *Il Corriere della Sera*. 'He is everywhere ... Can't you feel that he is listening to you?' Fifty people worked in the secretariat in the Palazzo Venezia answering the many thousands of letters addressed to him, many of them now expressing dissatisfaction with party bureaucracy, but seldom towards Mussolini personally, who was deemed to be somehow above it all.

Something of this frenetic desire to make Italians behave as proper Fascists was to be found in the films being made in Rome's newly opened Cinecittà. As Mussolini had been saying for years, film was '*l'arma più forte*', the strongest weapon of the regime, and some of Edda's best memories of the Villa Torlonia were the nightly film shows. At the beginning of the Fascist era, Italy's film industry had been in disarray. Though the country had been an early pioneer of silent films, lack of foreign markets, spiralling production costs and above all a failure of inventiveness had meant that the enormous appetite of Italians for cinema was fed by Hollywood. Audiences loved Charlie Chaplin, Mae West and Cary Grant, admired pencil moustaches and permed hair and plucked eyebrows, and they turned their backs on the pythons, witches, crocodiles and virgins shot for an Italian adventure film called *Siliva Zulu*. To counter the influence of the free, feisty American woman, the MinCulPop waged a constant battle to promote the florid, fecund *donna-madre*. What all the *gerarchi* agreed was that film, while eschewing propaganda, should convey a reassuring picture of Italian life, educated and cultured, in which the deserts of Africa had been transformed into the garden of Eden, and the countryside made the true repository of Italian values. '*Strapaese*', the glorifying of the homeland, would provide a bulwark against the invasion of foreign ways.

Then in 1934 a series of protectionist measures was introduced to limit foreign, and particularly American, imports into Italy. A genuinely radical school of experimental cinematography was established, and a number of film magazines and journals published. Private and state funds were granted to producers and distributors and a corporation was set up, bringing together film-makers, theatre owners, musicians and members of LUCE. Some of the impetus behind these moves came from twenty-two-year-old Vittorio Mussolini, who persuaded his father to let him go to the United States for discussions with Hal Roach, the producer of Mussolini's much-loved *Laurel and Hardy*. Vittorio was invited to tea at the White House, and came back saying that President Roosevelt had asked him to propose a meeting between Mussolini and himself in neutral waters in the middle of the Atlantic. The plan came to nothing, and Vittorio's dreams of ties with the Americans were soon crushed by the rivalrous Italian producers.

In September 1935, a fire destroyed the old Cines studios in Porta San Giovanni. The first stones were laid for Cinecittà on the Via Tuscolana, built in record time by fifteen hundred workmen, on the model of Hollywood. Posters showed a buxom woman, strong, sensual, energetic and beckoning. Prophetically, as the newspapers were quick to report, the day that Mussolini arrived for the official opening, 28 April 1937, gusts of strong wind and hail raged until his cortège swept up, when the Duce was bathed in sunlight.

Because Mussolini personally hated gangster films, comedies were favoured. A '*fascistizzazione sottile*', a subtle kind of pressure over themes and morality, was imposed. Drugs, orgies, relations between white and black people were vetoed. Within these constraints, however, the Italian film industry flourished. Under the rubric of '*telefoni bianchi*' – named after the boudoirs in which so many were set, with white as the symbol of modern chic – romantic comedies, sentimental and swashbuckling, celebrated femmes fatales, ingénues, honest fathers, sympathetic rogues, impeccably turned-out leading men and noble self-sacrificing mothers. And, in the scramble to find substitutes for Claudette Colbert and Bette Davis, they made a star out of the blue-eyed, small-waisted Assia

Noris, whose father was a count and who played middle-class fiancées, secretaries, nannies and shopgirls in need of protectors, and cast the homely, round-faced Maria Denis, with her pert nose and porcelain complexion, as the girl who stayed at home, helped her mother and played the piano. The sultry Luisa Manfrini, who took the name Ferida, had high cheekbones and long eyelashes and specialised in being the 'one real woman in a world of baby dolls', who, though fiery, was often wronged. Ferida's later lover, Osvaldo Valenti, son of a Sicilian baron, a restless womaniser and coke addict but possessed of elegant, clean looks and gentlemanly manners, made his name portraying virile, devious, highly strung, cruel villains. A Coppa Mussolini was set up, to rival the Oscars.

Vast sums of money were spent on locations: for an epic about Italian colonisation called *Abuna Messias*, eleven thousand men and four thousand horses were employed for a battle scene. And alongside these films, a new cinema sub-genre took shape, that of '*fotoromanzi*', magazines with stills taken from movies or in specially shot sequences with speech in bubbles as in comic strips. Their editors were desperate for stories about the starry Cianos. Any glimpse of Edda provided valuable photographs; the fact that she was often glowering made little difference.

The Italians loved the new movies just as they loved the whole panoply of Fascist theatre. In a single year, 310 million tickets were sold. The *gerarchi*, for their part, loved the starlets, courted them, made love to them, saw in their successes mirrors to their own. Cinecittà became a goldmine for Bocchini's spies, bit-part actors supplementing their incomes with regular reports on 'agents of corruption', wild decadent parties and anti-Fascist gossip. Starace himself was reported to be a 'big consumer of ballerinas'. But the control of public culture, whether in film, theatre or books, never reached the levels of Nazi Germany, where by 1937 Goebbels had banned hundreds of books, plays, films and paintings along with their creators. In Italy, gossip, cartoons and funny stories continued to circulate unpunished, providing a safety valve in a regime intent on portraying itself as powerful, modern, and free of vice, crime, poverty, broken homes and unemployment, yet at the same humorously conscious of human frailties.

Soon after his return from Ethiopia, Vittorio met a Milanese girl, Orsola Buvoli, and in February 1937, though he was not yet twenty-one, they married, like Edda and Ciano, in the church of San Giuseppe. Photographs show Ciano with a raffish grin, Rachele in a fur coat, her bosom drooping and Edda with her glaring eyes. But there was no grand reception in the Villa Torlonia, Rachele declaring that she would never go through that ordeal again. There were fewer extravagant presents, though Franco sent a gold cigarette case. Bruno, too, soon married, once again in San Giuseppe; his bride was Gina Ruberti, the daughter of an inspector with the Ministry of Education. OVRA spies reported that her family had 'exceedingly elevated Fascist feelings'. Starace presented Bruno with a newly invented Hoover. Both young men were involved in scrapes, though all were quickly hushed up. Bruno killed an elderly woman in a car crash, and also had an affair that led to a pregnancy. Vittorio had a summer romance with a married woman at Riccione. Though Mussolini complained that the Villa Torlonia was emptying of its life and did not want to see them go, the two young men and their wives moved into flats in central Rome. Sunday lunches, attended by the entire family, were not occasions that could be missed, not even by the often impatient and reluctant Edda.

In 1936, when Ciano was first appointed Foreign Minister, Mussolini was still playing with the idea of re-establishing a friendship with Britain, fractured by the Ethiopian war, and hoping to act as a balancing power in Europe. But Germany had been quick to recognise Italy as an empire, and Nazi power was obviously growing. On 1 November 1936 in Milan's Piazza del Duomo, Mussolini had first used the phrase that Rome and Berlin represented an 'axis', around which all European states 'that desire peace can revolve'. He was angered when the British invited Haile Selassie to the coronation of George VI in May 1937, and when the British and French signed an agreement to protect merchant ships in the Mediterranean from Italian submarines which, they claimed, had been 'conducting acts of piracy'. Ciano told Vittorio's friend Zangrandi that France and Britain were 'feeble, over-mature like rotten fruit and bladders of lard'.

Hitler, meanwhile, had been steadily courting Mussolini, playing up to Edda and Ciano and sending emissaries to Rome with invitations to Mussolini to pay a state visit to Germany. The

German embassy in Rome had been instructed to do all it could to exacerbate relations between Rome and London and to keep repeating that what Germany really wanted was to adopt many of the Fascist regime's ideas.

Mussolini demanded that he would not be forced to wear formal evening dress (in which he felt he did not look his best), and that he would be given the opportunity to meet ordinary Germans – the better to demonstrate his oratorial skill with crowds. The visit was set for 24 September 1937.

Meticulous care on both sides went into the preparations. Mussolini and Ciano arrived in Munich in their private train in gold and silver uniforms specially designed for the occasion and accompanied by a select group of Italy's most prestigious journalists. 'We must,' noted Ciano, 'look more Prussian than the Prussians.' No king had ever been received with such pomp and glory. Hitler and a vast entourage were waiting in the festooned and garlanded central station, also in uniform. Though the two dictators had met in Venice in 1934, this was the moment when their two nations and their two 'revolutions' really came face to face. For the assembled journalists, the encounter assumed enormous significance. A vast parade through the heart of Munich was followed by a display of naval manoeuvres in the Baltic Sea and a tour of factories in Essen. But it was Berlin that left both Mussolini and Ciano dazzled by German might.

As Mussolini's train approached the Heerstrasse station, Hitler's own train drew level on the adjoining track and for a quarter of an hour the two trains ran along, side by side, the two dictators standing at the windows and waving – an operation that had been exhaustively practised beforehand – until Hitler's pulled ahead so that he could be on the platform to greet Mussolini formally. The station had been upholstered in shining white silk and a double line of busts of Roman emperors laid out, with the clear suggestion that Mussolini was their successor. Steel-helmeted soldiers and immense cheering crowds lined the roads through Charlottenberg, the Tiergarten and the Unter den Linden, where German and Italian flags flew, the German eagle entwined with the Italian axe and fasces. On the rooftops crouched SS men with machine guns. The high point came the following evening when, after a parade of thirty-six thousand soldiers, a million people gathered in the

Olympia Stadium to hear Mussolini and Hitler speak, their words broadcast all over Germany and Italy. 'The strength of our two Nations,' declared Hitler, 'is the strongest guarantee for the preservation of a civilised Europe.' Though Mussolini's reply was partially drowned by a sudden downpour and booming thunderclaps, he too spoke of Italy and Germany being 'the greatest and most genuine democracies'.

A note of exaltation, almost religious fervour, crept into the journalists' reports. There was much talk of a sacred and heroic occasion and a 'tumultuous movement of the multitude'. Berliners were heard to describe Mussolini as 'bronzed, athletic and vivacious' with a 'radiant smile'. *Il Giornale d'Italia* noted that Mussolini had 'dominated the cheering multitude as a helmsman dominates the waves'. It was left to the irreverent Martha Dodd to remark that Mussolini's wild gesticulating and massive jaw made him look like 'a mad bulldog, both ridiculous and maddening'.

The visit had been choreographed to impress, and impress it did. Though Mussolini grumbled that Goering had allowed his pet lion to jump on him, and that Goering himself was 'flashy and pretentious', he came home stunned by the grandeur, the vast obedient crowds, the immaculately turned out and perfectly rehearsed parades. He had complained to Rachele that Italian soldiers marched as if they were carrying a suitcase on their way to catch a train, and now ordered his army to adopt the goose step, calling it the *'passo romano'* because, as he pointed out, the sacred Capitoline geese had saved Rome from the Gauls and stood in glory somewhere between the eagle and the she-wolf.

More importantly, on 6 November 1937, convinced by what he had seen of German might, he signed the Anti-Comintern Pact with Hitler. And on 11 December he took Italy out of the League of Nations. Italy, he said, would stand 'side by side' with Germany against Bolshevism. As he told the crowds, she would march with her new friend 'to the last', which came as something of a surprise to the Italians, told to think until now of the Fascist revolution as clean and salutary, and the Nazis as violent and uncouth and Hitler as a paranoid criminal. Ciano remarked that he had never seen Mussolini so relieved at not being isolated any longer, or so happy.

12

Death comes to Rome

Mussolini learnt that Edda was pregnant again when he saw her smoking at a reception, and went over to remonstrate with her, as he invariably did when he caught her with a cigarette. She was an adult, she told him, and she was having a baby, and she could do as she liked.

Marzio was born in the Via Angelo Secchi on 18 December 1937, three weeks after Italy signed a Tripartite deal with Germany and Japan. Ciano woke Fabrizio and Raimonda to tell them that they had a brother, with blue eyes and fair hair. Telegrams of congratulation arrived from Hitler, Goering, Hess, Goebbels and the entire Italian royal family. In the diary that he had started keeping soon after being appointed Foreign Minister, Ciano noted that Edda had chosen the name and that he liked its suitably political and prophetic war-like overtones. Marzio quickly became Mowgli, the boy cub in Kipling's *Jungle Book*. Dindina had been 'the child of error', Mowgli was to be the 'child of reason', the symbol of a stage-managed new closeness between Edda and her husband. Fabrizio would later say that the first time he realised that he and his brother and sister were not like other children was when one day his driver let him take the wheel on the way to school. He was seven and so small that it looked as if the car were driving itself. When they were stopped by a policeman and he saw who it was, he waved them on, halting the traffic for him.

As parents, the Cianos had fallen into a pattern. Ciano was the disciplinarian and, much like his father, was tough with his son, resorting to slaps which the little boy received stoically. He was gentler with Dindina, but she too was slapped when she angrily attacked Ciano for punishing her brother. Edda took the role of storyteller, the provider of fun and mischief, and the children called her by her Christian name, unusual for the time and a mark of the distance between herself and them. Nannies were never far away. There is little evidence that she ever took them on cultural outings. It was on Ciano's insistence that they never witnessed their parents' rows, some of which touched on Ciano's mother Carolina, who was known to tell friends that her daughter-in-law had forty thousand lovers. Either she locked herself away and read American novels, Carolina complained, or 'she takes off with the first man to hand'. When Edda travelled, she did not always remember to send the children postcards, though on one occasion, she planned to bring them home a charming calf that had taken her fancy. 'Do not want,' Ciano cabled her, 'to come home to find veal on my sofa.' But he was unable to stop her from returning with a small leopard and two boa constrictors. Animals interested Edda in ways that human beings seldom did.

Edda with Fabizio, Raimonda and Marzio

The fiction of the Cianos' new-found contentment was necessary. All Rome knew and gossiped about Ciano's infidelities and his many dalliances with society women, whom he entertained with stories about the politicians and diplomats he met, indiscretions quickly repeated back to Mussolini. These went to the Germans, too, who had learnt how to flatter him, while placing seductive women in his entourage, to act as spies. As reported back to Berlin, Ciano had referred to Hitler as a 'new Parsifal' and Goebbels as a 'cripple' out of a fourth-rate Nibelung legend. Edda, conscious of the dangers of these indiscretions, warned him to remember that he was a Minister of State, entrusted with secrets, and not to indulge in 'pillow talk'.

Gossip and envy swirled around those excluded from the Petit Trianon and the minor nobility and Fascist *gerarchi* who were not invited to the grander occasions took their revenge in venomous talk. Edda's own carefree manners, they said, were a corrupting influence on younger women. As one resentfully put it, the Cianos regarded the world as a vast hunting ground for pleasure and privilege, but only very few people were allowed to hunt there.

Elisabetta Cerruti, the Hungarian wife of Italy's former ambassador to Berlin, now somewhat out of favour, left a cold portrait of Edda at the time.* There was, she wrote, 'no convention on which she does not wage war' and 'she made a sport of behaving inconsiderately to elderly dignified people'. Capable of being charming and intelligent when she wished, 'her conversation was completely without wit', and the vehemence with which she dismissed France and Britain was proof that she had 'neither style nor sense of humour, only bitter sarcasm'. With her father's steady gaze and throaty voice, she was 'extremely authoritative'. But then Signora Cerruti had never liked Edda. Others, such as George Nelson Page, the Italo-American journalist now head of the inspectorate for television and radio in the MinCulPop, who did like her, later remembered small dinner parties in the Via Secchi which were lively and fun. The Duchessa di Sermoneta, the other keen and often malicious observer of Roman society in the 1930s, noted that both Ciano and Edda were at their best in their

* Martha Dodd, the American journalist in Germany, humorously said of the vast, paunchy ambassador that sparring with him would have been 'like licking an elephant's tail'.

own house, even though it was ugly and uncomfortable, and Edda made them play childish games.

Edda had returned to pay further visits to Germany and she remained friendly with Magda Goebbels, giving dinners for the senior Nazis when they came to Rome. Goering came in search of art, stayed at the Excelsior and went about dressed in white, with his Marshal's baton. His wife Emmy was planning to call her new baby Edda. Slowly waking to the realisation that the Nazis were not the charming hosts of her first encounters, but rather harsh and clear-eyed about what they wanted, some of Edda's own warmth towards them was fading. She noted that Goering was in fact the 'first parrot of Germany', faithfully repeating everything that Hitler said, and she had taken strongly against Ribbentrop, soon to be made Foreign Minister, saying that he made her 'nauseous'. From the first, Ciano and Ribbentrop despised each other, and even von Bismarck, Ciano's friend and the German counsellor in Rome, spoke of the about-to-be Foreign Minister as 'such an imbecile that he is a miracle of nature'.

Foreign newspapers made scabrous insinuations about Edda's visits to Germany, suggesting that she was a 'Messalina' who went in order to have affairs with Hitler's 'young, robust, tall, handsome and blond' bodyguards, and that she was the sort of woman who would not shy away from sleeping with either her father or her sons. To these stories, as to all the other accounts of the way she sought out solitary spots in which to pursue her nefarious adventures, Edda responded with exasperation and sourness. She knew how little she was liked, but refused to ingratiate herself by smiling on public occasions. She also realised that her dislike of compromise and bouts of exuberance made her seem more decisive, more sure of herself, than in fact she was.

One of Mussolini's mistakes had been to believe that Ciano was, and always would be, entirely loyal and uncritical towards him. Though suitably reverential and timid in the presence of his father-in-law, saying 'the truth is that one works for only one reason – to please him', Ciano was becoming distinctly more uncertain about Mussolini's foreign policy. And as the Duce became progressively more closed in and averse to all contradiction, so Ciano had no language with which to challenge him. A reciprocal unease was building up, a small shadow spreading between them, with Ciano ever more frustrated and Mussolini ever more isolated, and more convinced of his own exceptionalism. And as Mussolini was well aware through his spies, Ciano was setting his sights on succeeding him, and letting it be known to his friends that he regarded himself as his heir, his Dauphin. If at heart little interested in the ideology of Fascism, Ciano nevertheless saw himself as one of the new aristocrats of power; and in power he was deeply interested.

Ciano was also having to weather a wave of public dislike and disapproval. In June 1937, Carlo and Nello Rosselli, two of the leading Italian anti-Fascists, had been murdered in Normandy and though no immediate irrefutable evidence was produced of Ciano's involvement, it was widely suspected that he had ordered the killings. Observing his impulsiveness and lack of tact, his increasing ambition and sense of his own worth, Nelson Page put at least some of the blame on Dino Alfieri, Ciano's closest friend and now Minister at the MinCulPop, a man as cold and caustic as Ciano was ingenuous and credulous.

Nor was Ciano doing anything to make himself admired by the foreign diplomats in Rome, who were astonished by his arrogance and indiscretions. Jean-Paul Garnier, the first secretary in the French embassy, was only one of those who remarked on Ciano's way of 'aping his father-in-law' with his chin jutted out and his studied pronouncements. Joseph P. Kennedy, the US Ambassador to London, returned from a trip to Rome infuriated by the Foreign Minister's inability to concentrate on world affairs during a dinner, so taken was he by the pretty young women invited for his benefit. He had never come across, he said, a 'more conceited or pompous ass'.

None of this was lost on Mussolini, to whom Bocchini continued to feed daily briefings on the transgressions of his ministers. From anonymous letters that came directly to the Palazzo Venezia, he knew perfectly well that Ciano's antics were harming not only the family but also the image of the regime itself, and that Edda's abrupt and often graceless ways were making her enemies. One spoke of 'your son-in-law . . . a dickhead who makes the entire nation vomit . . . cuckolded, promoted, decorated' only through nepotism, while his wife was nothing but a tart. 'Our patience,' the anonymous correspondent warned, 'has its limits. Take care. You and him. But him first.' Have you no shame, asked another, to be the father of a daughter who is bringing 'dishonour to Italian women'? In OVRA's reports were many references to Edda's supposed use of alcohol and drugs, to a hoard of money hidden away in Brazil, and to the jewellery and gold she took abroad with her on her travels to deposit in foreign banks.

From an OVRA spy in Paris came a rumour that there were plans to 'eliminate' Edda by the extremist members of the French Front Populaire who considered Edda not just 'very intelligent' but the real architect of Italy's growing closeness to Germany. This was certainly an exaggeration, though her apparent friendliness towards the senior Nazis had been widely reported. When spy number 353 investigated further, he found the claim to be baseless. Nevertheless, Bocchini judged the threat 'extremely serious' and ordered extra security for the family. Ciano, on hearing the rumour, asked whether he, too, was on the hit list of possible people to assassinate and was very taken aback when word came that he was not considered important enough. Edda paid no heed, but it was a measure of how seriously she was perceived in the world of international politics.

Mussolini read the letters and the reports about his daughter's misdoings, but seems to have repeated little or nothing to Edda, instead telling a friend: 'Much is said, perhaps too much, about Edda's influence on me. She lives by her instincts. I love her, very much. I listen to her as I listen to everyone. But I take my decisions on my own.' They remained close, however, exchanging messages and telegrams on all occasions. 'Magnificent. You could not have been more "*Mussoliniano*" or the people more enthusiastic or more politically aware,' Edda cabled him after a speech in Genoa in the spring of 1938. 'I embrace you.' Mussolini had put her in charge of dealing with the requests – for pensions, holidays, medical help – that reached his desk every day. In the year 1937 alone, she paid out just over 12 million lire.

Deep in his romantic entanglement with Claretta Petacci, Mussolini himself was in any case poorly placed to lecture Edda. When their affair began, he was at the height of his power and prestige. He had given Italy an empire and he was revered, especially by infatuated women and young girls. It would later be thought that he had as many as nine illegitimate children by eight different women, with most of whom he remained on good terms, though their affairs were usually marked by casual, hasty, quickly bored sex, and the absence of all small talk or tenderness.

With Claretta, however, particularly in the early days, he was kind, loving, almost paternal. She was, he told her, 'my soul, my spring, my youth'. Wire taps on Claretta's phone revealed a new tone in his voice, solicitous and gentle, causing one of the older OVRA spies to exclaim: 'That woman will be the ruin of Mussolini and of Italy!' A direct line had been installed in her house, not to be used by the rest of her family. On a single day in 1938 he was recorded as having phoned her thirteen times.

Claretta's fiancé, Riccardo Federici, who had become her husband in the summer of 1934, had been posted to Africa and later to Tokyo as an air attaché. According to one of the rumours swirling around Rome, Mussolini had then formally asked Claretta's mother Giuseppina – an overbearing woman described by a spy as 'somewhere between a boxer and a caryatid' – whether he might make love to her daughter. Permission having been granted, a pattern was established. Claretta woke late, had breakfast in bed, curled her hair, made herself up with great care and waited for Mussolini's call. Most afternoons she arrived at a side entrance to the Palazzo Venezia, either in the chauffeur-driven family car or in the side car of a motorcycle, with a dust coat over her dress. She was shown to the frescoed Sala dello Zodiaco, with its blue and gold ceiling, two armchairs, a gramophone and a bathroom, and settled down to wait, sometimes painting delicate little pictures of her dreams. When Mussolini was kept by urgent matters, the wait might last for several hours, during which she made herself tea, furtively smoked a forbidden cigarette, touched up her make-up, looked through old photographs and tried on clothes she left there. As someone remarked after her death, Claretta's life had been one 'long wait'.

When Mussolini arrived, she did everything she could to distract and please him, noting later in her diary '*Si*' to record their lovemaking, and also where and when it took place. 'Like a madman,' she wrote one day. 'Like a wounded beast, it is divine.' Once he bit her, and she complained that he had severely injured one ear. Most often, the entries were ecstatic. He told her about his life, his family, his past; she listened. Edda's name came up frequently, Mussolini telling Claretta how intractable she was, how unsuited to 'worthy employment' and how much he disliked the Prussian nanny employed to tame his grandchildren. Edda, he said, was a 'really difficult woman, strange. But I dominate her.' He made it clear that, of his two daughters, Edda was the one he really loved and felt closest to.

Claretta, pretty if a little heavy, her hair cut fashionably short and curly, her blue eyes very bright and her wrists and fingers covered in bracelets and rings, was a woman you could not fail to notice. She was romantic, sensual and very feminine. Their affair was riven by fights and jealousy, Claretta deeply suspicious of other mistresses, Mussolini tormented by her possible infidelity. For a brief moment, she became infatuated with a rival suitor, a somewhat sad figure called Luciano Antonelli, who lived off jobs in bars and restaurants. Unfortunately, Giuseppina told her neighbour, who happened to be an OVRA spy, about the affair. The news travelled quickly to Mussolini, who summoned Giuseppina and threatened her. What became known as '*il caso Antonelli*' lasted a few weeks, with rows and tender scenes of making-up between Mussolini and Claretta, and it was followed by a period of passionate outpourings on his part. He and Claretta began to talk of finding her a house away from prying eyes, easily reachable by him. Sometimes they met at Ostia, where she would be rowed out to an agreed spot, and there picked up by Mussolini in a speed boat, after which they would lie in the sun and sip cognac. Mussolini always returned to the Villa Torlonia for dinner. Claretta, having been driven home, ate, then sat down to write to him on pink paper, added to her diary, and waited for a last, late, call. In his replies, Mussolini signed himself 'Ben'. It was to Claretta that Mussolini declared that the British were 'piggish' people, egotistic, drunk and brainless, and 'cretins' just like the French.

How much Rachele, with her own network of spies, knew about Claretta has never been established. Certainly, she made gnomic remarks about her husband. 'Just to have him with me,' she once said, 'I would accept to be blindfolded.' And to an interfering neighbour, who warned her to keep a closer eye on Mussolini, she replied: 'He's a good-looking man, and thank God not an "*invertito*" like so many of you.'

*

All through the winter of 1937 it was clear that Hitler had his sights on Austria. Mussolini met the Austrian Chancellor Kurt von Schuschnigg at La Rocca delle Caminate and told him that for all Italy and Austria's ancient differences, his support for Austria remained 'unchanged'. Schuschnigg, desperate to avoid an invasion, agreed to appoint an Austrian Nazi, Seyss-Inquart, as Minister of Interior, and announced that he would hold a plebiscite. Goering, on a visit to Rome, assured Mussolini that Germany would make no military move without first discussing it with Italy.

On 12 March 1938 German forces marched into Austria and declared it to be part of the German Reich. Mussolini received the news only as they crossed the border. A long placatory letter from Hitler, with protestations of lifelong friendship, did little to reassure him. But Mussolini decided not to react, only saying to Ciano in private that he feared that Czechoslovakia would be next. And the dangers of having a strong Germany expanding its borders to the Alto Adige, even if a supposed ally, was not lost on anyone.

Germany's invasion of Austria, the Anschluss, was, however, a severe blow. Mussolini had long thought it inevitable, but he had not seen it coming so soon, and now he had fallen into Hitler's net. He had hoped to make an accord with the British before it happened, to set up a Pact of Four which would ensure a long period of peace for Europe. Eden, now British Foreign Secretary and never willing to put any faith in the Italians, believed Mussolini and Ciano to be fundamentally irrational and vacillating. Saying that he would not deal with dictators, he had stalled over negotiations on the withdrawal of Italian troops from Spain and held back from recognising Italy as an empire. When talks about coming to an arrangement with Italy were conducted behind his back, Eden resigned. The news reached the Palazzo Colonna in Rome, and the dinner party taking place cheered. Lord Halifax, who replaced him, was more conciliatory. Grandi, as Ambassador in London and very keen to promote friendship between Italy and Britain, had gone to great lengths – beyond his orders – to portray the Italians as reasonable, and Chamberlain was moving towards a formula whereby Italy would remove her soldiers from Spain 'as soon as the civil war ends', and that recognition of the Italian empire would follow. An Anglo-Italian agreement was signed on 16 April 1938, regulating reciprocal interests in the Mediterranean, Africa and Asia. It provoked a request from France for negotiations. 'These dictators,' wrote Chamberlain to Sir Robert Vansittart, Under-secretary at the Foreign Office, 'are men of moods. They have to be caught at the right time.'

Until the end of 1937, Hitler had not particularly pushed for a military alliance with Italy, maintaining that his own forces were sufficient and remaining sceptical about Italian competence. Now, worried that the Anschluss might drive Italy towards a closer alliance with Britain and France, he began to make overtures. The Anschluss had not gone down well with the Italian public and Mussolini had difficulty in explaining it to parliament. But he was still not prepared to disengage from Berlin and clung to a recent report from an OVRA spy stating that Hitler showed no signs of wishing for war: he wanted a greater Germany and believed that he could achieve it by other means. When the British ambassador to Rome, Lord Perth, complained to Ciano about continuing Italian air raids in Spain, Mussolini observed that it made a change to be perceived not as a guitar player, but rather as a warrior.

Hitler's long-planned return visit to Rome was the grandest and most choreographed event to take place in Italy between the wars, a display of ostentation and magnificence that Mussolini intended

Goering, Mussolini, Ciano, Edda behind

to equal, if not outshine, that of his own visit to Germany. On 2 May 1938, three special trains, carrying five hundred people, including half the German government, most of the party leaders, prominent journalists and the wives of ministers, set out from Berlin for what Paul Schmidt, Hitler's interpreter, later called the 'invasion of Italy'. Frau Ribbentrop, who considered herself the first lady of the Reich, had requested that she be presented to the Italian royal family and asked Edda to show her how to curtsey. At the Brenner station on the Italian border, the platform had been carpeted, and formations of the Italian army and the Fascist Party were lined up to greet the Germans.

The trains reached Rome in the evening to find the King, Mussolini and their entourages waiting to meet them at Ostiense station, completely rebuilt for the occasion. Houses along the railway line had been repainted and the more dilapidated knocked down. A fleet of horse-drawn carriages, with Hitler and the King leading the way, processed past illuminated fountains, through the Arch of Constantine, and alongside the Colosseum, flood-lit in red so that it appeared to be on fire. On either side of the streets, which were filled with cheering crowds, flames flickered in ancient Roman amphoras, lighting up the ruins. Elisabetta Cerruti, watching from a balcony, noted that 'Death has entered our beautiful capital'.

A week of festivities followed. Under a cloudless sky, the sea dark and green, a naval parade of battleships, destroyers and cruisers was laid on in the Bay of Naples, where a hundred submarines dived simultaneously to resurface a few minutes later with perfect precision to fire their guns. As the battleship carrying Hitler passed Capri, Tiberius's villa was pointed out to him. He stared at it in silence. Care had been taken that all children presented to him were blond and blue eyed.

A gala dinner was held in the Sala dei Corazzieri in the Quirinale, with its frescoed friezes and Flemish tapestries, lit by candelabra and filled with a profusion of roses. It was made somewhat awkward by Hitler's unmistakable look of scorn as he surveyed the King and the elegant and bejewelled courtiers, and his obvious preference for Mussolini's company. When asked whether he would like to review the troops on horseback, according to Italian tradition, he replied that he hated horses. Rome's gossips put it about that before going to bed, he had asked for a woman – explained away by Ciano as a request for a maid to remake his bed – and that he had complained that the Quirinale reminded him of the catacombs. Hitler said later that he had found staying in the palace disagreeable and was furious when the footmen whisked away a plate of food that he was enjoying. Nor was he pleased to discover that the Vatican Museum was closed, and that the Pope had withdrawn to Castel Gandolfo to 'breathe the better air', having declared in a recent encyclical, 'anti-Semitism is inadmissible; we are all spiritually Semites'. The swastika, Pope Pius XI had observed, was a 'cross that is the enemy of the cross of Christ'.

The ceaseless round of engagements ended with a sumptuous, theatrical banquet in the Palazzo Venezia. The champagne flowed. Edda and Ciano led the line of dignitaries presented to Hitler, but Nelson Page noted that his expression remained somewhat mad and distracted. *Paris Match* devoted a cover story to the visit and was not the only paper to observe that Edda – though still only twenty-eight – was certainly now the most influential woman in Italy, and that she had inherited the rebellious independence of her forebears, along with the pride, ambition and passion that made her father great. Influence certainly, but actual power? As an onlooker on most international events, and a participant in some, she was extremely well placed to have her views heard, and she was never slow to tell both Ciano and her father what she thought. All through the anxious and uncertain days of 1938 and 1939 she spent most of her time in Rome, and some of it with her father in the Villa Torlonia. They spoke constantly, but just what she said, what she advised, was never written down.

The 'Italian invasion', for all its grandeur, had not gone quite as Hitler hoped. The programme had been deliberately planned by the Italians to leave no room for serious talk, and on the occasions when Hitler and Ribbentrop made it plain that they wanted a discussion, Mussolini and Ciano, fearing they might be called upon to commit Italy to moves they were reluctant to make, were evasive. The Germans had prepared a draft treaty for a German-Italian military and political alliance, one which would bind the two countries inextricably together, whether in secret or formally, as the Italians preferred. There was one uncomfortable and bad-tempered exchange between the two foreign ministers, during which Ribbentrop was stubborn and insistent and Ciano slippery. When an amended version was returned by Ciano to the Germans a few days later, it was found to amount to very little, and his subsequent words to Ribbentrop seemed only to emphasise the Italians' unwillingness to forge closer relations. 'The solidarity existing between our two governments,' Schmidt reported him as saying, with a 'sarcastic smile', 'has been so clearly evinced during these days that a formal treaty or alliance is superfluous.'

After the German contingent departed, the King was reported to have declared that Hitler was a 'kind of psycho-physical degenerate', while Mussolini told Ciano that he suspected that Hitler put rouge on his cheeks. The German post-mortem was just as sour. Goebbels remarked that Victor Emmanuel was far too small a man to sit on a throne. Hitler, for his part, referred to Ciano as a 'Viennese cafe ballerino', and would later call him 'the repulsive boy'. The German visit was said to have cost Italy 70 million lire and a square at Ostiense was renamed Piazzale Adolf Hitler. It had shown that Italy, too, could orchestrate a sumptuous and impressive display.

One thing that the state visit had revealed was the precariousness of the relationship between Mussolini and the King. On the surface, it was extremely cordial, the King ratifying Mussolini's laws with little protest, and Mussolini referring to their relationship as 'a double bedroom with two beds'. The army obeyed the King, the militia obeyed Mussolini and on public occasions both the 'Royal March' and 'Giovinezza' were played. But Mussolini, who was often heard to say that the monarchy was a 'useless superstructure', and the King a runt too ridiculous to learn the *passo romano*, had been extremely annoyed to find himself being constantly upstaged by the King during Hitler's visit, forced into the background while Victor Emmanuel and Hitler took the limelight together. In his diary, Ciano noted that Mussolini had taken to calling the King 'a dead tree', a 'bitter and untrustworthy little man' and 'an old hen'. The newly militant Italy, Mussolini now suggested, should in fact be under a single command: his own. The question was how to have himself raised from corporal to the same military rank as the King. Someone proposed that he be made a Maresciallo d'Italia, but there were several Marescialli already. Starace came up with the idea of making both Mussolini and the

King '*Primi Marescialli*', with special braids on their uniforms to indicate a parallel between them. The proposal was rushed through the Chamber and the Senate and quickly approved.

But no one had thought to consult the King who, when informed, was furious. He declared it to be a mortal blow against his 'sovereign prerogative' and said that he would have abdicated had not world affairs been so troubled. After much havering and consulting of the constitution, he was made to see that he had no choice but to sign. 'This is an insult to the Crown,' he told Mussolini. 'And it must be the last one.' It was from this moment, Mussolini's son Vittorio later wrote, that the King began to plot revenge, while Mussolini and Ciano felt ever more strongly that Italy should become a republic, as soon as was possible.

13

Wavering

Until his invasion of Ethiopia, Mussolini appeared to have shown little interest in race. But with fears that Italians in the colonies would mix too freely with Africans, he had decided that the time had come to impose 'racial discipline'. The Italians were more virile, fecund and intelligent than 'dark-skinned people', and doctors and historians were put to work to prove their physical and mental superiority. Orders and decrees on segregation were put into place, though not with much effect: in every colony Italian men were known to be having relationships with local women. The subject of race – discussed, disputed – was in the air, though not always to Italian advantage. A German musicologist, Hans Engel, produced a racial chart claiming to show that while Southern Italians, with their pointy heads, small bodies, excitable nerves and tendency towards pathos and bel canto, had 34 per cent musical talent, Southern Germans, with their 'average' heads and bodies, steady characters and 'merry dispositions' had 74 per cent.

The idea of the 'pure' Italian, one who had inhabited the peninsular for thousands of years, had, however, taken root among the *gerarchi*. Mussolini had originally been contemptuous of Hitler's anti-Semitism, and offended that the Germans believed the blond, blue-eyed Nordic Aryans to be superior to the darker, shorter Italians. But by 1937 'purity' was coming to include 'not Jewish'. It started with anti-Semitic articles in *Il Corriere della Sera* and *Il Giornale d'Italia*, campaigning against 'plutocratic-Jewish-Bolshevists' and making statements such as 'Jews do not belong to the Italian race'. Then it spread to a mishmash of so-called scientific studies, dealing with biology and anthropology along with the occult. Jews, warned the *Second Book of Fascism*, were 'exalters of dandyism, cultism, licentiousness, free love, feminism' and 'deriders of family and children' – in short, the very kind of Italian Mussolini did not want in his new Italy. Even fashion editors joined in. 'Good' fashion was Aryan, 'soft, maternal, opulent and sinuous', as opposed to overly thin, angular 'bad' Jewish fashion.

After 1945, attempts were made to absolve Italian Fascism of true racism by claiming anti-Semitism had been purely a German import. Certainly, it began gradually, both Mussolini and Ciano insisting that there would be no persecution of Jews. A census carried out in August 1938 had established that there were little more than fifty thousand Jews in Italy, of whom some forty-eight thousand were Italian nationals, long assimilated into Italian life, and a significant number of them Fascist Party members. Over two hundred of Mussolini's earliest supporters, all Jewish, had played a prominent part in his governments. On 3 December 1937, Ciano wrote in his diary: 'I do not believe that we ought to unleash an anti-Semitic campaign in Italy. The problem for us doesn't exist. There are not many Jews and, with some exceptions, there is no harm in them . . . the Jews should never be persecuted as such.' However, he also noted that Mussolini had referred to America as a country of 'niggers and Jews', whose 'acid corrosion' would destroy any country that allowed them to do so. Mussolini was also heard to say that Jews could be sent to Somaliland, where there was a 'shark frenzy', so that the Jews would be eaten. And the American Ambassador, William Phillips, reported a conversation in which Mussolini, discussing possible places for a Jewish state, announced: 'There is no room for Jews in Europe and eventually they will have to go.' During the discussion, Phillips noted that Ciano said nothing and that, 'He might as well have worn a livery!'

Among the *gerarchi* there was, however, a small number of avowed racists and anti-Semites. A Manifesto on Race was drawn up, closely vetted by Mussolini, and on 6 October 1938, the Grand Council voted a programme of systematic exclusion of Jews from many sections of Italian life – schools, the army, government service among them. The King, with characteristic pusillanimity, professed himself not to be anti-Semitic, but signed the decree into law and was reported as saying, 'The Jews are a wasps' nest, don't let us put our hand in it.' Pope Pius XI had condemned 'atheist, materialist' Nazi racism, but had fallen largely silent on the question of persecution and, in any case, the Vatican had its long record of anti-Semitism. By the end of the year many Jews had been sacked from their jobs, while their children were being educated at home. The exclusion of Jews was greeted with delight by the fanatical young members of the Gioventù Universitaria Fascista, who claimed that it would 'purify the atmosphere' and recommended that Jews wear brightly coloured bracelets to warn against 'the peril of infection . . . as with a rabid dog'.

The foreign Jews, many of whom had arrived in Italy as refugees from Nazi Germany, began searching for new places of asylum, and a number of Italian Jews began to think of emigration. One of these was Margherita Sarfatti, who, estranged from Mussolini, decided that the moment had come to leave Italy. 'La bella ebrea agli occhi azzuri' – the beautiful Jewess with the blue eyes – had fallen from grace. Talking to Claretta, Mussolini called her 'an ugly witch' whose flesh stank. There is a wholly improbable story that she was prompted to go after Edda arranged for her to be caught with a gigolo, taken to a police station and kept overnight in a cell because she had no document of identity with her. Sarfatti packed jewellery, money and a number of her more valuable pictures and crossed the border into Switzerland, before being warmly welcomed into France. Mussolini, another story goes, was furious and sent someone to bring her back. She refused to return.

As with many aspects of Fascism, even anti-Semitism was wavering and confused. One of the most unpleasant anti-Semitic gerarchi, a renegade priest called Giovanni Preziosi, was appointed to oversee the introduction of the new racial policies, but at the same time Bocchini was instructed not to enforce them too vigorously. Government offices were inundated with requests for exemptions, and some at least were accepted. Edda persuaded Ciano to intervene on behalf of her childhood Jewish boyfriend Dino Mondolfi after his mother told her that he was being held in San Vittore prison in Milan. When Capri's zealous bureaucrats prepared to deport the island's foreign Jewish population, Edda herself helped the German deaf and dumb painter, Hans Julius Spiegel, whose naked dances had entertained the locals since the 1920s, escape arrest, though he was later interned in Calabria. But the Cianos fell in line, apparently without protest, when the Pecci-Blunts arranged an eighteenth birthday party for their daughter, and informers reminded Bocchini that not only were there Jews in the family, but that they were of very dubious '*italianità*'. The warning came in time for all the Italian guests – including the Cianos – to back out, but not the foreign ones, who arrived from Paris and London in twenty-eight cars to find the family gone to the country and the party cancelled. Publicly, Edda said nothing, even if she had a natural, somewhat anarchical sympathy for people in trouble and would take up individual causes when something about them appealed to her.

The reaction to the new anti-Semitic laws among Italians was mixed, many expressing outrage. The inhabitants of Florence, Turin and Trento were especially outspoken. For a while, there were protests. But then, as with other Fascist decrees, the unrest died down. Or at least, it appeared to. Mussolini had also chosen this time to embark on an anti-bourgeoisie crusade, railing against complacency, compromises, defeatism and easy-living, claiming that years of 'Liberal' softness had rendered the country feeble and impotent. He needed warriors, not sheep, and only hardship would make them tough. Starace suggested doing away with the word '*insediare*' – to install – saying that it suggested a '*sedia*', a chair, and therefore lacked martial vigour. Feminine men, androgynous women, childless couples living in luxury with small dogs, homosexuals, 'inverts' did not belong in Italy. 'The credo of Fascism,' Mussolini announced, 'is heroism; that of the bourgeoisie egotism.' Farinacci declared that no true Italian could be anti-Fascist, because 'anti-Fascism, by definition, is not Italian', but rather foreign, Jewish or homosexual. Starace was heard to say that it was typical that when a Jewish editor from Modena committed suicide, he did it by jumping from a tower 'to save the price of a bullet'.

Combined with the *passo romano*, the '*anti-Lei*' (*Lei* was decreed to be foreign, servile, feminine and ungrammatical) campaign and anti-Semitism, this attack on the values and way of life that the Italians had come to enjoy – very little crime, no strikes, better living conditions, the celebration of family, God and *patria* – was disturbing, particularly as Mussolini put the new '*anti-borghese*' attack into the hands of the fussy, obsessive Starace, who caused much annoyance.

And it marked another step in the growing estrangement many Italians were beginning to feel towards the Fascist regime. After the Pontine Marshes south of Rome were drained and impoverished Northerners brought down to farm the reclaimed land, widespread publicity was given to their happiness and contentment. However, their initial pleasure was short lived. The farmers soon found themselves caught on a treadmill to pay back loans that grew larger with every year, with their families stuck in an 'isolated great ghetto' in which malaria was still rife. For all Mussolini's strictures, the countryside remained the place from which people wished to escape. The aftermath of the Depression had also put an end to the myth that Italy had become a great power, since it clearly remained subordinate to economic markets dominated by France, Britain, Germany and the US. Even the vast ceremonials so beloved by Mussolini, such as the fifteen thousand women from all over Italy – the rural housewives in their shawls, the girls from Tuscany in reds and sky blue, the women workers in blue overalls – brought to parade from the Circo Massimo down the Via dell'Impero, were beginning to seem hollow.

But the Italians had put up with the coercions of Fascism for more than fifteen years, not least by walling totalitarianism into one part of their brains, while continuing with their daily lives. They had grown accustomed to prospering in a world of constant low-level corruption, to plotting their way through cabals and vendettas, and to negotiating 'raccomodazioni', the labyrinth of patron-client arrangements. Anti-Semitism provided the more malevolent among them with another fruitful field for denouncing their neighbours. But even among the more moral, those who had spent the Fascist years lying low and waiting for better times, it did not lead to rebellion; at least, not yet.

Sometimes warm, sometimes chilly, Mussolini's endless dance with Britain and France went on, his changes of mood creating waves, moving towards Germany and then away from her, making peace then finding reasons for alienation. What Ciano referred to as the 'great European orchestra' played on. It would later be suggested that Mussolini's failure to grasp Hitler's true nature came in part from the collapse of Italy's formerly respected diplomacy, professional diplomats attuned to every nuance of power having been replaced by party stalwarts, who Mussolini in any case ignored. It came, too, from his visceral wariness of foreigners whose opinions he instinctively mistrusted. Malaparte wrote an imagined, comic exchange between Mussolini and the ambassador Lord Perth to illustrate the immense gap between their words and understanding. 'Mussolini says: "How do you do?" meaning "I want to know how you are". Lord Perth says: "How do you do?" meaning "I don't really want to know how you are" ... Mussolini says: "I want", Lord Perth says: "I would like" ... Mussolini says: "I think". Lord Perth says: "I suppose, may I suggest, may I propose, may I believe" ...' Mussolini's look, Malaparte continued, was that of a man who knew what was poker and what was not; Lord Perth's that of a man who knew what cricket was and what it was not.

Then Hitler announced that he would march into Czechoslovakia unless the Sudetenland, with its large German population, was immediately ceded to Germany. On 26 September 1938, Ciano wrote in his diary: 'It's war. May God protect Italy and the Duce.' On the 28th, at ten in the morning, four hours before Hitler's ultimatum was due to expire, Lord Perth informed Mussolini that Chamberlain wanted him to intervene and act as mediator. Delighted at the chance of becoming peacemaker, Mussolini agreed. After a flurry of calls, Hitler accepted a delay of twenty-four hours. By six thirty that evening, Mussolini and Ciano were on a train to Munich. Mussolini was in excellent spirits, lecturing his entourage on the decadence of the British, their frustrated spinsters and excessive love of animals. François-Poncet noted that he seemed to wear a 'Caesarian' mask and appeared totally at ease.

A deal was signed at 2 a.m. on the 30th. Even if what was agreed was the annexation of a large part of the Sudetenland, in return for an undertaking by Hitler that this was his last territorial claim in Europe, the illusion that war had again been prevented allowed Mussolini – as well as Chamberlain and Daladier – to return home to a hero's welcome. The USSR had not been invited to attend. The Czechs were not consulted.

As Mussolini's train travelled south through Italy, people knelt by the tracks. The King was waiting to receive him in Florence. In Rome, he emerged on to the balcony of the Palazzo Venezia to a reception as rapturous as that which had greeted his proclamation of empire. But the Duce was not altogether pleased. The deep public relief that there would be no war, confirmed by the many letters delivered to his office, as well as Bocchini's reports, seemed to him yet further proof that Italians were not warriors, but pacifists, about which he felt a sense of shame.

In earlier days, Mussolini had felt great fondness for France. Jean Valjean and Napoleon were his heroes, Sorel and Proudhon his intellectual mentors. But relations had soured and his former love had turned into mistrust and anger. France, he told Ciano, was a nation ruined by 'alcohol, syphilis and journalists'. There had been no French Ambassador to Rome since the French had refused to acknowledge Italy's empire, and it was only after the Socialist Leon Blum fell and a more conciliatory Edouard Daladier came to power that a new ambassador was appointed. The man chosen was François-Poncet, the courteous, wily former ambassador to Berlin, who was delighted to be in Italy, among less 'inhuman' men, after dealing with the 'lugubrious' Germans. He admitted that both dictators shared a passion for power, grandeur and glory and that both were jumpy, cynical, and skilled at dissimulation and oratory, but he greatly preferred the 'witty, seductive, quick' Italian, whose voice was 'sharp' and laugh 'truculent', to the stiff German with his 'flat, grey, globular eyes' and harsh, raucous voice. By the time François-Poncet took up his post, Mussolini was again vacillating between Germany on the one hand and Britain and France on the other, and his reception was cool. There was talk in Rome of banning French books, magazines and clothes.

New hopes for French concessions culminated in an unpleasant occasion, carefully engineered by Ciano and Mussolini, when Fascist deputies stood up in the Chamber in November 1938 in the presence of François-Poncet who had been invited on purpose, and began chanting 'Tunis! Savoy! Nice! Djibouti!' – the territories Mussolini had his eye on. Mystified journalists, dozing in the press gallery, woke up. François-Poncet walked out. Despite demonstrations in front of the French embassy, and insults shouted at him wherever he went, orchestrated by Starace, François-Poncet remained smiling and unperturbed. Roman society ignored the feud and continued to accept invitations to the French embassy, the exquisite Palazzo Farnese. In a letter, intercepted by the

Italians, François-Poncet wrote to the Quai d'Orsay that while in Germany he had dealt with 'real gentlemen, here I have to deal with servants who have become masters'. Ciano's ploy left a bitter taste among the French, while the Italian press was instructed to rail against France and demand that all forty-four million Italians spit on the French. Daladier remained firmly opposed to making any move towards rapprochement.

The dance went on. In January 1939, it was Britain's turn. On the 11th, Chamberlain and Halifax arrived in Rome, ostensibly as a sign of reconciliation between the two countries after the travails of Ethiopia and the League of Nations or, as the American correspondent William Shirer put it, 'to appease the Duce'. Chamberlain, Shirer noted, looked vain and birdlike as he walked, umbrella in hand, down the platform of Rome station, nodding to the assembled British residents. Mussolini was observed 'displaying a fine smirk' and exchanging comic asides with Ciano. For the reception at the Campidoglio, the renaissance palaces were hung with magnificent tapestries and lit by flaming torches which made the statue of Marcus Aurelius on his charger look 'gigantic and dimply golden'.

The British came bearing no gifts, but with the hope that they might keep Mussolini from inching further towards Berlin. Historians have disagreed as to whether Mussolini or Chamberlain believed that they had more to gain from the encounter. Certainly, Chamberlain and Halifax wanted Mussolini's help in avoiding war, and Mussolini hoped for material gains. When he broached the matter of Britain accepting a larger quota of Jews, Chamberlain said that he feared that it would only increase 'the anti-Semitism which already exists in many parts of the country'. After many banquets and much sightseeing, the British left believing that they had made steps in helping Mussolini 'escape from German toils'. As Chamberlain told King George VI, he had been 'favourably impressed' by Mussolini and found his sense of humour 'reasonable', though he had witnessed a 'thorough fit of sulks' at one banquet.

Having been informed that the person with the most influence in Rome was Edda, and that, having felt slighted during her visit to London, she had become strongly anti-British, Eden had bought the largest and most extravagant bouquet of flowers that Rome could provide and sent it to her with 'the PM's homage'. When they met, he found her friendly and hospitable, but he doubted, he told the King, that 'she bothers herself much with politics'. But then, he was not present during her têtes-à-têtes with her father; and Edda had perfected her air of inscrutability.

British restraint and understatement left Mussolini and Ciano convinced that the timidity and indecisiveness of Britain's statesmen was such that they had been reduced to a 'boundless apprehension of the ever growing strength of the Axis powers', an impression soon relayed to Berlin. While Mussolini sent Chamberlain a telegram expressing his faith in 'Italo-British friendship', Ciano phoned Ribbentrop to reassure him that the visit had been 'absolutely innocuous'. Too much was left unsaid and too little understood. Malaparte's parody was horribly accurate. Chamberlain and Halifax, Mussolini remarked to Ciano, were not made of the same stuff as Drake, but had become the 'tired sons of a long series of rich forebears'. When their train pulled out of Rome station, the British residents sang them on their way with 'For He's a Jolly Good Fellow'. Later, Sir Percy Loraine, who succeeded Lord Perth as Ambassador to Rome, would say that he thought that the British sanctions over Ethiopia had been the moment that Italy turned its back on Britain and that there was no going back.

In February 1939, Pius XI, the pope who had seen through the Lateran accords and on occasion stood up to Mussolini, making no secret of his horror at the German pogroms, died. His successor was Pius XII, the worldly, well-travelled, extremely diplomatic Vatican secretary of state, who came from a banking family, spoke eight languages and knew Germany intimately. An exchange of visits between the King and the new Pope, the first ever to be paid, was seen to herald a new era of peace between Church and Fascist state, after a period of disagreements over the control of the minds and souls of young Italians. It was a magnificent occasion, the court in full gala dress, with lace veils, tiaras, trains and decorations. The ladies had been instructed to go down on both knees when the Pope appeared. Laden down with finery, some were unable to get up again.

The appeasement of Hitler, and Mussolini's dash to Munich, had been an error. In September 1938 Germany would perhaps have been too weak to fight both France and Czechoslovakia, particularly with the Russians ready to step in. Having taken over the enormous and valuable Czech Skoda ironworks, thereby vastly increasing production for its military arsenal, the German army used the breathing space to increase its operational divisions from thirty to seventy-three. On 14 March 1939, once again without telling his ally Mussolini, Hitler marched into Prague, annexed Bohemia and made Slovakia into a German protectorate, thereby reneging on his Munich promises. 'Don't believe that this is the end,' noted Churchill. 'This is just the beginning.' To a furious Mussolini, it was another sign that Hitler was too strong to be stopped and that Italy would do well to stay by her side.

Even as Madrid fell to Franco's forces and the Spanish Civil War moved towards its desperate finale – Italy having lost 3,189 dead, 12,000 wounded, along with 759 planes, and accumulated a deficit of 40.4 billion lire – Ciano was responsible for another grave error. Fortune, he had written in his diary not long before, is a 'prostitute who offers herself fleetingly and then moves on to others. If you don't know how to grab her by the hair, you lose her.' On 7 April 1939, on the pretext that Germany's expansion in the Balkans had to be halted, and wanting to prove that Italy had its own military plans, Italian soldiers invaded Albania, the poorest and most backward country in Europe. King Zog was a personal friend of Ciano's who had been a witness at his wedding, and Albania had for many years been almost an Italian protectorate. For a moment, it seems, Ciano, who had convinced himself that the war would be quick and easy and bring Italy prestige, even spoke of 'eliminating' his friend the king, perhaps with poison.

The campaign went very badly. The expeditionary army was haphazard, the various Italian forces were ill coordinated, and the ships dispatched to ferry men and weapons found that the ports had too little clearance for them to enter. Had the Albanians had even a small army, the Italians could probably have been beaten off. King Zog, having refused an offer which effectively handed Italy total control, fled to Greece, and Albania's crown was offered to Victor Emmanuel. The port of Sarandë was renamed Port Edda. But Italy's chaotic aggression was enough to convince the British and the French that Italy was not in fact looking for peace. The two countries joined forces in guaranteeing support not just to Poland, clearly Hitler's next target, but also to Greece and

Romania, and began hesitant negotiations with the USSR towards a military pact. While Bocchini in Rome ordered that no one should in any way interfere with Albania, since it was 'Ciano's feud and I absolutely do not want trouble with him', Ciano professed himself delighted with his victory. He sent instructions to the MinCulPop 'not to be stingy with the typeface' when reporting his accolades from the Grand Council. But Albania, as many people had warned, was of very little use to Italy. Its oil was too costly to refine, and the conquerors derived nothing from the invasion, having to send money for the development of the country instead.

Mussolini, still wavering, still hoping to instigate another four-party conference and to win concessions from France, still oscillating between greed and fear, inched closer towards Germany. As an ally of Hitler, he believed that a larger slice of the cake was within his grasp. Italians needed to be seen, he said, not as 'tarts', but as 'new Fascist men', though in the Grand Council he was accused by Balbo of 'shining Germany's shoes'. He sent Ciano to meet Ribbentrop in Milan in May 1939 to conclude an alliance with Germany, which was signed in Berlin on the 22nd. Referred to as a 'pact of friendship and alliance', binding the two countries into mutual assistance in case of war, it was soon better known as the 'pact of steel'.

Though the pact's meaning was obvious, neither Ciano nor Mussolini appear to have thought through beforehand exactly what it would entail, and Ciano seems to have made no proper preparations for a meeting that he must have known was crucial. He came across as passive and distracted. During his talks with the senior Germans, he failed to obtain any kind of guarantee on when hostilities might begin, beyond Hitler's vague assurances that he himself did not want war for four or five years, and he did not demand one. Neither did he get any agreement on reciprocal consultation, or that any attack on Poland would not be the spark for a wider war. After the meeting was over, Eva Braun, Hitler's mistress, took photographs of Ciano from her window with a telephoto lens; she had wanted to be introduced to him, saying that she found him attractive, but Hitler refused. That night, after an evening in the Salon Kitty, where a group of pretty women who were trained in espionage were laid on to please him, Ciano, evidently finally aware of the day's implications, put his head in his hands and noted, 'This is not steel, it's dynamite.'

On 6 June 1939, having eaten a very large meal in a restaurant in Lucca, Ciano's father Costanzo had a heart attack and died. He was sixty-two. 'The cruel news of your death,' Ciano wrote in his diary sitting in his office in the Palazzo Chigi, 'struck me suddenly like a treacherous blow.' He spoke of it as an 'amputation'. His diary entry for that day runs to four awkward, highly sentimental pages addressed to his father, reminiscing about their times together. He does not mention his often coerced, bullying childhood.

Having given orders that Costanzo be dressed in his admiral's uniform, with full naval and Fascist decorations, Ciano joined the long cortège behind the coffin, borne on a cannon pulled by seven plumed horses. A tearful Victor Emmanuel greeted the coffin, lying in state in the Fascist headquarters, with a Roman salute. Every Fascist luminary was present. Even Edda, noted Ansaldo, 'was moved, and she was the person who prayed the longest'. Mussolini, who had flown in from Forlì, spent two hours by the coffin. While most of the congregation in Livorno's cathedral fidgeted, Ansaldo noted that Mussolini had trained himself to keep absolutely still. A naval squadron anchored in the bay fired its cannons. Ciano planned, as he wrote in his diary, to build a mausoleum for his father, 'so that we will all be reminded of your immortal spirit'. A veil was drawn over the fact that Costanzo had been extremely corrupt, even by Fascist *gerarchi* standards, having used his two brothers, both of them admirals, as front men for a vast array of companies, from shipyards to armaments, which made him one of the richest men in Italy. Mussolini knew it all, through Bocchini and his spies, but as with others who had remained loyal at the time of the Matteotti murder, he found it politic to say nothing.

When Ciano returned to meet Ribbentrop at his summer residence near Salzburg in mid August, he learnt that Germany was on the verge of invading Poland. Hitler, Ribbentrop informed him, had 'implacably decided to fight'. As disquieting, and more surprising, was the news that Germany was signing a non-aggression pact with the USSR, from which Italy was excluded and which gave Germany a free hand over Poland. Relations between the two men, never warm, turned icy. According to the notes he took, Ciano asked Ribbentrop: 'Do you want Danzig?' And Ribbentrop replied: 'More than that. We want war!'

All through the winter of 1938 and well into 1939, Ciano's doubts about an alliance with Germany had been growing steadily. Now he came back from Salzburg convinced that the Germans were traitors, 'possessed by the demon of destruction'. 'They have deceived and lied to us. And today they are about to drag us into an adventure that we do not want ... it would be a crime and the height of folly!' His diary increasingly records his hopes of keeping Italy out of the war, and his position distanced him ever further from Mussolini, who continued to swing between a desire to uphold Italy as a warrior nation and realisation that Italy was not in fact in any position to fight. At heart, Ciano wrote, Mussolini 'doesn't want to win this or that: he wants war'. Edda, too, appeared to want war and, more than ever, she and Ciano were now at odds. Following events closely, listening to her father and husband debate every twist and turn, she wrote later that Ciano 'fought against me, as I was trying to persuade my father to stand by Germany's side as a military ally'. But it was not just the might of Germany that appealed to her. There was also something profoundly impatient in her nature, and all vacillation irritated her.

However alienated Edda felt from Ciano, and however much she railed against the formality and tedium of official foreign trips, there were some that she could not avoid. She had accompanied him to Hungary, Yugoslavia and Poland in February 1939, to be met in Warsaw by a guard of honour, ostensibly to go hunting bison at the President's lodge, but also to show solidarity. Ciano took with him his usual retinue of journalists, and Ansaldo, now his official press officer, noted wryly: 'Pheasant hunts, hare hunts, wild boar hunts, wolf hunts ... Basta ... Let's hope we don't end with manhunts.' After days of banquets and receptions, and a visit in Krakow to the tomb of Jozef Pilsudski, the revered Polish statesman, Ciano kept his retinue up far into the night on the sleeper home. What he wanted above all, he told them, was to avoid war. 'He has grown above his stature,' observed one acid Roman acquaintance. He had fooled himself into thinking that he held in his hands all these foreign ministers who took him hunting.

Ciano and Edda on a hunting trip in Poland

Rather more enjoyably, Edda went off to Venice. She played poker with Nelson Page and lost 5,000 lire to him. At a lunch party given by Elsa Maxwell, her hostess told her that it pained her to hear so much German spoken in the streets. Edda, laughing, replied that in the 'next war', Italy and Germany would fight side by side, and that 'when we make war on England', she expected that the Americans would join them. She was still in Venice when she was handed a telegram from Rachele telling her that the King had awarded Ciano the prestigious Collare dell' Annunziata, the highest order in his gift, having been persuaded by Mussolini that not to bestow it after a successful foreign campaign would be an insult. Ciano, too, was now '*cugino*', cousin, to the King.

In Rome, in the summer of 1939, even as Europe hovered on the brink of war, there had never been so many splendid dinners given in private palazzi, with so much whisky obtained on the cheap through Vatican sources, so much silver and gold on display, or so many liveried servants. There was a craze for dancing, especially the Lambeth Walk, frowned on as a British import. There was, wrote the memoirist Claudia Patrizi, 'an air of falseness', the beautiful women who spoke English and the elegant men reminding her of an 'international mafia' sporting themselves as in the time of the Paris Directoire. 'The *nouveaux riches* were at their most snobbish, and the aristocracy at its most venal . . . lying and obsequious'. Everyone addressed each other as '*tu*'.

Conversation was all about sex and intrigues, and its frivolity had never seemed to Patrizi so absurd, as if to mock the austerity and prudishness of the regime and to keep at bay the thoughts of war. Husbands were decreed to be mere nuisances and wives were divided into three categories: the frigid, the accessible and the untouchable, deemed useless because already paired off. At midnight, Patrizi wrote, the musicians arrived in the grand palazzi and dancing began. Edda loved dancing. The few aristocrats from the *ancien régime*, invited to bestow respectability and style, tried but, too awkward and reserved, failed to join in the festivities. Bocchini's spies were present at all such gatherings, often in the guise of guests. Ciano himself had never seemed so vain, so full of energy, so triumphant as the *beau monde* pressed its invitations on himself and Edda – who seldom accepted – and pretty women vied for his attention. Foreign visitors spent nights in his *garçonnière* or in the Palazzo Chigi, where he kept a private room with a divan. The more the international political situation grew complicated and menacing, the more sure of himself Ciano seemed, whether at the Circolo della Caccia, the Palazzo Colonna or the golf club at l'Acquasanta, where his irresponsible indiscretions were assiduously noted and quickly relayed to the diplomatic community. His acolytes fawned, observed his moods, listened to his tirades against

Time Magazine, 24 July 1939

Mussolini – whom he now referred to as '*il vecchio*', the old man – and tolerated his capriciousness. Bocchini's spies listened and reported back. And he and Edda still shared jokes. At a reception one evening Ciano was kissing the hands of a long line of women presented to him but failed to notice that among them was an elderly, whiskery gentleman; to Edda's delight Ciano kissed his hand, too.

That March, *Newsweek* had put Ciano on their cover; in July, *Time* had put Edda on theirs. It was an extraordinary and telling accolade. 'Gaunt, pale faced' Edda, 'outstanding in ability, personality and intelligence' was, the *Time* reporter wrote, 'one of Europe's most successful intriguers and string pullers'. She wore the 'diplomatic trousers', had a 'somewhat mediocre husband' and had been overlooked by the regime because it refused to recognise women. Sometimes she was blonde and sometimes dark, and while in Vienna she had worn ermine, in Poland it had been mink. It was clear that she hoped to 'succeed to her father's power'. The *Sunday Mirror* referred to her as 'Italy's Number One Woman'. In a world in which women's talents remained largely unrecognised, these tributes have to be seen in context. But it was a mark of how far Edda had emerged on the international stage, how realistically onlookers had understood the influence she carried with both her father and her husband, and how widely she was now known not only in Europe but in the US. Often now her name was bracketed with that of Eleanor Roosevelt, and she had not yet reached her thirtieth birthday.

Edda, who was as averse to the social frenzy playing itself out in Rome as she was to high political intrigue, preferred to spend her time on Capri. Occasionally she took the children with her, but for the most part they stayed with their nannies. There had been fears that the Italian invasion of Albania would drive tourists away, and indeed some stayed at home, but on Capri, the summer of 1939 was more glamorous than any that had preceded it. The very rich, very pretty, green-eyed Mona Williams Bismarck held tennis parties for actresses and millionaires, while the serious-minded Alberto Moravia went off on a donkey to picnic in the hills. There was a film festival every evening. Capri was full of *dopolavoristi*, members of the after-work leisure clubs, brought down from the north by cheap *treni popolari*. At its peak, up to 4,500 trippers arrived on a single day, and steps were taken to reduce this 'indecorous, undisciplined spectacle, sowing confusion'.

Edda and one of her children, on Capri

Edda was observed to be behaving strangely. Ever the source of gossip, rumour, innuendo and spy reports, she was said to wander about on the rocks at night, often drunk. A doctor claimed that he had seen a scar on her temple, exactly like that left by a bullet. One zealous OVRA informer said that she was a '*spendaccione*', a heavy spender in the island's boutiques. The unreliable Malaparte insisted that he had met her one stormy night, jumping from roof to roof like a witch's cat, crying, tormented by attacks of depression. Edda reminded him, he said, of tragic heroines from the underworld, uttering funereal presentiments. He maintained that Mussolini and Ciano were both now totally dependent on her. More reliable friends noted that she felt that she had failed to achieve anything and that she deplored her own character, as being too weak to fight for the things she believed in – though with enigmatic Edda, just what these were was sometimes hard to see. She spoke of Ciano as small minded and faithless and told them that all that was now left for her was to devote herself to her family, a remark so out of character that it is hard to think she made it.

Earlier in the year, the Chamber of Deputies had been renamed the Chamber of Fasces and Corporations and the deputies, in their black uniforms, had given the Roman salute to the King on his throne and Queen Elena in the royal box. Despite the pact of steel, Mussolini continued to veer first one way and then the other between Germany, France and Britain; still believing that peace might just be possible, he had become more isolated than ever. The diplomat Bastianini left a telling portrait of him at this time. Mussolini, he wrote, had closed in on himself 'with the arrogance of a stoic and the pride of a cynic who believes that no one can understand him'. Restless, tormented, paranoid, perceiving the outside world as increasingly hostile, he had become convinced that the 'world has to be taken by assault'. While in the past he had tolerated a little argument and criticism, he now seemed to have taken on some of Hitler's abrupt and spiteful manner. Italians had to learn, he kept repeating, 'to grow less likeable and to become hard, implacable and hateful'.

When members of the Grand Council suggested that Italy should distance itself from the Axis, he replied: 'We are not political prostitutes.' Mussolini had been shaken by Hitler's failure to keep his promises, but withdrawing from Germany would have meant going along with his opponents and with the King, who had taken to referring to the Germans as 'ruffians and scoundrels', and it would have cast doubt on his own hold on politics.

For all his isolation and embattlement, Mussolini was too clever, and Bocchini too efficient an analyst of the strongly anti-German mood in Italy, not to know that a war would be deeply unpopular, that the army, navy and air force were fatally weak and that any war risked being long and terrible. But he was also convinced that France and Britain, tired liberal democracies lacking dynamism, would never go to war. When Chamberlain announced that Britain would fight if Poland were attacked, he chose not to take it seriously. He did not listen when Grandi pointed out that Britain always needed a moral reason to go to war. In 1914, they had had Belgium; now they had Poland. But visitors to the Palazzo Venezia reported that Mussolini appeared deeply apprehensive. 'Having provoked the wind, he now feared the storm.'

Hitler had long planned to take the free city of Danzig and the corridor which divided Germany from the province of East Prussia, since 1936 in the hands of a Nazi majority and an area described by François-Poncet as the 'symbol of the liberty of Europe'. Even as he appeared to be considering his next move, Hitler was marshalling his troops. Mussolini had been delighted by his role as peacemaker at Munich, and he now proposed a conference at San Remo at which the four great powers could review the Treaty of Versailles. Before it could take place, at four thirty on the morning of 1 September, the Wehrmacht invaded Poland. An ultimatum was issued to Hitler to withdraw his forces, after which discussions could go ahead. Hitler ignored it. 'The last note of hope,' Ciano wrote in his diary, 'has died.' On 11 a.m. on 3 September, Britain declared war; France followed at 5 p.m.

Italy, however, did not go to war. Hating the thought of neutrality, which he considered a sign of weakness, but wanting the breathing space to keep his options open, Mussolini settled on the word 'non-belligerency', described by some as a 'chef d'oeuvre of linguistic imagination'. Announcing his decision from his balcony over the Piazza Venezia, he looked pale. Hitler, having thought that Italy would follow him to war in spite of having turned down her request for a staggering 170 million tons of raw materials, and offering only a fraction of it, appeared to accept that she would not. Hitler said that he would crush Poland without Italian help, and then move on to defeat France and Britain.

The French and British ambassadors, summoned to hear the news from Ciano in the Palazzo Chigi, were surprised and relieved. Mussolini, the man who had once declared that it was better to live a single day as a lion rather than a lifetime as a sheep, now found himself uncomfortably among the sheep. But for Ciano, this was what he had wished for. He threw open the three large windows of his office and turned on all the lights. 'At least the Romans,' he declared, 'may see some light here.' As for Edda, she was relieved the waiting was over. She craved action, movement, certainty; but she thought little about where they led.

14

Waiting

For the next nine months, the Italians waited.

After a surge of relief, and a sharp rise in the stock market, they went about their ordinary lives, avoided talking about politics, enjoying the illusion that they would remain untouched. New babies were christened Roberto, after the Tripartite Pact Roma-Berlino-Tokyo. In Rome, they strolled up and down the Via Veneto in the early evenings and made excursions to Ostia to enjoy the last warm days of summer. The King and the court withdrew behind a wall of formality. There was a rumour that if it ever did come to war, the Vatican would ensure that the capital remained a '*città aperta*', an open city, inviolate. Men aged between twenty and twenty-five were called up, but immediately sent home again because there were no uniforms and nowhere for them to sleep. A few tram tracks were taken up for iron. Campaigns were launched about saving, not wasting, and making do.

Plans went ahead for a vast exhibition to be held in 1942, to mark the twentieth anniversary of the regime and for the opening of the new suburb of EUR. Rabbits were extolled, for food and for their fur. De Chirico offered to paint Edda and Ciano's portraits: Ciano, in full regalia, with medals and the Collare, took against his finished picture, but Edda's was judged an excellent likeness. She was shown in a long black dress, her hair reddish-brown, swept up and parted in the middle, handsome, almost beautiful.

The winter of 1939 was exceptionally cold. There were dinner parties every night in the Rome palazzi and the Cianos attended many of them. The gambling stakes were ever higher and even Ciano played *chemin de fer*, while pinching the bottoms, as the Duchessa di Sermoneta observed, of 'his young lovelies'. Coming away from a dinner given by the Cianos one night, she described a scene that made her think of Versailles before The Terror, with the footmen 'in their ill-fitting liveries' carrying trays laden with champagne, Ciano ruffling the hair of a young woman standing by him at the card table, which was scattered with banknotes, the air blue with smoke. She had nothing against either Edda or her husband, she added, 'except their manners'. Gabriella di Robilant, who also dined with the Cianos, put it more tartly. They had played the card game pinnacolo in 'absolute intimacy' and were 'such unpretentious hosts that you might almost have mistaken them for "*signori*"', that is to say, people of good breeding.

Mussolini was seldom seen. He moved between the Palazzo Venezia and Villa Torlonia, but refused to receive foreign diplomats or indeed his own *gerarchi*. The Grand Council meetings lasted barely an hour and Mussolini, sombre and bitter, was the only speaker. Sir Percy Loraine, the upright, dignified British Ambassador, considered less sympathetic to the Fascists than Lord Perth, found himself dealing only with Ciano. The two men got on well, met at L'Acquasanta and dined together at the Palazzo Colonna. But Ciano was also reading Loraine's intercepted letters and telegrams, while Ciano's doctor, who happened to be doctor to D'Arcy Osborne, British Ambassador to the Vatican, passed on valuable information about Ciano's circle, which quickly made its way back to London. Listening to the usual gossip, Loraine wrote to Halifax that Mussolini was said to be becoming senile. 'The only human creature he was really fond of, his daughter Edda, has disgraced him ... She has become a nymphomaniac and in an alcoholic haze leads a life of rather sordid sexual promiscuity.' Rome had lost none of its delight in malice.

Ciano's sister Maria Magistrati had been sickly since childhood. Their father Costanzo had forced her to eat, though she spat out everything she was given. She grew up frighteningly thin, with a horror of food, and would have pulled out of her marriage if Mussolini had not been invited to stand as witness. (Seeing her so thin, Mussolini had told Sarfatti, 'a woman without breasts is like a mattress without cushions, uncomfortable'). In October 1939, white as marble, she began to fade; two weeks later she died, ostensibly of tuberculosis. Her funeral, like that of Costanzo's a few months earlier, was held in Livorno Cathedral, attended by many *gerarchi*, diplomats and their families. Four veteran *squadristi* carried the coffin. Ciano was heard to say that he had lost 'the only person who really loved me'. François-Poncet, who had been friendly with Maria in Berlin, calling her '*élégante et séduisante*', found himself standing next to the new German Ambassador, Hans Georg von Mackensen, sent to replace von Hassell, whose distaste for Ciano and the Fascists had finally got him recalled.

At the end of the month came the sudden announcement that Mussolini was reshuffling his council of ministers. No reason was given. Starace, widely considered the most hated man in Italy for his draconian and ridiculous edicts, but in truth little more than Mussolini's shadow, was ousted as party secretary and sent to the Milizia instead. Hearing that he was to be sacked, he wrote to Mussolini: 'Forgive me, Duce. Forgive me ... and don't doubt me.' Even Ciano thought that he had been treated badly: when Starace came to the Piazza Venezia and begged to be received, Mussolini shouted to his secretary, 'Kick him down the stairs.' Bottai, the true believer in Fascist doctrine, left his post as a minister to found *Primato*, a cultural magazine intended to be a showpiece for the regime, but where, as a measure of the ambiguities of Fascism, he welcomed contributors known to be critical of the regime. Some called him a 'raptor' who viewed intellectuals as his 'prey'.

The change of guard brought in Ciano's friends and allies, among them Pavolini, who was made head of the MinCulPop, and Ettore Muti, a green-eyed, square-jawed hero of the Ethiopian war, who had the looks of a Greek god, but no great intelligence. Like the other newcomers, he was vain, egotistic, cold and politically naive, and still in his thirties, for Mussolini was now wanting to court the younger *gerarchi*. Rome talked openly about '*il gabinetto Ciano*', Ciano's cabinet. Edda seemed to have inched closer to the centre of power.

Ciano had in fact passed the months since war broke out, perhaps the clearest and most purposeful time of his life, engineering to keep Italy out of the war. Having spent his entire life trying to please, first his father, then Mussolini, he seemed at last to have found something that he believed in. He had become, as one historian put it, 'adamantine in his politics of neutrality'. It brought him a sudden burst of popularity and friendship from other like-minded *gerarchi* – Balbo, Grandi – who previously had no time for him. But it also increased the bitter hostility of the Germans, who professed themselves amazed that he had not already been sacked. The diplomat Friedrich von Schulenburg described the Ciano clan as 'sharks without scruples and with a self-destructive avidity', and Edda as 'a frenetic, obstinate nymphomaniac'.

In a two-hour speech Ciano gave to the Chamber in mid December, he paid tribute to 'Polish heroism' and warmly praised Mussolini's peace efforts. He did not mention the word 'Axis'. There were wild rumours that he was aspiring to take control of the government. For a moment, the pro-German lobby appeared to be beaten; the pro-Allies, pro-monarchy, pro-Vatican peacemakers were in the ascendant.

But then, early in 1940, the wind began to change. Mussolini emerged from hibernation, looking energetic, his expression 'dark and fierce'. Sumner Welles, the US Under-secretary of State, sent by Roosevelt to urge calm and restraint, was given a frosty reception. He found Mussolini 'ponderous and static', moving with 'elephantine effort', his face set in 'rolls of flesh', looking greatly aged. His meeting with Ciano went somewhat better and he left the Palazzo Chigi declaring, with some surprise, that the Foreign Minister was cordial and unaffected. Ciano had told him how profoundly he detested Ribbentrop, bitterly resented Hitler's lack of regard for the terms of the Axis treaty, and that he was doing all he could 'to mitigate German brutality'. Then there was an unfortunate incident, when thirteen Italian ships carrying coal from Germany were blockaded by the British in the Channel. Students paraded in front of the British and French embassies with coffins draped with flags. Romans observed the new wind, taking the temperature of Mussolini's moods. Germany had swung back into the ascendant.

After Rome, Sumner Welles went on to Berlin, where he noted that the faces of the storm troopers were 'subnormal in their startling brutality'. Flunkies in light blue satin liveries and powdered hair ushered him into Hitler's presence, and he attempted to lay down some basic understanding for a 'sane world'. Goering's hands struck him as being 'shaped like the digging paws of a badger'. He left Berlin concluding despondently that the future now lay in German hands.

Ribbentrop and Ciano at Rome Station

On 10 March 1940, Ribbentrop arrived in Rome, clearly intent on reminding the Italians of their Axis commitment to stand by their side. Ten days later, Hitler and Mussolini met on a snowy station on the Brenner Pass. Hitler, knowing precisely how to play on Mussolini's anxieties and ambitions, told him that he was soon to launch an offensive against the Allies, but assured him that he had no need of Italian help. The inference, that Mussolini was no longer an important player in any eventual war, was plain. It was all that the Duce most feared: missing out on the spoils that would surely follow a quick German victory. On the platform, Hitler harangued and Mussolini listened. 'As the dean of dictators,' noted Ciano, 'Mussolini was not used to such treatment.' When he and Ciano returned to Rome, he seemed preoccupied, soon writing to the King that Italy could not remain neutral for ever without becoming another Switzerland: 'The problem is not whether Italy will join or not . . . but only when.'

Ciano's mood was grim. He told friends that he was frightened that war would indeed come, that he hated the Nazis for their inhumanity, and that Hitler and Ribbentrop were 'two madmen . . . who wanted the destruction of the world'. Anfuso reported Ciano as saying about his father-in-law: 'He wants war like a child wants the moon.' At a dinner party in the Via Angelo Secchi one night, Ciano was silent, but Edda was in high spirits, insisting on playing pinnacolo after dinner, singing 'Boops-a-Daisy' and declaring that politics did not interest her and that she longed for it all to be over, so that she could travel again. Her apparent self-absorption and indifference to world events are not always easy to explain, but then, torn between her husband and her father's conflicting views, detachment may have been her only option.

When Daniele Varè, Ciano's boss in China, came to Rome to discuss the persecution of Catholics in Germany, he was struck by the contrast between the agitated, tempestuous mood in the Palazzo Venezia, and the subtlety, patience, worldly wisdom and finesse he met with in the Vatican. Bumping into Ciano, he asked him what Mussolini was doing. 'He is taking lessons in politics from the cat in the Villa Torlonia,' Ciano replied. 'The cat never makes mistakes.'

On 10 May, Ciano was a guest at a dinner given at the German embassy. As he left, Mackensen told him that he might have to reach him during the night. He rang at four to say that he needed to see Mussolini immediately. Germany, he informed the Duce and his Foreign Minister, was about to invade Belgium, the Netherlands and Luxembourg. When Mackensen left, Mussolini told Ciano that he had made up his mind: Italy would go to war. The waiting was over. Ciano protested. In his diary, he noted: 'He didn't deign to reply.' Even Edda was now pressing for war, telling her husband that Italy could no longer sit on the sidelines with honour. Ciano's entry was condescending: 'Too bad that even she, so intelligent, doesn't want to see reason.' He told her that, instead of meddling, she would do better to go to Florence to the annual music festival, noting smugly in his diary, 'I listened to her with impersonal civility.'

But he told his friend Orio Vergani that if Edda ever left him, he would be lost. Though he was indeed sick of her attacks on his 'Germanophobia', everything, he told his friend, 'depends on her'; she was the centre of his life. He had tried to explain to her how dangerous her behaviour could be, but 'with Edda you can't discuss things. She is a hard woman, strange. You never know what to expect. Sometimes she frightens me.' It was not Edda's only push for war. Not long before, she had been to see her father and berated him for 'this neutrality that looks so like dishonour'. That, wrote Ciano, 'is the kind of talk Mussolini wants to hear, the only kind he takes seriously'. Later, remembering that time, Edda sounded almost ashamed: 'I was extremely bellicose and Germanophile.' Edda's views were known to the *gerarchi*. As Enrico Caviglia, a distinguished soldier and shrewd observer of the Roman scene, wrote in his diary, Edda was unquestionably 'an influence on the weak spirit of her father'. When she visited Mussolini, she urged decisiveness. Rachele said little.

The German troops swept south through Belgium and France and Paul Reynard's government collapsed. In Britain, after a defeat in Norway, Chamberlain was replaced by Churchill. Mussolini, astounded that the Maginot Line had not held, prepared for war. Hitler had told him that it was a 'crossing of the Rubicon'. Letters from the Pope, from the French, from Roosevelt, from Churchill, arrived, offering concessions and begging Mussolini to stay out of it.

On 25 May 1940, the British Expeditionary Force began to withdraw from Dunkirk. On 29 May, Mussolini informed his assembled *gerarchi* that his decision was made: if Italy did not go in now, she would forfeit any chance at great power status. Some, such as Balbo, were appalled. The King, who had strongly opposed intervention, was persuaded that he had no choice but to sign the declaration of war: he too did not want to lose out on the spoils, and was in any case worried about the future of the House of Savoy. Mussolini's decision, Sir Robert Vansittart told Halifax, 'is a clear case of syphilitic paranoia'. On the evening of 9 June, Mussolini ordered Rome to be blacked out.

At four thirty on the afternoon of 10 June, Ciano received Loraine and François-Poncet in his office. He was dressed in the uniform of a colonel in the air force. François-Poncet told him that he could never regard an Italian as an enemy and both men were visibly moved. 'Don't get yourself killed,' François-Poncet told him. It was the last time they met. Loraine was 'laconic and inscrutable'. He hoped, he said, that Italy was not backing the wrong horse, as Britain was 'not in the habit of losing her wars'. 'Is it too late,' Churchill wrote to Mussolini, 'to stop a river of blood flowing between the British and Italian peoples?'

Towards six thirty that evening Mussolini came out on his balcony above the Piazza Venezia. It was a sultry evening and the sirocco was blowing. He looked corpulent and his voice was hoarse, but his eyes blazed. The crowd below, usually so jubilant at his appearances, seemed tense and sombre. Some carried placards with caricatures of Churchill and John Bull. 'We will win,' he told them. '*Popolo Italiano*! To arms!' The time had come to claim back the 'riches and gold' over which the Allies held a monopoly.

There was very little applause. In his diary, an academic historian called Piero Calamandrei noted: 'From today, whatever happens, Fascism is finished.' As François-Poncet observed, the 'declining autocrat' could not bear to miss his last great encounter with history. In his own diary, Ciano wrote: 'I am sad, very sad. The adventure begins. May God help Italy.' But Edda did not share his feelings. 'I was absolutely delighted,' she admitted later.

Next morning, taking her maid with her, Edda caught a train to Turin where she intended to join the Red Cross and took a room in the Albergo Principe di Savoia. She told no one what she was doing, but it was evidently something that she had long planned to do. She left a note for Ciano; both he and Mussolini were furious. That day, British bombs began to fall on Italian cities.

In some senses, Italy had been at war for the past five years. First Ethiopia and the sanctions imposed by the League of Nations, then the sacrifices demanded by the Spanish Civil War, had accustomed Italians to shortages and rationing. It was an unexpectedly cold, windy June. British and French diplomats boarded trains for home, while in London their Italian counterparts caught a train to Glasgow and then a boat to Lisbon, taking with them a Botticelli which had hung in the embassy and a fortune in cash. Thousands of Italians who had been living in England were sent to camps, and the more unfortunate were put on the *Arandora Star* to be interned in Toronto. The ship was torpedoed and all those on board died. In Rome, orders went out for foreign Jews, anti-Fascists and other 'dangerous' individuals to be detained, leading to a rush of denunciations.

LUCE began putting out triumphalist newsreels, showing the Italian soldiers as handsome, manly and victorious, the enemy as ugly, cowardly and nasty, and attributing the fall of France to the fact that the French consumed too much fat and alcohol, had too few children and indulged in inter-racial relationships. The fanatical young students of the Gioventù Universitaria Fascista volunteered in their thousands, declaring that war alone would return Italy to its days of heroic glory, under 'men of true moral worth'. Milan Cathedral replaced its great windows with canvas. Dance halls were closed. In the blackout, trams rumbled like ghosts through the darkened cities. After Turin, the RAF bombed La

Spezia, Livorno, Cagliari, Trapani and Palermo. People fled into the countryside.

Italian women, already used to substituting cotton and silk with synthetic fabrics, were told that henceforth they were to concentrate on 'autarchy', consuming only what was made in Italy. The *giubba d'orbace*, a jacket made out of the formerly despised rough Sardinian cloth, was decreed to be smart, as were women who gave up their silk stockings. Supplies of soap began to run out, then pasta, rice, sugar and bread. Even so, the Venice Film Festival was especially glamorous, though the films were almost all either Italian or German, and the Germans brought with them their viciously anti-Semitic melodrama *Jud Süss*. For a while at least, Italians were content to believe what they were told: that the war would be victorious and, above all, it would be short.

While Edda began her Red Cross training with the military hospital of San Giovanni Battista, a hotbed of fashionable high society, Ciano took command of a bomber squadron based in Pisa, reporting to Edda on his aerial triumphs. According to its OVRA spies, the air force considered him a 'dilettante and an incompetent'. He was ordered home by Mussolini to discuss the terms of the French armistice agreed between Hitler and Pétain when, hoping for a generous handout of concessions in France and North Africa, the Italians came away with almost nothing. The signing of the armistice in Rome on 24 June brought no booty. An Italian offensive in the Alps, under rain and snow, ended with further humiliation. Six and a half thousand Italians died, and over two thousand returned with frostbite.

What was clear now, as it had long been, was that Italy was in no position to wage any kind of war. Almost everything was lacking: fuel, steel, copper, zinc, weapons, artillery, uniforms, vehicles. The nine months of neutrality had been wasted in selling arms to the Allies and failing to invest the returns in badly needed raw materials or in building bomb shelters. Just nineteen out of seventy-four divisions were complete in either men or weapons, and there was only enough aviation fuel for two months. More damningly, there was no appetite for war, among either soldiers or civilians. As Mussolini noted, 'With an army like this, one can declare war only on Peru.' The speed of the German advance had shown a new face of a war that Italy could not compete with: speed, manoeuvrability, ferocious air power. Nor, as was soon apparent, was Italy any kind of match for the Allies. Edda was on board a hospital ship when an Italian flotilla, carrying a considerable cargo of supplies to the forces in Libya and accompanied by an impressive escort, came into contact with an Allied fleet heading to Malta with reinforcements. The ensuing Battle of Punta Stilo resulted in considerable Italian casualties. 'A nightmare,' wrote Edda later. 'That poor human flesh burnt, lacerated, shredded . . .' War was bringing out her more sympathetic side.

The war did not end, as promised by Mussolini, swiftly. On the contrary, it kept spreading. Ciano paid a visit to Berlin, where the interpreter Paul Schmidt remarked on the greed of his aspirations and Hitler warned him that it would be a mistake to light a fire in the Balkans, which would only provoke Russian retaliation. During one reception, Ciano selected one of the good-looking women guests 'as an antipasto', and took her out boating on the lake, in the pouring rain. A sharp-tongued diplomat recorded that the 'lady in question', though no nun, was extremely taken aback by his 'liberty of speech and ways'. The American correspondent, William Shirer, described Ciano at the time as 'ludicrous' with his 'snapping Fascist salute' and remarked that he was 'the clown of the evening'. Ciano returned to Rome professing a somewhat surprising change of heart towards the Germans: even Hitler now struck him as reasonable and high minded, though he entertained friends with an account of seeing Goering in pink and mauve pyjamas and an auburn wig, his face painted, seemingly totally unconcerned by the war.

Hitler's warning about the Balkans was ignored, as were reliable reports from the military attaché in Athens that the Greeks were well armed and ready to fight. Ciano, believing that backward Greece might prove an easy target, had plans to bribe Greek politicians and generals, but the money vanished. On 8 October the Germans – once again failing to inform or consult their Italian partners – invaded Romania and quickly took Bucharest, despite the fact that Romania had already allied itself with the Germans. Mussolini, much encouraged by Ciano, decided on a similar attack on Greece, both to demonstrate that Italy too could play at Germany's game, and because he feared the Peloponnesian ports becoming sanctuaries for the Royal Navy. Maresciallo Badoglio, Italy's chief of staff, insisted that the Greeks 'will resist like lions', but was over-ruled. Six hundred thousand Italian soldiers were mobilised. Ciano declared that it would be an 'Italian Blitzkrieg'.

The campaign started badly and then got worse. Rains delayed the attack by a few hours while the air force was grounded. The Italian troops had no winter clothing, their guns were inferior to Greek guns, and they were both fed and commanded appallingly. The roads were terrible, the terrain unfriendly and the distances daunting. The troops slithered through mud and their heavy vehicles sank and got stuck. In the high mountain passes, once the snows came, men were reduced to eating the food brought for the mules while they froze in trenches hacked out of the rocks. There was a rumour that Mussolini, hearing of the snow and ice, remarked: 'In this way the runts will die and this mediocre race will be improved.'

In January 1941 Mussolini suddenly decided that nine high-ranking ministers and Fascist officials should sign up and share the risks and tribulations of the soldiers. The sedentary *gerarchi* were outraged. The Chamber and the Senate were prorogued indefinitely. Ciano, ordering a very expensive fur coat, went off with his squadron to a base in Bari and Mussolini resumed control of the Foreign Ministry. One night there was a rowdy party in the Impero Hotel and Ciano was one of several officers who set off fireworks, sang war songs, played poker and pestered local girls, telling friends how much he enjoyed hotel life: 'more freedom and every night a whore'. He was angry when his father-in-law insisted that he appear before a commission of inquiry with the others, writing to Mussolini that his lack of trust in him had 'left a wound in my heart that can never be healed'.

Hitler had been on his way to a meeting with Mussolini in Florence when he received news of the attack on Greece. He was furious and incredulous. As Italian casualties mounted, and the offensive began to take the form of a retreat, Germany reluctantly dispatched reinforcements. Italy's position was shrinking fast to that of a despised, unruly, dissatisfied junior partner. The tide of the campaign turned to favour the Axis, and the Germans soon starved the Greeks of their dwindling supplies of food. The Greek campaign cost the Italians 13,755 dead and over 50,000 wounded, and they lost sixty-four aircraft and one submarine. Churchill taunted Mussolini for 'frisking up to the side of the German tiger', then having the audacity to pretend that the victory was his. On 27 April, the Germans reached Athens and a month later captured Crete. An armistice was signed, mortifyingly at first only between Greece and Germany, a puppet regime was installed and Greece divided up between Germany, Italy and Bulgaria. Italy's military failures were an ominous sign of what was to come.

During the spring offensive Edda passed her initial nursing exams and, though still far from fully trained, pulled strings to get herself on board a hospital ship, the *Po*, bound for Greece. Though she hated the smell of disinfectant and had practically stopped eating, she was proving a surprisingly popular and hard-working nurse. Red Cross life was not exactly to her liking, since the nurses were expected to represent the full dignity of Fascist womanhood, but it gave her the chance to prove her strength and effectiveness. And she relished action. Forbidden to enter cafés or speak to officers, the nurses were regularly inspected by the Red Cross president, the Princess of Piemonte, and a bevy of aristocratic ladies.

Edda as a nurse

On the night of 14 March, the *Po* was hit by two torpedoes as it lay at anchor outside the port of Vlorë on the Albanian Adriatic waiting to pick up casualties. Edda was in her cabin reading P. G. Wodehouse. She heard cries, wondered which of her coats to put on and searched for her lucky mascot, a cat with blue glass eyes, then went up on deck to find the ship listing and starting to sink, while most of the lifeboats had been damaged in the attack. She watched as the head nurse was swept away and swallowed up by the waves. A sailor shouted at her to jump and she climbed on to the rail and leapt into the icy water. There was a full moon and the sea was full of people trying to stay afloat. Later she described the scene: 'Santa Rita! I cried, help me! . . . I felt the cold creeping up my legs and feared getting cramp . . . As the ship keeled over I saw my friend, another nurse, crushed by the mast.' Santa Rita, fittingly, was the patroness of lost causes. The injured nurse was her closest friend, Ennia Tramontani, and twenty-two others drowned with her. A strong swimmer, Edda clung to a life-ring for five hours until a very overloaded lifeboat eventually made room for her and a sailor gave her a jacket and some cognac. She refused, she said later, surely embroidering her story, to think about death, instead looking at the moon and thinking that it was bright enough to read a newspaper by, while the waves reminded her of de Chirico's paintings. Emergencies brought out the best in her.

The Italian reporter Indro Montanelli – another often unreliable witness – who was on the shore when the survivors were brought in, described Edda as being both proud and shy. She was still wearing her camel coat and white gloves, but had lost her shoes. 'She sat on a seat smoking and sipping a mixture of rum and coffee,' he wrote, then answered questions reluctantly and with 'a lack of grace', evidently hating the role of heroine. Mussolini, who was in Albania at the time, hastened to Vlorë, and Ciano arrived the next day. Fifty-two telegrams were delivered, congratulating her on her escape. Later, Edda was one of fifteen nurses to be awarded medals for their 'keen sense of sacrifice' as the ship went down, but what she had actually done 'other than survive', as she put it, she never explained. Questions only elicited impatient replies. Danger, episodes of fate, were not things you dwelt on or indulged in. She would later say that working as a nurse was one of the happiest times in her life, 'away from the heavy atmosphere of Rome and living among intelligent people'.

Ten days later, Edda got herself transferred to a field hospital near the front at Dhërmi. 'We found the countess on the front line,' wrote a friend to Mussolini's secretary Sebastiani, 'in the full music of the cannons, and she is <u>very well</u>.' Action and usefulness were things that Edda craved. Danger was her antidote to boredom and languor.

The fiasco of the Greek campaign, into which Italy had thrown extravagant amounts of money, men and resources, was widely seen as Ciano's fault. 'Universal hatred rains on Ciano,' noted the journalist Ugo Ojetti, and people had started saying openly that he had now replaced Starace as the most hated man in Italy. And not only in Italy: the British hated him for having, as they saw it, tricked them into believing that he was on their side, and the Germans because they now regarded him as the leader of a hostile aristocratic mafia, composed of 'cretins, left over from a fossilised world from which Mussolini had been unable to free himself'. There were rumours that Edda was planning to leave him. In Rome, senators called openly for Ciano's dismissal.

Mountains of anonymous letters reached the Palazzo Venezia, portraying Edda as having lost all sense of family dignity since she had dedicated her life to alcohol and drugs, while the profiteering and parasitic Ciano was accused of 'immorality and depravity'. An OVRA spy reported that in the Palazzo Chigi there reigned 'an enormous spiritual anarchy: the chaos is total'. Whoever displeased Isabella Colonna was got rid of. Mussolini chose to do nothing.

Badly as the war had gone in Greece, it had gone even worse in North Africa. The ace pilot Balbo, who had strongly opposed the war but dutifully returned to his squadron, had been shot down in error by an Italian anti-aircraft battery as he was coming in to land at Tobruk. Mussolini appeared curiously unmoved, only remarking later that Balbo had been 'a fine soldier, a great aviator, an authentic revolutionary ... the only one who would have been capable of killing me'. Mussolini had always feared Balbo's popularity, and rumours circulated that the accident had been a plot to remove his rival.

By the middle of January 1941, even as catastrophic losses mounted in Greece, the Italian army, lacking the tanks or motorised infantry to fight a desert war, had stalled in North Africa, and the British were advancing on Cyrenaica. Seven ships sent to supply Libya were sunk, in spite of their convoy of destroyers. When in May Haile Selassie returned to his throne in Addis Ababa, Italy's brief moment as an empire abruptly ended.

Though rumours had reached Mussolini and Ciano of German plans to attack its ally Russia, news of the invasion, Operation Barbarossa, on 22 June, came as a surprise. It was delivered, as usual, with no warning, in the middle of the night, and for once Edda, Mussolini and Ciano were in agreement that the invasion was an error. As Edda wrote later, she could never forget Goering's remark to her that it would be a mistake to open a second front. At first, the Germans delighted in their swift advance towards Leningrad and Moscow, but by 1 July the Red Army had rallied and was resisting strongly. Italian troops, 62,000 men on 216 trains, were dispatched to support the Germans in the east, having been assured that the Russians were more like Africans than Europeans and would behave like 'sheep'. As with Greece, they soon discovered that their outdated weapons, broken radios, summer uniforms and insufficient ammunition were no match for the Russians, a discovery made all the more bitter when they were forced to watch the Germans flying past in their armoured cars, as they trudged through clouds of dust on foot. When winter came, bringing temperatures that dropped to 35 degrees below zero, many Italian soldiers died.

The strategic Libyan port of Benghazi had fallen to the British, and before Rommel arrived with reinforcements 130,000 Italians had been taken prisoner. 'Never,' remarked Eden, 'had so much been surrendered by so many to so few.'

The Mussolini family had its own share of tragedies. Rachele had always worried most about Bruno, now twenty-three and serving in the air force. She kept telling him that he was too bold and that he should take more care, to which he always replied that he was so cautious that he had 'snails' in his plane. It became their greeting. After the Greek campaign, Bruno spent a month in Germany, returning to speak with awe about German discipline and commitment. On 7 August, he went to Pisa with his squadron to test a new four-engine plane. It took off smoothly but as it returned to land, it crashed, scattering wreckage. Vittorio was watching. He took a bicycle and pedalled furiously to the scene. Bruno was still just alive, wrapped in the cords of a parachute, but died very soon after.

Mussolini rang Rachele, who was in Riccione for the summer, and the two hurried to Pisa. Both, suddenly, looked very old.

Mussolini stood stony faced. Rachele asked Gina, Bruno's wife, to go to the hotel where Bruno had spent the night and bring back his sheets. That night, she dreamt that Bruno told her that he was very cold. The funeral, in Predappio, was another opulent Fascist affair, with people lining the roads to watch the hearse pass. As he had done when his brother died, Mussolini sat down to write a memoir about his second son. The profits from *Parlo con Bruno*, an odd combination of sentimentality, tender reminiscences and bracing resolve, conjuring up a heroic figure not easily recognised by those who remembered him as timid and silent, went to the orphans of pilots. Bruno's daughter Marina had just had her first birthday and her mother pinned Bruno's medal on to her dress. Edda wrote to her younger brother Romano: 'I am completely crushed.' With true Mussolini restraint, she said no more.

After the Japanese attack on Pearl Harbor on 7 December 1941, bringing the Americans into the conflict, Mussolini declared war on the United States. The streets of Rome filled with *squadristi* carrying obscene cartoons of the Roosevelts, one of them of Eleanor wearing a lavatory seat as a necklace. Ciano was more pessimistic than ever. Looking out from his balcony in Palazzo Chigi towards the Via del Corso, he told a visitor: 'We will see American tanks drive up here.' Whenever she passed through Rome, Edda continued to distribute charitable donations, which increasingly went to prosthetic limbs for wounded soldiers. Much to her annoyance, Claretta had started doing the same thing and was calling herself '*Eccellenza*'.

In Italy, the production of new planes was derisory. The three battleships sunk by the RAF at Taranto in the late autumn of 1940 were followed six months later by three cruisers going down at Cape Matapan. The elderly military commanders appeared mired in bickering over useless statistical misinformation. As Italy lurched from disaster to disaster, its status reduced to little more than a satellite of the Third Reich, its soldiers unruly, despised by the Germans and mutinous, Mussolini spent his time not on the various military campaigns, but on what Italy would become once the war was over. His old ulcer plagued him constantly and one day Rachele's maid found him writhing on the floor. She thought that he was dying.

15

Dancing from one party to the next

In the early days of the war, the growing German community in Rome had been somewhat cold-shouldered by the *beau monde*. But now that they appeared to be on the winning side, the grand palazzi opened their doors to them. A concert performance of *Ariadne auf Naxos*, given in the German embassy gardens, delighted guests when nightingales joined in the singing. Prince Otto von Bismarck, grandson of the Iron Chancellor, arrived as Counsellor with his wife Ann-Mari, a 'Nordic, goddess-like beauty', sent to win Ciano's friendship. The princess, who was said to love parties, soon became very close to Filippo Anfuso, Ciano's dark, lacquer-haired Sicilian chef-de-cabinet.

The most beautiful of the group of Germans pressing their attentions on the Foreign Minister was Veronica Klemm, the wife of the economic adviser, who dressed in fashionable sailor suits. As the sharp-eyed Signora Cerruti remarked, they all 'danced, golfed and flirted while the world came nearer and nearer to tragedy'. A masseur called Felix Kersten, 'plump and gentle as a Buddha', had appeared in Rome as a gift from Himmler to his Roman friends. He soon joined the Petit Trianon, giving massages in the Grand Hotel, asking to be paid not in cash but in bolts of silk and boxes of chocolates.

A more ambiguous German figure was Eugen Dollmann, who had been doing historical research in Rome since the late 1920s and now regularly acted as interpreter when the senior Nazis came to Rome, having joined the SS in 1937. Dollmann was in his forties, cultured, clever, amiable, snobbish and suave, and he was a keen student of Italian social mores. He looked, not like a heroic German soldier, noted a visitor, but more like a Roman socialite, 'with his hair combed back and almost effeminate gestures'. Dollmann was close to the police chief Bocchini, and professed to find Himmler 'ludicrous and uncongenial', and Heydrich frightening, with his 'lily white hands' designed for 'prolonged strangling'.

Eugen Dollmann interpreting for the Nazi leaders, with Ciano, in Rome

The Roman princesses loved and feted Dollmann, who went everywhere with a large Alsatian, and commented that Italy's foreign policy under Ciano had developed into an 'erotically perfumed maze'. He had never liked the Foreign Minister, saying he was *un signore un po' soft*', but he did like Edda, and wondered how, 'tartly intelligent, capricious as a wild mare and endowed with a thoroughbred ugliness', she did not see through the rottenness of the corrupt Roman society and the danger of the encircling Nazis. With her 'Mussolini eyes that irradiated everything and everyone they looked at', Edda, at once fragile and powerful, intelligent and sceptical, was, he concluded, too wrapped up in her own private life and too intent on having a good time, though what he perhaps failed to detect was her determination to avoid seeing what was happening. Dollmann had no time for Rome's 'chatterers', dismissing them as 'frivolous, amoral, irresponsible, physically fascinating' but lacking in all intellectual qualities.

When Goering came to Rome on spending sprees, referred to by Elisabetta Cerruti as 'small raids', he brought with him presents of cigarette cases, decorated with a swastika and the Nazi Party badge – with gold and precious stones for the high-ranking

Fascists, silver with semi-precious ones for the more lowly. In his immense sable coat, he looked, thought Ciano, 'like something between a 1906 motorist and the tart at the opera'. By this stage, Ciano did not really care for any of the Nazi leaders, though, even as the war raged, he spent a week shooting with Ribbentrop and Himmler in Bohemia, bagging 620 pheasants; but he allowed them to court him, so that he could later repeat their absurdities around the Golf Club, while they relayed his to Berlin.

Listening to Ciano's indiscretions, Nelson Page wondered whether he should try to silence him, knowing that every word would be repeated verbatim back to Berlin. 'But it was too late,' he wrote later. 'And Galeazzo was already heading rapidly towards his destiny.' Ciano's dislike of Ribbentrop had grown stronger. He regarded him as a 'man of ice', bloated and affected after receiving the Collare dell'Annunziata from the King when the Pact of Steel was signed, and he was heard to refer to his German counterpart as '*il fesso*', the fool. Grandi complained that the German Foreign Minister had the tact of an 'elephant walking on plates'.

For their part, the Germans had initially regarded Ciano as a nuisance who had to be tolerated, but were now beginning to consider him very dangerous, especially in the light of the remarks about Germany repeated by their spies. Early in 1941, Hitler had apparently handed Mussolini a secret dossier – which later vanished and has never been found – containing accounts of Ciano's open contempt for the Axis and desire for peace at any cost, and also of his family's financial profiteering. It described, at great length, the parties thrown by Principessa Isabella Colonna, the scandalous affairs with actresses, and the corruption of the Petit Trianon. Himmler dismissed this as tittle-tattle but enjoyed referring to Isabella as '*la quinta colonna*', the fifth column. Hitler, however, took it all more seriously and it fuelled his already pronounced aversion to Ciano. When the memorandum was leaked, the Roman *beau monde* was at first afraid, then maliciously complacent, treating it as the ramblings of a disloyal servant playing dirty tricks. To his friends, Ciano boasted that Mussolini would 'never throw me to the wolves', but Malaparte observed that he was now looking frightened.

The dossier apparently also contained a great deal about Edda, her own indiscretions about Franco and Pétain and her ill-advised cracks about Himmler and Ribbentrop, along with her many supposed love affairs on Capri. What saved Ciano from dismissal, so it was said, was that the memorandum had been extremely hostile to Edda and that Mussolini had no intention of sacrificing his daughter. It was thought to be the work of an agent of Ribbentrop's, but just who all the informers were, in this city of spies, no one could quite work out. And so the *principesse* went on flattering their German visitors, despising Rachele as common, praying for the monarchy to endure, and dreaming of Ciano as a future Prime Minister with anglophile tendencies, while 'dancing their way from one party to the next'. And Edda went on with her own erratic, independent life, listening to no one, coming and going between Rome and her Red Cross duties, her children as ever left with their nanny, speaking out when she felt like it, but giving little impression of weighing her words.

It was at this time, reflecting on the cross-currents of talk sweeping through Rome, that an Egyptian magazine called *Images* described her no longer as simply influential but as 'the most dangerous woman in Europe'. Edda, it said, 'rules her father with an iron fist'. This, certainly, had become the accepted view in many circles, but as with so much else in Edda's life, it has to be seen in context. Her power was never of a concrete kind, not least because she was a woman, and because she was quickly bored with the minutiae of daily decisions. But her closeness to her father and Ciano's reliance on her, together with her impatience at equivocations, made her formidable, even when she was least aware of it.

In November 1940 the police chief Arturo Bocchini had collapsed with a cerebral haemorrhage during a Lucullan feast on the eve of his sixtieth birthday and died in the arms of his young mistress. His spectacular funeral had been attended by Heydrich and Himmler, to whom he had been sending cases of spaghetti and tomatoes every Christmas. It was a sumptuous affair: mounted police in dress uniforms, bands playing funeral marches, and a long cortège of *gerarchi*, civil servants, ministers, regiments of police and soldiers. Bocchini had asked that the words 'in difficult times, he did all the good, and as little of the bad, as possible' be written on his tombstone.

Since then, Bocchini's successor Carmine Senise had continued to report to both Mussolini and Ciano on the mood of Italy. In a safe in Bocchini's office, Senise had found twenty-one million lire in one-thousand-lire notes, and a great many incriminating documents. Ciano, mistakenly as it turned out, dismissed the crumpled, inelegantly dressed Senise as a 'good man, but a chatterbox, superficial and theatrical', but he was, in fact, both very canny and very dangerous. OVRA, which he inherited from Bocchini, now had fifty-six members of staff, 319 agents and a great number of sub-agents, busily tapping telephones, engaged in surveillance and bribing prostitutes and the mistresses of the *gerarchi*. It was from Senise that Ciano learnt that several of the senior Fascists were taking money from Jews in return for forged papers and protection.

Rome itself remained curiously unchanged. The capital had almost totally been spared the heavy Allied bombardments of other cities. Cinecittà was continuing to turn out escapist films showing Italians in a heroic light. American films were banned, but Goebbels sent Mussolini an early print of *Gone with the Wind*. The young director Rossellini worked on *Luciano Serra Pilota*, a film glorifying the air force, as did Vittorio Mussolini, and it won the Mussolini cup at the Venice Film Festival, sharing the prize with Leni Riefenstahl's *Olympia*. The spring of 1941 had seen the first bare breasts on screen, but who beat whom in the contest, whether the exotic, black-haired '*diva del regime*', Doris Duranti, or the smouldering, sensual Clara Calamai, no one was quite sure.

Ciano's protégé Pavolini had started an affair with Duranti, who thrived on the high life of the rich *gerarchi*, and he took her to Ciano's house in Livorno. At a party one night, when the guests demanded a 'naked minister', Pavolini was said to have taken all his clothes off. He was married with three children; Mussolini summoned him and told him that he had to give up Duranti. He refused. Mussolini watched one of her films, then told him: 'Now I understand.' Pavolini was another of the regime's more ambiguous *gerarchi*. He told a friend: 'I have climbed on to a tiger, and now I can't get off.'

With the war, cartoonists had grown bolder and more anti-Semitic. One produced a catalogue of social 'types', deemed to be 'spots, boils, cases of immorality, anomalies, inversions', to be derided, along with 'dapper dilettantes, flighty fashion consumers' and black marketeers, each type exaggerated and many given grotesque Semitic features.

The constant military defeats had caused a marked deterioration in Mussolini's health. His stomach pains had grown worse and more frequent. In her diary, Rachele noted how the attacks were sparked off by bad news from the war. After Bruno's death, his widow Gina had moved with Marina into the Villa Torlonia, as had Vittorio, who was now working with LUCE and the air force to record films of aerial attacks. Romano and Anna Maria were still at school, Romano no better a student than his older brothers and getting friends to do his homework, but Anna Maria was disciplined and diligent and 'full of curiosity'. She was still bent from the polio but ruthless with herself in not letting it get in the way of an ordinary life.

Rachele's own spy network flourished, with her informers bringing her endless tales of misdeeds. She took strongly against some of the *gerarchi*, and it was rumoured that she had engineered Starace's downfall, after dressing as a peasant woman and, taking her son Romano and his camera with her, visiting his house in Rocca di Papa, which she found full of incredible luxury. She also repeated to Mussolini that Starace was known to use militiamen to exercise his dogs. The passing of time had made her no less contemptuous of grandeur and when she attended a requiem mass for the Duke of Aosta, who had died in a prison camp in Kenya of tuberculosis and malaria, she arrived in simple mourning clothes, wept copiously and insisted on going home as she had come, on foot. Such simplicity was much mocked in the Roman palazzi.

But it also provided a clever cover for her acquisitiveness. When she decided to buy the villa the family rented every summer at Riccione and the owners refused to sell, she not only brought heavy and menacing pressure to bear, but forced them to give it to her at a fraction of its true cost. One neighbour's house was compulsorily knocked down so that she could build a tennis court, others nearby were bullied into selling adjoining plots. The outbreak of war did not check her property ambitions; between February and March 1942, Rachele bought two more villas at Riccione.

At Rocca delle Caminate – also now owned by her though a gift of the state to Mussolini – Rachele was often seen perched on a cushion on a hard bench in the central hall where Mussolini held his meetings, scrutinising the faces of the men present for signs of disloyalty. Ciano referred to her protégé, the unscrupulous architect Dino Prater, as the 'puny Rasputin of the Villa Torlonia', but Edda, never one to think deeply about the foibles of mankind, dismissed her mother's eccentricities as 'the consequences of the menopause'. Relations between Ciano and his mother-in-law, whom he described as living in a 'continuous and unjustified state of over-excitement', had grown no closer with the years.

Whenever she was given leave from the Red Cross, Edda returned to Capri, now largely emptied of foreigners, the houses shuttered, the English church taken over as 'enemy territory' and anti-aircraft posts set up along the Marina Grande. The Fascist authorities had drawn up lists of 'idlers' and those 'dedicated to debauchery'. In 1941 Edda had taken with her as her companion Emilio Pucci, a young air force officer, which whom she had skied at Cortina and visited Florence for the Maggio Musicale, and it was probably on Capri that they started an affair. Pucci, who was four years younger, was tall and extremely thin, with a long, melancholy and slightly horsy face; he called her *una divina piccola darling* and said that she was 'perceptive, loyal and direct'. Both of them very interested in fashion, they were spotted wearing matching clothes. Mussolini had forbidden dancing for the duration of the war: Edda kept dancing. He frowned on women in trousers: she wore little else. A spy reported that she and the children were eating refined white pasta, no longer available in shops, and going out in carriages drawn by English horses.

In May 1942 Edda was back with the Red Cross and decided to return to Germany to visit the bombed cities of Hamburg, Lübeck and Bremen, on her way to the Eastern Front. She waited irritably in Berlin for a pass, complaining that Ribbentrop, 'that parrot', was obstructing her until she finally badgered him into giving her a private carriage, though she continued to enjoy German society, and admired her friends' fortitude during bombardments. Hitler was reported to have been looking forward to her visit, saying that by contrast with the 'futile, degenerate' Italian aristocracy, it was a pleasure to talk to an 'intelligent and charming woman like Edda Mussolini'. Goebbels and Magda gave a dinner party for her, Goebbels noting later that he had found her 'exceptionally serious' and 'extremely clever'. Magda left a deep impression on Edda by saying that should Germany lose the war, 'we will all kill ourselves, including the children', and that she had the cyanide ready. Magda was forty, considerably older than thirty-one-year-old Edda, and the mother of an older boy and five small daughters.

A few days later, Ribbentrop met Ciano and complained that Edda had become 'intolerably capricious'. The same information reached the King, who repeated it to Mussolini, who in turn told Ciano to stop his wife's chatter. But by now Edda had already caused more trouble by visiting a labour camp for Italian workers, where she discovered appalling conditions and talked to a worker who had been badly beaten by a German supervisor. Before leaving for the Eastern Front, she berated Hitler for the treatment being meted out to Italian workers. 'Which will,' noted Ciano, 'change nothing.' Mussolini ordered her to tell no one what she had seen.

Overriding Hitler's warnings that the front was too dangerous, but accepting his offer of vaccinations by his private doctor, Edda set out for the east. She served in hospitals in the Italian sector and from the Dom basin wrote to Ciano that she had fallen in love with a blond, blue-eyed, two-year-old boy and that she wished to adopt him and bring him home. 'No, for heaven's sake,' Ciano hastily replied, 'that's all we need. We have enough problems as it is.' Commanding officers complained that her presence was disruptive, but sentimental, sugary accounts of her work made their way back to Rome. Edda said later that during her time on the Eastern Front she had lived in a constant state of fear about the many unexploded mines that lay all about; it was one of the very rare moments that she confessed to a lack of courage. The sunflowers were out, and she began to learn Russian from a young woman comrade. One day she watched a German panzer division rumble past on its way to Stalingrad. A German victory, she thought, was certain.

Edda's relations with her father had been growing strained. When on leave in Rome she would lecture him about the strictures on the lives of nurses, who were forbidden to wear trousers or dance with the soldiers. Both of them quick to lose their temper, their arguments often ended with Edda storming out. But something deeper had changed. Edda had long known about Claretta, and the knowledge that her father had someone closer to him than herself had driven an unhappy wedge between them, though the intercepts now picked up from Claretta's phone suggested that Mussolini's passion had diminished. Even as, distracted by the war, he pulled back, Claretta made melodramatic scenes, wept and wrote desperate and clinging letters. An ectopic pregnancy had ended in an operation; a second pregnancy was announced, but proved false.

On the ninth anniversary of their first encounter at Ostia, Mussolini gave her a bracelet with the inscription: 'Clara, I am you and you are me. Ben.' After the Petaccis moved into a sumptuous new 700-square-metre house, the Villa Camilluccia, with thirty-two rooms, for which the architects had given their services free of charge, rightly believing it would help their careers, Mussolini visited her there in the afternoons. A spy reported that he had been able to get inside the house and that there were crystal doors and frescoed walls, a black marble bathroom with a sunken mosaic bath, a completely pink bedroom and a swimming pool, 'all in very bad taste'.

The Petaccis had not wasted their time. Claretta's father had been given a column on the daily *Il Messaggero*, while her sister, eighteen-year-old Myriam, had got herself into the film studios at Cinecittà. Directors found her insipid but admired her generous bust. But it was Claretta's corrupt brother Marcello who made the most of his sister's liaison, winning unmerited promotions in his medical career and amassing fortunes in racketeering, money laundering and currency dealings. He was now head of surgery at a military hospital in Venice, which ensured that he did not have to report for military duty. His many business interests ranged from zinc and steel to sardines and cocoa. OVRA spies reported that Rome was rife with rumours about Mussolini's 'courtesan'. The Petacci clan, noted a senior police officer, was 'doing more harm to Mussolini than fifteen lost battles'.

The corrupt and greedy *gerarca* Guido Buffarini-Guidi was known to be Marcello's protector and was busy adding to his own income with a trade in documents for Jews to prove they were not Jewish, run by a colleague who had worked out a precise list of fees, according to wealth of client or type of document. Much the same was happening throughout the country: lawyers, professors and civil servants obligingly 'aryanising' citizens – for a fee. The atmosphere in Rome, wrote Ciano in his diary, had become like the decay 'of the late Roman Empire'.

Edda, picking up the rumours about Claretta, finally decided to act. News had reached her that people in Rome were openly calling Claretta's house 'the most important of the Ministries' because it was here that careers were said to be made and broken. Edda went to lunch with her father, told him what Rome was saying and urged him to put an end to all the scandals. Mussolini listened, agreed, and insisted piously that Rachele was the only woman in his life who mattered to him. But Claretta was not about to give up. The affair continued. She warned her lover against the 'dwarf King' and the meddlesome *gerarchi*, calling them 'a nest of filthy snakes'. As for Ciano, she declared, he was both unfaithful and treacherous.

Marcello was not giving up either. He arranged a very lucrative currency exchange with a well-placed crony in Spain and would have got away with another small fortune had a coffer containing 18 kilos of gold, entrusted to the diplomatic pouch, not fallen into the hands of a minister, who alerted Ciano. Ciano handed it to Carmine Senise, who paid the money into the Banca d'Italia. This time, there was no wriggling back. Marcello was ordered to join the navy in Taranto, though he continued to agitate for the return of his gold. Claretta was barred from the Palazzo Venezia. 'Petacci is an imbecile,' Mussolini declared. 'The woman will be liquidated and all these imbroglios stopped.' Except, of course, they were not. Telling him that he was treating her like a 'thief or a prostitute', Claretta was soon back with Mussolini, urging him to be 'the titan, the giant, the world dominator' and swearing vengeance.

16

Plotting

Mussolini had dreamt of entering Cairo on a white horse, claiming victory not for the Axis powers, but for the Italians. But on 23 October 1942, the British Eighth Army, under Montgomery, led a successful attack on the outnumbered and outgunned Italian and German troops at El Alamein; on the night of 7 November, the first Allied soldiers landed in Algeria and Morocco. In February 1943, after months of intense fighting, the surviving German forces in Stalingrad surrendered to the Red Army. Their long retreat westward turned into a rout, and they refused to give the Italians, retreating with them, petrol and denied them lifts on their trucks. In the Dom Basin, the Torino division lost nine out of ten of its men. The seventeen-month Russian campaign had cost Italy over 100,000 dead. Two thirds of the 70,000 men now taken prisoner would die, whether on forced marches or in Soviet prisoner-of-war camps. As news of defeats, and of soldiers tired, depressed and undisciplined, reached Rome, Mussolini turned his attentions from battlefront to battlefront, sometimes truculent, sometimes optimistic, sometimes accusatory, issuing orders, then immediately countermanding them.

He was clearly not well, trying to keep spasms of acute pain at bay by eating only vegetables and soup. His insomnia grew worse, and day by day he seemed to age. An OVRA intercept had picked him up saying to Claretta, 'I feel empty headed. I lose touch with ideas, with words.' Treatments by different specialists only appeared to make him worse. One told Rachele that he suspected that Mussolini was suffering from terminal stomach cancer, but new tests showed only gastritis and an acute duodenal ulcer. His weight kept falling. Gone were the days when chosen journalists were invited to watch him take his horse Thiene over the jumps in the park of the

Villa Torlonia. When Edda went to see him one day, she was struck by how ill he looked. Her father, she wrote to Ciano, was 'irritable, depressed' and also very angry. Then she added: 'I have a feeling of suffocation and fear.' When Ciano suggested to Mussolini that Italy should consider suing for peace, his father-in-law replied that he had made up his mind to 'march with Germany to the end'. Ciano himself, noted a senior civil servant in the Palazzo Chigi, was giving the impression of having completely lost his nerve, railing against the Germans, cursing, pacing, by turn angry and sullen, telling colleagues that 'it only remains to await the collapse'.

What Mussolini did now, taking everyone by surprise, was to reshuffle his cabinet. In what became known as the 'ministerial earthquake' of 6 February 1943, he suddenly announced that he was sacking four of the leading *gerarchi* and moving six others to different posts. The news reverberated round the European capitals, everyone trying to decipher what it meant. Ciano, Grandi and Bottai – the latter heard the news on Radio London – were among the casualties, and it was said that Mussolini had been swayed by information that the Germans had lost all confidence in Ciano. The men he brought in, though perceived as loyal, left him more isolated than ever. When Mussolini informed Ciano of his decision, he offered him the choice of the lieutenancy of Albania or Ambassador to the Vatican. Ciano opted immediately for the Vatican, where he would be free of Mussolini's tutelage yet well-placed to pursue independent peace overtures, and in any case he was persuaded that Rome was where the fate of Italy would be determined. Shrewdly foreseeing that Mussolini would realise what he had done and change his mind, he hastily made contact with the Vatican and had his new post as ambassador endorsed. When Mussolini did indeed tell him that he had changed his mind, it was too late.

Going to see the Duce to discuss his new appointment, Ciano told him that he had kept all the documents confirming the treachery of the Germans, in case he should have need of them. For all their disagreements, Ciano had never quite lost his veneration for his father-in-law. 'I like Mussolini,' he wrote piously in his diary. 'I like him very much, and what I shall miss most will be my contact with him.' In his luxurious new office in the Palazzo Borromeo on the Via Flaminia, soon known as '*il piccolo Palazzo Chigi*', he told friends that it was time to bring 'an end to the disaster of the war', and that he was now better placed to survive the inevitable crisis. He had taken with him sixteen volumes of his diaries, the earlier ones now hidden with his mother. To Bottai, watching him leave the Foreign Ministry, it seemed as if Ciano's earlier impatience with Mussolini was turning into visceral dislike.

Edda was increasingly suspicious and wary of the way things were going, and she blamed Ciano's removal from the Foreign Ministry on the Petacci clan, saying that it was their revenge for advising her father to get rid of Claretta. As Ciano prepared to take up his new duties, there was a comic moment when the official car failed to arrive to take the entire family for their first audience with the Pope. Ciano, in full ambassadorial regalia, Edda in floor-length dress and black mantilla, Dindina in her communion frock, and the two boys were forced to squeeze into Ciano's Topolino and race through the city. Once there, the day did not improve. During the audience, six-year-old Marzio, who was sitting on Edda's knee, made a grab for the Pope's gold telephone and for a few seconds the small boy and the pontiff tugged it backwards and forwards between them. The Pope cut short the audience. The Vatican was reported to be not altogether pleased with Ciano's appointment, saying that he had failed to curb Mussolini's bellicose tendencies. 'As for that toad Contessa Ciano,' an insider was heard to remark, 'they are saying that it is the duty of the Church to welcome sheep who stray.'

It fell to Vera, wife of Diego von Bergen, the German Ambassador to the Vatican, to introduce Edda formally to the papal ladies of the Black aristocracy. Vera consulted Dollmann who suggested that tea would be an appropriate occasion, providing that there were also cocktails and that at least a few of the guests were men. The papal ladies arrived at the Villa Bonaparte, once the residence of Napoleon's sister Pauline, at the appointed time, in sombre black, grey or violet high-necked dresses and gloves. They stood, in a yellow salon with frescoes by Perugino, and waited. For a long time, nothing happened. When Edda finally made her entrée, she was wearing gold sandals and ostentatious modern jewellery. She had no gloves. The ladies, visibly disapproving, sipped their tea. Edda refused tea but accepted a cocktail. Then, behaving exactly like her father, she turned her full attention to winning them over. She asked them questions about themselves, listened carefully, sympathised and smiled; she was modest and appreciative. One by one, the ladies melted. They stayed, charmed, until darkness fell.

Not long before the Cianos took up their new role, a police report had noted: 'Anti-Fascism is taking root everywhere – threateningly, implacably and silently.' Italy, people complained, was no longer a nation, but a 'field of plunder'. One journalist was heard to say that they should all enjoy themselves while they could 'because we are destined to end up hanging in the Piazza Venezia'. Roberto Rossi, spy 557, sent in a report on the fury of ordinary Italians at the 'inept, arrogant, often dishonest, always cowardly' *gerarchi* and their feeling that 'Fascism is finished, the nation is rotten'. It was true: the whole fabric of the twenty-year Fascist regime was unravelling. The heavy bombing of the cities – the Allies having decided that the best way of getting the Italians to reject Mussolini was by hitting their morale hard – had exposed the fact that air defences and air raid shelters were totally inadequate. Many parts of Milan, Turin and Genoa had been reduced to rubble, and frantic families had taken to breaking into the private shelters of the rich with pickaxes. The roads of Italy were full of people fleeing into the countryside, where they lived as if in the Middle Ages, bartering what little they had been able to salvage for food. At Easter, there were advertisements in the papers calling for the loan or rent of a chicken, so that children might have eggs.

People, everywhere, were hungry and becoming more so. There was nothing that was not rationed, except for potatoes, and rations provided barely a thousand calories per day. Every square inch of green land in Rome was under cultivation. The black market flourished and over telephones they knew to be tapped, housewives spoke of 'round things', which meant eggs, and 'white things' which were beans. Since there was no sugar, cake shops closed. In Rome, the Colonnas and the Dorias began dismantling and packing up their art collections. Ezra Pound, long an admirer of the Fascists, gave a series of broadcasts against Roosevelt over Radio Roma and orders went out that no photographs of Charlie Chaplin, Bette Davis or Myrna Loy were to appear (since they were Jewish).

Rome was placed under nightly blackouts and all lights, even in hallways and corridors, at petrol pumps and on electric clocks, were forbidden. The city was sombre, but Nelson Page continued to host parties for the gamblers, to which Edda came and lost money whenever she was in the city. If possible, the divide between the classes had become more extreme: when Gabriella di Robilant opened a new fashion house on the Piazza di Spagna – where Edda, along with the royal family and many film stars, was a regular customer – the Spanish embassy threw a sumptuous dinner, with servants in livery. It was, di Robilant thought, 'like the last days of Pompeii'. Romans, ever quick to ridicule and joke, coined names for well-known people and events. Edda became 'the girl in every port'; the Mussolini family, 'the flying devils'; victory, 'the eternal illusion'.

For a long time, Italians had blamed the inefficient, timorous generals and the untrustworthy, venal *gerarchi* for Italy's ills, saying that they were keeping the real facts of the war from Mussolini. 'If the Duce really knew . . .' And they were right to mistrust and despise them: many soldiers as well as senior Fascists were indeed profoundly corrupt, having spent their years in power amassing fortunes, rewarding their favourites, punishing their enemies and buying up swathes of real estate as Rome spread and grew. When Mussolini was informed that Fascism had become a *'mangiatoia'*, a trough, he was said to have replied: 'Perhaps, but it's important that it's not us doing the eating.' Mussolini had always been, and remained, a man of relatively modest tastes: of all his *gerarchi*, he was probably feasting the least.

The capital was full of *garçonnières*, bachelor flats, to which these men took the starlets from Cinecittà, leaving their offices in mid afternoon and making no attempt to conceal where they were going. As the Communist writer and politician Giorgio Amendola later wrote, what defined the Fascist regime in the end was not violence but corruption, a dark world of cynicism, extortion, a Darwinian struggle for survival and a virus from which few people seemed immune. Sleaze at every level: a police report noted that the Principessa Colonna continued to host dinners for 150 people, with no less luxury than before the war. As a close friend of Ciano's, she enjoyed 'special immunity'.

The myth of Mussolini's greatness and omnificence, the cult of him as father of the nation, which had endured so powerfully for more than two decades, was finally fading, with surprising speed, to be replaced by criticism and hostility. In bars and cafés, the whispers of dissent were growing louder. Even the faithful and devoted Bottai noted in his diary: 'The man who was always right is now almost always wrong.' People took to referring to Mussolini and his bald head as '*provolone*', after the round shiny cheese. After seventy British bombers dropped incendiary bombs on Milan, hitting two hospitals and killing forty-eight people, a scrawl in green paint appeared on a city wall: 'DUCE PORCO ASSASSINO'. Slogans such as 'believe, obey, fight', once so potent, were now regarded as ridiculous. The great Fascist experiment, which had promised stability, prosperity and a sense of direction, had, it turned out, been a mistake. The collapse of Fascist Italy had begun, and nothing seemed able to stop it.

The war news, meanwhile, was bleak. By May 1943, the Italian and German forces in North Africa had been caught in a pincer; on 12 May they surrendered and a little less than ninety thousand Italians were taken prisoner. In Russia, survivors of the defeat at Stalingrad were struggling home, telling their families that some of their comrades had preferred to kill themselves rather than face further fighting. From the labour camps in Germany came tales of German supervisors setting their dogs on Italian workers. There were now 270,000 Italian prisoners in Allied hands, and 45,000 more had disappeared. With Allied planes in reach of the Italian coastline, there was little to stop landings in Corsica, Sardinia or Sicily; it was a question now not of whether but when they would take place. Mussolini seemed to have lost trust in everyone around him, and sacked both his chief of staff, Ugo Cavallero, and his police chief, Carmine Senise. Himmler offered to train a special bodyguard for him, an 'M' Division, made up of young Fascists, equipped by the Germans.

In his office high above the Piazza Venezia, Mussolini alternated, Ciano noted, between a 'trance of optimism' and long periods when he realised the full disaster Italy was heading towards. Three people, Mussolini wrote to Claretta, 'are now the most hated: me, you, Count Ciano, who is perhaps the most hated of us all'. He told the *gerarchi* that if the enemy dared to land on Italian soil, they would be thrown back into the sea as corpses. But no more now than at any moment in his regime had Mussolini shown any real understanding of military strategy or priorities, preferring to advance in rapid jerks, shuffle around generals and troops, refuse to listen to experts unless they agreed with him, obsessed always with the memory of Italy's 'mutilated victory' at the end of the

First World War. He spent hours tinkering with the minutiae of public life, pondering such things as the date on which the guards in Rome should change into their summer uniforms.

Over one aspect of Italy's war, however, the vacillations at the heart of the leadership played a useful if unexpected part. The four years of the anti-Semitic laws had been filled with intense discrimination against the Jews, along with some internment and internal exile, against which neither the King nor the Vatican had made more than extremely feeble protest. But there had been very little physical violence other than by a few over-zealous Fascists, even if it was becoming harder to ignore the fact that anti-Semitism was now one of the most jarring points of difference with Germany.

As the Italian troops began to occupy Croatia, Slovenia, Dalmatia and Greece, so they also began to help and protect the Jews they found there, whether citizens or foreigners, from German round-ups and deportation. And when, on 11 November 1942, the Germans had swept south and occupied the whole of France, absorbing the Vichy-controlled areas and consigning the Alpes-Maritimes and Var, along with six other departments, to Italy, the Italian diplomats and police posted there acted in the same way. At this stage, some twenty thousand Jews were living in the South of France, and five thousand others had fled there, and the Vichy civil administration had already begun turning them over to the Nazis.

As a first step, the new Italian occupiers notified Vichy that they alone were entitled to arrest or intern Jews, irrespective of their nationality, in the departments they controlled. An Italian police inspector, Guido Lospinoso, was dispatched from Rome, ostensibly to bring order to Jewish affairs. But in practice, helped by a remarkable banker from Modena, Angelo Donati, and a Catholic priest called Père Benoit, he did the opposite. He obstructed, stalled, lost lists, forgot things. Jews were hidden, provided with false documents. Ribbentrop's angry demands for lists of Jews for deportation were met with stubborn obfuscation. When the German Foreign Minister eventually turned to Mussolini in person to sort things out, Mussolini equivocated, agreed, but did nothing, playing for time, caught between Hitler's wrath and what he feared would be hostility at home.

There is only sparse evidence either in the archives or in memoirs of the time as to the role played by Ciano in Italy's treatment of its

Jewish people, and even less about Edda's part. It seems to have been one of the many subjects she saw no need to concern herself with, beyond helping a few friends. But first as Foreign Minister, and then as ambassador to the Vatican, there can be little doubt that Ciano knew what was happening. In August 1942, his friend Otto von Bismarck told Ciano's chef-de-cabinet, Brasco Lanzo d'Ajeto, that the deportations of Jews from Croatia would lead to 'their dispersion and elimination'. Dino Alfieri, now Italian Ambassador to Berlin, confirmed that the SS were indeed carrying out mass executions. Ciano would have been informed about both. Even if the details of what would later be called the Holocaust were not fully known, there was certainly enough information for Ciano – along with the Vatican, the Pope, the Allies and the International Committee of the Red Cross – to be under no illusion that Jewish men, women and children were being systematically murdered. Faced with the choice of provoking Hitler or provoking the Italians, who continued for the most part to feel sympathetic towards the Jews, Ciano, like Mussolini, seems to have prevaricated and stalled.

Laval, Vichy and the Nazis, as well as a number of Ciano's friends in the Petit Trianon, believed that the instructions to protect the Jews came from Ciano himself. He was, they maintained, the 'inspiration' behind them. Cyprienne del Drago said later that 'though Galeazzo didn't like Jews very much . . . he helped to save them'. When told in December 1942 that the French Prefect in the Alpes-Maritimes had ordered Jews to register and move to German concentration camps further north, he instructed that 'the disposition regarding the Jews must be suspended'. These measures, the Prefect said, came 'personally' from Ciano, who had added that the Jews should be treated, as in Italy, 'humanely'. Heinz Röthke, the German head of Jewish affairs, also reported that Ciano was the 'inspiration' behind the orders, whether because he hoped to win sympathy for himself and for Italy, or because his home city of Livorno was, along with Ferrara, Rome and Venice, the 'Jewish city of the peninsula'. In Croatia, Greece and south-east France, Italian soldiers, diplomats and police continued to refuse orders to round up Jews. And, perhaps with no more than Ciano's tacit approval, for the seven months that ran from 11 November 1942 to the summer of 1943, Jews in Italian-occupied France for the most part survived.

*

At first, the Germans were delighted that Ciano had lost his powers as Foreign Minister, but they quickly perceived that he had in fact become more dangerous, more able to spread his efforts to take Italy out of the war now that he was free of Mussolini's control. The Germans believed that he had become the ringleader of the anti-Axis faction. 'Fascist corruption,' Goebbels noted, 'stinks to high heaven. Ciano has corrupted the entire crew.' Edda warned her husband that she had heard that the Germans were saying that Ciano had declared himself 'physically repulsed by them'. She seemed to friends to have become unnaturally thin, drinking too much whisky, smoking too many cigarettes, and living under a 'veil of tormented silence'. When she and Ciano were together, she watched him, her black eyes reflective, as if there was more, much more, that she wanted to say to him.

Ciano was too astute not to know the limits of friendship and loyalty within his little court, just as he knew perfectly well that he was now universally disliked. A poor public speaker, his voice sometimes hoarse, sometimes squeaky, he had never become Mussolini's 'man of the people'. But he continued to sit by the pool at L'Acquasanta, surrounded by pretty women, apparently incapable of not airing his doubts about Mussolini, about the war, about the need for peace. He seemed totally heedless of his own security. When his friend Vergani asked him why he did not resign, he replied that it was all too late, and that his duty now was to bring Italy out of the war. 'I'm frightened for you,' Vergani told him. 'For what is going to happen to you.' No one, Ciano replied, would ever now trust in his good faith. 'You have to prove it, even if it means paying with your person ... So many innocent people are dying. Why shouldn't I run the same risk?' He began to tell friends that they should not be seen in his company, as he was sure that the Germans were noting down their names. He had put on weight, looked more jowly, with deep black circles under his eyes that never went away. Later, Vergani would say that Ciano reminded him at this time of a 'boy who plays through the bars of a cage with tigers. Now it seemed to me that he had entered the cage of the great sleeping beasts armed only with a very thin whip.'

Rome was awash with gossip about the Cianos and their decadent lives. It was as if, after years of mostly suppressed animosity, Italians were now free to see Mussolini's favourite child as a metaphor for the country's ills. There were stories that Edda and the children ate steaks every day, while ordinary people never saw meat at all. An anonymous 'woman of the first hour' – that is to say a founder member of the Fascist Party – wrote to say that Edda's sleeveless low-cut dresses were 'worthy of a *cocotte*', a tart; another swore that she had hidden 10 kilograms of gold behind a wall in her flat. She was said to be surrounding herself with gigolos, and spending her nights 'playing dice like a Harlem negress' and not allowing her guests to win, and that she had always been at heart a *'vieille fille'*, for she had the 'wit, the temper and the capricious and despotic whims of an old woman'.

The malicious Malaparte said of her that she was in love with death. He claimed that meeting her one day in the Palazzo Colonna, she had said to him: 'My father will never have the pluck to kill himself.' He had replied: 'Show him how to shoot himself,' and, the next day, he had been visited by a police inspector who told him to avoid her in the future. The episode sounds implausible, but Malaparte also wrote that Mussolini felt that Edda was 'his only enemy, his real rival ... his secret conscience ... He can rule in peace, but can he sleep in peace? Edda is merciless, she obsesses his nights. Some day there will be bloodshed between father and daughter.'

Edda felt useless in Rome. The Duchessa di Sermoneta met her one day coming out of the hairdresser Attilio in the Piazza di Spagna, a hotbed of spies and informers, still in her curlers, dowdily dressed in a tartan skirt and thick woolly stockings. She seemed to have aged and was saying: 'What does it matter what I look like?' She decided to go to Sicily, to work with the Red Cross in a civilian hospital in Monreale, telling Ciano, who begged her not to go, that she 'wanted to see it through'.

She arrived in Palermo to find chaos and misery. People who had been bombed out of their houses were living in the gutters or under rocks; there had been no meat for five months, and there was now no bread because Palermo's three hundred bread ovens had all been destroyed. The telephones did not work and there was very little water. Soldiers were 'fleeing like hares into the mountains'. Edda talked to people, inspected the area, then wrote a report and sent it to Maria José, president of the Red Cross. She heard nothing back. So she sat down to write a long, detailed, urgent letter to her father. Even in Albania and Russia, she said, she had never seen such suffering or so much pain. He should now regard Sicily as a 'disaster area', much as if it had been hit by an earthquake. Send food, she wrote, above all pasta and bread, and send medicines. 'They are dying of hunger and cold. Literally ... The situation is extremely serious and from one moment to the next can turn into a catastrophe, even a political one ... What they are saying here is that the Duce doesn't know. But now you do know.' Again, misery and danger brought out the best in her. Mussolini sent her 50,000 lire to distribute and ordered the newspapers not to cover the situation.

One day Raimondo Lanza appeared in the hospital and took her back to the Castello di Trabia. It was hot and she plunged into the sea, and afterwards they lay on the rocks together, laughing and remembering the old times. It was a last carefree moment.

Mussolini sent desperate pleas for help to the Germans but Hitler, having suffered major losses in a tank battle at Kursk, had little to offer. Edda was back in her hospital ward when, on 10 July, the Allies landed seven infantry divisions on the shores of Sicily, using 4,000 planes and 285 warships. Operation Husky was the biggest naval assault ever carried out. The Sicilians, having endured months of heavy bombing and very short of food, put up no resistance. Edda was told to return immediately to Rome, in case Sicily was cut off from the mainland. Her sympathy for the Germans seemed to be rapidly disappearing, and the friend travelling with her on the train saw her make the disparaging sign for a cuckold, involving the index and little fingers, as a train full of German soldiers passed slowly by on the other track.

Hitler, Mussolini and Kesselring

On 19 July, Mussolini met Hitler near Feltre. Aides in an ante-room listened as Hitler lectured and ranted for two hours. Now that Mussolini was a beaten man, the contrast between them was glaring: Hitler cruel, vindictive, bombastic; Mussolini unsure and equivocating. Occasionally Mussolini was heard to sigh. He already knew that he would never get the planes, armoured divisions or war *matériel*, without which he could not continue the war. He had also had to stomach the fact that Field Marshal Kesselring had been put in command of joint German-Italian forces based at a headquarters at Albano, just south of Rome.

That day, as the two dictators talked, four successive waves of bombers brought death and destruction for the first time to Rome. In previous days they had dropped leaflets over the popular district of San Lorenzo; now they dropped bombs. Birds rose up from Rome's many gardens and flew agitatedly in great dark swirls above the city. The first radio reports put the number of dead at 300; it soon rose to 2,500. The attack was not as lethal as Hamburg or Dresden, but it sent a powerful message to the Italians. One of the main aqueducts, the Acqua Marcia, was hit and the water supply to the capital all but ceased. Pope Pius XII visited the scene and spent three hours wandering in the ruins, his white cassock smeared in blood. The people gathered round him and applauded. When the King came, he was jeered. That night the skyline of Rome was lit up by an immense fire and the dome of St Peter's was silhouetted in black against the crimson glow.

It was against this background – military defeats on every front, the Allied landings in Sicily, rising anger and disaffection throughout Italy, quarrelling and corrupt *gerarchi* – that the plots against Mussolini took shape. As Susanna Agnelli later said, 'Everyone was plotting. It had become the national sport.'

The plotters were many and varied. They included the King and the royal household; his unhappy daughter-in-law Maria José who had thrown in her lot with the anti-Fascists, but was considered 'meddlesome' by the others; the recently sacked and rumpled chief of police, Carmine Senise; a number of the senior *gerarchi* and generals, who had been discussing ditching Mussolini; and the Vatican which, since 1942, had been putting out feelers to the US about forming a new government in exile. Some wanted one outcome, others, a different one. But what all agreed was that Mussolini had to go, and that the next step would be to sue for a separate peace. From Vatican sources, they knew that the Allies had stated categorically that they would not negotiate with the Fascists, 'whoever they are, even Grandi and Ciano', and that the heavy bombardments would continue unless the Italians, and the King, acted. But though they all met, conspired, made promises and formed coalitions, none took steps. Almost all their moves were known to the Germans and to the Allies from their informers in Rome.

Through his own spies, Mussolini had been following the various plots, but he refused to take them seriously. He believed, after a recent audience, that the King esteemed him and would back him in the event of a coup. He also maintained that the *gerarchi* would not be able to operate without him, since they were of 'modest, extremely modest, intelligence, uncertain about what they believed in, and possessed of very little courage'. Hearing that Ciano had been speaking ill of him, that he had referred to his father-in-law as 'that mad tyrant who wanted this war', Mussolini summoned him to Palazzo Venezia but then seemed strangely credulous and forgiving when Ciano assured him of his total loyalty.

Ciano, as all Rome and even the Germans knew, had indeed been plotting, though at this stage Edda appears to have known nothing about it. He had talked to senior clerics in the Vatican, where he had good relations with Pius XII from the time before he had been made Pope. It seems clear that he had also made separate approaches to the British. He had met Maria José, and had in fact warned her of the imminent invasion of her country, Belgium, before it took place, to the fury of the Germans and causing Hitler to declare him 'a traitor to the Axis'. He had had audiences with the King, who was friendly but evasive. He had talked to the disaffected generals. His office had become a hub of intrigue. As his friend del Drago put it, everyone wanted this 'impulsive, exuberant, plucky boy on their side'. Ciano himself continued to feel oddly, absurdly, safe, thinking that his sacking as Foreign Minister had proved that he was not Mussolini's creature, and that, though the Italians hated him now, they would soon love him if he got Italy out of the war. There was, wrote Bottai, 'no bitterness in him, only a poisonous joy, a will of perdition or suicide'.

The paralysis into which the plotters seemed to have descended through June and July was at last broken when Mussolini returned from his meeting with Hitler near Feltre virtually empty handed yet still insisting that Italy would stand by Germany's side. The bombing of San Lorenzo was a vivid reminder of Italy's vulnerability. Days were spent in feverish clandestine talks. There were fears that the irresolute King would not find the resolve to play his part, and that Mussolini's well-known persuasiveness and intimidatory tactics were powerful enough to quell any rebellion. The first move was to get Mussolini to convene a session of the Gran Consiglio, which he agreed to do, setting the date for 24 July. The second was for Grandi and Bottai to settle on the wording of the motion they intended to put before it. It would be short and simple: Mussolini would be asked to step down, hand military authority over to the King and the affairs of state to a functioning body of ministers.

On 22 July, Grandi went to call on Mussolini to inform him about what would happen. Mussolini was glacial. That same afternoon, Grandi met Ciano and though there was no friendship between them, he suggested that, as Edda's husband and for his own safety, he should stand aside. Ciano refused, saying that his father Costanzo would have wanted him to act. Even Edda, who was in Livorno with the children and her mother-in-law, now believed there should be a change of government. 'If my father can hang on to power only because of German support,' she told Ciano, 'then it would be better if he broke away. It's no longer a question of being Fascist or anti-Fascist. Now we must only be Italians.' Grandi and a couple of other *gerarchi* worked on the motion, making it shorter and clearer, the crucial point being that Mussolini would hand all political and military power over to the King. Friends who saw Ciano that day found him nervous and agitated, but resolute.

It was Senise, with the help of the new like-minded police chief, Renzo Chierici, who was masterminding the events that were to follow the Gran Consiglio meeting. The King was now believed to be steady, telling an adjutant, 'The regime is no longer working. We must have a change, at all costs.' The plan was that, after talking to the King, Mussolini would be arrested by carabinieri loyal to the crown. But just how people would behave on the day – whether Mussolini's militia would intervene, whether the individual *gerarchi* would keep their nerve – no one knew.

None of this plotting had escaped Rachele's spies. She fretted and fumed and kept trying to put Mussolini on his guard, as did Claretta during their many daily conversations. Not long before, Rachele had summoned Eugen Dollmann, as enigmatic as ever as to his true feelings about the Italy he loved and the Germany he served, to see her at the Villa Torlonia. Pacing up and down in front of him, Rachele delivered a tirade on the disasters facing Italy and on the treacheries being plotted by the monarchy and the rivalrous *gerarchi*. It was very hot and her face powder formed rivulets that ran down her cheeks as she paced. It was Ciano, a man interested only in 'luxury, social fads and high living', she told Dollmann, who had brought unhappiness to her family. She had set her spies on him and knew now that he was among the conspirators. Edda was and had always been a Mussolini.

The 187th – and last – meeting of the Gran Consiglio opened at five fifteen on the stifling afternoon of Saturday 24 July 1943. Grandi, who had once written to Mussolini to say that all he wanted in life was to work 'near the Duce, warmed by his faith, invigorated by his energy, galvanised by his genius', would later claim that he had put two grenades in his pockets in case of having to fight his way out. There were twenty-eight men present, all in Fascist black, sitting around in a horseshoe with Mussolini in the middle on a raised platform. The Sala del Pappagallo had marble floors and walls upholstered in blue velvet, with heavy wrought-iron chandeliers. Mussolini opened the proceedings and tied down the discussion for almost two hours with military matters.

The conspirators, all of whom in their different ways were more concerned with their own personal interests than with the well-being of Italy, had decided that Grandi, Bottai and Ciano would speak. When finally allowed the platform, Grandi proposed that the current leadership should be re-examined. The regime, he declared, 'has destroyed and killed Fascism ... The responsibility for this disaster lies not with Fascism, but with the dictatorship.' Everyone was waiting for Ciano to speak; when he did so, he was clear and precise. Germany had deceived the Italians, he said, and Mussolini had been duped by Hitler. '*We* are not the betrayers, but the betrayed.'

Visibly angry, his jaw working as if he were mouthing furious replies, Mussolini kept his black eyes staring fixedly at his son-in-law. At midnight, he asked that the meeting be adjourned; Grandi insisted that they take only a thirty-minute break. In the lobby, some of the *gerarchi* seemed less sure where their loyalties lay.

After the break came more tirades from Mussolini. As Grandi later described it, the Duce, by turns angry, menacing, flattering and confiding, the 'magician and the master' to the end, denied all accusations and declared that Fascism, revolution, party, dictatorship and Mussolini were all 'inseparable'. Glaring icily around the room, he accused them all of corruption and of making illicit fortunes. Grandi offered Ciano another chance to step away; Ciano refused it.

Towards 2 a.m., after nine hours of talk, Grandi's motion was put to the vote, and one by one the men rose to declare their position. The plotters had expected that they would get twelve votes in favour. In the event, they got nineteen, with seven against and one abstention. Farinacci voted for a slightly different motion of his own. Among them were many who simply wanted some kind of change, without thinking through what it would entail. An elderly *gerarca* called Marinelli was too deaf to follow what was going on but voted with them anyway. As the vote ended, Mussolini, with apparent indifference, rose and said: 'You have brought about a crisis for the regime. The session is over.' He left behind him confusion and uncertainty; they had expected fury and resistance and did not know what to make of this calm resignation. Ciano, meeting friends, told them that there was no point in going to bed, as he was likely to be arrested, but that the King would remove Mussolini from power, and then 'I will be free'. As he left the Palazzo Venezia, one of the *gerarchi* said to him: 'Some things, you know, you pay for with your life.'

Later, the events of the night would be described as treason. But as a consultative body, the Gran Consiglio had no actual power, even if its proposals were perfectly legitimate. Mussolini could have had all its members arrested, which was exactly what Rachele begged him to do when he went home and described to her the night's events. When he got to the moment that Ciano voted against him, she shouted out: 'Him too!' Later she would say that of all the many blows dealt her husband, this was the worst, and later, too, people would wonder whether Mussolini's seeming indifference to the vote might not have been genuine, and that, looking for ways to get Italy out of the war, he perceived this to be his only option. At 3 a.m. Mussolini rang Claretta, saying that it was all over and that she should start thinking about saving herself.

Mussolini's bi-weekly audience with the King was scheduled for five on the afternoon of Sunday 25 July. He spent the day visiting the victims of the San Lorenzo air raids and receiving the new Japanese Ambassador, Hidaka. Before leaving for the Quirinale, he spoke to Claretta, sounding more hopeful. She, like Rachele, begged him not to go.

The King received him on the steps of the Quirinale. Mussolini's three cars, with his detectives and escort, remained outside the gate. The audience lasted barely twenty minutes. The rheumy-eyed King, with his beaky nose and prognathous jaw, was embarrassed but cordial, remarking that Mussolini was now the most hated man in Italy. He had, he announced, decided to replace him with Badoglio, the seventy-one-year-old Duke of Addis Ababa, a man widely regarded as calculating, greedy and incompetent. He was therefore asking Mussolini for his resignation. Several times, the King repeated, 'I am sorry, I am sorry. But the situation could not have been otherwise.' He would, the King assured him, guarantee the Duce's safety 'with my own head'.

As Mussolini walked down the front steps, preparing to make his way to his car, his way was barred by a carabiniere captain. 'His Majesty,' the man said, 'has ordered me to protect your person.' He steered Mussolini away from his car and towards a waiting ambulance and helped him get in. It set off at high speed, but just where it was going very few people had been told. No one – not the nearby divisions of militia, not the Fascist Party he had founded, not his presidential bodyguards – lifted a finger to protect him. What was happening was more than most of the *gerarchi* had expected or, as it turned out, wanted.

Part Three

EXODUS

17

Death walks on the roof

Edda, the three children and Ciano's mother had spent the night of 24 July in an air raid shelter in Livorno. It was only late on the night of the 25th, when she was in bed and asleep, that Ciano rang. He sounded agitated but suspected that OVRA's spies would be listening in. 'There is a *tramontana** blowing,' he said to her. 'But not especially at us. Come at once.' It was their code for trouble. Edda was not particularly surprised: she had been waiting for news that the King had taken over some of her father's powers. Ciano told her that he was sending a car for them. It failed to arrive, but carabinieri arrived to take them to the station to catch a train for Rome. Edda was more concerned with a painful boil, and the fact that her mother-in-law appeared to be dressed as for a cocktail party.

It was only when they reached the station and saw that someone had scrawled all over the carriages 'Down with Mussolini! Long live the King!' and painted crude pictures of her father, his jaw jutting out, that Edda began to feel apprehensive. They arrived in Rome very late, and were met by a car and a carabiniere escort to take them to the Via Angelo Secchi. 'Where is *nonno* Duce?' asked Fabrizio. 'I don't know, Ciccino, how could I?' Edda replied. The streets were in uproar. It might have been carnival time. Edda found Ciano almost in tears. 'We have to get out of Italy,' he said. 'Here they'll kill us.' Driving back to the Via Angelo Secchi very late the previous night, his car had been surrounded by angry, threatening crowds shouting, 'Down with the *gerarchi*!' Recounting the events of the Gran Consiglio, he insisted that he had never

---

* A cold strong northern wind from the Alps.

wanted to harm her father, but had sincerely believed some change in the structure of the government was essential for the survival of Italy.

Edda had not been able to reach Rachele since the lines to the Villa Torlonia had been cut. When she was finally able to talk to her, she found that her mother had been alerted to Mussolini's arrest by an anonymous caller, and that she had just had time to warn Vittorio, who had taken his Topolino, driven out by a back gate and disappeared. Since Anna Maria and Romano were in Riccione, with Bruno's widow Gina, Rachele was alone. As night fell on the 25th, hostile and jeering crowds had gathered outside the gates. For the moment she was safe, protected by soldiers sent by Badoglio to replace her normal guards, though the men also turned the Villa Torlonia over, looking for any possibly incriminating papers. When Anna Maria and Romano were told what had happened, Rachele noted that 'they were not frightened; fear in our family is a word that does not exist'.

Badoglio and Senise had prepared their coup with great care. Soldiers had disarmed the police, thought to be loyal to Mussolini, and taken over the telephone exchanges. After the King had made his announcement, at 22.45 on the Sunday night, that Marshal Badoglio was replacing Mussolini, Badoglio had made his own announcement. '*La guerra*' he declared, '*continua*': the war would go on. What exactly he meant by this he did not spell out, and his listeners chose to hear not his words but what they longed to hear, that Italy would now sue for peace. They embarked on a wild party. All over Italy, men and women who had sat through the two decades of Fascism with apparent approval set out on a riotous spree of destruction. Mussolini had wanted Italians not to think but to obey; once they realised they were free, their appetite for vengeance was uncontrollable.

In Livorno, a vast bust of Costanzo was knocked down, and someone wrote on a wall of the Via Costanzo, '*via anche il figlio*', let's get rid of the son, too. Statues of Mussolini were toppled, his pictures shredded, defaced and spat on, the Roman eagles smashed. An American woman, hiding in a convent in Rome, described torn fragments of Mussolini's portraits lying 'like snow on the pavements'. Giuseppe Graziosi's vast bronze statue of the Duce, which had been hauled over the Apennines by ox cart from Florence to

Rome, was attacked and Mussolini's head knocked off and dragged through the streets. People tore their Fascist Party badges from their lapels, and put away incriminating photographs of themselves with Fascist dignitaries. 'We thought,' wrote Gabriella di Robilant, 'that we would go mad with joy ... twenty-three years of servitude cancelled in a minute.' Cellars were broken into and people arrived with saucepans to carry the wine away. Mussolini's thirteen magnificent horses disappeared from their stables at the Villa Torlonia. But as joy gave way to a longing for revenge, known Fascists were pulled from their homes and beaten up. The Press Club, regarded as the centre of false news and Fascist propaganda, was ransacked. Overnight, Rome had become the 'great port of anti-Fascism', as opposition leaders emerged from hiding, older, greyer, filled with a desire for action, producing plans, proposals, competing views and gusts of political fervour, but agreeing on nothing. 'It is difficult,' wrote Corrado Alvaro in *Il Mercurio*, 'to be a free man.'

Even as Italy was revelling in its new perceived freedom, Badoglio was putting together a cabinet of sixteen ministers, most of them former high-ranking Fascists and six from the military, and all of them subservient to him. It did not include Grandi or any of the other plotters. Though political prisoners were indeed liberated over the next week, and the Special Tribunal which had sent so many political opponents to internment on the islands was disbanded, censorship remained in place and orders went out to shoot troublemakers, 'to kill, as in battle'. In the days that followed eighty-one strikers were shot dead and 320 more wounded. Marshal law was proclaimed and public gatherings banned, and though the anti-Semitic laws were not immediately rescinded, it was understood that they would no longer be applied. A new kind of dictatorship was taking shape.

The King, with 'Piedmontese coldness', had played a very clever game. Luring the plotters into thinking that they might enjoy a future under his auspices, he had effectively used them to get rid of Mussolini. But he had never planned to reward them. Instructions went out to arrest the 'traitors', the nineteen conspirators. Bottai, accused of 'plotting against the state', was caught and sent to the Regina Coeli prison. Farinacci took refuge in the German embassy. Grandi, after hanging on for a few days as the President of the

Council, fled to Portugal. Pavolini got himself to Germany, taking with him thirty-two gold sovereigns given to him by his lover, Doris Duranti. Ciano and Edda, though guards were posted outside their door, remained for the moment untouched, and a high-ranking courtier arrived to ask Ciano to remain at his post at the Vatican, saying that the King would protect all who belonged to the Order of the Annunziata. But Ciano knew that Badoglio was no friend and not to be trusted, since he was very well aware that Ciano had documents in his possession proving that the marshal had pulled off shady deals in Ethiopia and Greece.

It was only four days after the coup that Rachele finally heard from Mussolini. Having first been held in carabiniere barracks in Trastevere, he was now under close guard on the island of Ponza, a former prison for the anti-Fascists, and he asked her to send clothes, books and food. She put together a parcel of a chicken, tomatoes, tagliatelle and a present of some socks and a tie. He spent his sixtieth birthday on the island, receiving from Hitler the complete works of Nietzsche, which did little to counter the crushing boredom that oppressed him. He was at work on a slim volume of his thoughts, which he called *Pensieri Pontini*. Had the twenty years of Fascism, he asked himself, really been nothing but 'an illusion? . . . Superficial? Was nothing in them of real import?' He hoped, he wrote, to 'murder time, before it murders me'. In the evenings, he played cards with his guards. To his sister Edvige, he wrote: 'As for me, I consider myself three quarters defunct . . . The past is dead. I don't regret anything. I don't desire anything.' Claretta and her family had managed to escape to the Lago Maggiore, where her sister Myriam had a house, and from where she continued to write Mussolini passionate letters, which she was unable to post, since she had no idea where he was.

In August 1943, on Badoglio's orders, the whole Petacci family was arrested, ostensibly for stealing Persian rugs, and sent to Novara jail where the women were put into a cell with prostitutes and complained of fleas, scorpions and cockroaches. Signora Petacci had a 'crisis of hysterics'. Before leaving Rome, Claretta had been able to spirit away most of her valuables, along with two large leather suitcases with her ball gowns and fur coats. When the police arrived to sequester the contents of the Villa Camilluccia, they found it largely stripped of anything of value. In an overflow in the bathroom of Marcello's house, they found deeds to a recently bought castle.

For all their spies, the Allies, like the Germans, had not seen what was coming. To buy time, the Germans put out a communiqué saying that Mussolini had stepped down because of his health. In the war cabinet in London, Churchill speculated that Italy would now sue for peace, but then be unable to counter the inevitable German aggression. Debating whether to take what Macmillan described as a 'hard, soft or alternating' line, what was needed the British concluded, was more and heavier bombing of Italian cities, to ensure a rapid capitulation. The 'arch-devil Mussolini' and his 'demonic followers' would receive the punishment due to them. The British made it clear that they regarded the King as old and lacking in all initiative, his son Umberto as 'weak and irresolute' and the whole slew of Fascists as indulging in a 'collective delusion'.

Badoglio was in fact in an impossible position. Still, he did not handle it well. Neither he nor the King had actually planned what would happen next. The Allies had made it clear at Casablanca in January that they would accept nothing from Italy but unconditional surrender; the Americans might have softened but the British held firm. The days passed, while secret emissaries were dispatched from Rome to barter for better terms but returned, humiliated, with no concessions. The King and Badoglio procrastinated, talked, wondered how to prevent Mussolini from being rescued and how to keep the Germans from knowing that they were in fact making plans to break with the Axis powers. An absurd meeting between senior Italians and Germans, at which all those present were trying to mislead the others as to their real intentions, was described as 'an orgy of lying'. The anti-Fascists in Rome continued to jostle for power. Nelson Page, attending a meeting of these opposition leaders, said that he felt as if he were seeing 'a world of ghosts, ghosts seized by a sudden frenzy, who had been dancing a tragic, aimless, saraband'. All over Italy, factory workers came out on strike.

The King decided to rid himself of his meddlesome daughter-in-law, lest she further muddle his secret overtures to the Allies, and Maria José and her children were sent north, to spend the rest of the war in a hotel full of elderly ladies on the shore of Lake Thun.

He also took the precaution of sending to Switzerland several sealed carriages of his valuables; Badoglio had already purloined a secret account in Mussolini's name, said to contain $2.5 million, and had changed it into Swiss francs. Hitler, after a paroxysm of fury that no one had accurately anticipated the coup, threatened to send in an armoured division and arrest the King, the new government and even the Pope.

In the Via Angelo Secchi the mood darkened. For the first few days, Ciano had clung on to the hope that there might still be some role for him in the new Italian government. But it soon became apparent that he had enemies everywhere. One morning, the children woke to the smell of smoke: their parents were burning papers. Whenever they asked Edda where Mussolini was, she said vaguely that he was tired and resting. The Vatican made it known that they no longer wanted Ciano, and when he asked them to issue passports for himself and his family, they refused, saying that they could do nothing for a 'war criminal' wanted by the Allies. To his friend Anfuso, for whom he had done so much and who now declined to help, Ciano had become like a poker player, beaten in a hand on which 'he had wagered his whole patrimony'. What Edda found hardest was that the former friends now turning their backs on them 'like serpents' were the very ones who had fawned on them most during their years in power.

On 5 August, in response to a public that had grown angrier and more vengeful towards those they considered responsible for the crimes of Fascism – everyone conveniently forgetting their own illicit gains – a commission of inquiry into the wealth of the *gerarchi* was set up by Badoglio under the aegis of a senior judge, a risky move given his own excessively greedy past. Its remit was to look at everything that had been acquired between the birth of Fascism in 1922 and 24 July 1943. Denunciations began to arrive. 'We must make the greedy mob suffer,' wrote one furious informer. 'Just as we suffered in silence.' The new Minister for Foreign Affairs, Raffaele Guariglia, told Isabella Colonna that, since it was not possible to give Italians peace, they would give them 'Fascists to devour'. Among these titbits were the details of the *gerarchi*'s sexual adventures, displayed on the front pages of the newspapers. On 29 August, the long love affair between 'Clara and Ben' was recounted at length, together with descriptions of Angela Curti and

Mussolini's other mistresses. On being shown the articles, Rachele maintained that she had known nothing about any of it. Rome greatly enjoyed the revelations.

Foreign accounts, safe boxes and bank vaults were raided and silver, linen, fur coats and expensive art were confiscated. In the house of a senior Fascist in Turin was discovered a mountain of food, the hams, salami, sugar – and a veal tongue – long since missing from the shops. Farinacci's house yielded documents showing the ownership of a printing business, shares in a newspaper, a flat and a villa in Rome, another in Milan, a house in Naples and six million lire in gold and shares. His secretary's handbag revealed keys to more safe boxes and bank vaults. Pavolini was found to have spent 'vast sums' on Doris Duranti – though she later complained that he had never given her even a bunch of flowers – while other documents told of property in Lucca, a flat in Rome, antique furniture, furs and jewellery.

Soon, the inevitable happened: the commission turned its attention to the Ciano family, described as the most 'thieving' and possessed of 'spectacular riches'. Edda and Ciano were said to have buried untold wealth in chests in the garden of the house in Livorno. The fortune had been built up, the commission established, by Costanzo: the hero of the seas had been a serious profiteer and fraudster. But what he had left to Ciano, and that Ciano had since built on, included a number of enormous apartment blocks in Rome, shops, factories, villas and land, along with the very profitable *Telegrafo* and printing works in Livorno. Ciano was outraged by the publicity and wrote an angry and imprudent letter to Badoglio, trying to explain and minimise his wealth.

On 14 August the Allies carried out their threat and every large city in Italy was bombed. Churches, hospitals, museums, universities and cemeteries were flattened and destitute families took to the roads. There were rumours that explosives were being dropped in the shape of toys, dolls and pencils, the better to kill more citizens. As the *Gazette* of Lausanne observed, 'the Italians seem to be living in the aftermath of an enormous earthquake.' The summer was unnaturally hot, and the mosquitoes were ferocious.

Closely guarded in their apartment, the Cianos had grown fonder towards each other. Many former friends in the Petit Trianon ostentatiously dropped them, but a few remained loyal, especially the group of Anglophile aristocratic ladies. Daniele Varè's two daughters came to visit, and after Ciano quoted the lines from Kipling's poem: 'If you can meet with Triumph and Disaster / And treat those two impostors just the same', one of them remarked to her father that Ciano was confronting disaster with more dignity than he had ever shown during the years of triumph. When Susanna Agnelli went to call, she found Edda receiving in one room, Ciano in the other. Both looked pale and agitated. Ciano asked her: 'Tell me the truth: do you think they will kill me?' Agnelli replied, 'Yes, I believe they will.' And, Ciano went on: 'Will it be the Allies or the Germans?' 'Either one of them,' she said. She urged him to get out of Italy as quickly as possible, and went home fearing that even now he had not really understood the danger he was in. Edda informed everyone who called that she would always remember those friends who stood by her. Emilio Pucci arrived and told them that whatever happened, nothing had changed in his feelings towards them and that they could count on him if they needed help. Warned by his superior officers to keep away from them, he refused.

Then, on 24 August, Ettore Muti, whom Ciano had liked and promoted, was arrested in Fregene and shot dead in the pine woods, but whether on purpose or by accident was never established. But Muti's death unnerved them all, not least because they believed that of all the *gerarchi*, he might have been the one to rally supporters to Mussolini's side.

Getting out of Italy was proving impossible. Franco said he would take Edda and the children but not Ciano; friends suggested a private plane, but that would have meant just Ciano. One day he said to Edda, showing her a revolver: 'You must shoot me. Look, I'll sit on the bed and you shoot.' She decided that the moment had come for her to act. Once again, her strengths – decisiveness, boldness, determination – were coming into play. It was a bit as if, freed from the long ambiguity of her position, she was now not only in charge of events, but able to feel and express emotion long kept damped down.

She knew that Dollmann liked her and through Candido Bigliardi, a naval friend from Shanghai days, she got a message to him. No two versions of what happened next totally agree but it appears that Dollmann came to see her and she persuaded him to help, and that he in turn recruited Wilhelm Höttl, an SS officer with the Reich Security Main Office. At first, Hitler demurred, saying that he would save the 'Duce's blood relations', but not the treacherous Ciano. But then he seemed to relent. A second secret meeting took place between Edda and Herbert Kappler, a man with exceptionally small piercing eyes and a bony head, head of the SS in Rome. Though no one knew it, there was no time to spare: Badoglio had just ordered Ciano's arrest.

On the morning of 27 August, while her maid lured the guard posted outside their door into the park, Edda and the children set off for their customary morning walk. She wore a linen dress and sandals but had told the children to put on a double layer of clothes. Raimonda took with her a small toy duck. They were picked up by a car with false number plates and taken to the German academy where Ciano, who had escaped over a back wall and been collected by another car, joined them. A military truck took them to the airport of Pratica di Mare where a Junkers plane, its engines running, was waiting with Höttl on board. There was a terrifying moment during the drive when the truck was stopped by a roadblock, but the quick-thinking driver pulled rank and they were waved through. Edda and Ciano had stuffed their pockets with jewellery and money. The previous evening, a friend of Edda's was seen leaving the house in one of her more expensive fur coats, while a German officer, disguised as a man delivering flowers, carried away other valuables. Höttl, it later transpired, had used forged money to bribe the men guarding the Cianos, just as earlier he had used copious amounts of it on spies inside the Palazzo Colonna and elsewhere.

Edda had been told that the plane would fly them to Spain, from where they would be able to make their way to South America. Noticing that it appeared to be taking a different route, she was told that they would be stopping in Munich to refuel, before flying on to Berlin to pick up false papers and from there to Madrid. It was extremely cold on the plane, and they sipped the cognac provided by the Germans to keep warm. But when they landed in Munich, an SS general was waiting to take them to a villa on Lake Starnberg, where they were to be 'guests' of the Führer while their papers were sorted out. Their anxieties were somewhat allayed when Ernst Kaltenbrunner, Chief of the Reich Security Main Office, arrived to take their photographs for their new passports. Ciano sported a false moustache and was to be an Argentinian of Italian descent. Edda was Margaret Smith, an English woman born in Shanghai.

In Rome, when news came of their successful flight, Gabriella di Robilant wrote in her diary: 'It is certain that by fleeing Ciano has signed his own death warrant.' There was a rumour that Edda had died of a haemorrhage; another that she had committed suicide. Local Fascist thugs surrounded Carolina Ciano's house at Ponte a Moriano and threatened to burn her alive as the mother 'of a traitor who had got away'.

Then came word to the villa on Lake Starnberg that Hitler would like to see Edda – but not Ciano. On 3 September, she was flown in a small plane to Hitler's headquarters. It was very bumpy and she shared a bottle of cognac with another nervous passenger. Hitler was welcoming, assured her that he was working on a plan to rescue Mussolini and that he had no intention of keeping her in Germany against her will. As he had been heard to say, Edda was 'the most German of all Italians'. 'Whatever gave your father the idea of convening the Gran Consiglio?' he asked her. 'Mein Führer, I have no idea,' she replied. She spent the night on the Führer's train with Vittorio, who had been allowed to join her, having escaped from Italy and made his way to Germany.

Next day, Edda's thirty-third birthday, flowers arrived from Hitler, Himmler and Ribbentrop. When she met Goebbels again, she marvelled that she had ever liked or admired him. Their new-found antagonism was mutual. In his diaries, the Minister for Propaganda noted that he had come to believe the story that Edda's mother was in fact Angelica Balabanoff, which made her half Jewish; this accounted, as he put it, for her 'unbridled sexuality'.

Edda saw Hitler again, and once again he assured her that she had nothing to worry about. To the horror of the assembled Germans, she lit a cigarette, something no one ever did in his presence. And now she made what she later regarded as perhaps a fatal error. When Hitler suddenly said that he was confidant that Germany would win the war, she burst out: 'No! The war is lost!' and declared that all that was left was to make peace with at least one of the Axis' enemies. Hitler, clearly very angry, snapped back. She then made things worse by asking him to arrange to have the money she had brought out of Italy changed into pesetas. Vittorio, who was translating, was appalled by her outspokenness. After a few more harsh, accusatory exchanges, Edda left, also filled with rage, and she too now wondered whether suicide might not be their best option. Ribbentrop mollified her somewhat by telling her that the hated SS guards inside the villa could be replaced by servants and that what the Führer really wanted was to make certain the daughter of his best friend was properly protected.

Edda returned to the villa, determined to persuade herself of the Germans' good faith. The days passed. No passports came. From time to time there was a change of the guard outside. She realised how profoundly they had been turned into prisoners when a newly arrived SS guard casually killed a kitten that six-year-old Marzio had grown fond of, carrying him everywhere. Edda, restless, short-tempered, paced and railed; Ciano seemed apathetic. 'She had no half measures,' noted Höttl, 'either in matters of love or hatred.' The family clung together.

Rachele was still in Rome. After many days of silence and uncertainty, having lost all contact with Edda or Vittorio, she was abruptly informed that she was to be moved to the Rocca delle Caminate, where she would be reunited with Romano and Anna Maria. She suffered 'unspeakable indignities' during an unpleasant journey north by car, treated as a common criminal and pawed at by General Polito, the soldier who had accompanied Mussolini to Ponza. She found that the Rocca had been vandalised. The family was forbidden to leave the grounds and the telephone had been cut. Sixteen-year-old Romano spent the days playing the piano; fourteen- year-old Anna Maria read.

To all but a handful of people, Mussolini's exact whereabouts remained a mystery. There were rumours that he had been taken to Cyprus by the Allies. Terrified that the Germans were planning to rescue him, and suspecting that Ponza was not secure, the Badoglio government moved him first to the remote island of la Maddalena off Sardinia, then to a hotel high in the Abruzzi at Gran Sasso, a rocky hillside full of crevices 6,500 feet above sea level and accessible only by funicular. They were right to do so, as Höttl and his men were close on his trail.

In Rome, negotiations with the Allies were stuttering on,

Badoglio and the King proceeding with such deviousness that the British and the French felt confused and wary. Badoglio continued to take a nap in the afternoons, stall for time and pray for miracles. As one anti-Fascist campaigner put it, Badoglio had become the 'wiliest of deceivers'. The Italians had been informed that, whatever happened, they would not immediately be recognised as allies. But the secret discussions for an armistice continued with an understanding that an American parachute division would be landed over Rome to help defend the city against the feared vengeance of the Germans. On 3 September, in an olive grove at Cassibile in Sicily, the armistice between Italy and the Allies was finally – secretly – signed.

Rome, meanwhile, seemed to have filled with German men, posing as visitors, but so pale and with such a pronounced military gait that they were assumed to be soldiers. There was much talk between the King and Badoglio about the best timing for the announcement that an armistice had been signed, the Italians wanting the Allied parachute landing near Rome to take place first. When it became clear, however, that the Allies intended to make the landings coincide with the announcement and leave it up to the Italian army to confront the Germans on both sides of the Tiber, Badoglio prevaricated and asked for a postponement. Bluff followed bluff. Rudolf Rahn, a career diplomat who had served both the Weimar Republic and the Nazis, arrived to discourage the King and Badoglio from all thoughts of changing sides. The Allies were astonished by all the Italian bad faith and double dealing. And in any case, by now both the Allied invasion in the South and the timing of the announcement had been fixed. General Eisenhower cancelled the landing of the American airborne troops in Rome.

At six thirty on the evening of 8 September, with Badoglio protesting that the Allies had jumped the gun, Eisenhower announced over Radio Algiers that Italy had signed an armistice. The Allies, who had landed in Salerno five days earlier, began their push north up what Churchill called 'the soft underbelly of Europe'. At 7.43 p.m., Badoglio came on Radio Roma to confirm the joint agreement, taking less than a minute to say a curt seventy-five words. Once again, his words over the radio were ambiguous: Italians were instructed both to react to any attack, wherever it came from, and at the same time not to fight the Allies. For a while, people believed it was all some kind of trick. Then Frascati was bombed, killing four hundred Italians but missing Kesselring and the German headquarters.

What followed was further chaos and chicanery. Realising that the Germans were intending to occupy Italy and oppose the Allies every step of the way, the King, the royal household, Badoglio and many senior ministers crept out of Rome in a long cortège of cars before dawn on 9 September. They took with them servants, state papers and many suitcases filled with money and jewellery. Just outside Tivoli the pump on the Queen's car broke and the passengers moved to the other vehicles. The cars made their way to Ortona, where a boat was waiting for them, but since it could not take everyone, Badoglio had to choose from the jostling and frantic generals trying to board.

From there they sailed to Brindisi, where he and the King planned to set up their government, paying no heed to the fact that they were effectively condemning the Italians they had abandoned into becoming hostages for the enemy. Years of subservience to Fascism had robbed the King of any vestige of heroism. He and Badoglio left behind them no orders for the military, who, after a few valiant attempts at resistance on the edges of Rome, the men often armed with nothing but hunting rifles, capitulated to the Germans, while the terrified Romans tried to reassure themselves that the Allies could not be far away. The news that they were, in fact, far to the south was bad, but what was worse was watching lorries full of German soldiers roaring into the city from north and south and setting up machine guns on street corners. Soon, they were stopping people in the streets to strip them of their jewellery and watches and breaking into houses to loot the valuables. Someone scribbled on a wall: 'We don't want Germans or English. Leave us to cry on our own.' The Flora Hotel was turned into a military court. The mood was one of hysteria and abandonment.

The Germans had had forty-five days in which to prepare the army for the armistice they knew from their secret services was coming. They had used them well, securing the crucial Brenner Pass and transferring divisions down from the north of Italy. Now they moved quickly to occupy the telephone exchanges, police stations, electricity plants, ports and airports. Field Marshal Kesselring, with eight divisions, took command. A curfew was imposed;

newspapers were censored; orders went out that the Romans were not to walk near any of the German-requisitioned hotels and that no man was permitted to ride a bicycle. Posters were pasted to walls saying that snipers, strikers and saboteurs would be shot on the spot. The new announcer on Radio Roma spoke with a German accent. All inquiries into illicit Fascist gains were halted. The deer from the zoo were butchered and eaten by the new occupiers, along with the peacocks in the park of the German embassy. Italy, announced Kesselring, was now a war zone, subject to German military law. City after city fell. A reign of terror began.

Badoglio's few and opaque military orders, intended to confuse the Germans, had confused the Italians instead: Italian soldiers in their barracks all over Italy milled around, uncertain what to do. A few of the more resourceful slipped away, exchanged their uniforms for civilian clothes and set off for home to make plans for resistance. The unlucky, those who stayed in their barracks awaiting orders, were quickly caught by the Germans. Within days, trains were going north, carrying the men to prisoner-of-war camps in Germany. The staggering amount of booty left behind for the Germans included 4,553 planes, 15,500 vehicles and thirty-two million gallons of fuel. The 3,500-ton battleship *Roma*, pride of the Italian fleet, had set sail for an Allied port and was sunk by Junkers: 1,352 sailors, along with their admiral, were drowned. In Cephalonia, 8,400 Italian soldiers who tried to resist were killed, their bodies stacked up and set on fire.

On 10 September, the German Supreme Command put out a communiqué: 'The Italian armed forces no longer exist.' Italy was now a battlefield for the Germans and the Allies, in which a civil war between Italians and Italians – Mussolini's Fascist followers fighting the growing number of resisters – would soon take root, and the Germans would mercilessly exploit and plunder the country they occupied. From Brindisi, the King broadcast to his people: 'I know I can rely on you,' he declared, 'just as you can count on your King till the final sacrifice.' The Romans were disgusted. Capri was taken over by the Allies and Rear Admiral Sir Anthony Morse took up residence as Governor in Edda's requisitioned house. In Naples, a banquet was given for General Mark Clark. He had expressed a preference for fish, and since no fishing boats could go out because of mines, he was apparently given the prized baby manatee from the aquarium, boiled and served with garlic sauce.

Hitler kept his promise to Edda. In the frenzy of 8 September, Mussolini had been forgotten by the Italian leadership. He could have been taken south with the King, and handed over as agreed in the terms of the Armistice, to the Allies. Instead, a dramatic, flamboyant rescue operation was now staged. On 12 September, a six-foot-seven-inch SS officer called Otto Skorzeny with a strong, rugged face scarred by duelling wounds, who was a former engineering student and friend of Kaltenbrunner's, led twelve gliders and a reconnaissance plane to land, through banks of cloud, outside the hotel on the Gran Sasso. Though there were 250 carabinieri and police guarding the Duce, no shots were fired, and there was speculation later that the Italians had been complicit in the rescue – and, perhaps, in Ciano's rescue, too – fearing revelations either man might have made before a war crimes tribunal. The police chief, Carmine Senise, it was said, had suggested that a beaten and humiliated Mussolini would be better for Italy than a dead one and had radioed Campo Imperatore to put up no resistance. From the hotel, the Duce was hustled into the small plane, which took off, narrowly avoiding crashing into the escarpment. It bore him to an airport in the plains, then on to Germany.

Earlier that same day, German soldiers had arrived at Rocca delle Caminate and told Rachele and the children that they were to be flown to Germany. She was given fifteen minutes in which to pack. They left on a bomber from Forlì, and had to change course to avoid Allied planes. Rachele was at dinner in the Hotel Quattro Stagioni in Munich when an officer arrived to tell her that Mussolini had been freed and was on his way to Germany. She met him at the airport. He was, she wrote later, barely recognisable, very pale, very thin, wearing ski boots and an old coat. They spent the night in the magnificent Karl Palast Hotel, all chandeliers and thick-pile carpets, where Mussolini's room was so overwhelming that he chose to depart from habit and join Rachele in hers. He told her that even when driven away from the Quirinale on the afternoon of the 26th, he still had no idea what was happening. Next morning, he was taken to Hitler's headquarters. Goebbels referred to Rachele as '*una brava contadina Italiana*', a good Italian peasant. The meeting between Hitler and Mussolini, he added, was 'profoundly moving ... an example of loyalty between men and comrades'.

Edda learnt of the rescue on her own return to Munich. It took her several days of frantic demands and wheedling before she was allowed to see her father. She returned from their meeting relieved, saying that Mussolini seemed to accept that Ciano's vote at the Gran Consiglio had not been an act of treachery, but rather the expression of a desire to see things change. She and her father, she said, had 'found each other again', and she believed that if things went badly 'we would fight together side by side'. Ciano listened but remained extremely wary. The whole family then went off to meet Mussolini and Rachele in the Karl Palast Hotel. Edda, extremely thin and her eyes glittering, was tense and tentative; Ciano lashed out against Badoglio and vehemently denied that he had ever intended to betray his father-in-law. There was a very awkward lunch, with all twelve members of the clan now in Germany present. Mussolini seemed to be drowning in clothes that were much too big for him. Ciano looked sleek, in an elegant pale grey suit and exquisite pocket handkerchief. Her son-in-law reminded her, Rachele said later, of everything she had hated about the 'corrupt Roman aristocracy'.

The dining room was vast, with Flemish paintings of animals and flowers; Mussolini sat perched on a regal armchair at the head of the table. Ciano continued to protest his innocence and loyalty; Edda said little and ate nothing; Rachele, implacable, spoke out furiously, attacking her son-in-law. Mussolini seemed curiously forgiving. From time to time, marvelling that there could be such a meeting between a traitor and the father-in-law he had betrayed, German officers put their heads around the door to witness this strange kind of Italian theatre and the feebleness of the Italian soul. A chilly mist seemed to settle over the room. Edda asked whether the children could leave the room, and an SS officer escorted them out. 'If, after all his sad experiences,' noted Goebbels in his diary, 'the Duce puts himself once again into the hands of his daughter Edda, who is in truth a petty and vulgar harlot, in whose veins flows Jewish blood, there will be no way to help him politically.' He added that Hitler would have liked Mussolini to hand Ciano over to him so that he could have him shot immediately, and also to have Edda shut up in prison, where she might recover her wits. After the lunch, Vittorio later wrote, 'Death walked on the roof of our house.' In the car taking them back to their villa, Ciano said softly to Edda, 'Your father told me that he guaranteed my safety with his own head.'

Hitler had thought of replacing Mussolini with another *gerarca*, perhaps Pavolini, or even Farinacci – though Goebbels dismissed him as a 'clumsy idiot' – and setting him up in a new state over which he would have control. But he now turned back to Mussolini and proposed that he form a new government in the far north-east of Italy, in the tiny village of Gargnano on Lake Garda. The nearby town of Salò would give the new state its name, the Salò or Repubblica Sociale Italiana, which Mussolini liked since it seemed to stress its socialist, left-wing side. For all the talk of loyalty and comradeship, the terms offered by the Germans to the Italians were hard. Mussolini was to remain within the Axis; to provide Italian workers for the German war effort, along with machinery and goods; and Germany was to annex the two frontier provinces of Venezia Giulia and Alto Adige. Mussolini would, in theory, hold power; in practice he would be little more than a dutiful servant, his every move scrutinised, in a puppet state not unlike Vichy France. Furthermore, Hitler expected, he told Mussolini, the most exemplary punishment for the traitors of the Gran Consiglio, and especially for Ciano, who was a traitor four times over: to the Axis, to Fascism, to Italy and to his family. In his diary, Goebbels noted that Ciano was 'a traitor of unique proportions', and that this 'inflated football' of a son-in-law should rapidly be eliminated.

Several of the *gerarchi* had managed to escape to Germany and had been waiting for Mussolini's arrival. Farinacci and Pavolini were there, as well as Maresciallo Graziani, veteran of some of the worst atrocities in Ethiopia, and the men were moved to the castle of Hirschberg in the Bavarian pine woods to plan the new government. The constant presence of a German guard of honour and an SS officer, and the fact that their only link with the outside world was through a German military switchboard, was a reminder that they owed their existence to German sufferance. On 18 September over Radio Munich, Mussolini proclaimed his new Repubblica. His voice was at first flat and barely audible, but later picked up some of its old verve and firmness. After a period of 'moral isolation', he declared, he was once again establishing contact with the world.

18

What have we become?

Neither Ciano nor Edda was under any illusion: Ciano's position was extremely precarious. The days passed, Mussolini caught up with his political plans, Edda nagging at him to get the Germans to honour Dollmann's promise to let them leave for Spain, Rachele shouting at Ciano who, forbidden to leave the villa except under guard, was beginning to feel that he might be better off back in Italy than under house arrest in Bavaria. Rachele had taken to referring to her son-in-law as an 'arrogant whoremonger'. Höttl would later describe shopping expeditions into Munich, during which Ciano kept fishing for female company among the sales girls. Edda, noted Goebbels, was 'behaving like a wild cat ... whenever she is crossed, she breaks plates and furniture'. He said that he and Hitler had decided that it would be best if she were to be sent to a 'house of correction'. It would be Edda's fault, he added, if Ciano, 'that venomous fungus', was accepted back by Mussolini. Later, Daniele Varè would say that he was shown a copy of a long letter from Ciano to Edda, announcing that he planned to kill himself, and explaining the steps by which he had come to hate the Germans and believe that Italy had to save herself.

As the days dragged past and no passports came, Ciano and Edda began discussing the possibility of bartering Ciano's diaries for his safety, and even brought the matter up with Höttl. These diaries, they told the Nazi officer, not only contained details of diplomatic exchanges of every kind between European leaders during the years leading up and into the war, often of an unexpected and even disreputable kind, but they also threw new light on the various rivalrous German leaders who were jockeying for power, and particularly on Ribbentrop. Höttl expressed interest. Both he and Kaltenbrunner hated Ribbentrop and hoped to lessen his influence.

Ciano had left the diaries and other important material with his uncle Gino, who had been secretary to both Costanzo and to Ciano himself and of whom Edda was very fond, since he had bailed her out of gambling debts in the past. After much irritable badgering, Edda persuaded her German minders to let her go to Rome to retrieve the diaries. She travelled under the name of Emilia Santos, a nurse on a mission to Italy, and she was accompanied by two SS women, also posing as nurses, and a priest. She reached Rome at the end of September, hoping to stay with friends. Few were willing to take her in and, with varying degrees of abruptness, cut short her calls. Lola Giovinelli specifically asked her not to come to her house, so as to avoid 'awkwardness'. But Delia di Bagno immediately and warmly agreed to give her a bed, no small gesture in a city in which the name 'Ciano' had become poison.

Rome had been declared an open city, a *città aperta*, which made it theoretically protected from all military activity. In practice, the Germans roamed at will. The Commandant, General Mälzer, ruled with a certain leniency, but the real master of the city was Kappler, head of the SS, who used Italian policemen as his henchmen. The Gestapo had ordered the Jewish community to hand over 50 kilos of gold, warning that if they failed to do so their families would be taken hostage. The gold was collected, but on 16 October the Germans rounded up Jewish families just the same. A few mothers managed to hand their children to neighbours and friends before being put on to lorries destined for the camps in Poland.* Radio Roma was issuing attacks on the Allied leaders, referring to Churchill as a 'sad clown', a 'bad tempered podgy satanic Mephistopheles' with the face of a cow, Eden as an 'honorary Bolshevik' and claiming that Roosevelt was running the US 'with the synagogues ... and the stock exchange'. British women were described as having 'leathery elbows, boxers' hands, rough skins and voices like scratchy gramophone records'.

---

* Of the 1,023 deported, 207 were children. Only fifteen men and one woman survived.

Former Fascists, emerging from hiding, were now strutting down the streets in their black shirts, wearing German insignia and swastikas on their uniforms. The Palazzo Braschi, an old papal palace with a magnificent staircase, had been turned into a torture centre. The grand hotels had all been requisitioned. Bicycles were forbidden, but the crafty Romans had turned them into tricycles by adding pram wheels. Rome, a capital without a government, was grey, shuttered, miserable, short of food. Bread felt like glue, looked like mud and tasted of nothing.

Several members of the 'Ciano clan', his Petit Trianon, had been picked up and put in the Regina Coeli prison. 'Ah! How many there are!' wrote Gabriella di Robilant, referring to Ciano's aristocratic mistresses. Isabella Colonna, warned just in time, had taken refuge in the Spanish embassy, but Virginia Agnelli was being held in San Gregorio, a former Catholic school for children of good families, where she shared a room with Principessa Caetani. The ladies had their meals sent in from a restaurant. Prince Doria dressed as a priest and his tall, stately daughter and her mother dyed their fair hair black and posed as washerwomen.

The anti-Fascists, those who had been foolish enough to spend Badoglio's forty-five days deluding themselves that Italy was about to get out of the war, had crept back into the shadows. Many were being hidden in religious institutions, the convents, parish houses, pontifical seminaries, colleges, hospitals run for centuries by the Vatican on their extraterritorial land. Accustomed by long years of clandestine behaviour to living underground, those now once again on the run knew how to adapt; they grew beards, put on hats and wore glasses. Though the Germans were well aware of what was happening, Vatican immunity was for the most part respected, and as the weeks passed more and more former soldiers, Jews, industrialists, princes and writers slipped inside its walls, behind well-guarded lines.

In San Giovanni in Laterano, where the opposition leaders had taken refuge, they held their meetings in the sacristy, with a hidden radio in the basement. In one Vatican college, a thousand people now inhabited space for two hundred. The Carandini family had managed to find sanctuary not only for family members but for thirty prize Friesian cows and three bulls, which would otherwise have been seized by the Germans. What would play out in the months to come was a game of utter ambiguity, the Germans watchful, the Vatican intent on having its status respected while preventing insurrection before the arrival of the Allies. Rome had become a no man's land, in which everything could be bought and sold, with the Germans stripping the city of supplies, resources, food and gold from the Banca d'Italia, along with young men who they sent to labour camps in Germany. Cinecittà had been looted, its studios turned into depots for the German army. From time to time, Pius XII appeared at his window over St Peter's Square, to pray and comfort the faithful, among whom were many German soldiers.

Edda had reached Rome in early October. Gino had buried some of Ciano's papers under a tree in the garden of his house at Ponte a Moriano, near Lucca. Taking the faithful Emilio Pucci as her driver, Edda drove to collect them, only to discover they had disappeared. Carolina, her mother-in-law, suggested posting a reward for what she called the missing 'family papers', and next morning they were found left by the gate. Other papers, including Ciano's notes on talks with Ribbentrop and a file called 'Germania', were retrieved from a separate hiding place in Rome. Delia di Bagno, wrote Edda gratefully, had become her 'accomplice' and was doing all that she could to help.

The flat in the Via Angelo Secchi had been sealed by the police, but once again calling on their naval friend, who provided her with a strong sailor, Edda managed to break in and recover more valuables. Other friends, with whom she had left jewellery, returned it to her even though some refused to see her while doing so. 'She was depressed,' remembered Umberto Zanotti Bianco, a family friend as well as an anti-Fascist. 'She described horrendous things about Germany and said that she intended to stand by her husband and defend him.' Then she went off to Rocca delle Caminate where Mussolini, accompanied by a special escort of SS provided by Hitler, had arrived to continue talks on setting up his new government, and where he was to be seen pacing restlessly up and down the great hall, occasionally pausing to stare out at the distant Apennines. Not all of his former ministers and friends, he found, would even take his calls. Edda's meetings with her father were affectionate until she spoke of Ciano, pleading with him to protect the father of his grandchildren; then, he became icy. He told her that she would do well to check into a clinic to 'cure her shattered nerves'. Rachele remained hostile and implacable.

Edda was back in Rome again when, on 19 October, she heard that Ciano, having been told that he might return to Italy to enrol as a pilot for Mussolini's new republic, had flown back to Verona. He had been accompanied by heavily armed SS men, though there is some disagreement about whether he volunteered or was coerced to go. Before leaving, he was allowed to say goodbye to the children. '*Ciao, bambini,*' he said. 'We will not see each other for a while.' The children said nothing. Then he told Fabrizio: 'Ciccino, always behave with honour.' They stood watching silently as he was driven away.

When the plane touched down in Verona, the SS guards, saying nothing, handed him over to the Italian militia waiting at the airport. Later Ciano would say that, looking around at the rigid, impassive faces of the Germans, 'I had the immediate sense that I had made an enormous and irreparable mistake,' and that, in order to stay in power, 'that wretched Mussolini was not going to hesitate for a moment to offer my head on a silver plate to Hitler.' He was taken straight to the prison of the Scalzi, a former Carmelite nunnery.

Wearing a beige knitted turban, a rabbit-fur coat and red woollen stockings, Edda immediately set off again to see her father. She stormed into a meeting of *gerarchi*, stared fixedly at each in turn, and told Pavolini that this was not the moment to bear a grudge against his former friend. 'A grudge?' Pavolini replied. 'He deserves a great deal worse.' Edda sprang to her feet, tipping over her bag and exclaimed, 'I have a feeling that the worst is still to come, and it will be the worst for everyone, you'll see.' Mussolini's secretary Giovanni Dolfin was struck again by how similar she was in appearance to her father, particularly when she threw her head back and stared at the person she was addressing, waiting for an answer, full of scorn and impatience. She was now, Edda announced bitterly to the assembled gathering, ashamed to be Italian. Before leaving, she spent two hours alone with Mussolini, who informed her that there was going to be a trial for the traitors of 24 July; but, he added, everything would work out for the best.

*

For the first time in eighty-two years, Italy was again a divided country: a kingdom with a '*piccolo Quirinale*' in the south-east under Badoglio and the King, ruling over just four provinces; a new Fascist republic in the north-east; and the rest of Italy a battlefield as the Allies fought their way north and the Germans resisted them.

When the moment came for Mussolini to take possession of his state of Salò, he went ahead of Rachele and the children to Gargnano, to take up residence in the Villa Feltrinelli, a pretty house with pink marble floors, colonnades and a little tower set in the middle of olive groves. Cameramen from LUCE, which had also transferred itself to the north, filmed him in a handsome new military uniform. Offices were found in the nearby Villa delle Orsoline, and thirty men from Romagna were recruited to replace Mussolini's German guards. But the Germans were never far away. Rudolf Rahn, who had served in Vichy France and seen how to make a puppet government work, arrived from Rome as Hitler's personal emissary, 'not only to convey to Hitler Mussolini's never-ending problems and gripes', but to keep a close eye on 'this rather inauspicious experiment in political puppetry'. Rahn was a big, heavy man, with very pale eyes and bushy eyebrows, authoritarian and curt. He was also close to Ribbentrop. Mussolini was very irritated to discover that it took less than an hour for everything he said and did to be communicated to Berlin.

A few weeks later Rachele followed with Romano and Anna Maria, and they were soon joined by Vittorio and his family, as well as Bruno's widow and her daughter. The watchful Dolfin was struck by how profoundly Rachele had retained the manners and appearance of a Romagnola peasant: dynamic, brisk, impulsive, obsessed by cleanliness and order and absolutely averse to frivolity. Romano was sent to a nearby *lycée* and Mussolini sometimes bicycled with him to school. The new ministries were scattered around wherever space could be found – refugees from the bombed cities having taken over all the houses – and for a while the MinCulPop lived in a railway carriage on a disused line. Most of the nobility stayed behind in Rome, but a few wives and mistresses followed their *gerarchi* north, renting villas and spending their afternoons playing bridge. Mussolini had barely settled in when Edda appeared, like one of the Furies, and argued fiercely with her father, pleading with him to intervene on Ciano's behalf, before returning to a clinic at Ramiola, just south of Parma, where she had taken refuge. To his sister Edvige, Mussolini said that he could not understand why Ciano had not simply abstained from voting on the night of the Gran Consiglio.

Claretta, too, had chosen to follow her Ben, arriving ahead of Rachele. Freed from prison after Mussolini intervened, she had set up house in the pink four-storeyed Villa Fiordaliso, where Mussolini came to visit her two or three times a week. The locals christened it Villa dei Morti because no one was ever seen arriving or leaving.

To Lake Garda and the new Repubblica Sociale Italiana had come the hardest and most intransigent of the former *gerarchi*. The deeply corrupt Guido Buffarini-Guidi, who had made a fortune selling false papers to Jews, was made Minister of the Interior; Alessandro Pavolini became the new Fascist Party secretary. Vittorio was given the job of setting up a network of loyal collaborators, but he was regarded by his colleagues as arrogant and inefficient. He was, noted Dolfin, like a 'big, hefty boy' who had been asked to play a game whose rules he did not know. Rachele, busy re-establishing her own network of spies and informers, soon managed to get Dolfin replaced as Mussolini's secretary by Vittorio. She also acquired chickens, rabbits and a cow. Mussolini's immense archive, seized by Badoglio after the coup and sent north, had mysteriously disappeared. As its flag, Salò took the traditional Italian red, white and green, but instead of the Savoy arms, an eagle held the fasces in its claws.

Plots and cabals flourished. Giovanni Preziosi, the anti-Semitic former priest who had been responsible for the first Italian edition of the *Protocols of the Elders of Zion*, sent notes to Berlin on Mussolini and his circle. As Goebbels observed, Mussolini seemed to have learnt nothing: he was still surrounded by 'traitors, freemasons and Jew lovers', with Vittorio playing an 'odious' part, not through lack of character but through sheer stupidity. Shrewdly, however, the Duce let it be known that he was planning to continue the work of investigation into the illicit profits made by the *gerarchi*, so that he had some dirt and leverage over them. Tales of Guido Buffarini-Guido's speculations and trafficking soon landed on his desk. Pavolini was outraged when his own profiteering became known.

Two German officers watched closely over Mussolini at all times, and the Germans controlled his telephone switchboard with the outside world. They sat in on meetings, vetted everything that left his office as well as the newspapers and radio station transmitting from Salò. When Mussolini, humiliated and angry, sent Vittorio to Berlin to complain, Ribbentrop told him that the Italians would do better to prove their good faith by taking 'vigorous action against treachery and defeatism'. Following events in the Salò republic from Rome, Gabriella di Robilant noted, 'What have we become? What a calamity. What shame.'

Mussolini announced that he intended to pursue two policies: to return to his old socialist radicalism and nationalise Italian industry, and to create a republican army out of the Italian soldiers now interned in Germany. The Germans blocked both, though eventually and with great reluctance agreed to recruit four Italian divisions and train them themselves in Germany. They made little effort to conceal the fact that they regarded Salò as useful in helping run Italy, and as a provider of chemicals, industrial goods and food; but little else. To Mussolini's chagrin, the Vatican refused to recognise his new state; nor did Switzerland, Turkey, Argentina, Spain or Portugal.

By the end of October, the frenetic Pavolini had corralled twenty-five thousand people into a newly constituted Fascist Party, turning away all those who had flirted with Badoglio, along with 'plutocrats, the rich and the *nouveaux riches*'. Old diehards flocked to Salò, filling the northern cities with militias, private armies, mercenaries, adventurers, all of them angry and all intent on hunting down and punishing the 'enemies of Italy and of Fascism'. Just a couple of intellectuals, the philosopher Giovanni Gentile and the futurist F. T. Marinetti among them, followed. Pavolini talked about a return to the true soul of totalitarianism, combative, steely and ruthless.

On 10 November, a conference was held in Verona, which had become a fortress town for the Nazis and the Fascists, with a large arsenal and a jail, in which Ciano was now prisoner number 11,902. The plan was to lay down the foundations of the new Italian state, and the meetings were predictably chaotic, some calling for the abolition of private property, others for every citizen to carry a gun. The 'decadence of the monarchy' was loudly derided and the King declared 'a traitor and an outlaw'. There were many debates about Jews, both Italian and foreign, and it was decided to declare them 'an enemy people'. They were to be rounded up, put into camps and eventually deported. Tensions mounted when news came that a senior Fascist in Ferrara had been shot, and insistent calls for vengeance went up. A punitive expedition was immediately dispatched to Ferrara, and eleven of its citizens were picked up and shot at random. Their bodies were then hacked to pieces, setting the barbaric and frenzied tone for the months to come.

Though the hundred or so delegates finally came up with an eighteen-point manifesto, they seemed far more interested in how they were going to conduct the war on rebels and turncoats, and most of all in what was going to happen to the nineteen traitors of the 25th of July. There was a unanimous vote to set up a Special Tribunal, in order to bring them to trial and then to punish them. A roar of voices chanted: '*A morte Ciano! A morte Ciano!*' Pavolini, once Ciano's creature, pliant and servile, but now Jacobin in his harsh, almost mystical purity, was the one who called loudest for justice.

19

Doing one's duty

Edda had been assured by Mussolini that she would be allowed to see Ciano. She returned to Verona and went to the Carcere degli Scalzi, where the Italian warden was at first reluctant to let her in, but finally agreed to take her to Cell 27. An old *squadrista*, Luigi Chinesi, was detailed to sit with them. Edda was able to whisper to Ciano that the diaries were safe. Ciano asked her to arrange for his luggage to be sent from Germany, along with his Collare dell'Annunziata. Edda was allowed back the following day, and once again five days later, and they talked about the children. They were very affectionate with each other. This woman whose marriage had been marked by countless affairs and a friendly but distant comradeship seemed to discover a new kind of passion. It was as if, having for so long protected herself from his many affairs behind a wall of indifference, she now felt that she could really love him. The languor and cool eye with which she had surveyed the world around her vanished, to be replaced by urgency and warmth.

Hildegard Beetz had been the twenty-two-year-old secretary to Wilhelm Höttl at the time of the Cianos' flight from Rome, recently married to a major in the Luftwaffe. She was small, chestnut-haired, romantic, intelligent, and neatly dressed. Because she always seemed so cheerful, Kaltenbrunner, the head of the secret services, had given her the nickname Felicitas. After Höttl heard about the diaries, but before Ciano was returned to Italy, he had sent Beetz to the villa on Lake Starnberg to see what more she could find out, since her Italian was far better than his own. Her first impression of Ciano had been that he was vain, frivolous and too full of himself, though physically very attractive. Edda she had dismissed as a bad wife and a bad mother.

Hildegaard Beetz

But Frau Beetz had soon warmed to Ciano, saying that he was '*un uomo solo*', very much alone, and needed support. Whether or not, as people later claimed – and she later both claimed and denied – she fell in love with him is impossible to know. But what is known is that, once Ciano was a prisoner, she joined Edda in her battle to save him. Sent to Verona by Höttl to find a way of getting hold of the diaries now in Edda's hands, she became their go-between and lied, when necessary, to her superiors if she thought she had information that could harm him. When Ciano's school friend, Zenone Bernini, having turned himself into the police so that his family would not be taken hostage, arrived as a prisoner at Le Scalzi, Ciano told him that everyone knew that Beetz was a spy, 'but she's my spy'.

After their first three meetings, Edda was refused permission to visit Ciano until 27 November, after which she went to Gargnano to complain to her father that Ciano was not being permitted to leave his cell, even for exercise. Mussolini was surprised and said that he would look into it. Dolfin, who was present, described Edda that day: 'Dishevelled, pale, thin, she seemed to have great trouble concealing her agitation . . . She is suffering and her impul-sive nature needs an outlet.' After her visit to Ciano on November 27, she was barred altogether from the prison, with no explan-ation given. In the guard room, the men made disparaging and vulgar jokes about her. She banged on doors, raged and pleaded, but to no avail. Having intercepted one furious accusatory letter written by Edda to her father, Hitler and Goebbels asked themselves, 'What kind of an education can the Duce have given his daughter that she writes him a letter like this?'

Edda was still living in the clinic at Ramiola, under the name Emilia Santos. Fabrizio, Raimondo and Marzio were in Germany and she feared that Hitler might keep them as hostages. Dolfin wrote to her to say that Mussolini asked that she keep a very close watch over the children who might otherwise 'be exposed to hostile acts'. Unnerved, she now asked Vittorio to bring them to her in Italy. Vittorio drove to Berlin and met an under-secretary of foreign affairs during an air raid in a bunker under the Adlon Hotel. He was told that the children would not be permitted to leave Germany. When he returned to Ramiolo to tell Edda, she was reproachful. 'You promised me,' she kept saying. Vittorio had always been a little in awe of his older sister. He hitched a trailer on to the back of his car and set off once again for Berlin. This time he explained to the under-secretary that Mussolini needed to have his children and grandchildren around him, and that seeing the family together was important for Italians and would make them more resigned to the presence of their German occupiers. The under-secretary, somewhat reluctantly, accepted the story and gave him petrol for the return journey. Vittorio and the three children, their luggage in the trailer, immediately left for Italy. They kept driving until Bolzano, where they waited out a heavy American bombardment, the children cowering as explosions filled the sky above them. Edda was intensely relieved to see them, kissed each child in turn with her formal peck and thanked Vittorio, then turned to planning their escape to Switzerland. For all her new-found emotion, relief did not include displays of physical warmth.

The person she had recruited to help her was the faithful Pucci. They organised the children's flight with meticulous care, spending several days saying loudly in front of the staff and the other patients in the clinic that they intended to spend Christmas with Carolina Ciano in the Varese. There was no time to lose. One evening one of Pucci's most fanatical cousins arrived at the clinic, threatening to kidnap Edda and make her pay for Ciano's treachery. She just had time to hide.

Emilio Pucci

On 9 December, Pucci drove the three children from Ramiolo to Milan. Two family friends, one of whom was based at Como near the Swiss border, then took the children on to meet a smuggler. Edda had no actual money, but agreed to pay for their crossing with her jewellery, including the brooch given to her on her wedding day by the King and Queen. They spent a night in a shepherd's hut, Raimonda curled up in a large cradle. On the night of the 12th, Raimonda's tenth birthday, they crossed under the wire by a full moon, holding hands. The Swiss police were waiting, having been warned only to expect some children, and beckoned to them from the Swiss side. They gave them chocolate, which five-year-old Marzio later claimed he had never seen before.

After a night in the residence of the Bishop of Lugano they were taken to a convent in the nearby village of Neggio and given new names. Twelve-year-old Fabrizio became Jorge, Raimonda became Margarita and Marzio, Pedro. Their new surname was to be their mother's, Santos. Left behind in Italy, Edda was now free to concentrate all her energies on saving Ciano. As Carolina, who had always been extremely critical of her errant daughter-in-law, admitted, she would never have believed that Edda could be so devoted and single-minded.

On 18 December, Edda drove to Gargnano to confront her father again. He received her in his office, as if to underline that Ciano's fate was not a family matter. All her previous admiration for the Germans had disappeared. For two hours, the people in his outer office listened as she berated him for becoming Hitler's servant, and tried, with every argument that she could think of, to galvanise him into intervening in the forthcoming trial. At the very least, she said, it would prove he still had some control over events. Mussolini veered between silence and anger. There was much banging of fists on the table. At one point Edda said to him: 'You're mad. The war is lost. The Germans are now finished.' As she stormed out, she was heard to say: 'It's all over between us, finished for ever, and if you were to kneel before me dying of thirst, and beg me for a glass of water, I would pour it out on the ground before your eyes.' Dolfin, once again witnessing her departure, thought how formidable Edda could be, and how jealous and resentful she must have made other women. She 'defends her husband with every ounce of strength she has ... alone, in an atmosphere of hostility'. He found her appearance 'sloppy' and said that she had become even paler and thinner and now seemed incapable of keeping up her usual mask of indifference.

Mussolini was in an impossible position. Interrogation of the prisoners in Verona had begun a few days earlier, and he had been told that Ciano was laying the full blame for Italy's disastrous foreign policy decisions on his father-in-law. By accepting Hitler's offer to help him set up the new Salò government, Mussolini had told himself that he would be able to mitigate Germany's increasingly predatory and harsh treatment of the Italians. But to do so he would have to appear strong. Did he now think that if he showed weakness, Hitler would remove him and raze Italy to the ground? Mussolini looked older, battered both physically and mentally, slept little and had constant cramps. His skin was yellow. More tests had confirmed a duodenal ulcer. Hitler had sent him his personal physician, Georg Zachariae, who had changed his diet, eliminating the two litres of milk he had been drinking every day, and replacing them with fruit and fish, and many vitamins. His patient, the German doctor noted, was 'a wreck, evidently on the edge of the grave'. In 1937 Mussolini had told a visitor: 'I have never known gentleness, the serenity that comes with a happy childhood: this is why I am bitter, shut in, hard, almost savage.' Now he felt completely alone. The days passed quietly, with long periods of sadness and low spirits. Ministers, grave and silent, came and went. Mussolini had always hated lakes and he looked out with distaste on the still grey waters of Lake Garda.

Christmas was a mournful occasion, not improved when Romano, who had gone out on the lake with some of the Italian soldiers, failed to return. A storm blew up and rescue parties were dispatched to search for the missing boat. In the event, Romano was safe, the soldiers having found a safe harbour in which to anchor; but it was twenty-four hours before he was returned to his frantic parents.

Mussolini knew that Ciano was hated by everyone, by the Fascists who blamed him for bringing down the government and by the Germans who held him responsible for sowing anti-German feelings. On 10 December, he told the journalist Carlo Silvestri, referring to the forthcoming trial, that Edda was failing to understand his position. 'I have not been involved, I am not involved and I will not get involved.' Justice had to be allowed to take its course. In an undated note in his own hand, he wrote: 'It would be good if Ciano knew that despite everything, I did not abandon him.' Exactly what he meant by these words is not clear. And behind his agonising dilemma lay one simple fact: Edda was not just his favourite child, but one of the few people, perhaps the only one, whom he felt really close to. He loved her in a way that he had never really loved the other children; or even, perhaps, Rachele.

Still forbidden to exercise, Ciano's life in prison was much improved by the presence of Frau Beetz, who arrived at two most afternoons and stayed for five or six hours. They played cards and chess, made tea and toast and roasted chestnuts on a wood-burning stove he was allowed once it got cold and his bronchial asthma returned, and while he read, she sat silently. When they talked Ciano seemed to speak freely, saying how much he had always mistrusted the Germans and how contemptuous he had come to feel towards Mussolini and Rachele. Whatever her real feelings for Ciano, the position she now found herself in was both exciting and romantic. And Edda trusted her.

The Carcere degli Scalzi had been filling up with some of the other plotters, though most had managed to escape arrest. Tullio Cianetti, the Minister of Corporations, who, in the wake of the Gran Consiglio meeting had written a letter full of regret and apologies to Mussolini, arrived, and was followed by Carlo Pareschi.

Pareschi, who had been a friend of Balbo's and looked like a medieval warrior, had been absent from the chamber when Grandi's motion was read out, but hearing the others vote '*Si*' as he walked back in, had thought he should do the same. Starace had also arrived, though he had not been present at the Gran Consiglio, and he now spent his days running up and down the corridor to keep fit and writing begging letters to Mussolini, who did not reply. The prisoners were strictly forbidden from meeting one another. One night a party of drunken German officers brandishing pistols and bringing with them prostitutes forced their way into the prison, demanding to be shown 'the famous traitor'. They stripped the covers from the sleeping Ciano and one of the prostitutes made a mock curtsey, while an officer put a gun to Ciano's head and shouted, 'Bum! Bum!' Giovanni Marinelli, the eldest of the so-called conspirators, hearing the noise, called piteously for help, then fell to his knees.

During one of their stormy encounters, Edda had said to Mussolini that it would take just two determined men to free Ciano. It took no time for her words to be carried by spies back to Berlin, and the senior German officers in Gardone received a severe reprimand for having allowed Edda access to her father. Another somewhat enigmatic figure called Wilhelm Harster, a short, clever Bavarian with big hands, weathered skin and a slight limp, who was the head of the Gestapo in Italy, was now drawn into the affair of the diaries. Fearing any attempt at a rescue of Ciano, SS officers were sent to stand guard outside Ciano's cell. Taking it in shifts, the men were given a table and chairs in the corridor where they played cards. They had been told to shoot to kill if they spotted trouble. When Ciano saw them arrive, he said to Mario Pellegrinotti, one of the guards he had grown friendly with, 'Ahi! Ahi! This stinks of death.'

Edda was not allowed back to the prison. Ciano wrote to tell her the food was adequate, and that he 'read, read, read . . . I think about you a lot. With hope and with sadness . . . and always with infinite nostalgia.' Edda replied: '*Gallo mio*, stay calm and serene and believe me when I say that I feel not just profound sympathy for what you are going through, but absolute certainty that, if justice exists, it will all be all right in the end.' On 8 December, Ciano told her how he longed to see her, even if only for half an hour, in order for her to give him strength. 'The time never passes. Truly, boredom is an invincible enemy.' On 14 December, she replied. The children were well. 'I know how sad you must feel, but remain strong. I am always near you.' They had never sounded so close. Her letter of the 17th was sad. It was raining, the sky was grey and the trees were bare. She had once again been turned away from the prison. 'I am living a normal life because I don't want people to see on my face that I am suffering. There are horrendous days to come and we must be as iron to resist them.' 18 December was Marzio's sixth birthday; it was now two months since Ciano had seen his children. 'It's like black and red at roulette,' he wrote to Edda. 'It all depends on where the ball stops. All I believe in now is destiny. And I accept it.'

After a two-week break in Berlin, Frau Beetz returned to Verona depressed. The news about German intentions regarding the plotters had not been good, though the Germans had decided to stand back and leave matters entirely to the Italians, assured by the pitiless Pavolini that the trial would be brief and its outcome certain. Rahn was instructed not to intervene. Ciano told Beetz that he was now preparing for death. He spent the days correcting and editing an introduction to his diaries and writing letters to Mussolini and to Churchill, blaming 'one man only' – Mussolini – for leading Italy into the abyss for 'turbid personal ambition'. He told Churchill that he had made arrangements for his diaries and assorted documents to be handed over to the Allies. They would, he said, reveal all. To Edda, he wrote that he was finding the idleness and boredom 'overwhelming, subtle, penetrating, invincible' and deeply humiliating, since at no other moment in his life had he ever had nothing to do. He added: 'I think of you always with great love.'

Christmas had always been a good occasion for the Cianos, who never missed spending it all together. On Christmas Day, the prison chaplain, Don Giuseppe Chiot, was allowed to set up a table as an altar in the corridor, and the prisoners followed mass from their cells. That morning Edda arrived in Verona, determined to see Ciano. She knocked on every door, rang Mussolini but was not put through to him, and by nightfall had made no progress. She went to the prison. The warden, Sergio Olas, was a courteous and understanding man, but could do nothing. Then he remembered that Frau Beetz was with Ciano and summoned her.

The two women talked, held hands, then Edda handed her a bunch of flowers to give to Ciano, along with a box of cakes, a bottle of his favourite cologne and a letter. She also gave her a phial of cyanide, asked for by Ciano and obtained with some difficulty from the chemist in Ramiola. In return, Beetz handed her six new handwritten pages to add to the diaries. Edda's letter to her husband read: 'For the rest, neither walls nor men can prevent me from always being near you. We mustn't cry. Isn't that right, Gallo, that we mustn't, and above all we mustn't be seen to cry.' Even in these circumstances, the Mussolini lifelong determination to show no vulnerability did not weaken. But when he received it, Ciano cried. To his mother, Ciano wrote that he would never have believed that Edda would have done so much for him. She had shown herself, he said, to be 'an exceptional wife. An exceptional woman.'

Ciano in his cell

Edda paid one last visit to Gargnano. She and Mussolini had a final, furious, row; she called him Pontius Pilate. He told her that the trial was completely out of his hands. Having known and admired her father all her life for his strength and power, never questioned his ability to control the world around him, she did not believe him. Before she left the Villa Feltrinelli, Rachele shouted at her that of all the traitors, Ciano was undoubtedly the basest. On the 27th, in answer to a letter from Ciano bemoaning the fact that he had not left his cell in over seventy days, Edda wrote him a stern but loving letter: 'Stay calm and do not let yourself be beaten by discomfort and boredom. Knowing how to cope with boredom is an art.' Sounding somewhat comforted, he replied that what he missed most was fresh air and a visit from her. 'Dear, adored, Deda, I think about you all the time.'

Earlier, Claretta had blamed the 'vile, filthy . . . false' Ciano for having been the 'major actor' in the plot to bring down Mussolini, and declared that Edda, by standing by her husband, had forfeited all claims to pity, even if she were now penitent and supplicatory. Edda too, she said, was an infamous traitor. But now, as the trial approached, Claretta may have tried to intervene, writing a letter to Mussolini, though there are some doubts about its authenticity. 'Ben, save this man. Show the Italians that you are still master of your own life.' Ciano, learning what she had done, wrote to Claretta: 'The sentence is a foregone conclusion, but I will make sure the truth is known.' He intended, he said, to prove to his children that he had not been a traitor.

On 30 December, Edda wrote again to Ciano. 'I have just one wish for the New Year: that you are freed and that no one ever hears speak of us again. Gallo, my dearest, I hold you to me with infinite affection, as do the children. And I am still just as you know me.' This was a very different woman from her earlier cool, guarded days.

The trial had been set for 9 January. On 28 December, on her way to the Scalzi, Frau Beetz had been to see Wilhelm Harster, the SS chief now stationed in Verona. She warned him that if Ciano were executed, Edda would immediately hand all his papers over to the Allies, with possibly severe damage to the Germans, and even to Hitler himself. Harster was sceptical, but agreed to send a coded telegram to his superior, Kaltenbrunner, who took it to Himmler. The two senior Nazis, agreeing that the diaries might help them discredit Ribbentrop, decided on a rescue mission to spirit Ciano abroad. 'Operazione Conte' was launched. Hitler was not told.

Two Dutch SS arrived in Verona. The plan was for them to say they had come to help guard the prisoner. On the appointed day, posing as Fascist extremists determined to ensure that Ciano was properly punished, they would overwhelm the German guards and whisk Ciano, first to a friend's house in Hungary, and from there to Turkey. In exchange, Kaltenbrunner and Himmler would receive all Ciano's diaries and written documents, though precisely what they contained remained a secret. On New Year's Eve, Harster went to meet Kaltenbrunner in Innsbruck to exchange the contract, which had been signed by Ciano. Kaltenbrunner demanded to see evidence of his good faith. Frau Beetz hastened to Ramiola, told Edda, who was ill in bed, that the Germans needed proof that the documents were authentic. Pucci and Beetz volunteered to go to Rome to collect the material still hidden behind a secret wall in Uncle Gino's apartment. Two Gestapo officers accompanied them over the snowy mountain roads; the journey took sixteen hours. They collected the material and immediately set off back again. But the car soon stalled and got stuck in a snowdrift. They did not reach Verona until 6 January, and they found Edda in a state of nervous collapse, imagining that Pucci had been arrested. He had brought back with him eight volumes of diaries, sixteen others of meetings, and a briefcase, but kept the 'Germania' file hidden under his air force greatcoat as potential leverage. A sample from each was selected, copied and sent to Berlin. Evidently finding enough incriminating material in them to seem tantalising, Kaltenbrunner telephoned to say that the rescue should go ahead.

Edda was instructed to be at the 10 kilometre marker on the main road from Verona to Brescia at nine o'clock on the evening of 7 January. She was to bring as much money with her as possible, for Ciano to use in exile. That morning she and Pucci, full of excitement and optimism, gathered together money and documents and set out for the rendezvous. Then the back two tyres of Pucci's very ancient Topolino burst. Edda strapped everything she could under her dress, leaving the rest with Pucci, then flagged down a car, which took her to Brescia. It had in it two senior Fascists, but they failed to recognise her. From here she walked in her fur coat and turban, stumbling along the slippery roads and occasionally falling over, with a brief lift on the handlebars of a passing boy on a bicycle. She arrived at the rendezvous two hours late. There was no one there. The night was cold and foggy. She waited several hours, then made her way to Verona, to Frau Beetz's hotel. What she learnt, when Frau Beetz opened her door, was terrible. '*Operazione Conte*' had been cancelled.

There are different versions about the sequence of events that had led to the rescue being cancelled. The most likely is that Ribbentrop had somehow got wind of the plan, told Hitler, who had then summoned Kaltenbrunner and Himmler. The two men admitted that their intention had been to obtain material that might have proved incriminating and embarrassing to the German leadership, and said that they had thought it better to keep Hitler in the dark. Goebbels and Ribbentrop, who suspected that the diaries contained things that could indeed harm them personally, weighed in. Hitler cancelled the operation and warned Kaltenbrunner that he would be held personally responsible if Ciano got away. According to one German source, when told that if Ciano went to trial he would certainly be killed, Hitler said: 'Mussolini will never allow the father of his beloved grandchildren to be executed.'

Edda, on hearing what had happened, was distraught and accusatory. Frau Beetz handed her a letter from Ciano. '*Edda mia*, while you are still under the sweet illusion that in a few hours I will be free, for me the agony is now beginning. God bless the children.' He asked her to bring them up to respect the principles of honour imbued in him by his own father. He proposed that she have one final attempt at saving him by writing letters to Mussolini and to Hitler, and that then she should escape to Switzerland, taking the diaries with her. After she had finished reading his letter, Edda gave a moan: 'It's over. It's over.'

She returned to Ramiola and wrote three letters: one to Harster, one to Hitler and one to her father. To Harster, she said that if Ciano were not delivered to the station in Berne, within three days, she would make everything public and 'unleash the most terrifying campaign against the Axis'. Beetz, she instructed, was to accompany her husband to Berne, and would then receive all the papers, after which, she swore, they would never hear from her or her family again. They would disappear into silence. To Hitler, she wrote that she had made a terrible mistake in believing in his promises towards her family, 'and I was cheated'. She had hesitated to turn against the Germans earlier only because Italian and German soldiers were fighting and dying side by side. Addressing her father simply as 'Duce', she wrote: 'I have waited until today for you to show a minimum of feeling of humanity and justice. *Ora basta*.'

Unless Ciano lived, her vengeance would be merciless. Pucci took the letters to Frau Beetz.

At six thirty on the morning of 7 January 1944, having been given back their shoes, braces, belts and ties, Ciano, Marinelli, Pareschi, Gottardi, President of the Confederation of Industrial Workers, Tullio Cianetti former Minister of Corporations, and Marshal De Bono were driven to the Castelvecchio, a fourteenth-century fortress on the banks of the River Adige. The night before, the much decorated marshal, one of Mussolini's earliest comrades, had been brought to the Scalzi from a nursing home in Bergamo. He wore his military uniform and all his medals. Ciano had made his will 'on the eve of unjustly being condemned'. On the walls of Verona, people had scrawled 'Death to the traitor', and 'Edda Mussolini, daughter of a swine', but some had also written 'Viva Ciano'.

The trial was to take place in the same music hall that had hosted the Congress in November, a magnificent room with wood panelling, hung for the occasion with Fascist flags and banners. Pavolini had orchestrated the layout carefully to give the occasion a sense of menacing gravitas, with the judges sitting at a vast walnut table covered in a dark cloth, and behind them a great black cloth with the Fascist insignia and a crucifix. There was very little light. The trial was open to the public, but only by invitation, and the public gallery was filled with German officers and Fascist dignitaries, in their black uniforms. Outside, keeping back the crowds that had gathered, were three lines of armed guards. Not long before, Mussolini, pushed by the more unforgiving *gerarchi*, had summoned the President of the Tribunal, Aldo Vecchini, and told him to hand down justice 'without regard for anyone', and not to get bogged down in lengthy procedural arguments. 'Do your duty.' The fact that there was no legal case to answer, that the votes in the Gran Consiglio had merely expressed a view, that there was no evidence of any crime or of any collusion with the King, or that several of those who voted had not quite understood what they were voting for was ignored. And Mussolini knew it.

Among the accused, only Ciano feared the worst. As they filed into the courtroom there was a pause while the high-backed leather chairs waiting for them were replaced by more modest small wooden ones. De Bono looked stunned and absent, Marinelli on the verge of collapse. Ciano, in a pale mackintosh bought in Munich, sat in the middle of the second row. At nine, the judges arrived; all rose to give the Fascist salute. From the first, the proceedings were interrupted by constant shouts of 'traitor' and 'death' from the public gallery and the prisoners had trouble making themselves heard. All denied having plotted to bring down Mussolini and make a deal with the enemy. Three lawyer friends of Ciano's had refused to take on his defence, and the court-appointed lawyer was intimidated and incompetent. Ciano gave a dignified speech, denying everything that he was accused of, saying that he had never intended to betray either Mussolini or Fascism, but had simply wanted the King to take more control. His words were largely drowned by barracking. And more was at stake than the treachery or otherwise of the defendants. In the dock with the men was the whole gamut of the corruption and profiteering of the *gerarchi*; and the Italians, hungry, miserable, made destitute by the ceaseless bombing, needed scapegoats.

The first day ended with a splinter of hope. Mussolini had asked Dolfin to keep him constantly informed. The Duce, Dolfin wrote later, seemed 'crushed by suffering ... pale, exhausted, clearly making an enormous effort to appear calm'. The next day in court passed in a series of meaningless statements. On the morning of 10 January, the nine judges, not all of whom were in agreement about the death sentences, took three hours and forty minutes to reach a verdict. At first, several of them had voted to spare the lives of all but Ciano, but the president of the court told them to go back and try again until he got the vote he wanted.

Then, at one thirty, the judges came back in. There was total silence in the courtroom, even those in the public gallery holding their breath. When the leading judge spoke, it was to announce death for all but the repentant Cianetti. Pointing at him, Ciano said, 'Only he is saved. For us it is all over.' The elderly Marinelli fainted.

After waiting for two hours for the streets to be cleared of the crowds, the five men were driven back to the Scalzi. Nicola Furlotti, the head of the Verona police, went to the nearby barracks and asked the assembled men, 'Comrades, who wants to shoot Ciano?' Every hand went up. He selected thirty men, six of them marksmen, but none of the younger ones, saying that the honour should go to the veterans.

For several hours, Ciano refused to sign the plea for clemency that was to go to Mussolini. He was finally persuaded when the others said that it might compromise their own pleas. The cell doors were left open, and the men wandered up and down, trying to comfort each other. Only after much arguing, and several calls made to superior officers by Frau Beetz, was Don Chiot permitted to come and minister the last rites. Ciano wished, he said, to die in the 'Roman Catholic Apostolic Church'.

Ciano then wrote two letters. He told his mother that he hated causing her such pain, when all he had ever tried to do was to make her happy. 'I am preparing myself,' he said, 'for my departure with my soul serene.' To Edda he wrote: '*Edda adorata! Adorati bambini*! The pain of separating myself from you is too great for me to find the words I want to say to you.' Telling Edda that she was 'good, strong and generous', he consigned the children into her care and urged her to be brave during these coming hours of anguish. 'If, sometimes during our lives, I have been distant from you, know that I will now be with you, next to you, for ever ... *Addio, Edda cara. Addio*, Ciccino, Dindina, Marzio. I hold you to my heart with all my love.'

As with so much in this story, not everyone agrees on what happened next. Mussolini, having received Edda's last letter, apparently sat reading it in his office late into the night. Dolfin suggested to him that it was unlikely that Edda would really take her revenge. 'My daughter's character,' said Mussolini, 'is strong and violent. She is therefore capable of anything.' He did not sleep and his stomach cramps, which had improved, returned. Rachele listened as he paced up and down. At five in the morning, he made a call to the sinuous, Machiavellian General Karl Wolff, head of the SS in Italy. He began by asking the German what he thought he should do. 'Be inflexible,' answered Wolff. 'And what does the Führer think?' 'The Führer does not believe that you will go through with it.' Would a reprieve harm him in the Führer's eyes? 'Yes, considerably.' And what did Himmler think? 'Himmler believes that the executions will probably take place.' Mussolini thanked him and said that he would consider the options.

Whether Mussolini did or did not, as he always insisted, receive the pleas for clemency is another murky area. In Verona, once the condemned men had drafted them, there were debates about who was to be responsible for ensuring that they reached the Duce. Certainly Pavolini was determined to see his old friend and bene-factor Ciano die, and feared that at the last moment Mussolini would weaken. Mussolini himself may have longed for the matter to be taken out of his hands, and given out mixed messages to his staff; or he may simply have delayed too long. But as Harster remarked, Mussolini's wishes were paramount, and it was unlikely that anyone would have dared to disobey him if he had really wanted to intervene. A simple phone call would have secured par-dons for the men. In any event, no pleas seem to have arrived at the Villa Feltrinelli and Mussolini was able later to complain vehe-mently that nothing had reached him.

Having told those present that he wished to be buried alongside his father in the mausoleum in Livorno, Ciano returned to his cell and was handed the cyanide that Frau Beetz had brought him, concealed in a tube of toothpaste. He had told her that he was not afraid of dying, but dreaded the execution, which the Germans would certainly film and enjoy re-watching. He swallowed the cyanide and lay down, while Frau Beetz stroked his forehead. His heart raced violently. But nothing happened. He said to her: 'I will have to die again.' No one ever established why the poison did not work.

The men had agreed that if no one came for them by nine the next morning then they were probably safe. At five, hearing the church bells ring, they recited the Angelus together. As the hour approached their spirits rose, but Pellegrinotti, though he said nothing, had seen five coffins delivered to the jail. At five past nine, there were sounds of people approaching. The men returned to their own cells. Ciano was the first to be greeted by the Prefect and his men. The others, hoping to hear exclamations of pleasure, waited. There was silence. From Marinelli's cell now came a great shout of anguish and fear. Ciano burst out into furious accusations against Mussolini. Don Chiot, standing nearby, told him that the moment had come to forgive him. 'No! No!' exclaimed Ciano. But when Emilio De Bono said to him, 'Galeazzo, I have forgiven him.' Ciano paused and said: 'And I too will forgive him.'

The men were driven to the firing range of Forte Procolo. It was very cold, and a smattering of snow lay on the grassy slope. SS officers and senior Fascists were standing around in their great-coats. As traitors, the condemned were to be shot in the back, and chairs had been placed for them to sit on. When Ciano sat down, his chair tipped over and he fell to the ground; he was helped up again. All five men refused bands for their eyes. Marinelli, who was semi-conscious, murmuring the names of his wife and children, suddenly cried out, 'Don't do it! Don't do it! This is an assassination!'

The thirty-man firing squad took aim; a camera team, as Ciano had feared, began to film. The German officers took photographs. As the shots rang out, Ciano suddenly swivelled around to face the guns. He fell, whimpering, and a doctor ran up. Furlotti came and shot him twice more in the temple. Several of the others were still writhing and they too had to be finished off. As a German diplomat who was present remarked: 'It was like the slaughtering of pigs.'

Once the bodies were still, the Prefect ordered that the public be allowed to see for themselves that the 'Fascist *gerarchi* traitors' were really dead. It is unlikely that even with a pardon, they would have lived. Furlotti, the police chief, later said that his men would have killed Ciano themselves, had it looked as if he would be spared. 'We all wanted it. *E basta!*'

The burial place was to have been kept secret, but word got out and hundreds of people arrived carrying flowers. Don Chiot put a crucifix and rosary between Ciano's hands and surrounded the body with violets. Frau Beetz, her face covered by a veil, put a bunch of red roses on the coffin. Carolina, on hearing that the sentence had been carried out, fainted.

Mussolini had been sitting in his office since five o'clock. At ten, Dolfin arrived to tell him that the executions had been carried out. There was a long silence. Then Mussolini said that though reasons of state had decided the fate of the plotters, their blood would remain on his hands. 'The Germans needed this tragedy, this blood, to persuade them of our good faith.' No more was said and the council of ministers arrived for their regular meeting. As Vittorio said later: 'With the Verona trial, the Mussolini family paid up.' And Mussolini himself had effectively killed the husband of the child he loved.

*

Edda knew nothing of this. On 8 January she asked the Melocchi brothers, who owned the clinic at Ramiola, to keep and hide all the Ciano documents, except for the diaries, along with some jewellery, furs and her own personal papers. A perfect spot was found behind the high-tension electricity cabin in the basement. Leaving a sign on her bedroom door that she was ill and exhausted and not to be disturbed, she slipped out of a door in the cellar and walked across fields to where Pucci was waiting for her with his car. They drove to the Hotel Madonnina at Cantello, very close to the Swiss border, and spent the night there. The hotel, an old coaching house, belonged to a family Edda had known since childhood. She was given a suite, with a bath in the bedroom, art deco furnishings and a terrace. Arrangements had been made with a smuggler, but at the last moment, discovering who he was taking across, he demanded a sack of rice on top of the money promised him. Somehow, the rice was found. Pucci cut the leg from his pyjamas and sewed into it the five most important diaries, covering the war years.

On the afternoon of 9 January, as night was falling, Edda attached the bundle of diaries to a belt under her dress and followed the smuggler across an open field towards the border, which was heavily patrolled by the Swiss on the one side, the Germans and the Italian Fascists on the other, dozens of them armed men with dogs. A wire fence, several metres high, with barbed wire along the top and bells that rang if attempts were made to breach it, acted as the demarcation line. A German patrol was heard approaching and the smuggler made Edda lie down until it passed. It was a bright moonlit night. When the smuggler whispered that she should go, Edda began to walk, very upright, towards the wire, saying later that she had reached a state in which she had ceased to care what happened to her. She found a little gate cut in the wire. The frontier guards had been warned to expect a crossing.

Edda told them that she was the Duchessa d'Aosta, but that she was too frightened to say more. After consultations with superior officers, the border police allowed her through. It was then that she handed them her passport, told them her real name and asked for asylum, on the grounds that if caught by the Fascists or the Germans she would certainly be arrested, and possibly shot. Asked in traditional Swiss fashion what money she had with her, she said she had jewellery worth seven million lire, and over half a million in cash. She was given coffee and allowed to sleep in a storeroom.

She had indeed escaped just in time. At 7 a.m. on 9 January, Kaltenbrunner had sent a telegram to Harster telling him that, if Edda showed any signs of trying to leave Italy, she should immediately be detained. Getting hold of Ciano's papers now became a priority for the Nazis. Harster dispatched SS officers to Ramiola. At the clinic they were told that Edda was sleeping. It was only towards evening that the men, having knocked repeatedly, forced the lock on her door and discovered that the room was empty. Orders went out, to both German and Fascist patrols along the border, to find and apprehend a 'tall woman, with a large square face'. But Edda was gone.

Pucci, however, was now in great danger. Having waited by the border for an hour to make certain that Edda was safely across, he set off back for Verona in his Topolino with two of her suitcases. He saw Beetz, gave her Edda's three parting letters – the ones that she had written to Hitler, Mussolini and Harster – and turned back towards the border in order to make his own escape. But he had been awake for almost twenty-four hours and was exhausted, so he pulled over to sleep. When he woke at four, still in the pitch black, he found that his car would not start. Hearing a vehicle approaching, he stood on the road and waved his arms. It was one of the German patrols out searching for Edda and with the description they had been given of her companion the soldiers recognised him immediately. They knocked him about, demanding that he tell them where Edda was and where the diaries were hidden. Pucci said nothing. Finally they drove him to the Gestapo headquarters in Verona, where he learnt that Ciano had just been shot.

It was in the San Vittore prison in Milan, to which he was now transferred, that the real torture began. Pucci had resolved that, whatever happened, he would say nothing. On the first day, he was tortured for eight hours. Three men thrashed him with whips and put screws on his fingers and wrists. He passed out. When he was finally taken back to his cell, he decided to kill himself. He had hidden a razor blade in his underpants and though handcuffed managed to work it loose, planning to hold it between his teeth and cut a vein in his arm. After making his mouth and lips bleed profusely, he tried for a vein on his neck, but by now he was too weak. Next morning, as he was being dragged back to the torture chamber, he tried and failed to throw himself from the balcony. He was tortured again all day until he lay unconscious in a pool of blood. When he came round he was pushed against a wall and told that he had thirty seconds in which to speak. He fainted. Pucci's devotion to Edda seems to have been inexhaustible. But then, it also says much about her charm and ability to inspire it.

Precisely how and why he was freed is another mystery in the story. One version has it that Himmler decided that Pucci should be sent to find Edda and tell her that if she ever spoke out against Germany, or published any incriminating stories from Ciano's diaries, she and the children would be hunted down and killed. Another is that Frau Beetz somehow intervened to have him spared. A third is that Mussolini wanted to save the man who had helped his daughter. On 18 January, Pucci left the San Vittore and friends helped him get a boat across the lake to Switzerland. For three days, suffering terrible headaches, he tried and failed to discover where Edda had gone. Then he collapsed. He was taken to a hospital in Bellinzona, where doctors found a ruptured eardrum, fractures to two parts of his skull, and severe bruising all over his body.

With Edda and Pucci gone, the Gestapo turned their attention to those who had helped them. They returned to the Hotel Madonnina, arrested the owner, the manager and the local priest, who had been party to the escape. They were transferred to the San Vittore and tortured. The priest died.

20

A gangster's moll on the run

Edda had crossed into Switzerland enveloped in a capacious peasant dress, the bulky diaries strapped around her waist making her
look heavily pregnant. A senior inspector was summoned in order
to determine her future, and his task was not an easy one. By the
winter of 1943, Switzerland had all but closed its borders to refugees fleeing Nazi-occupied Europe and was moreover extremely
nervous about accepting anyone who might prove politically
threatening to Swiss neutrality. Mussolini's daughter could only
spell trouble. On the other hand, the Swiss prided themselves on
their long-held reputation for providing asylum to those who genuinely needed it. To put a refugee back across the border to
probable death was not a decision to be taken lightly.

At 8.40 on the evening of 10 January, Edda's interview with
the Swiss authorities took place. Asked whether, as a supporter of
the Axis powers, she would not, in fact, be perfectly safe in Italy, she
replied that hated by everyone, by the Salò Fascists as well as by the
Nazis, she would be in grave danger, particularly as the Germans
'know precisely what I think of them'. She had believed in her husband's honesty and supported his change of heart over the wisdom
of an alliance with Germany. Her father, she added, was now
powerless, an impotent 'rag in the hands of the Germans'. Where
did she hope to go? She would prefer French-speaking Switzerland,
since neither she nor her children spoke any German. What money
did she have with her? Edda repeated that she had brought valuable jewellery and a considerable amount of cash. The interview
over, she was taken to one of the guards' houses to wait while the
matter was referred up to the Federal Department of Justice. She
still knew nothing about events in Verona or Pucci's capture.

The Swiss verdict came quickly. Edda and her children would be permitted to remain, provided that she adopted a new false name, Elsa Pini, deposited all her money in a Swiss bank, and agreed not to use a telephone, write a letter, listen to the radio or read the newspapers. She accepted and was driven the few miles up into the mountains to the convent of the Casa di San Domenico at Neggio, where she was reunited with the children. It had been almost two months since they had seen their mother, and Fabrizio later wrote that she looked smaller and older, 'very thin and devastated'.

On the afternoon of 12 January, a local priest was sent to break the news to her. Later, Edda would say that, with everything that had happened to her, she had thought that she was unbreakable, with nerves of steel. But Ciano's death overwhelmed her. She decided to be honest with the children. 'I wanted,' she wrote later, 'what I had to say to be heard against a clear and clean background.' That afternoon, she led them to the top of a nearby hill; it was very cold and the ground sparkled with frost. She drew the three of them close to her and told them that their father had been executed. 'Papa is dead . . . They shot him . . . he's gone.' Then she fell silent, before adding: 'He was innocent . . . it was absolutely not his fault.' As she described it later, Fabrizio and Raimonda 'stared at me, petrified, then their eyes filled with tears'. She thought that Marzio had not taken it in. He asked, 'Which Papa?' But then he ran off, saw a flower, picked it and handed it silently to her. 'He too had understood.' She turned it over in her fingers and said, 'Let's go now.' That night, she tried to appear cheerful and strong, but Raimonda locked herself in the bathroom and began sobbing and beating her head against the wall, and a gardener had to be found to break down the door. Edda led her gently out, but the little girl went on sobbing.

Four days later, Edda was visited by the Italian consul general in Lugano. Though ostensibly an old friend of the family, and a member of Ciano's cabinet, his report to the Swiss authorities on Edda and her children was not friendly. He had found her 'cunning, shrewd and her language coarse' when reprimanding Marzio for something. Fabrizio, though clearly intelligent, seemed curiously unmoved by his father's death, saying only, 'What do you expect? It's all about destiny.' Edda railed against both the Germans and the Axis powers, but remembered to be appreciative and flattering about Switzerland. 'The woman in question,' wrote the consul, 'apart from being sly . . . is also devious and dangerous.'

Neggio was considered too close to the border, especially since there was already a rumour that the Germans intended to track Edda down and kidnap her, fearing that she might produce 'sensational revelations'. Another convent, deeper into Switzerland, at Ingenbohl on the lake of Lucerne, was found. The nuns in Neggio were longing for her to leave since they had already had to stop her several times trying to escape into the village to buy newspapers. Local schools were arranged for the children. On 18 January 1944, the family caught a train to Brunnen and from there were driven to the convent, where they were given two rooms: a bedroom with two beds and a sitting room. A Major Reding was detailed to watch over them.

The Swiss were desperate to keep Edda's presence a secret. It only took a few days for the news to leak out. '*Wo ist die Gräfin Ciano?*' asked several newspapers, thereby launching a deluge of articles and letters, some hostile and others welcoming. A Swiss reporter was quoted as saying that Edda was 'a gangster's moll on the run, with teeth and claws still sharp'. Why, asked another, should the 'Fascist Countess Ciano' be allowed to live in idle luxury, while other refugees were sent to work camps? This '*perle latine*' was a viper and should have her head shaved. In the last week of January, no less than eight British newspapers joined in the frenzy, and their comments were far from warm. 'As one of the most powerful women in Europe,' wrote the *Daily Express*, 'she used all her influence against Britain.' It was wrong to regard the 'first lady of the Axis' as a distraught and lonely woman pleading for Ciano's life, since she had done nothing but 'impose her will on her mediocre, flashy husband and urge her ageing father to excesses'. Edda's fame – and infamy – had spread widely.

A convent on the edge of a dark grey Swiss lake, surrounded by high mountains, where everyone spoke German and she was allowed no contact with the outside world, was everything that Edda most dreaded. Even in the heat and sunshine of Italy, surrounded by friends, she was restless and demanding. This felt like prison. She was sad, angry and profoundly bored. One night, Fabrizio woke to find her apparently reading *The Pickwick Papers*;

only she was not actually reading but crying, silently, her shoulders shaking. In true Mussolini fashion, he said nothing.

To her brother-in-law, Magistrati, now Italian Ambassador in Berne, she wrote miserably: 'I beg you to come at once. I have decided to leave Switzerland, and this world, and to die in Italy.' Somewhat reluctantly, having been warned that Edda was in a highly nervous state, he asked the federal authorities to be allowed to visit her, and was granted permission. He found her grateful for her safety and she told him that the children were happy, but said that she was horribly lonely and felt herself to be a victim. Never maternal, and never without nannies to care for them, she was also discovering that she had little aptitude for bringing up children. When he left, Magistrati promised to try to find a French-speaking visitor for her, as well as to ask permission for her to leave the convent grounds and go for walks. But for this, he told her, she needed to obey the rules.

Edda found rules intolerable. She had never once thought that they applied to her. Almost the only events that now broke the monotony of her days were the repeated visits of the police authorities, come to check on her behaviour. An inspector arrived one morning at ten thirty to find her still in bed. On being informed that the interview would take two hours, she invited him into her bedroom, and proposed to stay in bed while he perched by her side, using the bedside table to type on. The inspector meekly agreed. Edda then talked at length about Ciano, described every step of her escape, but when asked about politics or the war insisted that she had never had anything to do 'with affairs of state'. The policeman left having learnt nothing new.

But soon after, an 'absolutely trustworthy source' informed the Swiss secret services that a man posing as an almoner had requested a passport from the Vatican in Rome, and was thought to be heading for Switzerland to assassinate Edda, 'since she knows things that people want to stop her revealing'. Security round her was increased, many of her new privileges rescinded, and with it all came a stronger sense of having been made a prisoner. She looked out over the deep grey lake, round which she was no longer allowed to walk, and mourned.

Visits from friends were absolutely forbidden, 'given the meddling and overheated nature of the woman concerned', noted the head of the Federal Political Department, Marcel Pilet-Golaz. As a neutral country, Switzerland could not risk the kind of political talk that Edda would certainly engage in. 'She is a schemer on whom we have to keep a close eye, and the fewer her contacts with the outside world the better.' He recommended opposing all 'excess of liberty'. The following day, he added to his report. 'We must not forget that she is altogether undesirable. Edda must be prevented from pulling strings or "committing indiscretions".' In fact, her 'regime must be much closer to that of detention than liberty'. Edda was not an easy or amenable guest; but there was something implacable and unforgiving about her Swiss hosts.

One of the very rare letters that was allowed to get through to her came from Pucci, still in Switzerland and slowly recovering from being tortured. It ran to ten pages and told her in detail everything he had learnt about Ciano's death, and about his own persistent headaches and loss of memory. Kiss the children with infinite tenderness, he wrote. 'I am always, constantly, close to you, with devoted thoughts and eternally faithful.' In her reply, Edda told him that what she missed most was the sun. 'This climate makes me ill. I feel profound nostalgia for Capri.'

If Edda found her enforced stay in Ingenbohl deeply trying, it was nothing to the mounting irritation of the mother superior of the convent, Diamira Brandenberg. 'The behaviour of the Contessa leaves much to be desired,' she wrote to the federal authorities. 'The discipline of the convent does not allow for the life and customs of a hotel.' Edda 'smokes incessantly, orders cognac and drinks a litre of wine every day'. She seldom rose before midday, and she let the children run wild 'without any attempt at maternal care'. Could somewhere else, she asked plaintively, not be found for this depressed and eccentric guest? For the moment, there was nowhere else for her to go.

'I am so desperately alone,' Edda wrote soon after in one of the very few letters to a friend that she managed to get out. 'And even though I am a good warrior, I still have moments of horror.' She added that were it not for the three children, she would certainly kill herself. 'Dying is little – it is living that is so difficult.'

The day after Ciano's execution, Mussolini had been shown copies of his final letters to Edda and to his mother. His hands were seen to tremble as he read them. To Carolina, Mussolini wrote somewhat curtly that she was 'too intelligent a woman not to understand the way things had to be'. To others, like Ciano's Spanish friend, the Minister for Foreign Affairs Ramon Serrano Suñer, who had written to offer condolences, he replied that the day that Ciano had died had been the 'most dramatic chapter' of his life, in which state and personal feelings had clashed fatally. To Don Chiot, who he summonsed to tell him about Ciano's death, he reportedly said: 'The day of his death, I died too.'

With Edda, it was not so straightforward. What could he possibly say to bring her back to him? The first letter that he wrote to her, early in March, using as go-between Don Pancino, a childhood friend, is missing from any archive. But her answer is not. She instructed Don Pancino to tell her father that 'only two solutions could redeem him in her eyes: flight or suicide'. During their brief meeting, Edda seemed to the priest distraught and shattered. Having heard the rumour that she seemed immensely fat when she crossed the border, he now asked with some embarrassment whether, given her condition, she should not be thinking of getting married? When he returned to Italy and visited Mussolini, he found him reduced to a 'larva of a man', shrunken and emaciated, so pale that the veins stood out blue on his nose. On his way back to Salò, he had stopped in Milan to consult Cardinal Schuster about what exactly he should tell Mussolini. The cardinal told him to tread gently, not to further enflame Mussolini's anguish.

Don Pancino returned to Edda on 28 March with another letter. In it, Mussolini wrote that he hoped that the day would come when she would understand the painful and impossible 'personal and political' situation in which he had found himself. In the letter she handed the priest to carry back to her father she wrote, 'The injustice and villainy of men, and of you in particular, have made me suffer so intensely that nothing could ever be worse. I pray that it all finishes soon.' More bitterly, she went on: 'I bear the bloody name of my husband with pride. And this counts for you, for your servants and for your masters.' When Don Pancino repeated her words to Mussolini, he demanded every detail of the visit, finally shaking his head and saying: 'No, no, not that.'

*

In Rome, reactions to Ciano's death were mixed. Daniele Varè wrote that he had never personally believed that Ciano's friends and former colleagues would really try to save him. His vulgarity and bad manners had been tiresome, noted the acerbic Duchessa di Sermoneta, but his real sin had been not standing by his father-in-law. There were displays of grief from the ladies of the Petit Trianon, some of whom took to carrying about in their handbags the letters of farewell he had written to them. 'Le belle amiche,' wrote Gabriella di Robilant, 'are all in tears.' The Italian secret services, meanwhile, cooperating with the Germans, began to draw up lists of Ciano's closest friends, noting that it was not always easy, given that most were aristocrats, to penetrate their social circle. A few found it prudent to go into hiding.

Among the diplomats, the verdict on Ciano was on the whole unforgiving. Sir Miles Lampson, who had known Edda well in China, noted in his diary that Ciano's days of greatness had 'completely spoilt him', adding that 'he is largely responsible for the ills that have overtaken Italy'. The Romans were more generous. Gabriella di Robilant said that Ciano had been made a scapegoat, perhaps a necessary one, and that his death had been not a judicial execution but an assassination. Though never one of his close friends, she remembered the pleasure she felt whenever she saw him, 'always dear and full of life'. Malaparte wrote that Ciano had been 'fat, rosy, smiling and despotic', but that he pitied him. And all, critics and friends alike, agreed that he had died 'as a man and with profound dignity and resignation', showing more at the end than he had ever shown in his life.

The Romans, in any case, had other things to think about. On 22 January 1944, the Allies landed thirty-six thousand men at Anzio and Nettuno, planning to move swiftly to liberate Rome. But Kesselring, initially caught unprepared, brought every unit that could be spared into a defensive ring and rained shells on the beach, the harbour and the surrounding marshes. The Allies stalled.

Rome was running out of food, and the Vatican arranged for 150,000 kilos of flour to be sent from Umbria. The Collegio Urbano di Propaganda Fide on the Janiculum had become a Noah's Ark, an extraterritorial haven crammed to overflowing with people on the run, along with chickens, pigs, mules, two peacocks, a race horse and an astrakhan goat. There was no salt to be found in the city. Ration books were useless. Refugees wandered the streets, famished, having long since sold anything of value. In the Abruzzo, people froze to death in their ruined houses. All that mattered now was survival. With the total absence of rubber and spare parts, the buses and trams came to a halt. Everyone, noted the writer Marjorie Jebb, seemed to have aged by fifteen years. The Wehrmacht and the SS had taken over the summer palace of the Doria Pamphili and were using the Roman statues for target practice. A second torture house was set up in the Pensione Jaccarino. When one day they broke into the Fascist headquarters in the Via Braschi, they found half-dead, tortured anti-Fascists in chains and mountains of sugar, flour, cheese and ham, along with looted gold and jewellery. Eden had suggested dropping food into the famished city, but Churchill replied: 'It's with pain that I write these words. Rome must starve till freed.'

In the vast Renaissance palazzi, with their high ceilings, marble floors and ill-fitting windows, the cold was ferocious. Rome had become a warren of hiding places, in attics, cellars, behind cupboards, in churches, for Jews, for resisters, for young men avoiding German forced labour. Ever since the Congress of Verona in November, itself a city with a large Jewish population, there had been an unremitting hunt for Jews, and concentration camps in various parts of Italy had become way stations to the gas chambers. There were too few Germans to conduct house-to-house searches, but many Roman Fascists, young men who had grown up knowing nothing but Fascist imperatives, had served in the violent campaigns in Ethiopia and Spain, and who looked with admiration on German Nazism, became enthusiastic helpers in the round-ups. In the Vatican, Pius XII steered his own path, 'with painfully nuanced shades of grey', issuing no directives, making no denunciations, confining himself to giving tacit support to the activities of those of his priests and nuns involved in rescuing the Roman Jews.

Then, on 23 March 1944, came an attack on the Germans, followed by an atrocity that stunned the Romans, already inured to the brutality of the German occupation. That day, as 156 men from a German police regiment marched up the Via Rasella, the Italian partisans detonated a 40-pound bomb. The explosion was heard all over Rome. Thirty Germans were killed, and their bodies laid out in rows on the pavement and covered with flowers, along with two Italian civilians; 110 people were wounded. The German response was immediate: 335 people, whittled down from many more when suitable hostages could not be found, were rounded up and taken to a disused quarry on the edge of Rome, known as the Ardeatine Caves. The firing squad, given cognac to stiffen them, shot them in groups of five. They were told that if they baulked, they would be shot too.

When that seemed to take too long, the prisoners were ordered to kneel on the backs of their dead comrades. When all were dead, the entrance to the caves was sealed by exploding mines, but a young man burrowed his way in and brought out the body of his father. Later, Romans flocked to remove the stones and replace them with flowers. Seventy-five of the dead were Jews.

The Allied 'Operation Diadem', the assault on the enemy south of Rome, was launched on 12 May. The weather was fine, but the Germans put up fierce resistance. Mile by mile, the Allies crawled forward, leaving in their wake a trail of burnt vehicles, smashed gun carriages and villages and houses torched. It was not clear until the very end whether or not the Germans would defend Rome. On 3 June, with the Allies just 20 kilometres away, streams of lorries and tanks began to leave the city, heading north towards Tuscany. Rome, noted an inhabitant, felt as if it were throbbing. Desperate Fascists, fearing what liberation would bring, tried to get lifts with the Germans but were rebuffed. There was a continual sound of gunfire.

On the night of 3 June, suddenly everything was still. The Americans had arrived. The bells on the Capitol began to toll. One by one, all across the darkened city, windows and shutters were thrown open and people began to call out. Then came the sound of thousands of feet, as they rushed down the stairs and into the streets. Next day, as Ciano had prophesied, jeeps and tanks rolled up the Via dell'Impero towards the Piazza Venezia. The Romans sat in the sunshine on the steps of churches and along the pavements to watch them. 'A rain of roses fell on men, guns, tanks and jeeps,' wrote the diarist who went by the name of Jane Scrivener. By next morning, the city was full of dusty, unshaven, battle-worn and smiling Allied soldiers. The Scots gave a concert with pipes in the Piazza Venezia, wearing kilts. A little-known film director called Roberto Rossellini began to make *Roma, Città Aperta*. Rome was free.

But the war was not over. As the Allies began the long, tough march to reach the north and the Salò republic, they left behind them poverty, lawlessness, danger and hunger. 'We were free, in a devastated land,' wrote the anti-Fascist Giuliana Benzoni. The Allied strategy had been to draw German divisions into Italy and tie them up the length of the peninsula, but it had tied up the Allied forces, too, and they would now be forced to take Italy village by village. As Major General J.F.C. Fuller, the military historian and strategist, put it, Churchill's 'soft underbelly' had turned into a crocodile's back. While opposition politicians wrangled over coalitions, and the monarchy still based in the south struggled to survive, the civil war continued and with it a painful and often savage reckoning with Fascism. Rome remained without water, electricity, gas or the telephone, and there was no food.

Edda's friend Virginia Agnelli, herself emerging from hiding, was standing with a friend outside the Hotel Flora on the Via Veneto when guests began to arrive for a reception given by the Americans. Smartly dressed, their hair impeccable, wearing a colourful assortments of hats, gloves, bags and shoes, these were the Italian men and women who had spent the 1930s enjoying the pleasures of Roman Fascist society, grateful for the sense of stability, accommodating themselves to its rituals, corruption and sleaziness. Agnelli watched as they looked around a little furtively, a little defiantly, with expressions that suggested that they felt that they had survived the worst, and that they could now start their proper lives again. At some imperceptible signal, they began to file into the hotel, taking 'little bird-like steps' as if they had been deposited there by the wind, 'so light and ephemeral' that they seemed hardly to touch the ground. 'We recognised them,' she wrote. 'We counted them. They were all there.' Except, of course, for 'Galeazzo Ciano, because he was dead'.

21

Edda is willing

In Ingenbohl, despite the arrival of books, crossword puzzles and a gramophone sent up by her lawyer in Geneva, Edda grew increasingly depressed. The nuns remarked that she no longer came to her window to smoke and look out. A Dr Réal, called to see her, reported that she had a history of pleurisy, bronchial catarrh, pneumonia and colitis, and that she had become lethargic and anxious and was barely eating. 'She came to Switzerland,' he wrote, 'to find freedom, only to be constantly watched.' The mother superior, Diamira Brandenberg, wrote to the police authorities, saying that '*questa povera signora*' needed more freedom, some sunshine and above all company. Edda herself sent a beseeching letter to the Berne chief of police, Dr Balsiger: 'I ask myself what I am guilty of . . . to be treated so harshly . . . I have never been a hysteric or a fanatic . . . and I am not without intelligence.'

Then she turned once again to Ciano's brother-in-law, Magistrati. 'I'm ill,' she told him. 'There is no part of me that does not bother me.' Her eyes were swollen, she was seeing black spots and her teeth hurt. She was, she said, being treated as a '*cretina*', which was one thing that she was not. In fact, she insisted, she was one of very few women who possessed a sense of discipline and honour, and for whom 'yes is yes and no is no'. If the Swiss refused to move her somewhere freer, where she could speak French, then she would prefer to be sent back to Italy to take her chances with the Germans. Resorting to one of her bouts of histrionics, she wrote that she was now more of a burden to her children than a mother, and would in any case soon probably die. 'If I must die, I would rather die surrounded by my own people, by Italian art under an Italian sky', even if it meant being taken out and shot.

One day, conscious that she was running out of money, Edda asked the children whether they thought they should save what they had left or buy a radio? They were now thirteen, eleven and seven. They voted for the radio, went to the village, had a wonderful lunch and came home with their radio, on which they now followed the course of the war. Not long after they heard a strange noise in the garden late one evening. Edda looked out, saw nothing, then heard a whisper: 'Calpurnia. Calpurnia.' Edda smiled. It was the code that she and Don Pancino had used as children. She opened the window and called: 'Where are you?' The priest was perched in a tree. He told her that he was secretly bringing her money from Mussolini, from the sale of *Il Popolo d'Italia*. She took it and told him that she intended to pay it back one day, since she refused to accept anything given to her by her father.

In May, Don Pancino arrived again with another letter from Mussolini, bringing her news of the family, and a suitcase of things. 'I would be really pleased,' Mussolini wrote, 'if you were to write to me. I embrace you, *tuo papà*.' But Edda remained unforgiving. Before he left, she gave Don Pancino Ciano's diaries to put in a safe box in Crédit Suisse in Berne and told him that they were to be published in the event of her death.

Finally, after many discussions at federal level, the Swiss authorities relented. Seven minutes up a private road outside the village of Monthey near Fribourg was a Maison de Santé called Malévoz. It was run by Dr Répond, a psychiatrist who had written a paper on psychosis in prisoners-of-war in the First World War, and who was described by a grateful patient as 'having an expansive personality, open and extremely fascinating'. Dr Répond had expressed an interest in 'the case of this refugee'; he was known to favour shorter stays for patients, and more agreeable conditions. Malévoz stood in its own seven hectares of land, with no fences, and its individual villas looked more like holiday houses than a sanitarium. There were no dangerous inmates, and few people except parties of schoolchildren ever passed that way. Leaving the three children in their boarding schools, and accompanied by a senior policeman and a 'trustworthy woman', Edda arrived at Malévoz on 21 July.

Edda was given a spacious apartment with its own front door. Dr Répond had already selected a twenty-five-year-old

French-speaking girl to be her constant companion and ensure that 'Mme Pini does not indulge in regrettable acts'. Three nurses had signed confidentiality agreements. Once again, there were rules: strict control over the telephone and visits; no political activity of any kind; walks only with permission. Dr Répond saw Edda for an hour every day. 'The patient is less depressed, more lively,' he wrote to Dr Balsiger, who had asked him to provide fortnightly reports, 'and is starting to show an interest in reality' though her appetite remained poor and she continued to sleep very badly. He described her as of 'middling stature, broad shouldered, with good proportions, very thin, brown hair, looks pale, dry eyed, clear voice and strong'. She was not, he asserted, 'sexually frigid', but appeared to be suffering mainly from 'mental and physical exhaustion'. Edda told him: 'I'm not mad.' 'I know, I know,' he replied.

By the summer of 1944, rumours had begun to spread about Ciano's diaries and what they might contain. The day the Allies entered Rome, the Communist *L'Unità* reported that 'interested parties' were blocking their publication. Evidently in answer to an enquiry from Mussolini, Edda replied that her intention was to vindicate Ciano: 'Do not hope, *padre mio*, that you or your friends will get your hands on my husband's diaries.' When, in August, some tantalising fragments were published, with Edda's permission, in a Roman journal called *Risorgimento*, then picked up by a Spanish Catholic paper, uneasy interest in what they might divulge increased, among both the Allies and the Axis partners.

The diaries themselves had already had a number of adventures. The papers in Harster's hands, delivered to entice the Germans before the failed rescue plan, had been partially translated, typed up and despatched to Kaltenbrunner in Berlin. Those left with the Melocchi brothers at Ramiola behind the electricity box, together with two volumes of the diaries hidden behind books, were as yet unfound, despite a visit and a search by Harster's men, convinced that the best material was still to be discovered. But at the end of August, a man claiming to be the nephew of an eminent Milanese gynaecologist arrived at the clinic with a letter, purporting to be from Edda, instructing the Melocchis to hand over everything to him for safekeeping. Convinced that he was an impostor, the brothers denied all knowledge of any diaries. A few days later, the SS came to arrest the Melocchis and, afraid of being tortured, they produced the documents, together with Edda's handbag. The Germans now had five or six volumes of diplomatic exchanges, the two diary volumes for the years 1937 and 1938, and a third, labelled 'Germania'.

Frau Beetz was asked to make a summary of the newly seized material, then ordered to return to Weimar, where she was to make a full translation of the entire collection of papers. Each night, her work was locked away in the Gestapo safe. As the Nazi regime was crumbling, Hitler ordered all the documents, together with their translations, to be destroyed. However, Frau Beetz, telling no one, had made an extra carbon copy of everything. In due course, she buried the copy in her garden, where it would soon be given the name of 'The Rose Garden Papers'.

But the Americans, too, were interested. While no one yet knew exactly what the papers and diaries contained, or even if they were of much interest, they believed that they just might be helpful in shaping Allied policy in Italy and in deciding whom they could trust in the ever-shifting Italian political world. Preparations were already being made for future war crime trials, and it was thought that Ciano's diaries might provide possible evidence for the conviction of senior Nazis and Fascists. Edda and Ciano had been right to believe that as bargaining tools, they might just have saved his life. 'Operation Edda C. Diaries' was launched.

Through her friend Virginia Agnelli, Edda had been introduced to Frances de Chollet, an American married to a Swiss banker, also known to Pucci. Towards the end of October, Pucci was permitted to visit Edda and together they discussed ways to contact the Americans. He had received furious letters from his relations, accusing him of having behaved disgracefully by helping Edda, thereby jeopardising his whole family, and they wanted no part 'in your ruin'. 'Ah Emilio,' they wrote, 'to have behaved like this you must have been bewitched.' A correspondent for the *Chicago Daily News* in Berne, Paul Ghali, investigating a rumour that Edda was about to marry Pucci, was astonished when suddenly told that Pucci wanted to see him, with Madame de Chollet acting as go-between. What Ghali learnt was, as he said later, the scoop of his life. Pucci told him that Ciano had instructed Edda to deliver the diaries either to Churchill or to Roosevelt, and he now asked Ghali to find out whether Allen Dulles, the New York lawyer and diplomat currently running the Office for Strategic Studies in Berne, might be interested. Ghali agreed to become a messenger, but only on condition that Edda accepted to sell newspaper rights to the *Chicago Daily News*. Edda agreed.

When Ghali and de Chollet met Edda secretly in the buffet of Monthey station, they found her 'gaily dressed in a Swiss idea of a Scotch plaid' with a 'brilliant and misplaced love of colours' and rather too much green mascara. She regaled them with stories about Ribbentrop and Himmler, whom she blamed for the Cianos' misfortunes, and about Eva Braun, about whom little was still known, and whom she described as 'vulgar and uninteresting'. She wanted, she said to 'give the Boches what they deserve', and for people to realise that it had only been Ciano who had really fought against Italy entering the war, 'and he was alone'. De Chollet noted that Edda's character was a 'delightful mixture of childishness, love of beauty, laziness'; she was a 'dreamer', always honest, a 'charming companion' and she never complained.

As a senior American working semi-clandestinely in Switzerland and as a friend of the Italian anti-Fascists, Dulles could not afford to be seen with Edda. By the winter of 1944, Berne had become a hub for the secret services of both the Allies and the Axis countries, attracting spies and informers of every kind. But Edda categorically refused to use any further go-betweens. As Dulles wrote to his superiors in Washington, she was a 'psychopathic case . . . whose motives and connections' were dubious. He had been told that she was asking for a considerable amount of money. 'Naturally the matter requires most discreet handling from every view point.'

On 7 January 1945, Dulles decided to risk a meeting. Taking Ghali and de Chollet with him, he drove to Monthey. Edda had managed to slip out of the clinic unobserved and met them in the railway buffet. Her face was so thin that her eyes looked enormous. Dulles found that once she relaxed, she talked freely, with occasional bursts of 'feverish gaiety'. Her mind was quick but she leapt from topic to topic. De Chollet, who took notes on their meetings, observed that Edda was 'very vain and very afraid of adverse criticism' and that she wanted to be liked. She told de Chollet that her father had made a big mistake in going to war but that 'all great people make mistakes'.

Edda, clearly craving company, insisted on telling them her story before talking about the diaries. Then she asked to see Dulles alone. In exchange for all the papers she had, she wanted him to use his influence to obtain Swiss asylum for her mother, brothers and sister, and to help get her and her children out to Spain or Portugal. She also asked to keep the newspaper serialisation rights of the diaries. Dulles told her that he had no interest in bargaining, but that she could keep the serialisation rights, providing the American government could publish anything that might help them in their war. After further exchanges – in which the diaries were referred to as 'the chocolates' – a deal was struck. Dulles cabled Washington: 'Edda is willing'.

Since it was important for Edda's status as a refugee to keep the Swiss in the dark about these transactions, an American army captain working for OSS arrived late one night at Malévoz to photograph the diaries secretly in her room. Though he was not detected, he succeeded in blowing the clinic's electrical fuses without completing his task. Dulles now decided that the safest thing would be to smuggle Edda out of the clinic one night, drive her to de Chollet's house at Fribourg, 80 kilometres away, photograph the 1,200 pages of the documents there, then return her to her room by dawn. The mission all went to plan, though Edda was seen entering her room at five in the morning, thereby fuelling stories among the locals of her wayward behaviour. By 20 January, the photographed papers were on their way to the US. Since she was very short of money, the Swiss keeping her on a tight allowance, Dulles gave Edda an advance of 3,500 Swiss francs against future royalties. He wanted Washington to make the diaries public at once, but the State Department decided to keep them for the Nuremberg trials. The de Chollets advanced her money against the jewellery she had deposited in the bank.

Various newspapers now started a bidding war, but on 9 April Edda signed a contract, as promised, with the *Chicago Daily News,* which agreed to match the highest offer of $25,000, a respectable sum for the time. Meanwhile, Dulles set about tracking down the documents she had left at Ramiola, though Edda's evasiveness made it difficult. It was only some time later, after the German capitulation, that he was able to visit the Melocchis and learnt that the SS had got there first. As the CIA report put it, 'the chocolates' had been 'gobbled up'.

Fabrizio, Raimonda and Marzio had been allowed to join Edda, and she told de Chollet that, having arrived looking 'perfectly awful', they were now 'almost human again'. Here at Malévoz, she added, except for the occasional row, 'life goes on peacefully and sleepily'. She was feeling much better and dreaming of a future 'somewhere else, free, with no money worries and a few friends around me. I am a human being again. You can't possibly imagine what it means.'

Mussolini was also feeling better. Zachariae's diet and regime of hormones and vitamins had stopped his stomach cramps and, since he refused to eat any food that others could not get hold of, Rachele had bought a cow and made butter. She had brought her maid Irma with her to the Villa Feltrinelli and together the two Romagnole women made fresh pasta. Mussolini was much attached to his daughter-in-law Gina and her little girl. Elena, his daughter by Angela Curti, had followed him to Salò and read the papers to him while he sat in his armchair. He was always cold, and wanted the heating to be kept very high. Later Zachariae described long discursive talks with the Duce about philosophy, literature and politics. He had come to admire and feel affection for his patient, saying that he was 'courageous and strong', a man of boundless optimism but childishly credulous.

Nothing else, however, was better. The northern cities were awash with German SS and mercenaries waging war on the increasingly well-armed and well-organised resistance and carrying out reprisals against civilians. Spies and informers were growing rich on extortion and every police station was receiving anonymous denunciations of hidden Jews and partisans. In June, Pavolini had drawn forty thousand of the most ardent Fascists, '*i puri e i duri*', into a new force, the Brigate Nere, to bring some order to the proliferating lawless bands. But in practice, far from being pure, these men were ruffians and torturers. Pavolini had become obsessed with death. This once dapper man had given up shaving, become dour and brusque, and now sped about the countryside in an open car, with his bodyguard, inspecting his men. The civil war had entered its bloodiest phase.

On the afternoon of 20 July, soon after Claus von Stauffenberg's bomb exploded during a briefing in Hitler's headquarters, killing four people but only slightly wounding the Führer, Mussolini had arrived in Germany. He was angry about the atrocious conditions in which the Italian forced labourers were being kept in Germany, about the now regular deportations of Jews from northern Italy to the death camps, and about Germany's encroachment on Alto Adige and Trieste. Hitler made promises, but he did not keep them. 'It is too late,' Mussolini had come back saying. 'I have drained the poisoned chalice to the dregs.' He looked pale and wretched and told Rachele, 'The defeated have no friends.' Mussolini had been many things: Romagnolo, populist, elitist, socialist, dictator. For almost twenty years he had enjoyed the adulation normally given only to film stars. But he had allowed himself to be seduced, choosing to believe that with Germany at his back, he could make Italy a real player on the international stage. Now Hitler had Mussolini in his fist, a grey puppet of the Germans, trying to court his remaining followers with promises that he knew he could not deliver.

Mussolini's spirits had revived briefly when, on 13 November, General Alexander, commander of the Allied Armies in Italy, faced by mud and torrential rains, called a halt to the winter campaign in Italy and dug in to await the spring and better conditions, instructing the Italian resistance, now left very vulnerable, to do the same. The Duce began to think that Hitler's much-vaunted secret weapons could bring the Allies to a conference table, where they just might regard Mussolini as a valuable ally in the fight against communism. On 16 December, he had rallied himself and spent three days in Milan, speaking at the Teatro Lirico to cheering crowds and then touring the city in an open car. He had not quite lost his magic.

With Edda in Switzerland and closed off to him, Ciano dead, his brother Arnaldo long since gone, and easy access to mistresses barred, Mussolini's relationship with Claretta had grown more loving. 'You are my heart,' he told her, 'you alone.' There were furtive visits to the Villa Fiordaliso. But Rachele and her spies were watchful. Discovering that Claretta had been making copies of Mussolini's letters, she dispatched a team of police to investigate. Then she decided to act. In Rachele's own version of events, she told Mussolini that she was off on a '*spedizione punitiva*' to the Casa dei Morti. He told her: 'Do as you wish.'

Dressing with care, avoiding belts or sashes that Claretta could grab hold of, Rachele put on stout rubber-soled shoes, summoned her driver and set off, taking a revolver with her. It was eight o'clock on a stormy evening. Having collected the deeply reluctant Buffarini-Guidi – who had kept in with Claretta and her family – she had herself driven to the gates of the darkened Villa Fiordaliso. She rang the bell repeatedly, pounded on the gates, and forced Buffarini-Guidi to crawl through a gap in the fence, tearing his trousers in the process. The villa was dark and no one answered. Finally, a German officer appeared at a window, and agreed to let them in.

Rachele was shown into a small sitting room. Fifteen minutes later, a pale Claretta, clutching her handkerchief, appeared. Rachele told her that she must leave the area immediately, since she was 'upsetting the serenity of my family'. Claretta wept. Rachele hated women who cried. She shook her, then followed her upstairs to her bedroom, with its vast canopied bed, and Claretta produced the copies of Mussolini's letters, before sinking feebly back on to the bed. Buffarini-Guidi produced some brandy, and she took little sips to revive herself. She told Rachele that Mussolini could not live without her. Rachele rang Mussolini to prove that she was indeed in the Casa dei Morti. Then, after a further barrage of insults, telling Claretta that everyone hated her and that she would certainly 'come to a bad end', Rachele swept out.

But the evening's drama had not yet played itself out. In the Villa Feltrinelli, Rachele locked herself in the bathroom and drank bleach, but not so much that she could not be revived. Mussolini spent the rest of the night by her side. 'I understood,' she noted somewhat smugly later, 'that I had not lost my man.' But nor, it transpired, had she quite recovered him. The furtive visits to Claretta, who had moved to another house, continued; as did the letters between her and Mussolini, with their usual swings between passion and jealousy. Having listened over the radio to his speech in Milan, Claretta wrote to him: 'On my knees before you ... I sustained you with my soul, with the violent beating of my heart, as I listened, enraptured.'

Mussolini's brief hope that all might still be well was short lived. By March 1945, just as Edda was concluding her deal with Dulles, it was clear that the Allies, advancing steadily towards the north, were on their way to victory. Mussolini sent Vittorio on a secret mission to Milan to ask Cardinal Schuster to approach the Allies on his behalf, with a view to some kind of negotiated peace, but the Vatican, to whom the request was forwarded, replied that they had been informed that the British and the Americans were interested only in unconditional surrender. When Don Pancino, on another visit to Edda, told her about Mussolini's overtures, her reaction was telling. Suddenly, she no longer seemed angry. 'Is there then hope? Will he be able to save himself?'

On his return to the Villa Feltrinelli Don Pancino repeated her words to Mussolini, who seemed to find consolation in them. But as the priest left, Mussolini said: 'Father, let's say goodbye now, because I know that I will be killed.' Don Pancino urged him to think about his soul. Mussolini smiled but said nothing. He was spending hours looking out over the silent grey lake, brooding, his face livid and tired. Lakes, he said, were neither seas nor rivers, 'but a sort of betrayal'. He told his sister Edvige, 'like Hamlet, the rest is silence'. He had been ready for some time, he said, to 'enter a great silence'.

On April 14, before a group of assembled Germans and *gerarchi*, Pavolini outlined a plan for a last redoubt of Fascism in the Valtellina. Two days later, Mussolini told the last council of ministers: 'Whatever the place, Fascism has to fall heroically.' But it was a fantasy, and time was running out. In the Villa Feltrinelli, Rachele began packing. Papers and documents were destroyed; the *gerarchi* began sending their families abroad.

On 19 April, as the Allies reached the Po Valley, Mussolini returned to Milan to meet the Resistance leaders in Cardinal Schuster's palace. He offered to have his Fascist army lay down their weapons, in return for safety for himself, his family and the senior *gerarchi*. What he did not know was that in Caserta in the south, German generals were negotiating an armistice, and that Wolff had told Dulles that Mussolini was 'now of no consequence in the matter of surrender'. When told, he exclaimed, 'The Germans have stabbed us in the back ... they have always treated us like slaves.' He could have remained in the safety of the cardinal's palace, where he would ultimately have been handed over to the Allies. Instead, he stormed out and returned to Como. Vittorio had come up with a plan for a submarine to spirit them to Argentina, where Peron would give them asylum; Luigi Gatti, Mussolini's secretary, suggested that a sea plane land on the lake and take them to Spain. Claretta proposed that a motor boat take Mussolini and herself across the lake to Switzerland, and that from there they should somehow get to Australia, leaving Rachele and the children behind. To them all, he said: 'No one can help me.' He told Rachele that he would never let himself fall into the hands of the Allies, for they would only put him on show 'like a freak'. He spent 25 April calmly receiving visitors and preparing to leave for the north.

'The important thing', Pavolini told the three thousand or so Fascists who had answered his call to come to Como, 'is to die well'. Most chose not to and slipped away. At five thirty on the morning of 27 April, twenty-eight cars, lorries and armoured vehicles set out in a long convoy along the west bank of Lake Como. There were 177 Germans and 174 Italians, many of them the wives and children of the senior Fascists. Mussolini was among them, but not Rachele, Romano or Anna Maria, who had been moved some days before to a villa nearby. But Elena Curti went with them, as did Claretta, wearing overalls over a suit and her hair in a pilot's cap, and her brother Marcello. For a moment, she took Elena for another mistress and made a scene. Claretta had written to her sister, 'Who loves, dies. I am following my destiny, which is his.'

They were soon stopped by a partisan roadblock. After negotiations, the Germans were allowed to pass and proceed towards Germany. The Italians were held. In the village of Dongo, Mussolini, wearing a German greatcoat that was much too big for him and a helmet, was recognised. The partisans feared a rescue attempt so he was taken early next day to a peasant's cottage near the village of Giuliano di Mezzegra. A shrill and tearful Claretta insisted on going with him. There are many versions about who, precisely, gave the orders for their execution, and many conspiracy theories to prove and disprove them. But on the afternoon of 28 April, a group of men under the command of a partisan who went by the name of Valeria shot Mussolini and Claretta by the gates of a villa outside Mezzegra. Claretta was wearing her mink coat and high-heeled shoes. It was later said that she had tried to shield his body with her own.

Fifteen of Mussolini's henchmen, Pavolini among them, were

executed in the main square at Dongo. At the last moment, Pavolini had joined the convoy in his own car. What he had felt about the betrayal of his great friend Ciano he never said. Though Marcello managed to escape and plunge into the lake, he was shot in the face and died. At four o'clock on the morning of 29 April, twenty-three corpses were unloaded from the back of a lorry in the Piazzale Loreto in Milan, where anti-Fascists had been massacred the previous year. In a gruesome finale, Mussolini and Claretta were hanged upside down from the roof of a garage after the crowds had urinated and spat on their bodies. Starace, the man who had venerated Mussolini and tried to turn Italy into a Fascist barracks, was rounded up nearby and shot. As he died, he raised his arm in a Roman salute to Mussolini's dangling corpse. Farinacci, caught by the partisans as he tried to reach the Swiss border, attempted to commit suicide but failed, and was dragged barely conscious to his own execution, his shirt torn, having lost one of his shoes. The hatred now felt by many Italians towards the Fascists was overwhelming.

Edda heard of her father's death over the radio. 'I stood absolutely still, unable to move,' she said later. 'In my whole life, I have never fainted . . . but I felt as if I had been turned to stone. I could neither lift my finger nor blink. Doctors came and sedated me and put me to bed.' For several days, she avoided all newspapers, and kept everything from the children. Then, not wanting them to learn from others of '*nonno Duce's*' gruesome end, she summoned them, as she had after Ciano's death, and told them the truth. Fabrizio thought: 'They have killed another member of my family.'

When Edda visited the local village again, she could not avoid seeing the photographs of Piazzale Loreto in all the newspapers. 'Him and that poor woman . . . and the others,' she said, 'just like a slaughterhouse.' When Don Chiot later offered to tell her the details of her father's death, she stopped him, saying that if she knew them, she would not be able to bear it. But Edda was never able to forget the photograph of a young woman partisan, looking at the body of her father: 'Smiling, smiling . . . I could have understood hatred, triumph, contempt. But not that smile, satisfied and peaceful.'

22

Settling scores

In the space of fifteen months, Edda had lost her husband, executed with the connivance of her father; and her father, executed by the partisans. She was thirty-four, with three young children, all of them refugees, and she had no idea whether her mother, sister and two brothers were alive. In the aftermath of Italy's civil war, to be called Ciano or Mussolini was perilous. It was just as well, as she said herself, that she was a fighter.

Operation Sunrise, the German surrender in Italy, was signed secretly on 29 April and formally on 2 May. The talks in Switzerland had started several months earlier between the SS commander Karl Wolff and Allen Dulles, and they probably saved Wolff, perceived as a peace broker in the negotiations, from the Nuremberg trials and execution. By bringing the fighting to an end they also saved countless lives and the total destruction of industry and infrastructure in the north. There was real fear on the Allied side that the Communists might sweep to victory in post-war Italian elections, and the Germans knew that anti-communism was their strongest card. In the event, Operation Sunrise was simply a pause, a moment between the end of the Second World War and the start of the Cold War, when the enemy became no longer Germany but the Soviet Union. With the spring ending and the summer coming, Italy began its painful reckoning, not just with its civil war and the penury to which the country had been reduced, but with its '*ventennio Fascista*', Mussolini's two decades of Fascist dictatorship. There were many scores to settle. On 7 May, Germany unconditionally surrendered to the Allies; but it would be September before Japan followed suit.

*

While the closing weeks of the war had seen Edvige's son Pino and Rachele's nephew Germano shot by the partisans, Rachele and her children were still alive. Late on 23 April they had been driven, through a stormy night, without headlights because of enemy planes, to Milan. There she received word that they were to join Mussolini in Como. The night of the 26th they were in a friend's villa when a letter was delivered from Mussolini. At least, that is what Rachele later maintained and Romano confirmed; but no one else ever saw it and there were grave doubts that it was ever written. In it, according to Rachele – who said that she memorised every word before destroying it – Mussolini asked her to forgive him 'for all the harm I have heedlessly done you ... you have been the only woman I really loved. I swear it before God and on Bruno at this supreme moment.' True or false, it seemed a final revenge on Claretta. Mussolini told her to ask for asylum from the Swiss, and if they refused, to hand herself over to the Allies. According to Rachele, he spoke to her once again over the phone to say, 'You'll make a new life.' Then she heard no more from him.

When Rachele and the children reached the border, the Swiss said that they would take in only Anna Maria, on account of her polio. Having lost none of her feistiness, Rachele told them that by refusing them entry, they were in fact doing her a favour, as she would far rather be in Italy. They all returned to Como to wait for news. There was still nothing from Mussolini. That night they heard shooting: the Americans had arrived. From a window, Rachele watched the celebrations over the fall of the Fascists explode into a desire for revenge and saw a young man in his pyjamas being lynched. At midday on the 29th their host brought her a copy of the Communist paper, *L'Unità*. Its whole front page was taken up with the words 'Benito Mussolini has been executed'. It came as a terrible shock.

Fearing a mob might attack her and the children, Rachele had sent word to the Resistance leadership and three partisans arrived to take them to police headquarters. There the children were removed and Rachele was driven to the prison of San Donnino. One of the partisans, rifling through her luggage for valuables, had found a little portrait of Bruno and taken it, saying that, like all the Mussolini possessions, it rightfully belonged to the people.

Rachele, icily, had said: 'We gave the people my son's life.' The partisan handed it back. From her cell, she had listened to shots in the courtyard, assuming that it would soon be her turn. When the children, distraught and shivering, were briefly brought to see her, she concluded that her end had come. Later, Romano and Anna Maria would say that their mother had suddenly looked smaller, shrunken; but utterly resolute.

But Rachele was not executed. Instead, on another night of wind and rain, she was driven to a villa along the lake, where an American officer with an umbrella led her to a room in which 'Singing in the Rain' was playing on a radio. The Americans, who had then collected Romano and Anna Maria, were courteous and friendly. The British, to whom they were all turned over on 10 May, were formal and cold. They took the family to Terni, where a rubber factory had been turned into a concentration camp for the Fascists. They were given rooms attached to the camp hospital. Romano was about to turn eighteen; Anna Maria was sixteen. When news of their presence got out, anonymous little presents from surviving diehard Fascists began to be delivered: clothes, shoes, scent, a straw hat for Anna Maria, a fountain pen for Romano. Twenty-seven cases of the Mussolinis' belongings had been handed over to the Allies and inventories drawn up, listing everything from a silver coffee pot to two pairs of used woollen socks, an accordion and a canister with beans and flour.

A stringer for the United Press managed to slip into the camp. Rachele refused to discuss Edda, beyond saying that 'she certainly had a great influence [over Mussolini] but mostly against him'. Finding her enforced idleness intolerable, Rachele was allowed into the kitchens, where she and Principessa Pignatelli made tagliatelle for the camp, and soon took over the entire catering. In the evenings, she regaled her fellow prisoners with stories of life in the Villa Torlonia. Three months later, on 26 July, Rachele, Romano and Anna Maria were sent to a semi-detached, partially derelict little house overlooking the sea at Forio on the island of Ischia. Its window panes were broken and there were no plates or linen. 'My house is empty,' she complained to the authorities, 'there is nothing in it.' She begged to be allowed at least their warm winter clothes. Later, she would say that the box containing money, jewellery, Mussolini's gold chain and Marshal's baton had been stolen, along with the revolver encrusted with precious stones given him by Franco. And Rachele had always hated islands.

Vittorio had also survived. Knowing himself to be on the partisans' wanted list, he had taken refuge with a cousin and a friend in the sanatorium of a college in Como. He had with him a little radio, on which he heard the news of his father's death. Vittorio spent the weeks trying to keep fit by walking round and round his bed. After three months, local people becoming suspicious, the monks judged it no longer safe and Vittorio moved first to an orphanage in Rapallo, then by bicycle to Genoa, and from there to a college run by French priests in Rome. He grew a beard, to conceal the famous Mussolini jaw, and wore a cassock. He was there when he heard that Gina, Bruno's widow, had had her hair shaved by the partisans, but had then been released, only to drown in Lake Como when the motor boat in which she was going to a wedding with some British officers overturned. Four-year-old Marina was now an orphan.

The question now, for the Swiss, was what they should do with their unwanted Fascist guests. Alfieri, Bastianini and Volpi had all managed to escape Italy across the border and found asylum. Given that even minor former Fascists were being hunted down and executed, how could the Swiss authorities return them to Italy? The war in Europe might have ended, but retribution was pitiless. Edda, the most prominent of them all, posed the biggest problem.

Edda herself was watching events with growing apprehension. On 15 May, she wrote to Dr Balsiger: 'The war is over, thank God', but since it would clearly not be safe for some time for herself and the children to go home, might she rent somewhere, perhaps on Lake Leman, where her mother-in-law Carolina could join her? Carolina had, in fact, tried to slip into Switzerland in early April, but asylum had been refused and she had been sent back, the policeman who interviewed her noting that 'her head is not exactly clear'. Edda, choosing deftly to gloss over her past, reminded Dr Balsiger that whatever anyone said, she herself had never been involved in politics. 'More than ever I want a peaceful life, but this perhaps is a fantasy.' Neither Dr Balsiger nor Dr Répond was against the plan, agreeing that she should be allowed to find somewhere remote, where she could 'roam free', though they worried that if her whereabouts became known she would be 'challenged and abused' by the anti-Fascist Italians who had found asylum from Mussolini's spies in Switzerland. But the federal authorities were adamant: Edda had to stay at Malévoz.

Life in the clinic had become increasingly disagreeable. There was a patient whose fiancé had been killed and who wandered the grounds, asking everyone she met to help her find her head, telling them that the Germans had cut it off. One day Fabrizio was standing at a window when a schizophrenic girl jumped from the fourth floor and crashed to the ground in front of him. Of the three children, he was the one who had found Switzerland the hardest, frequently crying himself to sleep at night. While still in his boarding school, he had run away in his pyjamas and slippers and made his way, frozen and desperate, to Edda. He would later say that his father's death had been 'like an earthquake in my heart', and that he had come to hate his grandfather. The three children were known locally as '*les trois gamins*' since Raimonda had cut her hair to look like a boy.

Both the Swiss press and the local people, voicing the general feeling of revulsion towards the former Fascists, now went on to the attack, with considerable viciousness. There were rumours, avidly repeated around the village, that Edda had flaunted herself in a flaming red dress on the day that her father had been executed, that she regularly got drunk and that she had been spotted in villages and towns all over Switzerland. A particularly vituperative article appeared in the *Feuille des Amis de Monthey*, written by a journalist who had never met her, saying that she spent her days in 'an establishment' in town – he did not spell out which one but the meaning was clear – that she received young men in her room in the clinic and that she was generally 'behaving scandalously'. In *France Soir*, a reporter wrote sneeringly about this 'ex-femme fatale of Europe who pretends that she is ill and ruined'. The Swiss *Die Nation* claimed that she had taken part in a black mass, an 'orgy worthy of Nero's times'.

So poisonous did the stories become that an Inspector Muller was dispatched from Berne to Malévoz to investigate. He found that three-quarters of the local people had no idea who Edda was and did not care. Over the course of the winter she had in fact left the clinic just five times to visit nearby towns and, accompanied by her female guard, she had taken the children once to a café. On one day, she had been out bicycling. True, she had been spotted walking barefoot, and had occasionally strolled in the woods in the evening, but the opprobrium she had attracted was making her extremely distressed.

Dr Répond was also driven to intervene. On 1 June, he presented a long report to the federal authorities, based on the many hours he had spent with Edda. It is a fascinating, if curiously guileless, document. In keeping with his interest in psychoanalysis, it draws together the different strands of Edda's life, dissecting her relationship with her parents, and the picture it gives is sympathetic. Edda, he wrote, was 'a very rich and generous personality, who could be both loyal and capricious'. She hated making people unhappy and was quick to ask forgiveness. 'Introverted, not very communicative, hypersensitive,' she fled from confrontations, intrigue and power games; she was also full of self-doubt and 'tormented by feelings of inferiority'. He bought her story that she was not interested in politics and observed that she had been schooled since early childhood to stay out of things that did not concern her. She had, he continued, a 'quite limited and odd view' about many things as well as 'a sense of reality' that many Swiss would consider abnormal, which made her appear both naive and cynical. He blamed her mood swings between depression and euphoria for making her seem strange, undisciplined and hard to fathom. But she was categorically 'neither a Lucretia Borgia nor a Cleopatra'.

As for her family, Dr Répond considered that it would be a grave mistake to offer Rachele asylum, since he understood from Edda that far from being an innocent victim, her mother was 'mischief-making and impulsive' and had played a hidden but important part in Mussolini's life, often treating him like an idiot in front of the children and the servants, shouting at him like a fishwife with her hands on her hips. Mussolini, whom Edda had described to him as 'feeble and authoritarian', with the mind of a provincial school teacher, may, he speculated, have been driven to take up with other women by this 'lamentable conjugal existence', and it was very possible that it was precisely this that had scarred her. For Edda, his dismissal of her mother was a pleasing revenge.

On the other hand, Dr Répond blamed Mussolini for Edda's

insomnia (by keeping her up late as a child) and her pickiness over food (caused by digestive problems inherited from him), and above all for her violent mood swings. Despite her 'lively intelligence, lucidity and perceptiveness', she had become a 'serious neurotic'. Changing his mind about her behaviour with men, he now believed her to be 'absolutely frigid'. Her inability to love fully, to give herself to a man, was in fact the 'catastrophe' of her life and it had also been the cause of her terrible reputation, for she enjoyed her friendships with different men and felt protected from them by her own coldness. From their talks, Répond concluded that being naturally timid, she had hated Roman society, and especially all the flattery and sycophancy that surrounded her family. The happiest time in her life, she told him, were her years in Shanghai. 'Her manner is simple and without airs, without the least trace of snobbery', and she was so sensitive that criticism made her literally ill. Rather than face reality, she preferred to turn into an ostrich.

Challenged by Répond, Edda willingly accepted that she had been a poor mother, and very bad at keeping discipline. Because of the violence of her own upbringing, she had retained the rebelliousness of an adolescent, which had made her strongly resistant to taking orders from anyone, and incapable of imposing order on her own family. In short, she was 'untidy, undisciplined, wilful', but could also be charming, thoughtful, considerate and kind. The doctor, it seems, had fallen somewhat under Edda's spell.

Edda had told Dr Répond that she despised and hated her father for having deceived her and letting Ciano die; and that she would never forgive him. And yet, the psychiatrist concluded, she remained profoundly attached to him, and his death had affected her deeply.

When news reached the federal authorities, and then the press, that Edda was selling off family papers to a foreign publisher for a 'colossal' sum, the campaign to get her expelled from Switzerland intensified. Journalists descended on Monthey and, forbidden access to Edda, talked to the locals, who were only too happy to repeat and embellish the already colourful rumours. A young police officer in the village called a meeting to vote on her expulsion. Edda said that she now felt like a football, kicked by everyone.

But she did little to help her cause. After Répond felt obliged to allow her a little more freedom, hoping that she would use it discreetly, she disappeared for twenty-four hours with a former male patient at the clinic. Then it turned out that she had become close to another patient, a good-looking, feckless alcoholic and epileptic, who had been dismissed from the army. Dr Répond felt betrayed and furious. Given the constant press attention, and the bad reputation that it was giving his clinic, he wrote angrily to Dr Balsiger to ask him to have Edda removed. She was too thoughtless, too rebellious, too irresponsible, and she was clearly incapable of learning from experience.

At federal level, plans were now being put into place for the return home of the forty-five thousand or so Italian refugees who had spent some of the war in Switzerland. A meeting held on 20 August voted that Edda should be made to leave, but that her children would be allowed to stay with their governess Frau Schwarz until things were clearer. Edda protested that she would be treated as a war criminal, saying that evidently the Swiss considered her one, and wrote to Dulles: 'If they send me back to Italy, I'll know the meaning of death soon enough.' But a date had been set – 29 August – and the Italian Foreign Ministry had given assurances that there would be no summary justice. Like her mother, Edda was to be sent to a concentration camp 'for her own security'.

Dr Répond now relented and said that she could stay. But it was too late. The Italians had made arrangements to take her back, and the Americans had agreed to 'arrange reception and delivery'. Edda's fears were not misplaced. A *New York Times* reporter writing from Rome said that the Italians now regarded her as the 'very hub' of a Fascist world of social and political intrigue comparable only to the 'era of the Borgias', and that many bore her a personal grudge. 'Should the patriots find her,' he prophesied, she would surely 'suffer the same fate as her father'.

Edda spent the evening of the 28th at the station buffet in Monthey with her children and various friends. Pucci, recovered from his injuries, had also been given permission to see her off. At two thirty on the afternoon of the 29th, she boarded a train for Berne; Dr Répond, Fabrizio and Raimonda, Pucci and mademoiselle Schwartz accompanied her on the first leg of the journey. At Vevey, Virginia Agnelli was waiting with flowers. At Fribourg, Madame de Chollet joined the train. The party had dinner together in the restaurant car.

Every step of the way had been meticulously orchestrated by Dr Balsiger, the Swiss border guards and the US Legation in Berne. At Bellinzona, the frontier with Italy, Edda said goodbye to her children. She gave Raimonda her watch. There was the usual lack of emotion displayed on public occasions and they recited to each other the phrase that had become their family mantra: 'God send you a good journey and no wind.' An American jeep was waiting. The barrier to Italy opened and, with Edda on board, it sped through, followed by a van with her luggage. Inspector Muller, who was present, noted that Edda was a 'little less eccentrically dressed than sometimes in Monthey', and that she showed 'great discretion and dignity' and no shred of 'despair or dejection'. But then, whatever her feelings, she would not have shown them in public.

Edda had not been informed where she was going. After three bumpy hours in the jeep, through countryside littered with the debris of war, she found herself at Linate airport in Milan. On the walls of the towns she passed through she saw scrawled, 'Fascists! Remember the Piazzale Loreto!' Next morning she was flown on to Orvieto where she was handed over to the Italians. Her reception was chilly. She was ordered to undress and was then thoroughly searched, naked, in a room with an open door. The policeman who took charge of her was Polito, the man who had pawed Rachele on the drive to Rocca delle Caminate.

Polito began with a formal interrogation. Who were her parents? Edda told him. Not so, said Polito smugly, we know exactly who your mother is – referring to the absurd rumour about Angelica Balabanoff. Well, replied Edda coldly, 'since I was so young at the time of my birth, I can't quite remember. Perhaps you'll be kind enough to tell me?' A military plane flew her on to Catania and from the window Edda looked out on Capri below. Finally, Polito consented to tell her their destination: the island of Lipari, former detention centre for anti-Fascists sent into internal exile by Mussolini, and now turned into a similar holding pen for the fallen Fascists. It was 1 September, Edda's thirty-fifth birthday. Her thirty-third had been spent with Hitler; her thirty-fourth, as she put it, in a lunatic asylum.

Lipari, the largest of the Aeolian Islands, was considered by the exiles to be the best of the penal settlements. It had two ports, a number of hamlets scattered over the hillsides, and a mild climate. Its only industry was pumice. Cypresses, palm trees, eucalyptus, medlars and lemon trees grew in profusion, along with bushes of capers with their distinctive purple leaves. But modern life had somehow passed it by. There were almost no cars, no tarmac roads and very little electricity, and it was sparsely populated, generations of impoverished islanders having left to seek their fortunes in the New World. Few of the fishing boats had motors. The Liparesi, both the men and the women, were thin from childhood malnourishment but nimble and muscular. When Edda stepped off the naval corvette, accompanied by soldiers and officials, she was seen to walk hunched over, holding on to someone's arm. She looked pale, almost emaciated; her weight was now just 42 kilos. She was given a little house with two rooms; four carabinieri were detailed to guard her in shifts.

It was some time before she was able to discover the charges against her. They fell under four headings: favouring Fascism and behaving in 'an immoral Fascist way'; contributing to the decision to go to war; befriending senior Germans and furthering the alliance between Italy and Germany; and telling Mussolini that neutrality was a *'vergogna'*, a disgrace. The telephone taps discovered when Rome was liberated had revealed the full extent of favours and cronyism in high places, and Edda, it appeared, was not altogether guiltless: one report had it that a man she had helped acquire four scarce Fiat trucks in Predappio had given her five leopard skins.

The exact truth of the various charges against Edda is hard to pin down. Certainly, her interest in politics had been considerable, whatever her protestations, and she had much enjoyed the power and privilege that came with them. She had also, for a period, been friends with the leading Nazis and urged her father to go to war on their side. Had he listened? Had she actually influenced the tide of history? Her accusers chose to believe she had. Edda was sentenced to spend two years *in confino*, under 'special surveillance number 1', as 'dangerous to the exercise of democratic freedom'. An official document spelt it out more fully. Edda had in fact been partially responsible for the 'military and economic disaster' of Italy's entry into the war, and her 'dissolute tenor of life' had played a part in 'all the sufferings of the Italian people'. Reading these charges, Edda remarked drily: 'It wasn't as if I was Helen of Troy.'

Fearing that worse awaited her, that with her father and husband dead she might be made to pay the price for their mistakes,
and that Lipari was merely a stage on the way to a war crimes trial
and execution, Edda threw herself into establishing her innocence.
She could hardly deny that she had attended meetings with leading
Nazis, but insisted that her role throughout had been 'purely
social'. In a long memorandum sent to the authorities in Rome, she
repeatedly downplayed her own presence to that of an obedient
wife and daughter, uninterested in politics, but useful in arranging
the seating at official dinners. She insisted that she had held no
party card until forced to do so by Starace in 1936. Since she spoke
no German, she pointed out that it would not have been possible
for her to have friends among the Nazis.

Though happy to lie when the occasion demanded it, there had
always been, as Dr Répond had realised, a strong streak of candour in Edda's make up. Towards the end of the memorandum, she
admitted: 'I honestly believed in a German victory', and felt that
Italy's undertaking to support Hitler, once made, had to be honoured. But were these really war crimes? The police came back
with a stern report of their own. Edda's 'vices, capriciousness and
her abnormal sexual sensibility' should never be forgotten or forgiven. Were she to be allowed to go free, there was every chance
that she might 'spark a dangerous resurgence of neo-Fascism'. And
it was all very well for her to say that she believed that Italy's
promises to Germany had to be honoured – but whose promises
were they? 'Not those of the Italian people, but of the Mussolini-
Ciano dynasty.'

It was at a meeting in the port on food shortages in Lipari that
Edda was introduced to Leonida Buongiorno, son of Edoardo, the
trombone-playing Communist who owned a local boat agency
and who had helped Carlo Rosselli and his anti-Fascist friends
escape from *confino* in 1929. Leonida, also a party member, was
not long home from serving with the Alpini in Greece and France,
then with the partisans in the north. He would later say that his
first impression of Edda was of a 'wounded swallow'. Leonida was
thirty-four, a year younger than Edda, with a degree in economics,
and he spoke several languages; he was witty, ironical and had a
will of iron.

Soon after, Edda sent him a note. Would he like to pay her '*une *petite visite*'? She felt melancholic and longed to hear 'fantastical, tender, cheerful, funny stories'. He came, found her in bed under a mosquito net, felt briefly embarrassed, but stayed. They began to talk. Among Leonida's many qualities were warmth, exuberance and intimacy, things that Edda had long been deprived of. They wrote each other letters, in French and Italian. She called herself Ellenica; he became Baiardo after the horse in *Orlando Furioso*. He told her about a recent failed love affair and she teased him for taking it too seriously. He showered her with flowers. She said that she was not given to yielding herself to anyone, because what she valued most was 'feeling clean inside'. They exchanged kitsch little cards and talked about Homer, Leonida reciting to her long passages from the *Odyssey*.

The Buongiorno family owned a villa, larger and more comfortable that the one she had been allocated, whitewashed and with a terrace under the eaves. She was allowed to move into it and christened it '*la petite Malmaison*', after the Empress Josephine's house outside Paris. Though both were wary of getting involved – who, after all, could be less suited than a Communist Party member and an unrepentant Fascist? – the conversations soon became an affair. Leonida had a boat and took Edda to swim from the beach at Lazzaretto, where, to the amazement of the islanders, she wore a bikini and lay for hours in the sun. One day he drew her naked with a black charcoal pencil before framing it in red mahogany. She worried that she looked old and was pleased only with her legs. She craved his kindness, and there was something quite new to her in his lack of artifice.

One morning, they went to the neighbouring island of Vulcano, where the sand was black and the air smelt of sulphur. Her police guards kept at a discreet distance. 'Ellenica is chaste,' Leonida observed, suggesting that she had kept herself pure not out of religious scruples or any sense of morality, but because 'of a certain cast of mind and a horror of promiscuity'. Under his loving gentleness, Edda thrived. She took sulphur mud baths, put on weight and grew brown in the sun. Her unkempt hair and casual clothes suited her. One night they did the foxtrot on the empty stage of the village theatre.

Their affair was not always smooth. The two could not have been more different: Leonida was excitable, talkative, full of optimism and plans; Edda was restless, brooding, haunted. She missed the children and complained about her sentence. Her mood would suddenly darken and she would storm and rage. Leonida, soldier, partisan, Sicilian, accustomed to uncomplicated affairs, found her waywardness and profound insecurity baffling; but he comforted her and urged patience. She begged him to love her, to give her strength and show her tenderness. This was another Edda, loving and unguarded, freed from the constant need to play a part, perhaps even a stranger to herself.

In June 1946, Palmiro Togliatti, the leader of the Communist Party and Minister of Justice in the broad-based post-war coalition government, unexpectedly announced an amnesty for most Fascist crimes. Edda was having dinner in a restaurant in the port when her guards appeared and told her that she was on the list for immediate release. She had served just ten months of her two-year sentence. She greeted the news, as she greeted most things when in public, impassively. She was not, however, altogether delighted, for she felt content on Lipari, where the islanders had warmed to their 'elegant' guest. But she was free. And for the first time since she could remember, there would be no one to follow, monitor or spy on her.

Leonida suggested that she go to Rome, to take stock of her situation and begin to prepare for the return of the children. She hoped – imagined – she might find friends there, but in the event few seemed prepared to be seen in her company. Virginia Agnelli, who had done so much for her in the past, had recently been killed in a car crash in Pisa. She missed Leonida and 'Lipari's blue water'. In Rome, she wrote, 'you have the feeling that you are living in an enormous lunatic asylum. Everyone is overexcited, agitated, nervous, breathless.' She hoped that he was missing her and 'very unhappy and very jealous'.

The police had informed her that she would not be allowed to re-enter Switzerland. Instead, the children were brought to Carolina's house at Ponte a Moriano, staring from the train windows at the devastated countryside and sleeping in the luggage racks. Edda had not seen them for almost a year. Wisely, the rumour that Fabrizio had tried to kill himself – a fabrication – had been kept from her. But she found them wild, disobedient and very reluctant to study, and soon felt restless and dejected in their company. The locals made no attempt to conceal their distaste for her presence and the Questore in Lucca suggested that she should consider emigrating, for her own safety. 'Dear Friend,' she wrote to Leonida, 'will I ever have a moment of truce? Will the swallow ever have a nest?' She addressed her letters to her 'dearest and only communist', and her 'fiancé'.

Having paid Leonida a brief visit in October, their affair mysteriously still kept secret from the press by the islanders, she went on to Ischia to see her mother. They had not met or spoken since Rachele had pressed so hard for Ciano's death. Edda had thought that they would never speak again, but there was something about Rachele's poverty that touched her. The little house was still almost bare of furniture, with doors that would not shut and pieces of ceiling that fell down, even though Rachele assured her that in comparison with the early days, it was now 'all roses and flowers'. Listening to her mother talk agonisingly about Mussolini's last days, Edda felt guilty and saddened that her father had minded so acutely about the breach between them. 'And I too,' she told Leonida, 'wept.' Ellenica, she said, was filled with sadness.

Romano was beginning to show real talent as a jazz musician, and though Anna Maria seemed to have retreated into herself and spent much of the day reading comics, both children had made friends. And the islanders had been kind to Rachele. To her mother, when she learnt that her sister-in-law Gina had drowned boating on Lake Garda, Edda wrote, 'The moment you begin to find your feet again, there comes another hammer blow ... If you wish to stay upright, then you must dress in red and sing. And you must never cry, not even if your heart is bursting.'

Leonida was never going to leave Lipari, and Edda and her children had no future there. There were a few more visits, a few secret encounters on the mainland, but the tone of Edda's letters grew anxious. Leonida sent her loving postcards, in English and in French. One evening, Edda met Leonida's brother Giovanni for dinner. In the course of enjoyable gossip about Lipari, he let slip that Leonida was seeing a new woman. Edda knew all about jealousy, saying frequently that she had tamed it years before in Shanghai over Ciano. But this was very hard to take. One day she wrote to Leonida: 'Come with me. Don't throw away the happiness that the Gods have offered you. They rarely give one such a gift. And never twice. Leave the island. The family. Your fiancée. Love knows no regrets.' Edda had never written with such naked tenderness. 'I want to murmur to your lips: I love you.'

For a while, their correspondence ceased. Edda's hair began to fall out, and as more and more disappeared, her hairdresser suggested that she should shave it all off before becoming completely bald. With no hair, the resemblance to her father was startling. She sent a lock to Leonida, describing it as a 'relic', and took to wearing turbans, which suited her handsome bony face. Then her hair grew back with what she jokingly called 'neo-Fascist vigour'. But Leonida remained largely silent. A 'terrible barrier of ice' seemed to settle between them. 'They say,' she wrote, 'that silence is golden; but you exaggerate.' And later, 'Everything is dark . . . everything weighs on my shoulders. I am desperately alone . . . My nerves are stretched taut and my heart trembles.'

The break was not total. They continued to write to each other sporadically, and even to meet. Leonida married his girlfriend, was elected to the local council and entered politics. Many years later, as a memento to their love affair, he had engraved on a wall in Lipari the verses from the *Odyssey* in which Circe tells Odysseus why it is impossible for him to return to Ithaca. Underneath were the words: 'To Ellenica – L.B.'

Edda returned to Capri. The barrage of mines laid around the island were gone, the restaurants had opened, the tourists were back, there were drinks parties in the main square in the evenings, and long swims to the Blue Grotto. The main piazza was once again '*il salotto del mondo*'. Not everyone greeted Edda and the children warmly, but the loyal Chantecler did everything he could to make them welcome and the barman at the Quisisana provided her with the ration books the state refused to give her. She was beginning, she told Leonida, to live again, 'even quite well', if somewhat bored by what she called 'monstrous happiness'. But then, Edda had always been deeply suspicious of happiness. As she said, '*la felicità abbrutisce*' – happiness stupefies, dazes, numbs. 'To fight is to live.'

23

L'Aquilaccia

Edda was back in Rome over the winter of 1946, but Rome in the late 1940s was a poor and angry city, trying to come to terms with twenty years of Fascism and eight months of Nazi occupation. There were still vendettas to be settled, and little had been done to put to rights a city impoverished and battered by war. Within families, fractured between Fascism and anti-Fascism, there was much that needed sorting out. Speaking to a British officer in the camp where he was being held by the Allies, Eugen Dollmann, describing Roman society in the late 1930s, said that he had 'never known a social group which so prostituted itself'. Edda had told Leonida that when she looked behind her, what she could see was a desert filled with graves; when she looked ahead, she saw a storm over a rough sea. She was right: there were to be many stormy times ahead.

Vittorio, still on the run, was preparing to leave Italy for a new life in Argentina. There was a family picnic to say goodbye to him in the ruins of Pompeii, and Rachele, Anna Maria, Romano and Edda all came. They had not met since Ciano's and Mussolini's deaths. Vittorio came in disguise, wearing a priest's cassock and a red baseball cap. The mood was wary. In true Mussolini fashion, little was said.

For Edda, there was now the question of where she and the children would live. The flats in the Via Angelo Secchi had been sequestered and the villa in Capri was still requisitioned by the Allies, and she embarked on a series of court cases against the government to win them back. She was already suffering, she said, from 'lawyer phobia'. '*La figlia della povertà*', as her father had called her, was not, however, any longer poor, whatever she sometimes maintained. The sum of money he had sent her from the sale of *Il Popolo d'Italia* alone was said to have amounted to five million lire.

Rome was rife with litigation. As part of its programme of '*defascistazione*' the commission on illicit gains by the Fascists had resumed its investigations and the surviving families of the *gerarchi*, like Edda, were fighting for at least part of their fortunes to be returned to them. Both Farinacci's widow and Claretta's parents and sister wanted to claw back the villas, farms, apartment blocks, shares, jewellery and art, tucked away in numbered accounts and bogus companies. Their lawyers would be busy for decades to come.

There was also the question of hunting down the army of secret spies, informers and blackmailers who had provided OVRA with so much harmful and incriminating information and who had contributed so profoundly to the malaise of Fascist Italy. In contrast to the denunciations lodged in Nazi Germany or the Soviet Union, where informers gave their names, 80 per cent of those in Italy had been anonymous. Soon after the liberation of Rome, orders had gone out for the arrest of all OVRA and secret service agents. A list of 815 names was drawn up – there was no category, age, class or occupation not represented, from call girls to generals, porters to priests – but most found ways to wriggle their way to freedom, helped by the fact that so many pseudonyms had been used. Files were mysteriously lost or mislaid. In the dock, witnesses lied, falsified, misremembered. In the event, just 162 sentences, for the whole of Italy, were handed down, and many of those who went to jail were soon set free. Early in July 1946, the Gazzetta Ufficiale published a list of 622 names, with dates of birth and even addresses of the informers; but in the mood and chaos of post-war Italy, few people seemed to care. Togliatti's amnesty for Fascist collaborators, reducing most sentences and removing others, was another step in national forgetting.

In his tribute to his brother Arnaldo, Mussolini had written that it would be presumptuous to imagine that he himself would be left in peace after his death. 'Around the graves of leaders of those great transformations called revolutions, there can be no peace.' The story of his own remains was gruesome. Edda and Rachele were both haunted by not being told where Mussolini had been buried. Their repeated requests were met only with assurances that they would be informed 'once political passions had died down'.

Then, in April 1946, Rachele read in a newspaper that his coffin had been buried in grave number 384 in the cemetery of Musocco outside Milan, but without a piece of his brain, which had been taken by the Americans for medical research. But this was only the beginning. She learnt that Mussolini's body had been dug up one night by Fascist extremists outraged by what they called the 'cannibalism' perpetrated on the Duce's corpse and claiming that 'out of love' they could not leave it where it was. The rotting body was heavy and at one point the grave robbers, wheeling it through the cemetery on a barrow, the head lolling to one side, dropped the corpse. They had also taken one of Mussolini's boots, to make later identification easier. The corpse had spent several months in a house in the country, until its owner had been arrested, but not before it had been spirited away in rubber sacks by two monks who had buried it in a box wrapped in plastic sheeting under the altar of the Certosa at Pavia. In due course the monks agreed to hand the body back to the authorities, on the condition that it was given a proper Christian burial. However, the police then hid it again, under the label of 'Documenti Provinciali', and all requests by Edda and Rachele for its return were met by the same refusal: to bury Mussolini in a known grave would only become a pretext for political agitation.

Along with the battle for the return of her father's body, Edda was dealing with the repercussions of Ciano's diaries, now available for publication, but also the subject of some confusion. When, in June 1945, Don Pancino was interviewed by the Americans, he told them that he had been acting as a spy for the Germans, in order to help them get hold of the diaries, in return for money and the promise of ecclesiastical promotion. But this, he soon admitted, was a lie. He had in fact been trying to get the diaries for Mussolini, to use as a bargaining tool in the last months of Salò. The Duce, too, had believed them valuable.

As the diaries began to be published, both in English and in Italian, the question posed by readers and critics – and never properly answered – was the extent to which Ciano himself had doctored, revised or rewritten them, as well as substituted pages, in order to present himself in a more favourable light. Those who had known him wondered how a man who had seemed to them so frivolous could have kept such a concise, clear-headed account of years filled with uncertainty and turbulence. And to what extent had he been playing a double game, courting both the Axis and the Allies until victory became clear? Certainly the man who emerges from its pages is more likeable, perceptive and serious than his reputation; but also curiously indifferent to the huge numbers of casualties and atrocious conditions of Italian soldiers in a war for which, as Foreign Minister, he had to take at least some responsibility.

Goebbels once claimed that it was Ciano and not Grandi who was in fact the leader of the conspiracy against Mussolini. The diaries suggested otherwise. Ciano, in the early days totally subservient to Mussolini's wishes, genuinely seems to have wanted to keep Italy out of the war on the Axis side; but when it came to the coup, he failed to think through the consequences, either for Italy or for himself. The perceptive, worldly wise François-Poncet, who had got to know and like Ciano, believed the diaries to be faithful to events and to a 'reality, as interpreted by Ciano, that is to say, coloured by his feelings and his prejudices'.

The diaries, so eagerly sought after by both the Allies and the Germans, so desperately clung on to by Edda as barter for Ciano's life, ultimately contained no major revelations. There was nothing in them that could have changed the course of the war. But they did show the futility of the efforts made by the liberal Western democracies to detach Italy from Germany. 'The whole sad structure of pre-war Europe,' wrote Malcolm Muggeridge in a long introduction to an English edition, 'is contained in them – appeasers and appeased moving with the inevitability of a Greek tragedy to a common ruin.' And as a portrait of Mussolini, with all his sudden rages, his sentimentality, capriciousness, flashes of insight and narcissism, it has no equal. The men he surrounded himself with, 'brainless, egotistical, cowardly, corrupt and criminal', do not emerge well. Ciano was proud of his diaries. He wrote them rapidly, but with great care and style. They were to be his testament. But they are striking for one other thing: beyond a handful of fleeting asides, Edda, in their many hundreds of entries, is nowhere to be found.

Since their publication had unleashed a fury of press hostility towards her, Edda had begged her mother not to speak to journalists. But in February 1946, Rachele, still in Ischia, agreed to talk to a reporter called Bruno d'Agostini. And once she started talking, she could not stop. For four days, she poured out her life, her fears, her memories, seeming to relive her childhood, her life in Villa Torlonia and Salò. 'My husband,' she told d'Agostini, 'seemed to be a lion, but instead, all things considered, he was *"un pover'uomo"'*, a poor kind of man.

Like Edda, Rachele was soon allowed to return to live on the mainland. She fought to get back the Villa Carpena, and when she managed to secure it, she busied herself turning it into a shrine to the past. She kept chickens and rabbits, went back to speaking Romagnolo and for a while ran a restaurant where she served *tagliatelle alla Rachele*. Small and seemingly fragile, she remained as strong and competent as ever. Locally she was known as Donna Rachele.

Edda, too, got some of her properties back, agreeing on a sum to the government that returned to her the flats in the Via Angelo Secchi and her villa on Capri. She found the villa dilapidated, dirty and stripped of anything of value, and tried to raise money by getting Chantecler to sell Ciano's Collare dell'Annunziata. As defiant as ever, when the local municipality decided to rename the public road leading up to the house Viale della Liberazione, she went out one night in the dark and removed the sign.

In the spring of 1947, Italy's supreme court retrospectively absolved Ciano of all crimes against the state of Italy, stating that, on the contrary, he had distinguished himself in the 'struggle against the German invaders'. In a remarkable, indeed improbable, turnaround, he was totally 'rehabilitated' and his name added to the lists of 'martyrs of the war of liberation'.

Edda was only thirty-six when she returned to Rome. She had her children, still all of school age. She played solitaire, read, did crossword puzzles, travelled and kept a Yorkshire terrier and a Siamese cat, Pippo, to whom she wrote postcards when away, instructing her maid to put them on the floor for the animal to sniff. She had promised herself that she would take exercise, but soon gave it up. She slept badly. 'I write, I dream, I drink, I smoke,' she wrote to Leonida. 'I stay up till dawn. All this is bad. Particularly for the skin, without counting the heart and the liver.' She remained very superstitious, about black cats, hats on beds, umbrellas in houses, spilt salt, and she fulminated over loud noises, bores and speed restrictions. When angry, she threw things. She never learnt to cook, but her two servants produced excellent meals. She remained a somewhat partial mother to her children, saying that she saw herself more as their friend and telling her mother-in-law that she wanted them to grow up 'cynical and insensitive' in order to protect themselves from an inhospitable, alien world. They called her Edda, or Eddazza and sometimes l'Aquilaccia, queen of the mountains, able to fly even after the world collapsed around her.

Edda changed very little in the Via Angelo Secchi: the blue porcelain plates from Peking were there, the screens from Shanghai, the bits of Roman sculpture and the de Chirico portrait of Ciano. To all of these she added cats, in ceramic and bronze, along with the stuffed cat with the blue glass eyes, clung on to when her Red Cross ship was sunk in Albania. She did not marry again. To prepare herself for a serene old age, as she put it, she took up the piano and began to learn Russian and golf, but she seldom stuck at anything for long. Edda kept some of her friends, with whom she played backgammon, canasta and gin rummy, though others crossed the road to avoid having to greet her. When in company, her eyes cold and gleaming with irony, she impressed her listeners with her prodigious memory. Occasionally, she spoke well of Hitler, and said that her father's greatest mistake had been to allow himself to fall for the adulation of the Italian people. She was certainly lonely.

On 9 May 1944, King Victor Emanuel, after forty-six years on the throne, abdicated. His son Umberto was lieutenant-general of the realm for twenty-three months and King for just thirty-four days: in June 1946 Italians voted by 12.7 million votes to 10.7 million to turn Italy into a republic. Princess Mafalda, caught in the net of Italy's switch of alliance in 1943, had fallen into German hands and died in Buchenwald. The austere little King died soon after the war in Egypt, in 1947; Queen Elena survived him by five years.

By the late 1940s, Cinecittà was again in full swing, turning out the films set among the poor and the oppressed that would define the post-war years, along with spectaculars such as *Quo Vadis*, for which thirty-two thousand costumes were made. But there was no place in neo-realism for the languid, sulky starlets of the late 1930s and most disappeared into obscurity. Pavolini's mistress Doris Duranti tried but failed to commit suicide. Osvaldo Valenti and Luisa Manfrini, 'the dandy and the peasant', having drifted into Fascist violence in Salò, were caught and shot by the partisans. Luisa was two months pregnant.

Isabella Colonna, queen of Ciano's Petit Trianon, slipped smoothly into the role of social queen of the new republic. The aristocracy, like an incoming tide over a sandy shore strewn with rubbish, closed over the years of Fascism. It was as if they had never happened and the Cianos, with all their vulgar vitality and hunger for happiness and success, had simply not existed. Like so much else in post-war Italy, they became a part of the unremembering. Very few ever joined in the memoir-publishing fever that followed the war. Fascism was cast as a blip of history many preferred to forget.

Edda kept her own counsel over not talking to journalists and she was infuriated by the endless vituperative descriptions of the Mussolinis put out by the drivers, secretaries and servants who had worked for them. She told her mother that it was like 'spitting poison'. When her wider family began publishing memoirs and autobiographies she stayed silent. As she did when the photo magazines so beloved by Italians – such as *Gente*, *Tempo*, *Epoca* and others – put out innumerable articles on the lives of the Mussolinis and the Cianos. It was not until 1959 that she relented and agreed to talk, to 'put things straight' and prove that she was not and had never been a '*pazza isterica*', mad and hysterical. 'We never liked exhibitionism,' she told an interviewer, 'and still less sentimentality.'

To the end of her days, Edda refused to believe that either Ciano or those shot with him had been traitors. Her husband, she would say, had kept faith with his beliefs all along, supporting the Pact of Steel when he thought it best for Italy, fighting to keep Italy out of the war when he came to believe that the country was in no position to fight. 'You cannot change fate. You reason, you struggle, you torment yourself over what is right and wrong. You try to do your best and sometimes you make mistakes.' How had she survived? 'Reflecting. Reading. Above all with pride.' She had always wanted, she said, to be different and she had not been cut out to be a 'perfect and ordinary little woman'.

Afterword

Towards the end of August 1957, Edda received a call from the police. After twelve years of the family begging, cajoling and arguing, the Christian Democrat Prime Minister, Adone Zoli, whose own ancestors were Romagnoli, had finally agreed to return Mussolini's body to be buried in the family vault. She was on Capri and left immediately with her children for Predappio. Rachele joined her from Ischia, where she was still spending much of her time. The two women had been instructed to keep the internment in the family tomb totally secret, in order to prevent crowds gathering. But the news had got out. When Edda arrived at the crypt in San Cassiano she found the cemetery overflowing with people, many of whom had brought wreaths and flowers. As she approached, she heard murmurs: '*Il Duce è tornato*!', the Duce has come home.

What followed was a macabre ceremony. Mussolini's remains had been delivered packed inside a wooden crate, bound together with metal strips. When it was moved, the crate rattled. Prising open the lid, the family discovered a small glass jar, containing part of Mussolini's brain, the rest having been taken away in 1945 by the Americans, who wanted criminologists in Washington to examine it for possible insanity brought on by syphilis.

Rachele had embroidered a funeral shroud and insisted on wrapping it around what remained of Mussolini's body before consigning it to its resting place in the crypt, in front of a vast bust of his head and neck. There were speeches and many tears. But Mussolini's prophecy that his corpse, like that of all the leaders of great revolutions, would find no peace, proved true. In 1966, an American official knocked on the door of the Villa Carpena and handed Rachele the missing segment of his brain, wrapped in cellophane with the word 'Negative' stamped on it. No syphilis had been found. Then, at Christmas 1971, a bomb exploded next to the crypt, causing extensive damage, but leaving Mussolini's remains untouched. In 2015 came news that yet another sliver of brain had been offered on eBay for 15,000 euros. Today the crypt is open only on the anniversaries of Mussolini's birth and death, and on 28 October every year, when the faithful, those who yearn for the days when Fascism ran their lives, gather in Predappio to remember the March on Rome.

Edda lived on until 9 April 1995, when she died after an operation to remove an abscessed kidney in a Roman clinic. She was eighty-four. At her funeral in the Basilica del Sacro Cuore Immacolato di Maria in Parioli, many mourners gave the Fascist salute. Edda had tried and failed to prevent Dino De Laurentiis making a film about her and Ciano, saying that 'it treads on our sorrow'. She remained unrepentant about the past, saying that she thought it deeply hypocritical to pretend, as many did, that they had never known the Nazi leaders. 'Hitler? Goering? Goebbels?' she would say. 'I knew them all.' She was fierce when questioned about her role in Italy's years of Fascism, strongly denying that she had ever been her father's *eminence grise*, or any kind of 'arbiter in Italy's international politics'. As she grew older, she admitted that even with the passing of time, she continued to remember and dwell on the tragedies of her life. 'And yet,' she would add, 'I continue to live, not vegetate ... There are women who have a vocation for being a widow. I am not that sort of woman.'

Edda's children did not find much happiness. Fabrizio coped with the stigma of his parentage by emigrating to Venezuela, staying out of Italy for nine years, then joining the neo-Fascist Movimento Sociale Italiano, campaigning for a seat in parliament with the slogan 'I am the son of a Fascist who made a mistake and paid for it'. His political ambitions came to nothing, and nor did those of his brother Marzio, the most sensitive and unpredictable of Edda's three children, who grew up to be a short, brown-haired man with an uncanny resemblance to Mussolini and a warm, raucous voice, and whose wife left him for his brother Fabrizio. Marzio drank heavily and died in April 1974 at the age of thirty-six. Raimonda, their sister, also drank heavily. In 1952 she married the son of a former senior Fascist and went to live in Brazil. But that marriage failed and she was often to be found staying with her mother on Capri. Raimonda died in 1998, and Fabrizio in 2008. Neither had children; Marzio had two sons.

The Mussolini siblings fared a little better. Vittorio spent eleven years in Buenos Aires, with a wife and two children, working in journalism, textiles and insurance; but that marriage eventually broke up as well. Romano made a modest success as a jazz player, married Sophia Loren's sister in a magnificent ceremony in Predappio attended by film stars and veteran Fascists, and had two children. After his marriage, too, ended in divorce, he married again and had a third daughter. Their sister Anna Maria, the 'most loved and most unlucky' of the Mussolini children, gruff and obstinate, but also strong and combative, carved out a small career as an interviewer. In 1960 she married Nando Pucci, a presenter of variety shows, in a long veil and flowing dress that covered her slight physical deformity. She died at thirty-nine, having caught chicken pox from one of her two small daughters. It was Romano who put into words what he saw as the fate of the Mussolini children: though Italy tolerated them, there were clear limits to what they could do before doors were slammed in their faces. Interestingly, none of them changed their names. And two of Romano's daughters, the half-sisters Alessandra and Rachele, have found a place in Italy's right-wing politics.

Rachele lived on until 1977, cooking, visiting her son Bruno and her husband in the crypt at San Cassiano every day and bad-mouthing Claretta to anyone who asked about her past. With the Palazzo Venezia and Rocca delle Caminate returned to the state, and the Villa Torlonia to the prince, the Villa Carpena became the place where the Mussolinis gathered. In 1957, the magazine *Oggi* published Rachele's version of her story in sixteen episodes, selling a million copies and many more in translation. Between them all, the Mussolinis and the Cianos wrote – or had written for them – well over a dozen memoirs and autobiographies: Rachele four, Vittorio three, Edda two and Romano one. Fabrizio called his *When Grandpa had Daddy Shot*. Their descendants are still continuing with the tradition.

The Mussolinis' wider circle had predictably uncertain lives. After the coup in 1943 Bottai, generally accepted as the most cultured of the *gerarchi*, moved from hiding place to hiding place, often dressed as a priest, before enrolling for 'moral redemption' in the Foreign Legion. When pardoned by the Italian state for his part in Fascist crimes, he returned to Rome and pursued a career in journalism. Grandi, the real architect of the coup against Mussolini, sat out the war in Portugal then lived for twenty years in Brazil. In his memoirs he concluded that the Duce had been a great man who had committed unpardonable errors.

Margherita Sarfatti went back to Rome in 1947 to be cold-shouldered by many of the intellectuals who had fawned over her during her years as Mussolini's mistress. Her verdict on Mussolini was unforgiving: he had indeed been a 'good tyrant', bringing genuine social reform to Italy, but by the end he had turned Fascism into a grotesque deformation and degenerated into someone so lonely, so vain, cynical and touchy that his ultimate ruin was inevitable. As for Claretta, her remains were finally handed over to her family in the mid 1950s, to be buried in the Petacci family tomb. Her sister Myriam, when allowed back to Italy from Spain, launched proceedings to recover Claretta's voluminous letters and diaries, and devoted part of her life to constructing a popular narrative that her sister had been Mussolini's one and only great love.

Neither of Ciano's two close friends survived for very long. Raimondo Lanza di Trabia, the master of subterfuge, was found dead under the window of his room in the Hotel Eden in Rome in 1954. He had been negotiating the selling of his sulphur mines in Sicily and no one believed it was suicide, but rather the long hand of the Mafia. Malaparte, increasingly embattled, continued to write about poverty and oppression and published a successful novel about Naples, *La Pelle*. But while on a visit to China he was diagnosed with lung cancer and died in 1957 at the age of fifty-nine.

The Germans who had served in Italy for the most part got off lightly. General Wolff, whose words may have persuaded Mussolini not to intervene to save Ciano's life, was sentenced to four years in prison in 1949, but served fifteen more when, in the wake of the Eichmann trial, cases were reopened against Nazis guilty of war crimes. Field Marshal Kesselring's death sentence was commuted to life, but he was freed in 1953. Hildegard Beetz married twice more after her first husband was killed on the Eastern Front. She went to considerable lengths to avoid reporters, but eventually capitulated and became the subject of news stories and a book.

And one of the more bizarre stories, concerning Churchill and Mussolini, was only finally laid to rest some seventy years after the war. Immediately after the liberation of Italy, rumours began that the two leaders had exchanged letters which compromised Churchill and rehabilitated Mussolini by obfuscating his role in dragging Italy into the war. There was talk of a trove of papers, burnt by Romano along with others in case they should fall into the wrong hands. In the event, what papers existed were shown to be forgeries or reconstructions based on false material. Churchill and Mussolini had in fact exchanged just two letters: Churchill's imploring Mussolini to stay out of the war; Mussolini replying two days later that his mind was already made up.

The end of the war found Italy politically, economically and socially exhausted. Many hundreds of thousands of people were homeless, 250,000 hectares of land were heavily mined, there was famine in the south and Italians, rancorous, miserable, poor, vengeful, felt betrayed. In 1947, the Marshall Plan began restoring Italy's ruined infrastructure.

It suited almost everyone to forget the past, even the partisans who longed to put the terrors and deprivations of the war years behind them. The right in particular wanted to paint a picture of a less violent Fascism, and themselves as having 'loyally dissembled', professing allegiance to Mussolini on the one hand, while remaining sceptical and detached on the other. There was a scramble to erect a firewall that ensured very little scrutiny of the *ventennio Fascista*. The Togliatti amnesty of 1946, by allowing some of the worst crimes to go unpunished, effectively slowed down the democratic process. Fascism was derided as a false religion, a parody of government; anti-Fascism as purifying and redemptive. Mussolini himself, with all his busts and statues, was presented as a figure of ridicule. The 'redeemed' reinvented themselves as left-wing intellectuals. The line between history and memory, too painful and too damaging to dwell on, became blurred.

What was conveniently forgotten, however, was that for those twenty years, Mussolini had been revered by many, perhaps most, Italians with an almost mystical devotion. His genius had been to understand that faith allows people to really believe that mountains can be moved. 'Illusion,' as he said long before he came to power, 'is, perhaps, the only reality in life.' He knew how to speak to them, play on their bad sides, their weaknesses and credulity, their scant political education, their tendency to bully and prevaricate and to prize above all the appearance of things. *Mussolinismo* was a rite, a liturgy. And while social reforms were changing the lives of many Italians, they enjoyed the sense of success, the sporting triumphs, the paid holidays, the feeling that they had joined the Great Powers, that Italy belonged to them, 'the aristocracy of healthy ordinary people' and not to the decaying nobility. They were proud to be Italians. Mussolini's error was to be seduced by Hitler and allow himself to be convinced that weak, impoverished Italy could actually have any sway over a country as large and powerful as Germany; and to misread the Italians' aversion to racism, and their attachment to the '*spirito borghese*', the comforts and reassurance of bourgeois life. They had not wanted to be warriors, new men, or breeders of little soldiers.

Yet not quite all Italians, it turned out, wanted to put the Fascist years behind them. The monarchy had gone, a new constitution was in place, Italy had joined NATO and become a democracy and a successful industrial country, but the sense of power and entitlement experienced by a whole generation who had known nothing but Fascism was hard to relinquish. Even as the war ended, a far-right Movimento Sociale Italiano was formed among surviving Fascist veterans. Though after 1950 the party changed its name, was absorbed into other groupings, which themselves dissolved then came together in other forms, the spirit of *Mussolinismo* never quite went away. The fortunes of these parties fluctuated over the years, but the elections of March 2018 saw gains for a centre-right coalition that brings together the Fratelli d'Italia, the Lega and Berlusconi's Forza Italia. Of the 630 seats in Rome's Chamber of Deputies, the coalition took 265; in the Senate, it holds 137 of the 315 seats. All far-right candidates insist that they have no thought of returning to the politics of Fascism. Yet many of its worst aspects – nationalism, xenophobia – are to be found on their agendas.

For the fifty years that were left to Edda after the war was over, she resolutely stood apart from Italian politics. But her name and her presence remained beacons for the far right, especially once the photo magazines started publishing stories showing the Mussolinis and the Cianos in a softer, more human light. Edda never stopped believing in her father. For the Italians who mourned him, she was all that Fascism might have been; and, briefly, what it actually was.

Prominent among the photographs that she kept on her grand piano and in her bedroom in Rome were photographs of Mussolini. She told friends that she had hated him, 'really hated him', and that you could only feel deep and proper hatred 'for someone you had once really loved'. But then one day, to a writer who came to interview her, Edda said that her father 'was the only man I ever really loved'.

Acknowledgements

First and foremost I am very grateful to Rachele Mussolini and Gloria Ciano, and to Emma Moriconi, co-author with Edda Negri Mussolini of a family memoir, who all talked to me about the Mussolini and Ciano families. Gloria Ciano's help in particular was invaluable.

I would also like warmly to thank Bill Savadove who, when I was unable to get to Shanghai, provided me with crucial research and information about the city in the 1930s, and helped me track down elusive sources. In Germany, Gerd Stratmann and Ingrid von Rosenberg were as always enormously helpful in every way. Guillermo Gil helped me with Spanish translations. I thank them all very much.

My thanks go to Jacqueline de Chollet, for her permission to quote from her unpublished memoir; Benedetta Polk, for her permission to quote from the papers of her father, Daniele Varè; the di Robilant family, for allowing me to quote from their grandmother's unpublished memoir.

The following people all helped me during the course of my research and I want to thank them: Giovanni Aldobrandini, Giuseppe Aprea, Catherine Bailey, Ludina Barzini, Peter Baring, Luciana Castellina, Mauro Canali, the late Nicola Caracciolo, Orsina Cerulli, Anna Chimenti, Aimee Corsini, Benedetta Craveri, Jonathon Dora Pamphilj, Santa Ercolani, Paul French, Gelasio Gaetani d'Aragona, Jon Halliday, Luigi Lembo, John Moorehead, David Macfadyen, Andrea di Robilant, Filippo di Robilant, Laudomia Pucci, Principe Ruspoli, Marcello Sorgi, Inigo Thomas.

Because of Covid restrictions, access to libraries and archives was extremely limited. I am therefore especially grateful for the help I received from the following people and institutions, without whom I would not have been able to complete this book: Beatrice di Pinto, Marina Turchetti and Daniela Loyola and the Archivio Nazionale dello Stato, Rome; Ignazio Pintus and the Archivio Cantonale of Bellinzona, Ticino; Paola Busonero and the Ministero degli Affari Esteri, Rome; Desirée di Stefano and the Biblioteca Nazionale Centrale di Roma; Carmelina Fiorentino and the Biblioteca del Centro Caprese Ignazio Cerio; Alan Brown and the Bodleian, Oxford; the staff of the Biblioteca Minerva del Senato, Rome; the National Archives, London; the British Library, London; the Swiss Federal Archives, Berne; the Archives of RAI, Rome; the Biblioteca della Camera, Rome; the Biblioteca di Storia Moderna e Contemporanea, Rome.

I paid several visits to the Villa Carpena, the Mussolini family home at Forlì, now a museum, and would like to thank its director, Adele Grana, for all her help.

Richard Bosworth and Anne Chisholm kindly read the book in manuscript and I am extremely grateful to them. I would also like to thank my travelling companions during my research: Miles Morland, Michela Wrong, Guy Slater, Patricia Williams.

All the translations in the book are my own.

As ever, my warmest thanks go to my editors, Poppy Hampson, Jennifer Barth, Pamela Murray, Mary Gaule and Greg Clowes; to my very kind picture editor, Jo Evans, and copy-editor, Alison Tulett; and to my wonderful agent, Clare Alexander.

List of Illustrations

Select Bibliography

Afeltra, G., *La spia che amò Ciano*, Milan, 1993
Agnelli, S., *Vestivamo da marinara*, Rome, 1975
Agostini, B. d', *Colloqui con Rachele Mussolini*, Rome, 1946
Alatri, P., *Mussolini*, Rome, 2004
Alfieri, D., *Dictators Face to Face*, London, 1954
Anfuso, F., *Da Palazzo Venezia al lago di Garda*, Rome, 1950
Ansaldo, G., Il *Giornalista di Ciano 1932–43*, Bologna, 2000
Ansaldo, G., *In viaggio con Ciano*, Rome, n.d.
Antonazzi, G., *Roma città aperta. La citadella sul Gianicolo*, Rome, 1983
Aroma, N., d', *Mussolini segreto*, Rome, 1959
Assia, E. d', *Il lampadario di cristallo*, Rome, 1992
Bacci, A., *Mussolini, il primo sportivo d'Italia*, Rome, 2014
Bastianini, G., *Uomini, Cose, Fatti. Memorie di un ambasciatore*, Milan, 1959
Balabanoff, A., *My Life as a Rebel*, London,1938
Begnac, Y. de, *Palazzo Venezia. Storia di un regime*, Rome, 1950
Behan, T., *The Italian Resistance. Fascists, Guerrillas and the Allies*, London, 2009
Benini, Z., *Il carcere degli Scalzi*, Florence, 1994
Benzoni, G., *La vita ribelle*, Bologna, 1985
Bertoldi, S., *Camicia nera*, Milan, 1994
Bertoldi, S., *I tedeschi in Italia*, Milan, 1964
Bertoldi, S., *L'Ultimo re, l'ultima regina*, Milan, 1992
Bianda, R. et al., *Atleti in camicia nera: Lo sport nell'Italia di Mussolini*, Rome, 1983
Bilski, E. & Braun, E., *Jewish Women and their Salons*, New York, 2005
Black, P., *Ernst Kaltenbrunner: Ideological soldier of the Third Reich*, Princeton, 1984
Bloch, M., *Ribbentrop*, London, 1992
Bosworth, R.J.B., *Claretta: Mussolini's Last Lover*, London, 2017
Bosworth, R.J.B., *Mussolini*, London, 2014
Bosworth, R.J.B., *Mussolini's Italy: Life under the Dictatorship*, New York, 2006

Bosworth, R.J.B., *Mussolini and the Eclipse of Italian Fascism*, New Haven, 2021

Bosworth, R.J.B., *Whispering City: Modern Rome and its Histories*, New Haven, 2011

Bottai, G., *Diario 1935–1944*, Milan, 1982

Bottai, G., *Vent'anni e un giorno*, Milan, 1949

Bottai, M.-G., *Giuseppe Bottai, mio padre*, Milan, 2015

Broggini, R. & Vignanò, M., *I sentieri della memoria nel Locarnese*, Locarno, 2004

Brunetta, G.-P., *Cent'anni di cinema italiano*, Rome, 2003

Burdett, C., *Italian Travel Writing between the Wars*, Oxford, 2007

Canali, M., *Le spie del regime*, Bologna, 2004

Canali, M. & Volpini, C., *Mussolini e i ladri di regime*, Milan, 2019

Caracciolo, N. (ed.), *La mia vita. Edda Mussolini*, Milan, 2001

Caracciolo, N., *Tutti gli uomini del Duce*, Milan, 1982

Carafoli, D. & Bocchini Padiglione, G., *Il Vice-Duce. Arturo Bocchini: capo della polizia Fascista*, Milan, 2003

Casagrande, O., *Quando si spense la note*, Milan, 2018

Caviglia, E., *Diario. Aprile 1925 – Marzo 1945*, Rome, 1952

Cerruti, E., *Ambassador's Wife*, London, 1952

Charles-Roux, F., *Une grande ambassade à Rome, 1919–1925*, Paris, 1961

Cianetti, T., *Memorie del carcere di Verona*, Milan, 1983

Ciano, F., *Quando il nonno fece fucilare Papà*, Milan, 1991

Ciano, G., *Diary. 1937–1943*, London, 2002

Ciano, G., *Diplomatic Papers*, London, 1948

Ciano, G., *Autobiografia*, Milan, 1983

Collie, C., *The reporter and the Warlords*, London, 2013

Colombo, P., *La monarchia Fascista, 1922–40*, Bologna, 2010

Coote, C. R., *Italian Town and Country life*, London, 1925

Cordova, R. (ed.), *Uomini e volti del Fascismo*, Rome, 1980

Corner, P., *The Fascist Party and Popular Opinion in Mussolini's Italy*, Oxford, 2012

Craig, G. A. & Gilbert, F., *The Diplomats 1919–39. Vol 2. The Thirties*, New York, 1965

Curti, E., *Il chiodo a tre punte. Schegge di memoria della figlia segreta del Duce*, Pavia, 2003

Davis, M. S., *Who Defends Rome? The Forty-five Days: July 25 – September 8 1943*, London, 1972

Deakin, F. W., *The Brutal Friendship. Mussolini, Hitler and the Fall of Italian Fascism*, London, 1962

Deakin, F. W., *The Last Days of Mussolini*, London, 1962

Dodd, M., *My Years in Germany*, London, 1939

Dogliani, P., *Il Fascismo degli Italiani: una storia sociale*, Milan, 2008

Dogliani, P., *L'Italia Fascista – 1922–1940*, Milan, 1999

Dolfin, G., *Con Mussolini nella tragedia*, Rome, 1949

Dollmann, E., *The Interpreter*, London, 1967

Dollmann, E., *Call me Coward*, London, 1956

Dosi, G., *Il mostro e il detective*, Florence, 1973

Douglas, N., *Siren Land*, London, 1911

Ducci, R., *La bella gioventù*, Bologna, 1996

Duggan, C., *Fascist Voices. An Intimate History of Mussolini's Italy*, London, 2012

Dulles, A., *The Secret Surrender*, London, 1966

Dutton, D., *Anthony Eden: A Life and a Reputation*, London, 1997

Emiliani, V., *Il fabbro di Predappio. Vita di Alessandro Mussolini*, Bologna, 2010

Emiliani, V., *Il paese dei Mussolini*, Turin, 1984

Fallaci, O., *L'Italia della dolce vita*, Milan, 2017

Farrell, N. & Mazzuca, G., *Il compagno Mussolini*, Soveria Mannelli, 2013

Fattorini, E., *Pio XI, Hitler e Mussolini. La solitudine di un papa*, Turin, 2007

Felice, R. De, *Storia degli Ebrei Italiani sotto il Fascismo*, Turin, 1961

Felice, R. De, *Mussolini il rivoluzionario 1883–1920*, Turin, 1965

Felice, R. De, *Mussolini il Fascista 1: la conquista del potere 1921–1925*, Turin, 1966

Felice, R. De, *Mussolini il Fascista 11: l'organizzazione dello stato Fascista 1925–1929*, Turin, 1986

Felice, R. De, *Mussolini il duce 1: gli anni di consenso 1929–1936*, Turin, 1974

Felice, R. De, *Mussolini il duce 11: lo stato totalitario 1936–1940*, Turin, 1981

Felice, R. De, *Mussolini l'alleato 1: l'Italia in guerra 1940–1943*, Turin, 1990

Felice, R. De, *Mussolini l'alleato 11: la guerra civile 1943–1945*, Turin, 1997

Festorazzi, R., *Margherita Sarfatti. La donna che inventò Mussolini*, Vicenza, 2010

Forcella, E., *La resistenza in convento*, Turin, 1999

Forgacs, D. & Grindle, S. (eds), *Mass Culture and Italian Society from Fascism to the Cold War*, Bloomington, 2007

François-Poncet, A., *Souvenirs d'une ambassade à Berlin*, Paris, 1947

François-Poncet. A., *Souvenirs d'une ambassade à Rome*, Paris, 1961

Franzinelli, M., *Il Duce e le donne*, Milan, 2013

Franzinelli, M., *I tentacoli dell'OVRA. Agenti, collaboratori e vittime della polizia politica Fascista*, Turin, 1999

Franzinelli, M., *Squadristi, protagonisti e tecnici della violenza Fascista*, Milan, 2003

Franzinelli, M., *Delatori: Spie e confidenti anonimi: l'arma segreta del regime Fascista*, Milan, 2012

French, P., *City of Devils*, London, 2018

Fromm, B., *Blood and Banquets. A Berlin Social Diary*, London, 1943

Fucci, F., *Le polizie di Mussolini. La repressione dell'antiFascismo nel 'ventennio'*, Milan, 1985

Fucci, F., *Ali contro Mussolini*, Milan, 1978

Galeotti, C., *Achille Starace e il vademecum dello stile Fascista*, Catanzaro, 2000

Garnier, J.-P., *Excellences et plumes blanches*, Paris, 1961

Gilmour, D., *The pursuit of Italy*, London, 2011

Goebbels, J., *Diaries 1939–41*, London, 1982

Goebbels, J., *Tagenbücher. 1897–1945*, Hamburg, 1977

Golsan, R. (ed.), *Fascism, Asthetics and Culture*, London, 1992

Gooch, J., *Mussolini's War*, London, 2020

Grandi, D., *Il mio paese. Ricordi autobiografici*, Bologna, 1985

Gravelli, A., *Mussolini anecdotico*, Rome, n.d.

Grayling, A. C. and Whitfield, S., *China: a Literary Companion*, London, 1994

Grazia, V. de, *The Perfect Fascist. A Story of Love, Power and Morality in Mussolini's Italy*, Harvard, 2020

Grazia, V. de, *How Fascism Ruled Women, Italy 1922–1945*, Berkeley, 1992

Grazia, V. de, *The Culture of Consent. Mass Organisation of Leisure in Fascist Italy*, Cambridge, 1981

Grindle, S., Duggan, C. and Pieri, P., *The Cult of the Duce. Mussolini and the Italians*, Manchester, 2013

Guariglia, R., *Ricordi 1922–1946*, Naples, 1950

Guerri, G. B., *Italo Balbo*, Milan, 2013

Guerri, G. B., *Giuseppe Bottai. Un Fascista critico*, Milan, 1976

Guerri, G. B., *Il Malaparte illustrato*, Milan, 1998

Guerri, G. B., *Un amore Fascista. Benito, Edda e Galeazzo*, Milan, 2005

Guerri, G. B., *Galeazzo Ciano. Una vita 1903–1944*, Milan, 1979

Guerri, G. B., *L'Arcitaliano. Vita di Curzio Malaparte*, Milan, 1990

Guerri, G. B., *Fascisti. Gli italiani di Mussolini*, Milan, 1995

Guerri, G. B. (ed.), *Rapporto al Duce*, Milan, 1978

Guspini, U., *L'Orecchio del regime. Le intercettazioni telefoniche al tempo del Fascismo*, Milan, 1973

Hagen, W., *La guerra delle spie*, Milan, 1952

Hahn, E., *China to Me*, New York, 1944

Hay, J., *Popular Film Culture in Fascist Italy*, Indiana, 1987

Hassell, U. von, *Diaries 1938–1944*, London, 2011

Hassell, F. von, *A Mother's War*, Brescia, 1987

Hazzard, S., *Greene on Capri*, London, 2000

Heymann, C. D., *Poor Little Rich Girl. The Life and Legend of Barbara Hutton*, London, 1985

Hibbert, C., *Benito Mussolini*, London, 2008

Hitler's Table Talk, London, 1953

Innocenti, M., *Le signore del Fascismo*, Milan, 2001

Innocenti, M., *Edda contro Ciano. Una storia di odio e amore*, Milan, 2003

Innocenti, M., *Lui e loro. Mussolini e i suoi gerarchi*, Milan, 2012

Innocenti, M., *Ciano il Fascista che sfidò Hitler*, Milan, 2013

Insolera, I., *Roma Fascista nelle fotografie dell'Istituto Luce*, Rome, 2001

Ivone, D., *Raffaele Guariglia tra l'ambasciata a Parigi e gli ultimi 'passi' in diplomazia*, Naples, 2005

Jebb, M., *Tuscan Heritage*, London, 1976

Jocteau, J. C., *Nobili e nobiltà nell'Italia unita*, Rome, 1997

Koon, T. H., *Believe, Obey, Fight. Political Socialization of Youth in Fascist Italy, 1922–43*, London, 1985

Lamb, R., *Mussolini and the British*, London, 1997

Lampson, Sir M., *The Killearn Diaries*, London, 1972

Landy, M., *Fascism in Film*, Princeton, 1986

Leone de Andreis, M., *Capri 1939. L'isola in bianco e nero*, Naples, 2002

Leone de Andreis, M., *Capri 1943. C'era una volta la guerra*, Naples, 2007

Leone de Andreis, M., *Capri 1950. Vita dolce vita*, Naples, n.d.

Lessona, A., *Memorie*, Florence, n.d.

Luciolli, M., *Palazzo Chigi: anni roventi*, Milan, 1976

Ludwig, E., *Talks with Mussolini*, London, 1932

Luna, G. De, *Donne in oggetto. L'antiFascismo nella società italiana.1922–39*, Turin, 1995

Lupano, M. & Vaccari, A. (eds), *Una giornata moderna. Moda e stile nell' Italia Fascista*, Bologna, 2009

Lussu, E., *Marcia su Roma*, Ontario, 1992

Mack Smith, D., *Mussolini*, London, 1981

Magistrato, M., *L'Italia a Berlino 1937–1939*, Milan, 1956

McGaw Smith, H., *Secrets of the Fascist Era*, Illinois, 1975

McLean, E. K., *Mussolini's Children: Race and Elementary Education in Fascist Italy*, London, 2018

Malaparte, C., *Kaputt*, Milan, 2009

Mangilli-Climpson, M., *Men of Heart: Red, White and Green. Italian Anti-Fascists in the Spanish Civil War*, New York, 1985

Mannucci, E., *Il marchese rampante*, Milan, 1998

Marinelli, M. & Adornino, G., *Italy's Encounter with Modern China. Imperial Dreams, Strategic Ambitions*, London, 2014

Mayer, D., *La verità sul processo Verona*, Rome, 1945

Megaro, G., *Mussolini in the Making*, London, 1938

Money, J., *Capri. Island of Pleasure*, London, 1986

Monticone, A., *Fascismo al microfono. Radio e politica in Italia 1924–45*, Rome, 1978

Moseley, R., *Mussolini's Shadow*, London, 1999

Mussolini, B., *Pensieri pontini e sardi*, Rome, 2019

Mussolini, E., *My Truth*, New York, 1976

Mussolini, E. Negri, *Donna Rachele. Mia nonna, la moglie di Benito Mussolini*, Bologna, 2015

Mussolini, Edvige, *Mio fratello Benito*, Florence, 1957

Mussolini, R., *The Real Mussolini*, Farnborough, 1973

Mussolini, R., *La mia vita con Mussolini*, Milan, 1948

Mussolini, R., *Benito, il mio uomo*, Milan, 1958

Mussolini, R., *Benito ed'io. Una vita per l'Italia*, Paris, 1948

Mussolini, Rachele, *Mia Nonna e il Duce*, Milan, 2011

Mussolini, Romano, *Benito Mussolini: apologia per mio padre*, Bologna, 1969

Mussolini, V., *Vita con mio padre*, Milan, 1957

Mussolini, V., *Mussolini: The Tragic Women in his Life*, London, 1973

Navarra, Q., *Memorie del cameriere di Mussolini*, Milan, 1972

Ortona, E., *Diplomazia di guerra. Diari 1937–43*, Bologna, 1993

Ottaviani, G., *Cucina di guerra: ricette e rimedi al tempo del Fascismo*, Rome, 2014

Ottaviani, G., *Il controllo della pubblicità sotto il Minculpop*, Rome, 2016

Packard, R. & E., *Balcony Empire: Fascist Italy at War*, London, 1943

Page, E. N., *L'Americano di Roma*, Milan, 1950

Papa, E. R., *Fascismo e cultura*, Venice, 1974

Patrizi, C., *Quegli anni*, Milan, 2007

Pellegrinotti, M., *Sono stato il carceriere di Ciano*, Milan, 1975

Pensotti, A., *Le Italiane*, Milan, 1999

Petacci, C., *Verso il disastro. Mussolini in Guerra. Diari 1939–1940*, Milan, 2011

Petacci, M., *Chi ama è perduto – mia sorella Claretta*, Guardolo di Trento, 1988

Petacco, A., *Pavolini: l'ultima raffica di Salò*, Milan, 1982

Petacco, A., *Come eravamo negli anni di guerra. 1940–45*, Novara, 1984

Petacco, A., *Il prefetto di ferro*, Rome, 1975

Petacco, A., *Riservato al Duce. I segreti del regime conservati nell'archivio personale del Duce*, Milan, 1979

Phillips, W., *Ventures in Diplomacy*, London, 1955

Pirelli, A., *Taccuini 1922–43*, Bologna, 1984

Pizzo, R., *Panni sporchi e Cinecittà. Scandali, misteri, amori e dolori della Hollywood italiano*, Florence, 2008

Poliakov, L., *La condition des Juifs en France sous l'occupation italienne*, Paris, 1946

Quazza, G. (ed.), *Fascismo e società*, Turin, 1973

Rienzo, E. Di, *Ciano*, Rome, 2018

Ripa di Meana, M. & Meccucci, G., *Virginia Agnelli. Madre e farfalla*, Bologna, 2010

Rosengarten, F., *The Italian AntiFascist Press 1919–45*, Cleveland, 1968

Sachs, H., *Music in Fascist Italy*, London, 1987

Sandomenico, C., *Donne di Capri – passioni, arte, stravaganze*, Naples, n.d.

Sarazani, F., *Alla corte del Duce: l'aristocrazia romana e il Fascismo*, Rome, 2015

Sarfatti, M., *Dux*, Milan, 1926

Savio, F., *Cinecittà anni trenta*, Rome, 1979

Schmidt, P., *Hitler's Interpreter*, London, 1951

Schnapp, J. T., *Staging Fascism*, Stanford, 1996

Scrivener, J., *Inside Rome with the Germans*, New York, 1945

Seldes, G., *Sawdust Hitler*, London, 1935

Senise, C., *Quando ero capo della polizia. 1940–43*, Rome, 1946

Sergeant, H., *Shanghai*, London, 1991

Sermoneta, V., Duchessa di, *Sparkle Distant World*, London, 1947

Serrano Suñer, R., *Entre les Pyrénées et Gibraltar*, Geneva, 1947

Settimelli, E., *Edda contro Benito*, Rome, 1952

Sheridan, M., *Romans: Their Lives and Times*, London, 1994

Shirer, W. L., *This is Berlin*, London, 1989

Shirer, W. L., *Berlin Diary*, London, 1941

Signoretti, A., *'La stampa' in camicia nera 1932–43*, Rome, 1967

Simoni, L., *Berlino ambasciata d'Italia 1939–43*, Rome, n.d.

Sofri, G., *Gandhi in Italia*, Bologna, 1988

Sorgi, M., *Il grande dandy*, Milan, 2011

Sorgi, M., *Edda Ciano e il communista*, Milan, 2009

Spinosa, A., *I figli del Duce*, Milan, 1983

Spinosa, A., *Alla corte del Duce*, Milan, 2000

Spinosa, A., *Edda: una tragedia Italiana*, Milan, 1993

Stille, A., *Benevolence and Betrayal. Five Italian Jewish Families Under Fascism*, London, 1992

Susmel, D. (ed.), *Carteggio Arnaldo-Benito Mussolini*, Florence, 1954

Susmel, D., *Vita sbagliata di Galeazzo Ciano*, Florence, 1962

Tamagna, F., *Italy's Interests and Policies in the Far East*, New York, 1941

Tannenbaum, E. R., *The Fascist Experience: Italian Society and Culture 1922–45*, London, 1972

Trevelyan, R., *Rome '44. The Battle for the Eternal City*, New York, 1981

Treves, P., *What Mussolini Did to Us*, London, 1940

Varè, D., *Laughing Diplomat*, London, 1938

Vecchioni, D., *Le spie del Fascismo*, Florence, 2005

Venè, G. F., *Coprifuoco*, Milan, 1989

Venè, G. F., *Mille lire al mese*, Milan, 1988

Venè, G. F., *Il processo di Verona*, Milan, 1963

Verdone, M., *Feste e spettacoli a Roma*, Rome, 1993

Vergani, O., *Ciano, una lunga confessione*, Milan, 1974

Welles, S., *The Time for Decision*, New York, 1944

Wood, F., *No Dogs and Not Many Chinese. Treaty Port Life in China 1843–1943*, London, 1998

Woodhead, H. G., *A Journalist in China*, London, 1934

Zachariae, G., *Mussolini si confessa*, Rome, 1948

Zangrandi, R., *Il lungo viaggio attraverso il Fascismo*, Milan, 1962

Zanotti-Bianco, U., *La mia Roma. Diario 1943–44*, Rome, 2011

Zucotti, S., *The Italians and the Holocaust. Persecution, Rescue and Survival*, London, 1987

Zucotti, S., *Under his Very Windows. The Vatican & the Holocaust in Italy*, New Haven, 2000

SELECTED ARTICLES

Bosworth, R.J.B., 'Per necessità famigliare: hypocrisy and corruption in Fascist Italy', *European History Quarterly*, July 2000, Vol 30

Edwards, P. G., 'The Foreign Office and Fascism 1924–29', *Journal of Contemporary History*, 1970, Vol 5

Gentile, E., 'La politica estera del partito Fascista 1920–1930', *Storia Contemporanea*. 1995, Vol 26

Giuliani, G. et al., 'Tavola rotonda: vissualizzare la razza e costruire la bellezza in Italia 1922–2018', *Italian Cultural Studies*, 2018, Vol 72

Grindle, S., 'Laughter Under Fascism: Humour and ridicule in Italy 1922–43', *History Workshop Journal*, 2015, Vol 79

Jocteau, G., 'I nobili del Fascismo', *Studi Storici*, 2004, Vol 3

Kesevich, C., 'The British Labour Press and Italian Fascism 1922 –1925', *Journal of Contemporary History*, 1975, Vol 10

Lefebvre, F., 'Dino Grandi, la "carriera" e la "Fascistizzazione" del Ministero degli Esteri', *Nuova Rivista Storica*, 2012, Vol 2

Luzzatto, S., 'The political culture of Fascist Italy', *Contemporary European History*, 1999, Vol 8

Mallett, R., 'Fascist Foreign Policy and Official Italian Views of Anthony Eden in the 1930s', *The Historical Journal*, 2000, Vol 43

Newham, F., 'The White Russians of Shanghai', *History Today*, 2005, Vol 55

Niccoletti, A., 'The Decline and Fall of Edda Ciano', *Collier's*, 1946, 20 & 27 April

Ortona, E., 'L'esodo da Londra dell'ambasciata Italiana nel 1940', *Storia Contemporanea*, 1990, Vol 21

Serri, M., 'The Redeemed: Intellectuals who gained a second life', *Telos*, 2007, No 139

Stone, M., 'Staging Fascism: the exhibition of the Fascist revolution', *Journal of Contemporary History*, 1993, April

Zuccotti, S., 'Pope Pius XII and the Rescue of Jews in Italy: Evidence of a Papal directive?', *Holocaust and Genocide Studies*, 2004, Vol 18

Zuccotti, S., 'L'Osservatore Romano and the Holocaust 1939–1945', *Holocaust and Genocide Studies*, 2003, Vol 17

SELECTED SOURCES

The literature on Mussolini, his family and the Fascist years is vast and the Archivio Centrale dello Stato (ACS) in Rome has an enormous holding on the dictator and Fascism generally; in particular the Segreteria particolare del Duce carteggio riservato and ordinario, Ministero dell'Interno; Ministero della Cultura Popolare. The following are the historians whose works have been most consulted in this book: R.J.B. Bosworth; Mauro Canali; F. W. Deakin; Christopher Duggan; Renzo De Felice; Mimmo Franzinelli; Giordano Bruno Guerri; Christopher Hibbert; Denis Mack Smith; Ray Moseley; Arrigo Petacco; Antonio Spinosa; Eugenio Di Rienzo. The Mussolinis themselves were prolific writers. Books by Mussolini himself, his wife Rachele, his sons Vittorio and Romano, his granddaughters Rachele and Edda, all feature largely, as do, of course, the memoirs of Edda herself. Mussolini's complete works are to be found in thirty-six volumes in Opera Omnia (eds E. and D. Susmel) published between 1951 and 1962.

Notes

Chapter one

p. 3 'I never felt liked ...' See *Epoca*, 14 September 1974
p. 5 Edda's grandmother ... Rachele Mussolini, 1948, p10
p. 5 Dinner was often ... See Christopher Hibbert, *Benito Mussolini*, 2008
p. 7 he began to explore the art of propaganda ... Balabanoff, 1938
p. 7 He liked to think of himself ... Megaro, 1938, p. 75
p. 9 He was ruthless ... Edda Negri Mussolini, 2015, p. 50
p. 9 His own articles ... See Farrell & Mazzuca, 2013
p. 9 His voice veered ... Megaro, 1938, p. 321
p. 9 Alessandro's health ... Emiliani, 2010, p. 126
p. 11 Rachele's hair ... Balabanoff, 1938, p. 107
p. 12 A small boy ... Spinosa, 1993
p. 14 Writing most of *Avanti* ... See Bosworth, 2014
p. 14 Courted by both sides ... Gilmour, 2011, p. 287
p. 15 Neutrality, he told his sister ... Edvige Mussolini, 1957, p. 50
p. 15 He now kept a revolver ... Caracciolo, 2001, p. 101
p. 16 As Rachele described it ... Rachele Mussolini, 1958, p. 45
p. 16 In April 1915 ... Gilmour, 2011, p. 287

Chapter two

p. 17 'I live for tomorrow ...' Farrell & Mazzuca, 2013, p. 215
p. 18 Taking Edda with her ... See Edda Negri Mussolini, 2015
p. 18 At three o'clock ... Spinosa, 2000, p. 106
p. 18 Edda, at four and a half ... Rachele Mussolini, 1958, p. 46
p. 19 When he returned ... Edda Negri Mussolini, 2015, p. 17
p. 19 the police became involved ... Grindle et al., 2013, p. 63
p. 20 One day, seeing ... Rachele Mussolini, 1948, p. 48
p. 20 Many years later ... See Caracciolo (ed.), 2001
p. 20 A photograph ... See Guerri, 2005
p. 20 The government refused ... Gilmour, 2011, p. 89
p. 21 To deny these men ... Emiliani, 1984, p. 126

p. 24 She gathered up the children . . . Edda Negri Mussolini, 2015, p. 83

p. 24 Edda became distraught . . . Guerri, 2005, p. 21

p. 24 Mussolini had started . . . See Bosworth, 2017

p. 25 They spent most of their . . . Farrell & Mazzuca, 2013, p. 251

p. 26 The first *squadristi* . . . See Franzinelli, 2003

p. 27 Italy, he wrote . . . Alatri, 2004, p. 69

p. 28 On 12 December . . . Hibbert, 2008, p. 44

p. 28 There were yet more . . . Sarfatti, 1926, p. 202

p. 28 Another was Italo Balbo . . . See Guerri, 2013

p. 29 For Edda . . . See Edda Mussolini, 1977

p. 29 By the summer of . . . Tannenbaum, 1972, p. 76

p. 32 By train, by car . . . Spinosa, 2000, p. 35

p. 32 Edda and Vittorio . . . See Edda Mussolini, 1977

Chapter three

p. 33 There was a profound . . . See McLean, 2018

p. 34 Rome itself . . . See Insolera, 2001

p. 35 And there was the Vatican . . . See Bosworth, 2011

p. 36 He intended, he announced . . . Antonio Munoz, *Roma di Mussolini*, 1935, p. 59

p. 36 On 16 November . . . Mack Smith, 1981, p. 58

p. 36 After his first . . . Lussu, 1992, p. 81

p. 37 The themes of blood . . . Simonetta Falasca-Zamponi, 'Of Story Tellers', *Social Science History*, 1 Dec. 1998, p. 434

p. 37 'Our myth . . .' Koon, 1985, p. 9

p. 38 There was talk of him . . . Rachele Mussolini, 1948, p. 50

p. 40 As one British visitor . . . Coote, 1925, p. 241

p. 41 The family spent the summers . . . Rachele Mussolini, 2011, p. 41

p. 41 He had asked for . . . Tannenbaum, 1972, p. 43

p. 42 To contain the violence . . . See Vecchioni, 2005

p. 42 In pursuit of creating . . . Papa, 1974, p. 268; see also Festorazzi, 2010

p. 43 He called her Vela . . . Spinosa, 2000, p. 34

p. 43 'Culture', in Gentile's credo . . . R.J.B. Bosworth, 'Mussolini's Cultural Revolution', *Journal of Contemporary History*, July/October 1972

p. 44 No proof was ever . . . Guerri, 1995, p. 106

p. 44 He also brought in a decree . . . Treves, 1940, p. 12

p. 46 Fascism was back in control . . . Richard Washburn Child (ed.), *Benito Mussolini. My autobiography*, 1928 p. 8

p. 46 After one particularly . . . Caracciolo (ed.), 2001. p. 7

p. 47 The school Mussolini chose . . . see Edda Negri Mussolini, 2015

p. 48 He received a slight wound . . . Vittorio Mussolini, 1957, p. 32

p. 50 But Edda and Rachele . . . See Vecchioni, 2005

p. 50 A career rising . . . Carafoli & Padiglione, 2003, p. 47

p. 50 Seldom rising . . . See Franzinelli, 2012; see also Canali, 2004

p. 52 Meanwhile, in Rome . . . see Guspini, 1973

p. 52 Hand in hand . . . Adriano del Pont, *I lager di Mussolini*, 1975, p. 35

p. 52 Mussolini, constantly receiving . . . Spinosa, 1983, p. 39

Chapter four

p. 54 Edda was . . . ACS Carta Riservata del Duce, F22b113

p. 54 She blushed easily . . . Renata Broggini, *La Famiglia Mussolini. I colloqui di Edda Ciano con lo psichiatra Svizzero Répond*, n.d., p. 358

p. 54 wrote one reporter . . . *Chicago Daily News*, 24 June 1926

p. 55 One summer they wrote . . . Spinosa, 1983, p. 35

p. 55 When they saw photographs . . . Rachele Mussolini, 1958, p. 99

p. 55 At first, it nuzzled . . . Vittorio Mussolini, 1957, p. 36

p. 55 Conradi, who had . . . ACS Carta Riservata, F22b 113

p. 56 At eighteen, Edda . . . *Il Corriere della Sera*, 23 January 1929

p. 57 Occasionally, if the road . . . Rachele Mussolini, 2011, p. 52

p. 57 Rachele was driven . . . Rachele Mussolini, 1973, p. 150

p. 58 There had already been . . . Grindle et al., 2013, p. 41

p. 58 'an aristocratic plebeian . . .' Sarfatti, 1926, p. 10

p. 58 Now, alone . . . Bosworth, 2017, p. 64

p. 58 Magda Brand . . . see Navarra, 1972; see also Nino d'Aroma, *Mussolini segreto*, 1958, p. 208

p. 60 To keep the singing . . . See Carafoli & Padiglione, 2003; see also ACS. *Un' altra Italia nell'Italia del Fascismo*, 2006

p. 60 upstaged by a mafioso . . . See Petacco, 1975

p. 61 Nothing of what Mussolini . . . See Dogliani, 2008; see also Petacco, 1979 and 1982; Caracciolo, 1982

p. 63 Then there was . . . Guerri, 1976, p. 107

p. 63 as the most devoted . . . Bottai,1982, p. 6

p. 63 And there was . . . See Grandi, 1985

p. 63 Some were freemasons . . . Bertoldi, 1992, p. 145

p. 64 Arnaldo remained . . . See Susmel (ed.),1954

p. 65 It was also . . . Guerri, 1995, p. 148

p. 65 With the signing of the Concordat . . . De Felice, 1974, p. 227

Chapter five

p. 67 He was not present . . . Edda Negri Mussolini, 2015, p. 107

p. 68 Bruno and Vittorio . . . See Zangrandi, 1962

p. 68 Most evenings . . . See Vittorio Mussolini, 1957

p. 69 The summers were . . . *Prager Tagblat*, 23 July 1929

p. 70 Edda found him . . . Caracciolo (ed.), 2001, p. 30

p. 70 Evidently preferring . . . ACS Carta Riservata, F22b

p. 71 Galeazzo Ciano . . . See Moseley 1999; Di Rienzo, 2018; Guerri, 1979

p. 71 His mother Carolina . . . See Festorazzi, 2010

p. 71 As the only one with money . . . See Vergani, 1974

p. 72 In 1926 . . . See Varè, 1938; see also unpublished family papers

p. 73 Two years later . . . See Maria Rosa Oliver, *La vida cotidiana*, 1969

p. 73 Ciano leant across . . . Edda Mussolini, 1977

p. 73 After this matter-of-fact . . . Spinosa, 1993, p. 66

p. 73 Edda toyed with . . . Edda Negri Mussolini, 2015, p. 131

p. 74 Vittorio and Bruno . . . Edvige Mussolini, 1957, p. 125

p. 74 In her diary . . . Rachele Mussolini, 1948, p. 71

p. 74 The one person who . . . Guerri, 2005, p. 62

p. 74 Edda was, in short . . . Edda Negri Mussolini, 2015, p. 131

p. 75 Presents began to arrive . . . ACS Carta Riservata, F22b113; see also *Il Corriere della Sera*, 25 April 1930

p. 75 Edda wore a pale . . . *Il Popolo*, 16 May 1930

p. 76 Edda, with a veil . . . *L'Illustrazione Italiana*, 4 May 1930

p. 76 Her witnesses were . . . See Di Rienzo, 2018

p. 77 Edda, healthy, virtuous . . . See Spinosa, 1983

p. 77 When in Milan . . . Angela Curti, *Oggi*, Nov/Dec 1949

p. 78 But her parents' . . . Broggini, *La famiglia Mussolini*, n.d.

Chapter six

p. 79 While Ciano waved . . . Spinosa,1983, p. 87

p. 79 He took them . . . Varè family papers

p. 79 Skyscrapers stood . . . Sergeant,1991, p. 19

p. 80 'Shanghai,' wrote the reporter . . . see Hahn, 1944

p. 80 The Italian consulate . . . ACS. Carte Riservate. b115

p. 81 Italy was looking . . . Ministero degli Affari Esteri. Ministero Estero Rapporto 1870–1953, Busta 191

p. 81 What Edda discovered . . . See Wood, 1998

p. 82 Though very modest . . . Ministero degli Affari Esteri. Rapporto diplomatico Cina-Busta 99; see also Orazio Coco, 'The penetration of Italian Fascism', *The International History Review*, 23 April 2020

p. 83 Away from the frenetic . . . See French, 2018; see also Julia Boyd, *A Dance with the Dragon*, 2012; Shirley Ann Smith, *Imperial Designs*, 2012

p. 84 Daniel Varè observed . . . Family papers

p. 85 Known for his . . . see Woodhead, 1934

p. 86 Then she discovered . . . *North China Herald*, 1 October 1930

p. 87 She learnt to deal . . . see Pensotti, 1999

p. 87 Signing himself . . . Telegrams of 8 February 1931 and 1 September 1931

p. 87 Every day, Arnaldo . . . Edda Negri Mussolini, 2015, p. 140

p. 88 Not long after reaching . . . Telegram of 20 April 1931

p. 88 Sending her . . . ACS. Segreteria particolare del Duce. b115

p. 89 Mussolini was extremely ... ACS. Segreteria particolare del Duce. b11

p. 90 But on 18 January ... See Tamagna,1941

p. 91 It was in the Cathay ... *Oggi*, 10 September 1931

p. 93 Edda would deflect ... Edda Mussolini, 1977, p. 76

p. 94 A report sent back ... Ministero degli Affari Esteri. Rapporto diplomatico Cina-Pekino, Busta 100

p. 94 With Ciano kept ... See Hui-Ian Koo, *An Autobiography*, 1943

p. 95 A letter full of ... Ministero degli Affari Esteri. Rapporto diplomatico Cina-Pekino, Busta 170

p. 96 Orders finally came ... Spinosa, 1983, p. 91

Chapter seven

p. 100 In the new Foro ... Burdett, 2007, p. 34; Munoz, 1935

p. 102 In the Villa Torlonia ... Vittorio Mussolini, 1957, p. 57

p. 102 As reluctant as ever ... See Rachele Mussolini, 2011

p. 103 To the pleasure ... Sofri, 1988, p. 70

p. 104 Mussolini ate rapidly ... See Navarra, 1972

p. 106 Even the young ... See Dogliani, 2008; see also Tannenbaum, 1972

p. 106 Having created ... *Gente*, 19 June 1973

p. 107 To help Italians feel ... Bosworth, 2006, p. 210

p. 107 The new vogue ... See Grindle et al., 2013

p. 108 After this came ... Emiliani, 1984, p. 77

p. 109 To the German writer ... Ludwig, 1932, p. 26

p. 109 He had said as much ... See Festorazzi, 2010

p. 109 Mussolini once told ... See De Felice, 1974

p. 110 Several of these had been ... See Bosworth, 2017

p. 112 What one remembered ... See Ortona, 1993

p. 112 She hated it ... See Vergani, 1974

p. 112 Contacts between ... De Felice, 1974, p. 421

p. 114 He had, however ... Petacco, 1979, p. 147

p. 115 Edda fulfilled her mission ... ACS Carta Riservata, b115

p. 116 She reported that ... Edda Mussolini, 1977, p. 114

p. 117 Ciano's proposals ... Guerri, 1979, p. 82

p. 117 In September, the Presidential ... See Elsa D'Annibale, 'Ciano e la nascita del Ministero', *Nuova Rivista Storica*, Mar/Apr 2017

p. 117 *Fascistizzazione* was to ... De Felice, 1974, p. 182; see also 'Today Italy. An American Enquiry', September 1929

Chapter eight

p. 118 A very small number ... See Sorgi, 2011

p. 119 As the half-English ... Sermoneta, 1947, p. 94

p. 119 The collaboration ... Colombo, 2010, p. 169

p. 119 Crown Prince ... Bertoldi, 1992, p. 58

p. 120 As one American . . . Sermoneta, 1947, p. 118

p. 120 With these various forces . . . Ripa di Meana & Meccucci, 2010, p. 24

p. 120 It became expedient . . . See Gian Carlo Jocteau, 'I nobili del Fascismo', *Studi Storici*, Jul/Sep 2004

p. 120 George Nelson Page . . . See Page, 1950

p. 122 Edda was certainly . . . See Lupano & Vaccari, 2009

p. 123 In his new offices . . . See de Begnac, 1950

p. 124 Having studied . . . See Ottaviani, 2016

p. 126 Malaparte was a . . . See Agnelli, 1975

p. 126 He allowed himself . . . Guerri, 1998, p. 33; see also pp. 56, 112, 179

p. 126 For the subtitle . . . Guerri, 1990, p. 102

p. 128 The Palazzo Colonna . . . ACS Ministero dell'Interno. PolPol. Fasc. Pers. F320; See also Ducci, 1996, p. 195

p. 129 The princess, wrote . . . See Malaparte, 2009

p. 129 To their friends . . . Innocenti, 2001, p. 22; see also Moseley, 1999

p. 129 But since Rome thrived . . . ACS Ministero dell'Interno. PolPol. Fasc. Pers. 298

p. 129 As an obedient Fascist . . . ACS Ministero dell'Interno. PolPol. Fasc. Pers. 431

p. 130 Relations between . . . Guerri, 2005, p. 140

p. 130 He would have wished her . . . See Spinosa, 1993

p. 130 When asked . . . *Oggi*, 10 September 1959

Chapter nine

p. 132 Fascism, as Mussolini . . . See Ruth Ben Ghiat, *La cultura Fascista*, 2000

p. 133 Since youth . . . McLean, 2018, p. 38

p. 133 After a brief moment . . . See de Grazia, 1981 and 1992

p. 133 In place of suffrage . . . See Dogliani, 1999; see also De Luna, 1995

p. 135 Men, women and children . . . See Lupano & Vaccari, 2009

p. 137 As Federale . . . Schnapp, 1996, p. 49

p. 138 Of all the activities . . . Bacci, 2014, p. 56; see also Patrizia Dogliani, 'Sport & Fascism', *JMIS*, Vol 5, Fall 2000

p. 139 After his triumphant . . . See Caracciolo, 1982; see also Guerri, 2013

p. 141 He was a man . . . See Galeotti, 2000

p. 141 Bocchini was now . . . Dollmann, 1967, p. 52

p. 142 Bocchini's fief . . . Franzinelli, 1999, p. 147

p. 142 Bocchini visited . . . ACS Ministero dell'Interno, PolPol 241

Chapter ten

p. 146 Mussolini was . . . De Felice, 1974, p. 569; See also the *Observer*, 24 July 1932

p. 147 Under their desks . . . Vittorio Mussolini, 1957, p. 306

p. 147 At seven thirty that evening . . . See Leone de Andreis, 2002

p. 148 The reaction from the . . . See Lamb, 1997

p. 148 The Italians rapidly . . . See Packard, 1943

p. 149 When it was noticed . . . Trevelyan, 1981, p. 342

p. 149 A delegate from . . . Caroline Moorehead, *Dunant's Dream*, 1998, p. 310

p. 150 Ciano, Vittorio . . . Canali & Volpini, 2019, p. 84

p. 152 Later, Lord Perth . . . David MacFadyen (ed.), *Eric Drummond and his legacies*, 2019, p. 25

p. 152 A British journalist . . . Stephen Potter, *New Statesman*, 20 April 1935

p. 152 But as General . . . Gooch, 2020, p. 33

p. 153 The *Frankfurter Zeitung* . . . 4 June 1936

p. 154 Soon after Edda's arrival . . . Fromm, 1943, p. 192

p. 155 Edda herself said . . . Moseley, 1999, p. 29

p. 155 Goering took her . . . Edda Mussolini, 1977, p. 143

p. 155 footnote . . . Malaparte, 2009, p. 316

p. 156 She left immediately . . . *Sächsische Volkszeitung*, 1 July 1936

p. 157 But Anna Maria . . . Spinosa, 1983, p. 117

p. 157 Anna Maria had . . . Vittorio Mussolini, 1957, p. 68

p. 157 Goering then held a ball . . . François-Poncet, 1947, p. 265

p. 159 A vicious militia leader . . . Moseley, 1999, p. 27

p. 160 As for Edda . . . Spinosa, 1983, p. 145

p. 161 For his part . . . Anfuso, 1950, p. 24

Chapter eleven

p. 163 By 1936, the old . . . F. L. D'Ovidio, 'Dino Grandi', *Nuova Rivista Storica*, Maggio/Giugno, 2012

p. 163 But in practice . . . See Ducci, 1996

p. 163 He was 'elegant' . . . Innocenti, 2012, p. 39

p. 164 (But as an unsigned . . .) ACS Min dell'Int, PolPol. Materia Ministero degli Esteri. Busta 169

p. 164 Of all Ciano's . . . Sorgi, 2011, p. 113

p. 164 Lanza's life . . . ACS.Min Dir Gen Pub Sic, PolPol. Fasc. Pers. 700

p. 165 When speeches were shown . . . See Bastianini, 1959

p. 165 Ciano was heard to . . . Ramon Serrano Suñer, *Entre Hendaya y Gibraltar*, 1973, p. 325

p. 165 There were rumours . . . ACS Min dell'Int, PolPol. Ministero degli Esteri, Busta 169

p. 166 He came away more . . . Phillips, 1955, p. 92

p. 166 Another important diplomat . . . von Hassell, 2011, p. ix

p. 166 The Petit Trianon . . . See Page, 1950

p. 167 As Rachele said . . . *Oggi*, 24 June 1947

p. 167 The centre of power . . . Vergani, 1974, p. 52

p. 168 When the Duke . . . See Heymann, 1985

p. 169 Many years earlier . . . Money, 1986, p. 56

p. 169 As Norman Douglas . . . See Norman Douglas, *Footnote on Capri*, 1992.

p. 170 With generous funds . . . See de Leone Andreis, 2002

p. 171 Pagano, as he . . . Bertoldi, 1964, p. 233

p. 172 Things got so bad . . . See Dosi, 1973

p. 172 Dosi's behaviour became . . . ACS. Personale versamento.1973. Fasc Dosi b226

p. 174 Edda was only one . . . Author interview with Giuseppe Aprea

p. 174 In keeping with . . . Guerri, 1990, p. 111

p. 175 They spied on Edda . . . See Sandomenico n.d.

p. 176 And they spied . . . ACS Min del Int, PolPol. Fasc. Pers. 205

p. 176 Because there had never . . . Quazza (ed.), 1973, p. 232

p. 176 The Duce was . . . Hay, 1987, p. 223

p. 177 'Where is the . . . ' . . . Grindle et al., 2013, p. 131

p. 177 Something of this frenetic . . . See Brunetta, 2003; see also Landy, 1986

p. 178 Drugs, orgies . . . see Pizzo, 2008

p. 178 And, in the scramble . . . See Maria Casalini (ed.), *Donne e Cinema*, 2016; see also Stephen Grindle & Michele Zegna, 'Art, entertainment and politics', *Historical Journal of Film, Radio and TV*, Vol 40, 2020

p. 179 The Italians loved . . . De Luna, 1995, p. 266

p. 179 Cinecittà became a goldmine . . . ACS Min dell'Int, PolPol. Fasc. Pers. 183

p. 179 Soon after his return . . . Spinosa, 1983, p. 27

p. 181 'We must,' noted Ciano . . . Diary, 27 August 1937

p. 181 Steel-helmeted . . . Fromm, 1943, p. 221

p. 182 Though Mussolini's reply . . . Schmidt, 1951, p. 73

p. 182 It was left to . . . Dodd, 1939, p. 182

Chapter twelve

p. 183 Mussolini learnt . . . See Guerri, 2005

p. 184 All Rome knew . . . See Page, 1950

p. 186 Foreign newspapers . . . Spinosa, 1993, p. 142

p. 186 A reciprocal unease . . . De Felice, 1974, p. 807

p. 187 From anonymous letters . . . ACS Min dell'Int, PolPol. Materia, Busta 87

p. 188 From an OVRA . . . ACS Min dell'Int, PolPol. Materia, Busta 87

p. 189 With Claretta . . . Bosworth, 2017, p. 68

p. 189 Wire taps . . . Innocenti, 2001, p. 48

p. 189 Mussolini had then . . . Canali & Volpini, 2019, p. 170

p. 190 I would accept . . . See Rachele Mussolini, 2011

p. 191 Mussolini received . . . ACS Min dell'Int, PolPol. Materia, Germania, Busta 41

p. 192 'These dictators' . . . Lamb, 1997, p. 183

p. 193 Hitler's interpreter ... Schmidt, 1951, p. 80

p. 193 A gala dinner ... See Page, 1950; see also Sermoneta, 1947

p. 194 The 'Italian invasion' ... See De Felice,1981

p. 196 'This is an insult' ... Vittorio Mussolini,1957, p. 319

Chapter thirteen

p. 197 A German musicologist ... Sachs, 1987, p. 190

p. 197 the idea of the 'pure' ... See De Felice, 1961

p. 197 It started with ... Tannenbaum, 1972, p. 242

p. 197 Jews, warned the Second ... Koon, 1985, p. 153

p. 198 However, he also ... Ciano, Diary, 6 September 1937

p. 198 And the American ambassador ... Phillips, 1955, p. 121

p. 199 and recommended that Jews ... *Il Lambello*, 10–25 June 1941

p. 199 Talking to Claretta ... Bosworth, 2017, p. 68

p. 199 Government offices were inundated ... ACS MinCulPop. Gabinetto B. b196

p. 200 Mussolini had also chosen ... Dogliani, 2008, p. 306

p. 201 Sometimes warm, sometimes ... De Felice, 1981, p. 513

p. 201 It would later be ... See Craig & Gilbert, 1965

p. 202 Malaparte wrote ... See Malaparte, 2009

p. 203 France, he told ... Ciano, Diary, 13 May 1938

p. 203 The man chosen ... François-Poncet, 1947, p. 295

p. 203 New hopes for ... Packard, 1943, p. 43

p. 204 Ciano's ploy ... Shirer, 1941, p. 123

p. 204 The British came bearing ... See Paul Stafford, 'The Chamberlain-Halifax visit to Rome', *The English History Journal*, Vol 98, 1983

p. 204 Having been informed ... National Archives, PREM 1/327

p. 205 Later, Sir Percy ... National Archives, FO 1011/204

p. 206 Even as Madrid fell ... Ciano, Diary, 23 February 1938

p. 207 Mussolini, still wavering ... Guerri, 1995, p. 232

p. 208 When Ciano returned ... Lamb, 1997, p. 253; see also Bloch,1992

p. 209 'possessed by the demon' ... Ciano, Diary, 11 August 1939

p. 209 Ciano took with him ... Ansaldo, 2000, p. 150

p. 209 'He has grown' ... Patrizi, 2007, p. 180

p. 212 On Capri ... Leone de Andreis, 2002, p. 144

p. 213 The unreliable Malaparte ... Guerri, 2005, p. 166

p. 214 Mussolini, he wrote ... De Felice, 1981, p. 802

Chapter fourteen

p. 216 For the next nine ... Spinosa, 2000, p. 284

p. 216 Ciano, in full regalia ... Vergani, 1974, p. 113

p. 216 The winter of 1939 ... Sermoneta, 1947, p. 174

p. 217 Listening to the usual ... Sheridan, 1994, p. 103

p. 219 The diplomat Friedrich ... Festorazzi, 2010, p. 350

p. 219 In a two-hour speech ... National Archives, GFM 36/8

p. 219 Mussolini emerged from ... François-Poncet, 1961, p. 173

p. 219 He found Mussolini ... Packard, 1943, p. 80

p. 219 Sumner Welles went on ... Welles,1944, p. 90

p. 220 When he and Ciano ... National Archives, GFM 36/7

p. 220 'As the dean of' ... Ciano, Diary, 17 March 1940

p. 221 he was struck by ... Varè, family papers

p. 221 That, wrote Ciano ... Diary, 10 May 1940

p. 221 As Enrico Caviglia ... Caviglia, 1952, p. 337

p. 222 He looked corpulent ... Vittorio Mussolini, 1957, p. 364

p. 223 British and French ... See Ortona, 1993

p. 224 Italian women, already ... Petacco, 1984, p. 18

p. 224 According to its OVRA spies ... ACS Segreteria Particolare del Duce. Carte Riservate, Busta 115

p. 224 The speed of the German ... Gooch, 2020, p. 70

p. 225 'A nightmare,' wrote ... Sorgi, 2009, p. 53

p. 226 One night there was ... Spinosa,1983, p. 167; see also ACS Min. dell'Int, PolPol Fasc. Pers. 298

p. 227 She heard cries, wondered ... see Pensotti, 1999

p. 228 'We found the countess' ... ACS Segreteria particolare del Duce. Carta riservata, Busta 115

p. 229 Mountains of anonymous ... ACS Min. dell'Int, PolPol. Fas. Pers. 298; see also ACS Segreteria Particolare del Duce. Carta riservata, Busta 115

p. 230 Italian troops ... Nuto Revelli, *La guerra dei poveri*, 1979, p. 7

p. 230 The Mussolini family ... Edda Negri Mussolini, 2015, p. 195

p. 231 Looking out from his balcony ... Guerri, 1979, p. 625

Chapter fifteen

p. 232 In the early days of the war ... See Sermoneta, 1947

p. 232 Prince Otto ... See Hagen, 1952

p. 233 The Roman princesses ... See Dollmann, 1967

p. 233 When Goering came ... Cerruti, 1952, p. 174

p. 234 Ciano did not ... Bloch, 1992, p. 342

p. 234 Ciano's dislike of ... Anfuso, 1950, p. 24

p. 234 Grandi complained that ... Lamb, 1997, p. 190

p. 234 When the memorandum ... Malaparte, 2009, p. 408

p. 235 And so the *principesse* ... Dollmann, 1967, p. 139

p. 235 an Egyptian magazine ... *Images*, 16 February 1942

p. 235 In November 1940 ... See Carafoli & Padiglione, 2003

p. 236 He told a friend ... Petacco, 1982, p. 144

p. 237 She took strongly ... See Rachele Mussolini, 1973

p. 238 Relations between Ciano ... Moseley, 1999, p. 133

p. 238 In 1941 Edda had ... See Agnelli, 1975
p. 238 He called her *'una divina'* ... Mannucci, 1998, p. 75
p. 238 A spy reported ... ACS Min.dell'Int, PolPol. Fasc. Pers. 431
p. 238 Hitler was reported ... *Hitler's Table Talk*, 1953, p. 194
p. 238 Magda left a deep ... Edda Mussolini, 1976, p. 126
p. 239 She served in ... Innocenti, 2003, p. 115
p. 239 The sunflowers were out ... *Oggi*, 10 September 1959
p. 240 A spy reported ... Canali & Volpini, 2019, p. 166
p. 241 The atmosphere in Rome ... Ciano, Diary, 10 April 1942

Chapter sixteen

p. 242 Mussolini had dreamt ... Lamb, 1997, p. 303
p. 242 Their long retreat ... National Archives, GFM 36/609
p. 243 Ciano had never ... Ciano, Diary, 8 February 1943
p. 244 'As for that' ... Ortona, 1993, p. 252
p. 245 One by one ... Dollmann, 1967, p. 56
p. 245 Not long before ... Pirelli, 1984, p. 401; see also Corner, 2012, p. 268
p. 246 If possible, the divide ... ACS Min.dell'Int, PopPol. Fasc. Pers. F320
p. 246 Romans, ever quick ... Franzinelli, 2012, p. 105
p. 246 'Perhaps, but it's' ... Cordova, 1980, p. 192
p. 246 As the Communist ... R.J.B. Bosworth, 'Everyday Mussolinism', *Contemporary European History*, 2005, Vol 14
p. 247 Even the faithful and devoted ... Spinosa, 2000, p. 293
p. 247 After seventy British ... See Gabriella di Robilant, *Diari di Guerra*, unpublished memoir
p. 247 The war news ... National Archives, GFM 36/9
p. 247 But no more now ... Gooch, 2020, p. 411
p. 248 He spent hours ... Senise, 1946, p. 122
p. 248 Over one aspect ... See de Felice, 1961; see also Zucotti,1987 & 2000
p. 249 Laval, Vichy and the Germans ... Moseley, 1999, p. 153
p. 249 These measures, the Prefect ... Poliakov, 1946, p. 61
p. 250 At first, the Germans ... Corner, 2012, p. 288
p. 250 Goebbels noted ... *The Goebbels Diaries*, 1982, 13 February 1941
p. 250 When she and Ciano ... Vergani, 1974, p. 172
p. 251 An anonymous 'woman ... Di Rienzo, 2018, p. 102
p. 251 Another swore that ... ACS Min.dell'Int, PolPol. Fasc. Pers. 298
p. 251 'his only enemy' ... Malaparte, 2009, p. 277
p. 253 That night the skyline ... Sermoneta, 1947, p. 199
p. 253 The plotters were ... Benzoni, 1985, p. 108
p. 254 There was, wrote Bottai ... Bottai, 1949, p. 373
p. 255 There were fears that ... Grandi, 1985, p. 623
p. 256 The regime, he declared ... Deakin, 1962, p. 486
p. 258 He would, the King ... Vittorio Mussolini, 1957, p. 393

Chapter seventeen

p. 261 'There is a *tramontana*' ... Spinoza, 1983, p. 191

p. 262 When Anna Maria ... Edda Negri Mussolini, 2015, p. 209

p. 262 In Livorno ... Garnier, 1961, p. 183

p. 262 An American woman ... See Scrivener, 1945

p. 262 Giuseppe Graziosi's vast ... Grindle et al., 2013, p. 201

p. 263 Overnight, Rome became ... Davis,1972, p. 208; see also Venè, 1989

p. 264 To his sister ... Edvige Mussolini,1957, p. 201

p. 264 Before leaving Rome ... *Il Corriere della Sera*, 28 August 1943

p. 265 For all their spies ... Di Rienzo, 2018, p. 533

p. 265 An absurd meeting ... Bloch, 1992, p. 380

p. 266 Denunciations began to arrive ... Edda Mussolini, 1976, p. 192

p. 267 On 14 August ... Claudia Baldoli et al., 'Italian society under Anglo-American bombs', *The History Journal*, 2009, Vol 52

p. 268 Daniele Varè's two ... Varè family papers

p. 268 Both looked pale ... See Agnelli, 1975

p. 270 There was a rumour ... ACS Min.dell'Int, PolPol. Fasc. Pers. 298

p. 270 Local Fascist thugs ... *Gente*, 23 October 1953

p. 270 Hitler, clearly very ... Vittorio Mussolini, 1957, p. 189

p. 271 To all but a handful ... ACS Min.dell'Int, PolPol. Fasc. Pers. 298

p. 273 The news that they ... See Sermoneta, 1947

p. 274 He had expressed a prefence ... Money, 1986, p. 214

p. 275 Earlier that same day ... Rachele Mussolini, 1973, p. 266

p. 276 She and her father, she said ... Afeltra, 1993, p. 34

p. 276 'If, after all his sad' ... *The Goebbels Diaries*, 1948, p. 469

p. 277 Furthermore, Hitler ... See Anfuso, 1950

Chapter eighteen

p. 279 Radio Roma ... Monticone, 1978, p. 240

p. 280 Several members of the ... di Robilant, unpublished memoir, p. 151; see also Sermoneta, 1947, p. 217

p. 280 Prince Doria ... Trevelyan, 1981, p. 343

p. 280 The anti-Fascists ... See Forcella, 1999

p. 281 Other friends ... Zanotti-Bianco, 2011, p. 97

p. 282 Before leaving, he was ... Fabrizio Ciano, 1991, p. 84

p. 282 Later Ciano would say ... Afeltra, 1993, p. 49

p. 283 When the moment came ... See Deakin, 1962

p. 284 He was, noted ... see Dolfin, 1949

p. 284 Shrewdly, however, the Duce ... Canali & Volpini, 2019, p. 57

p. 285 When Mussolini, humiliated ... See Bloch, 1992

p. 286 There was a unanimous vote ... Cordova, 1980, p. 231

Chapter nineteen

p. 289 Unnerved, she now asked . . . Vittorio Mussolini, *Epoca,* June 1958

p. 290 On 9 December . . . Moseley, 1999, p. 202

p. 291 on 18 December . . . Rachele Mussolini, 1948, p. 222

p. 291 His patient, the German . . . *L'Illustrazione Italiana*, May 1957; See also Zachariae, 1948

p. 292 The Carcere degli Scalzi . . . Pellegrinotti, 1975, p. 93

p. 295 To his mother . . . Guerri, 2005, p. 236

p. 298 There are different versions . . . Hagen, 1952, p. 287

p. 299 The trial was to take place . . . see Venè, 1963; see also Renzo Montagna, *Mussolini e il Processo di Verona*, 2001

p. 301 Ciano then wrote two . . . Carolina Ciano, *Gente*, 23 December 1957

p. 304 On 8 January she asked . . . See Mannucci, 1998

p. 304 A wire fence . . . See Broggini & Marino, 2004

p. 305 Orders went out . . . Archives Bellinzona. Internati 22, 1943–945; Archives Berne. EP(D) 3EDP1943-45.269

p. 306 With Edda and Pucci . . . Author interview with hotel manager

Chapter twenty

p. 307 Edda's interview . . . Archives Berne. AFBE4320(B)1991/243 Dossier 1

p. 308 On the afternoon . . . *Gente*, 9 July 1969

p. 308 She decided to be honest . . . Edda Mussolini, 1976, p. 248; see also Fabrizio Ciano, 1991, p. 99

p. 309 A Swiss reporter . . . *Daily Dispatch*, 25 January 1944

p. 309 'As one of the most' . . . *Daily Express*, 27 January 1944

p. 312 To Carolina . . . *Gente*, 23 October 1957

p. 312 To others, like . . . Serrano Suñer, 1947, p. 280

p. 312 When he returned to Italy . . . *Oggi*, 23 September 1954

p. 313 In Rome, reactions to . . . See Jebb, 1976

p. 313 The Italian secret services . . . ACS Min.dell'Int, PolPol. Fasc. Pers. 298

p. 313 Sir Miles Lampson . . . Lampson, 1972, p. 278

p. 313 Rome was running out . . . Antonazzi, 1983, p. 182

p. 314 Eden had suggested dropping . . . Trevelyan, 1981, p. 265

p. 314 Ever since the Congress . . . See Zuccotti, *The Italians and the Holocaust*, 1987; see also Fattorini, 2007

p. 314 Then, on 23 March . . . See De Felice, 1961

p. 315 Later, Romans flocked . . . Scrivener, 1945, p. 143

p. 316 The Allied strategy . . . Davis, 1972, p. 468

Chapter twenty-one

p. 317 The mother superior . . . Archives Berne. E4320 (B) 1991/242 Dossier 2

p. 318 Edda looked out . . . Fabrizio Ciano, 1991, p. 106

p. 319 'The patient is less' . . . Report by Dr Répond, 15 September 1944, in Broggini, *La famiglia Mussolini*, n.d.

p. 319 Edda replied . . . ACS Segreteria Particolare del Duce. b122

p. 319 The diaries themselves . . . See McGaw Smith, 1975

p. 320 Through her friend . . . Frances de Chollet private papers, author interview with Jacqueline de Chollet

p. 320 He had received furious . . . Archives Bellinzona, Internati 22. 1943-45

p. 321 they found her 'gaily dressed' . . . Jacqueline de Chollet, unpublished memoir

p. 321 As a senior American . . . US National Archives, OSS RG226 E124 Folder 1343

p. 322 After further exchanges . . . US National Archives, OSS RG226 E124 Folder 1345

p. 322 The de Chollets . . . Berne Archives. E4320. (B) 1991/243 Dossier 2

p. 323 Fabrizio, Raimondo . . . Letter from Edda Mussolini to Frances de Chollet, December 1944, Princeton University Library, Special Collections.

p. 324 He was angry about . . . Lamb, 1997, p. 284

p. 324 He looked pale and wretched . . . See D'Agostini, 1946

p. 326 He told his sister . . . Edvige Mussolini, 1957, p. 227

p. 326 'Whatever the place' . . . McGaw Smith, 1975, p. 171

p. 327 'The important thing' . . . Petacco, 1982, p. 12

p. 328 But Edda was never . . . *Gente*, 9 July 1969

Chapter twenty-two

p. 330 While the closing . . . See Giorgio Pini & Duilio Susmel, *Dall'Impero alla Repubblica*, Vol IV, 1953

p. 330 In it, according to . . . Rachele Mussolini, 2011, p. 158

p. 331 A stringer for . . . ACS Min.dell'Int. Div.Pubblica Sicurezza. Categoria B. Famiglia Mussolini

p. 332 The question now . . . Archives Bellinzona. Fondo internati italiani, 1943–45. SC 22 fasc.1

p. 334 Dr Répond was also . . . Broggini, *La famiglia Mussolini*, n.d.; see also Archives Berne. E4320 (B) 1991/243 97b

p. 336 Edda's fears were not . . . *New York Times*, 10 June 1945

p. 338 It was some time before . . . ACS Min dell'Int. Div. Pubblica Sicurezza Categoria B, 15 December 1945

p. 339 It was at a meeting . . . See Sorgi, 2009

p. 343 The barrage of mines . . . Edwin Cerio, *L'Ora di Capri*, 2000. p. 64

Chapter twenty-three

p. 344 Speaking to a British . . . See Dollmann, 1956

p. 344 there was now the question . . . See Franzinelli, 2012

p. 346 As the diaries began to be ... See Ciano, *Diary, 1937–1943*, 2002; Ciano's Diplomatic Papers, 1948

p. 348 Like Edda ... Author interview Adele Grana

p. 350 It was not until 1959 ... Edda Mussolini interview with Anita Pensotti, *Oggi*, September 1959; see also RAI interviews with Nicola Caracciolo, 1969

Afterword

p. 352 Edda's children ... Author interviews with Gloria Ciano; Rachele Mussolini; Emma Moriconi

p. 353 It was Romano ... See Romano Mussolini, *Il Duce Mio Padre*, 2004

p. 354 Her verdict ... See Margherita Sarfatti, *Acqua Passata*, 1955

p. 355 One of the more bizarre ... Author interview with Mimmo Franzinelli

p. 355 There was a scramble ... Serri, 'The Redeemed', *Telos*, 2007; see also Mimmo Franzinelli, *L'amnistia Togliatti*, 2006

p. 355 Fascism was derided ... See Guerri, 1995

p. 355 What was conveniently ... See Dogliani, 2008

p. 355 'Illusion,' as he said ... Speech of 18 July

Index